THE WORLD ACCORDING TO TRUMP

VOLUME II

ECONOMY, IMMIGRATION, AND MORE

2017, 2018, 2019

ACTUAL QUOTES OF
PRESIDENT TRUMP BROKEN
DOWN AND CATEGORIZED BY
SUBJECT MATTER

ISBN: 978-1-64973-002-2

Arc Manor
P. O. Box 10339
Rockville, MD 20849-0339
www.ArcManor.com

These are the direct quotes of President Trump. We have made every effort to check accuracy and no quote is included without a direct reference to the source material. We apologize for any typos or mistakes inadvertently introduced into the compilation of a project as large as this (nearly 1,000 pages between the two volumes).

We have attempted to include all his direct quotes readily accessible, but due to the volume of material had to eliminate obvious repetitions. No attempt was made to correct original typos or usage for the sake of authenticity...all quotes are presented as they were originally referenced.

Contents

China/Tariff/Trade—2017 News Quotes

Remarks after meeting with President Xi Jinping of China, April 7, 2017.

Source: https://www.whitehouse.gov/briefings-statements/
remarks-president-trump-meeting-president-xi-china/

"I just want to say that [Chinese] President Xi [Jinping] and all of his representatives have been really interesting to be with. I think we have made tremendous progress in our relationship with China. My representatives have been meeting one-on-one with their counterparts from China. And I think, truly, progress has been made. We'll be making a lot of additional progress.

"The relationship developed by President Xi and myself I think is outstanding. We look forward to being together many times in the future. And I believe lots of very potentially bad problems will be going away.

"So, I just want to thank President Xi for being with us in the United States. It's a tremendous honor for me and all of my representatives to host the President and his representatives. And again, progress has been made."

Response to a question from John Dickerson of CBS News, April 30, 2017.

Source: https://www.cbsnews.com/news/face-the-nation-transcript-april-30-2017-president-trump/

"You can never be sure of anything, can you? But I developed a very good relationship [with China]. I don't think they want to see a destabilized North Korea. I don't think they want to see it. They certainly don't want to see nuclear on, from their neighbor. They haven't liked it for a long time. But we'll have to see what happens. The relationship I have with China, it's been already acclaimed as being something very special, something very different than we've ever had. But, again, you know, we'll find out whether or not President Xi [Jinping] is able to effect change."

Response to a question from John Dickerson of CBS News, April 30, 2017.
Source: https://www.cbsnews.com/news/face-the-nation-transcript-april-30-2017-president-trump/

"But when they talk about currency manipulation, and I did say I would call China, if they were, a currency manipulator early in my tenure. And then I get there. Number one, they, as soon as I got elected, they stopped. They're not going, it's not going down anymore, their currency."

Response to a question from John Dickerson of CBS News, April 30, 2017.
Source: https://www.cbsnews.com/news/face-the-nation-transcript-april-30-2017-president-trump/

"No, they [China] were doing it before. I mean, there was no question. I mean, they were absolute currency manipulators before. But somebody said, "Oh, you didn't call him a currency manipulator." Now, you and I are just talking about how he's working. I believe that President Xi is working to try and resolve a very big problem for China also. And that's North Korea. Can you imagine if I say, 'Hey, by the way, how are you doing with North Korea? Also, we're going to announce that you're a currency manipulator tomorrow.' So, the mainstream media never talks about that. They never say that. And that's, you know, unfortunate. It's just one of—[Dickerson interrupts.]"

Response to a question from John Dickerson of CBS News, April 30, 2017.
Source: https://www.cbsnews.com/news/face-the-nation-transcript-april-30-2017-president-trump/

"OK? You understand what I'm saying. And if I can use trade as a method to get China, because I happen to think that China does have reasonably good powers over North Korea. Now, maybe not, you know, ultimate, but pretty good powers. Now, if China can help us with North Korea and can solve that problem… [Dickerson interrupts; Trump continues.] …that's worth making not as good a trade deal for the United States, excuse me, right?"

Response to a question from Laura Ingraham of FOX News, November 2, 2017.

Source: https://www.youtube.com/watch?v=yTdDH-o_ICM

"It's not in a total vacuum. And [Chinese] President Xi [Jinping] has been pretty terrific. Most people have been saying, you know, whether it's cutting the banking system off from North Korea, whether it's cutting the oil down to North Korea, or cutting supplies down.

"And I must tell you, North Korea is a thing that I think we will solve, and if we don't solve it, it's not going to be very pleasant for them. It's not going to be very pleasant, I guess, for anybody. But China is helping us."

China/Tariff/Trade—2017 Tweets

March 30, 2017

5:16 pm[1]: The meeting next week with China will be a very difficult one in that we can no longer have massive trade deficits…

…and job losses. American companies must be prepared to look at other alternatives.

April 8, 2017

9:50 am to 9:51 am[2]: It was a great honor to have President Xi Jinping and Madame Peng Liyuan of China as our guests in the United States. Tremendous…

---

1   All Tweets are listed using the Eastern Time Zone, which is the same time zone as the White House in Washington, D.C.

2   As of late 2017, Twitter allowed 280 characters per Tweet—double its previous 140-character limit. Sometimes, U.S. President Donald J. Trump writes

…goodwill and friendship was formed, but only time will tell on trade.

April 11, 2017

6:59 am: I explained to the President of China that a trade deal with the U.S. will be far better for them if they solve the North Korean problem!

April 13, 2017

8:08 am: I have great confidence that China will properly deal with North Korea. If they are unable to do so, the U.S., with its allies, will! U.S.A.

April 16, 2017

7:18 am: Why would I call China a currency manipulator when they are working with us on the North Korean problem? We will see what happens!

April 21, 2017

8:04 am: China is very much the economic lifeline to North Korea so, while nothing is easy, if they want to solve the North Korean problem, they will

May 12, 2017

8:20 am: China just agreed that the U.S. will be allowed to sell beef, and other major products, into China once again. This is REAL news!

July 5, 2017

6:14 am: The United States made some of the worst Trade Deals in world history. Why should we continue these deals with countries that do not help us?

---

consecutive Tweets on the same issue. The timing for multiple, consecutive Tweets will be reported in this manner (post time of the first Tweet in a series to post time for the last Tweet in a series) throughout this book.

6:21 am: Trade between China and North Korea grew almost 40% in the first quarter. So much for China working with us—but we had to give it a try!

July 12, 2017

3:20 pm: "After 14 years, U.S. beef hits Chinese market. Trade deal an exciting opportunity for agriculture." https://t.co/gDGgejqFMs

July 29, 2017

6:29 pm to 6:35 pm: I am very disappointed in China. Our foolish past leaders have allowed them to make hundreds of billions of dollars a year in trade, yet…

…they do NOTHING for us with North Korea, just talk. We will no longer allow this to continue. China could easily solve this problem!

September 13, 2017

9:22 pm: China has a business tax rate of 15%. We should do everything possible to match them in order to win with our economy. Jobs and wages!

October 25, 2017

2:24 pm: Spoke to President Xi of China to congratulate him on his extraordinary elevation. Also discussed NoKo & trade, two very important subjects!

November 9, 2017

6:39 pm: I don't blame China, I blame the incompetence of past Admins for allowing China to take advantage of the U.S. on trade leading up to a point where the U.S. is losing $100's of billions. How can you blame China for taking advantage of people that had no clue? I would've done same!

6:44 pm: My meetings with President Xi Jinping were very productive on both trade and the subject of North Korea. He is a highly respected and powerful representative of his people. It was great being with him and Madame Peng Liyuan!

December 28, 2017

11:24 am: Caught RED HANDED—very disappointed that China is allowing oil to go into North Korea. There will never be a friendly solution to the North Korea problem if this continues to happen!

China/Tariff/Trade—2018 News Quotes

Remarks at a rally in Tampa, Florida, July 31, 2018.

Source: https://www.tampabay.com/florida-politics/buzz/2018/08/01/
heres-a-full-transcript-of-president-trumps-speech-from-his-tampa-rally/

"We rebuilt China paying hundreds of billions of dollars a year with nobody there to protect your money. But you're there now, we are protecting your money.

"And I want to thank our farmers, our farmers are true patriots.

"Because China and others have targeted—China and others, remember this, have targeted our farmers.

"Not good, not nice. And you know what our farmers are saying? 'It's OK, we can take it.' These are incredible people. 'We can take it.'

"You know why? They target our farmers because they know it's one of our great strengths. It's us, it's not me, it's us altogether. They know it's one of our great strengths.

"We won every farm state, you're going to see that middle of that map, wasn't even the middle, it was about everything but a little corners of each side. But you have to see, that is all red, Republican red, beautiful, Republican red.

"And remember this, remember this. Farms have been on a decline—I mean it's been for 15 years. I've only been here for, you know, it's pretty soon going to be close to two years.

"But if you look at soybeans, big crop. If you go back to Election Day and then move back five years, so five years before Election Day, soybeans dropped 50% in price. I wasn't even here, so now we're going to open up markets, We're going to do it the way it should be. And all of this stuff, you're going to make it back and it's going to be made back faster than anybody would know.

"But we haven't been treated right. We're going to make it back nice and quickly. Nice and quickly.

"Now, after years of rebuilding foreign countries, it's time to finally rebuild our country, right? Wouldn't you say? Right?"

Remarks at a rally in Tampa, Florida, July 31, 2018.
Source: https://www.tampabay.com/florida-politics/buzz/2018/08/01/
heres-a-full-transcript-of-president-trumps-speech-from-his-tampa-rally/

"We've taken the toughest-ever actions in response to China's abusive trade practices. And we're doing very well with China, very well. And I have a lot of respect for China. And I have tremendous respect for President Xi of China.

"But this has been too many years of abuse, $500 billion a year. $500 billion. We've helped rebuild China. We can't do that anymore.

"We can't do that anymore. And our farmers understand it, and our workers understand it. And, frankly, our companies understand it. I was with one of the greatest companies in the world. The chief executive officer, very short while ago. And it really affects him. He said, 'You know what, this does affect our company. But, Mr. President, keep going. You're doing the right thing.' I thought it was great.

"I thought it was great.

"A great company, one of the greatest. He said, 'You're doing the right thing.' And I said, 'I appreciate it.'

"Thanks to our powerful trade policies, the trade deficit is falling and falling and falling. And, boy, did it fall this quarter.

"The days of plundering American jobs and American wealth, those days are over; they're over."

China/Tariff/Trade—2018 Tweets

March 2, 2018

5:50 am: When a country (USA) is losing many billions of dollars on trade with virtually every country it does business with, trade wars are good, and easy to win. Example, when we are down $100 billion with a certain country and they get cute, don't trade anymore-we win big. It's easy!

8:01 am: We must protect our country and our workers. Our steel industry is in bad shape. IF YOU DON'T HAVE STEEL, YOU DON'T HAVE A COUNTRY!

8:57 am: When a country Taxes our products coming in at, say, 50%, and we Tax the same product coming into our country at ZERO, not fair or smart. We will soon be starting RECIPROCAL TAXES so that we will charge the same thing as they charge us. $800 Billion Trade Deficit-have no choice!

March 3, 2018

12:43 pm: The United States has an $800 Billion Dollar Yearly Trade Deficit because of our "very stupid" trade deals and policies. Our jobs and wealth are being given to other countries that have taken advantage of us for years. They laugh at what fools our leaders have been. No more!

12:53 pm: If the E.U. wants to further increase their already massive tariffs and barriers on U.S. companies doing business there, we will simply apply a Tax on their Cars which freely pour into the U.S. They make it impossible for our cars (and more) to sell there. Big trade imbalance!

March 4, 2018

7:10 pm: If the E.U. wants to further increase their already massive tariffs and barriers on U.S. companies doing business there, we will simply apply a Tax on their Cars which freely pour into the U.S. They make it impossible for our cars (and more) to sell there. Big trade imbalance!

March 7, 2018

10:10 am: China has been asked to develop a plan for the year of a One Billion Dollar reduction in their massive Trade Deficit with the United States. Our relationship with China has been a very good one, and we look forward to seeing what ideas they come back with. We must act soon!

March 14, 2018

9:37 am: We cannot keep a blind eye to the rampant unfair trade practices against our Country!

April 4, 2018

6:22 am: We are not in a trade war with China, that war was lost many years ago by the foolish, or incompetent, people who represented the U.S.

Now we have a Trade Deficit of $500 Billion a year, with Intellectual Property Theft of another $300 Billion. We cannot let this continue!

8:20 am: When you're already $500 Billion DOWN, you can't lose!

April 6, 2018

6:11 am: Despite the Aluminum Tariffs, Aluminum prices are DOWN 4%. People are surprised, I'm not! Lots of money coming into U.S. coffers and Jobs, Jobs, Jobs!

April 7, 2018

1:03 pm: The United States hasn't had a Trade Surplus with China in 40 years. They must end unfair trade, take down barriers and charge only Reciprocal Tariffs. The U.S. is losing $500 Billion a year, and has been losing Billions of Dollars for decades. Cannot continue!

April 8, 2018

7:12 am: President Xi and I will always be friends, no matter what happens with our dispute on trade. China will take down its Trade Barriers because it is the right thing to do. Taxes will become Reciprocal & a deal will be made on Intellectual Property. Great future for both countries!

April 9, 2018

5:03 am: When a car is sent to the United States from China, there is a Tariff to be paid of 2 1/2%. When a car is sent to China from the United States, there is a Tariff to be paid of 25%. Does that sound like free or fair trade. No, it sounds like STUPID TRADE—going on for years!

April 16, 2018

7:31 am: Russia and China are playing the Currency Devaluation game as the U.S. keeps raising interest rates. Not acceptable!

May 8, 2018

6:22 am: I will be speaking to my friend, President Xi of China, this morning at 8:30. The primary topics will be Trade, where good things will happen, and North Korea, where relationships and trust are building.

May 14, 2018

3:06 pm: ZTE, the large Chinese phone company, buys a big percentage of individual parts from U.S. companies. This is also reflective of the larger trade deal we are negotiating with China and my personal relationship with President Xi.

May 15, 2018

7:35 am: ZTE, the large Chinese phone company, buys a big percentage of individual parts from U.S. companies. This is also reflective of the larger trade deal we are negotiating with China and my personal relationship with President Xi.

May 16, 2018

8:09 am: The Washington Post and CNN have typically written false stories about our trade negotiations with China. Nothing has happened with ZTE except as it pertains to the larger trade deal. Our country has been losing hundreds of billions of dollars a year with China…

…We have not seen China's demands yet, which should be few in that previous U.S. Administrations have done so poorly in negotiating. China has seen our demands. There has been no folding as the media would love people to believe, the meetings…

…haven't even started yet! The U.S. has very little to give, because it has given so much over the years. China has much to give!

May 21, 2018

6:21 am: I ask Senator Chuck Schumer, why didn't President Obama & the Democrats do something about Trade with China, including

Theft of Intellectual Property etc.? They did NOTHING! With that being said, Chuck & I have long agreed on this issue! Fair Trade, plus, with China will happen!

6:27 am: China has agreed to buy massive amounts of ADDITIONAL Farm/Agricultural Products—would be one of the best things to happen to our farmers in many years!

6:31 am: On China, Barriers and Tariffs to come down for first time.

6:40 am: China must continue to be strong & tight on the Border of North Korea until a deal is made. The word is that recently the Border has become much more porous and more has been filtering in. I want this to happen, and North Korea to be VERY successful, but only after signing!

8:16 am: Under our potential deal with China, they will purchase from our Great American Farmers practically as much as our Farmers can produce.

May 25, 2018

6:07 pm to 6:13 pm: Senator Schumer and Obama Administration let phone company ZTE flourish with no security checks. I closed it down then let it reopen with high level security guarantees, change of management and board, must purchase U.S. parts and pay a $1.3 Billion fine. Dems do nothing…

…but complain and obstruct. They made only bad deals (Iran) and their so-called Trade Deals are the laughing stock of the world!

June 2, 2018

12:51 pm: The United States must, at long last, be treated fairly on Trade. If we charge a country ZERO to sell their goods, and they charge us 25, 50 or even 100 percent to sell ours, it is UNFAIR and can no longer be tolerated. That is not Free or Fair Trade, it is Stupid Trade!

3:57 pm: Why is it that the Wall Street Journal, though well meaning, never mentions the unfairness of the Tariffs routinely charged against the U.S. by other countries, or the many Billions of Dollars that the Tariffs we are now charging are, and will be, pouring into U.S. coffers?

4:23 pm: When you're almost 800 Billion Dollars a year down on Trade, you can't lose a Trade War! The U.S. has been ripped off by other countries for years on Trade, time to get smart!

June 4, 2018

7:41 am: China already charges a tax of 16% on soybeans. Canada has all sorts of trade barriers on our Agricultural products. Not acceptable!

7:43 am: The U.S. has made such bad trade deals over so many years that we can only WIN!

8:47 am: Farmers have not been doing well for 15 years. Mexico, Canada, China and others have treated them unfairly. By the time I finish trade talks, that will change. Big trade barriers against U.S. farmers, and other businesses, will finally be broken. Massive trade deficits no longer!

July 20, 2018

7:43 am to 7:51 am: China, the European Union and others have been manipulating their currencies and interest rates lower, while the U.S. is raising rates while the dollars gets stronger and stronger with each passing day—taking away our big competitive edge. As usual, not a level playing field…

…The United States should not be penalized because we are doing so well. Tightening now hurts all that we have done. The U.S. should be allowed to recapture what was lost due to illegal currency manipulation and BAD Trade Deals. Debt coming due & we are raising rates—Really?

8:04 am: Farmers have been on a downward trend for 15 years. The price of soybeans has fallen 50% since 5 years before the Election. A big reason is bad (terrible) Trade Deals with other countries. They put on massive Tariffs and Barriers. Canada charges 275% on Dairy. Farmers will WIN!

13

July 24, 2018

6:29 am: Tariffs are the greatest! Either a country which has treated the United States unfairly on Trade negotiates a fair deal, or it gets hit with Tariffs. It's as simple as that—and everybody's talking! Remember, we are the "piggy bank" that's being robbed. All will be Great!

July 25, 2018

6:01 am: Every time I see a weak politician asking to stop Trade talks or the use of Tariffs to counter unfair Tariffs, I wonder, what can they be thinking? Are we just going to continue and let our farmers and country get ripped off? Lost $817 Billion on Trade last year. No weakness!

6:20 am: China is targeting our farmers, who they know I love & respect, as a way of getting me to continue allowing them to take advantage of the U.S. They are being vicious in what will be their failed attempt. We were being nice—until now! China made $517 Billion on us last year.

August 04, 2018

2:47 pm to 2:52 pm: Tariffs are working far better than anyone ever anticipated. China market has dropped 27% in last 4months, and they are talking to us. Our market is stronger than ever, and will go up dramatically when these horrible Trade Deals are successfully renegotiated. America First...

...Tariffs have had a tremendous positive impact on our Steel Industry. Plants are opening all over the U.S., Steelworkers are working again, and big dollars are flowing into our Treasury. Other countries use Tariffs against, but when we use them, foolish people scream!

2:58 pm to 3:03 pm: Tariffs will make our country much richer than it is today. Only fools would disagree. We are using them to negotiate fair trade deals and, if countries are still unwilling to negotiate, they will pay us vast sums of money in the form of Tariffs. We win either way...

...China, which is for the first time doing poorly against us, is spending a fortune on ads and P.R. trying to convince and scare our politicians to fight me on Tariffs-because they are really hurting their economy. Likewise other countries. We are Winning, but must be strong!

August 5, 2018

6:59 am to 7:06 am: Tariffs are working big time. Every country on earth wants to take wealth out of the U.S., always to our detriment. I say, as they come, Tax them. If they don't want to be taxed, let them make or build the product in the U.S. In either event, it means jobs and great wealth...

...Because of Tariffs we will be able to start paying down large amounts of the $21 Trillion in debt that has been accumulated, much by the Obama Administration, while at the same time reducing taxes for our people. At minimum, we will make much better Trade Deals for our country!

August 15, 2018

10:04 am: Our Country was built on Tariffs, and Tariffs are now leading us to great new Trade Deals—as opposed to the horrible and unfair Trade Deals that I inherited as your President. Other Countries should not be allowed to come in and steal the wealth of our great U.S.A. No longer!

August 20, 2018

12:14 pm: It is outrageous that Poisonous Synthetic Heroin Fentanyl comes pouring into the U.S. Postal System from China. We can, and must, END THIS NOW! The Senate should pass the STOP ACT—and firmly STOP this poison from killing our children and destroying our country. No more delay!

September 8, 2018

10:45 am: Apple prices may increase because of the massive Tariffs we may be imposing on China—but there is an easy solution where there would be ZERO tax, and indeed a tax incentive. Make your products in the United States instead of China. Start building new plants now. Exciting! #MAGA

September 9, 2018

8:49 am: "Ford has abruptly killed a plan to sell a Chinese-made small vehicle in the U.S. because of the prospect of higher U.S. Tariffs." CNBC. This is just the beginning. This car can now be BUILT IN THE U.S.A. and Ford will pay no tariffs!

9:01 am: If the U.S. sells a car into China, there is a tax of 25%. If China sells a car into the U.S., there is a tax of 2%. Does anybody think that is FAIR? The days of the U.S. being ripped-off by other nations is OVER!

September 13, 2018

9:15 am: The Wall Street Journal has it wrong, we are under no pressure to make a deal with China, they are under pressure to make a deal with us. Our markets are surging, theirs are collapsing. We will soon be taking in Billions in Tariffs & making products at home. If we meet, we meet?

September 17, 2018

5:11 am: Tariffs have put the U.S. in a very strong bargaining position, with Billions of Dollars, and Jobs, flowing into our Country—and yet cost increases have thus far been almost unnoticeable. If countries will not make fair deals with us, they will be "Tariffed!"

September 18, 2018

7:50 am to 7:55 am: China has openly stated that they are actively trying to impact and change our election by attacking our farmers, ranchers and industrial workers because of their loyalty to me. What China does not understand is that these people are great patriots and fully understand that...

...China has been taking advantage of the United States on Trade for many years. They also know that I am the one that knows how to stop it. There will be great and fast economic retaliation against China if our farmers, ranchers and/or industrial workers are targeted!

September 26, 2018

12:26 pm: China is actually placing propaganda ads in the Des Moines Register and other papers, made to look like news. That's because we are beating them on Trade, opening markets, and the farmers will make a fortune when this is over!

October 22, 2018

2:18 pm: The Fake News Media has been talking about recent approval ratings of me by countries around the world, including the European Union, as being very low...

...I say of course they're low—because for the first time in 50 years I am making them pay a big price for doing business with America. Why should they like me?—But I still like them!

October 23, 2018

11:43 am: Billions of dollars are, and will be, coming into United States coffers because of Tariffs. Great also for negotiations—if a country won't give us a fair Trade Deal, we will institute Tariffs on them. Used or not, jobs and businesses will be created. U.S. respected again!

November 1, 2018

9:09 am: Just had a long and very good conversation with President Xi Jinping of China. We talked about many subjects, with a heavy emphasis on Trade. Those discussions are moving along nicely with meetings being scheduled at the G-20 in Argentina. Also had good discussion on North Korea!

November 29, 2018

7:32 am: Billions of Dollars are pouring into the coffers of the U.S.A. because of the Tariffs being charged to China, and there is a long way to go. If companies don't want to pay Tariffs, build in the U.S.A. Otherwise, lets just make our Country richer than ever before!

December 3, 2018

7:54 am: China has agreed to reduce and remove tariffs on cars coming into China from the U.S. Currently the tariff is 40%

8:01 am: Farmers will be a a very BIG and FAST beneficiary of our deal with China. They intend to start purchasing agricultural product immediately. We make the finest and cleanest product in the World, and that is what China wants. Farmers, I LOVE YOU!

8:18 am: President Xi and I have a very strong and personal relationship. He and I are the only two people that can bring about massive and very positive change, on trade and far beyond, between our two great Nations. A solution for North Korea is a great thing for China and ALL!

December 4, 2018

9:30 am to 10:03 am: The negotiations with China have already started. Unless extended, they will end 90 days from the date of our wonderful and very warm dinner with President Xi in Argentina. Bob Lighthizer will be working closely with Steve Mnuchin, Larry Kudlow, Wilbur Ross and Peter Navarro…

…on seeing whether or not a REAL deal with China is actually possible. If it is, we will get it done. China is supposed to start buying Agricultural product and more immediately. President Xi and I want this deal to happen, and it probably will. But if not remember,…

…I am a Tariff Man. When people or countries come in to raid the great wealth of our Nation, I want them to pay for the privilege of doing so. It will always be the best way to max out our economic power. We are right now taking in $billions in Tariffs. MAKE AMERICA RICH AGAIN

10:10 am: …But if a fair deal is able to be made with China, one that does all of the many things we know must be finally done, I will happily sign. Let the negotiations begin. MAKE AMERICA GREAT AGAIN!

December 5, 2018

7:46 am to 7:49 am: "China officially echoed President Donald Trump's optimism over bilateral trade talks. Chinese officials have begun preparing to restart imports of U.S. Soybeans & Liquified Natural Gas, the first sign confirming the claims of President Donald Trump and the White House that…

…China had agreed to start "immediately" buying U.S. products." @business

8:44 am to 8:51 am: One of the very exciting things to come out of my meeting with President Xi of China is his promise to me to criminalize the sale of deadly Fentanyl coming into the United States. It will now be considered a "controlled substance." This could be a game changer on what is…

…considered to be the worst and most dangerous, addictive and deadly substance of them all. Last year over 77,000 people died from Fentanyl. If China cracks down on this "horror drug," using the Death Penalty for distributors and pushers, the results will be incredible!

December 6, 2018

7:56 pm: Statement from China: "The teams of both sides are now having smooth communications and good cooperation with each other. We are full of confidence that an agreement can be reached within the next 90 days." I agree!

December 11, 2018

8:19 am: Very productive conversations going on with China! Watch for some important announcements!

December 14, 2018

11:25 am: China just announce the there economy is growing much slower than anticipated because of our Trade War with them. They have just suspended U.S. Tariff Hikes. U.S. is doing very well. China wants to make a big and very comprehensive deal. It could happen, and rather soon!

December 29, 2018

11:03 am: Just had a long and very good call with President Xi of China. Deal is moving along very well. If made, it will be very comprehensive, covering all subjects, areas and points of dispute. Big progress being made!

China/Tariff/Trade—2019 News Quotes

Response to a question from A.G. Sultzberger of *The New York Times*, January 31, 2019.
Source: https://www.nytimes.com/2019/02/01/us/politics/trump-interview-transcripts.html

"So, we just had, this is from, they just delivered that to me from President Xi [Jinping of China]. You'll get a transcript of the meeting. The press was here. A lot of the press was here. A nice letter. They have a nice way of giving letters.

"But we're doing very successfully."

Response to a question from Peter Baker of *The New York Times*, January 31, 2019.
Source: https://www.nytimes.com/2019/02/01/us/politics/trump-interview-transcripts.html

"Well, we're getting closer. It's a big deal. It's a big deal. And we're going comprehensive. We're not just—He [President Xi Jinping of China] announced that he was buying today a tremendous amount of soybeans and various farm products. And I think you'll be given that information in a little while, too. But he announced. What he did was the vice premier came in. He was here for two days having meetings. He's leaving tomorrow. They're meeting again now. And negotiations are going very well.

"That doesn't mean there are any guarantees. But I will say there's a very good feeling. There's a very good relationship. This is the letter. You can actually read it. This is the translated version. So you can get a print out of that. But that was given out, and it was also, I guess it was read. They had the interpreter read it."

Response to a question from Peter Baker of *The New York Times*, January 31, 2019.
Source: https://www.nytimes.com/2019/02/01/us/politics/trump-interview-transcripts.html

"It's possible. It's a very short period of time for a deal this big. But it's very possible. But many of the points were agreed to. And some haven't been. I believe that a lot of the biggest points are going to be agreed to by me and him [President Xi Jinping of China]. In other words, they're just not going to be authorized to agree to certain things that you folks write about and read about: intellectual property and lots of other things. And I think that will be agreed to by me and him at the right time. Like when you make a big deal, or a big scoop, you have to approve that little thing. And I think they're probably waiting, they're waiting for me and him to sit down and agree on five points at the end, or 10 points at the end."

Response to a question from Peter Baker of *The New York Times*, January 31, 2019.
Source: https://www.nytimes.com/2019/02/01/us/politics/trump-interview-transcripts.html

"Well, I think control is very important. I think the checking to make sure that—We're putting in a very strong system of checks and balances so that when we make a deal we know that it's happening. In other words, that it's being followed. And we've asked for the most stringent controls on that, because there's been difficulty over the years with certain places. And that's a very important element that's been agreed to. But you have to get it down in writing.

"You're going to have intellectual property. You're going to have theft, because so many things have been, in theory, done a little bit differently. And I think that in the end we're going to have something that's going to be very special, if it happens.

"I could have had a deal done, if I wanted to make—You know, most people thought it was going to be a deal where they buy a tremendous amount of corn and soybeans and that'll be it and everybody's happy and the farmers are happy. But he [President Xi Jinping of China] actually announced today—I wish you were here, because it was sort of a great thing to watch. The press was packed. A lot of Chinese press, too. And he announced that he's buying a massive amount of soybeans and various other farm products today. Starting immediately. And that's going to make a lot of farmers very happy. So you know, that was very nice."

Response to a question from Peter Baker of *The New York Times*, January 31, 2019.
Source: https://www.nytimes.com/2019/02/01/us/politics/trump-interview-transcripts.html

"Peter [Baker of *The New York Times*], without the tariffs, we wouldn't be talking. And I make this point clear to them. We've never had a deal with China. We've never had a trade deal with China. You have the World Trade Organization, which is a disaster for the United States. The World Trade Organization is probably the worst trade deal ever made with NAFTA being second. The World Trade Organization helped create China. If you look at China, it's flatlined. And from the day the World Trade Organization came into existence, it's a rocket ship. But just the opposite for the United States. That was a terrible deal for the United States and it was an unbelievably good deal for China."

Response to a question from Peter Baker of *The New York Times*, January 31, 2019.
Source: https://www.nytimes.com/2019/02/01/us/politics/trump-interview-transcripts.html

"Yeah, sure. We have 25% now on $50 billion. And by the way, Peter [Baker of *The New York Times*], that's a lot of money pouring into our

Treasury, you know. We never made five cents with China. We're getting right now 25% on $50 billion. And then I was putting 25 percent at a later date, which date came and went: 25% or $200 billion."

From State of the Union address, February 5, 2019.
Source: https://www.whitehouse.gov/briefings-statements/
president-donald-j-trumps-state-union-address-2/

"To build on our incredible economic success, one priority is paramount: reversing decades of calamitous trade policies.

"We are now making it clear to China that after years of targeting our industries, and stealing our intellectual property, the theft of American jobs and wealth has come to an end.

"Therefore, we recently imposed tariffs on $250 billion of Chinese goods, and now our Treasury is receiving billions of dollars a month from a country that never gave us a dime. But I don't blame China for taking advantage of us; I blame our leaders and representatives for allowing this travesty to happen. I have great respect for President Xi [Jinping], and we are now working on a new trade deal with China. But it must include real, structural change to end unfair trade practices, reduce our chronic trade deficit, and protect American jobs."

Response to a question from Catherine Herridge of FOX News, May 2, 2019.
Source: https://www.foxnews.com/politics/transcript-fox-news-interview-with-president-trump

"I see where [Joe] Biden[3] put in a statement, or a strong statement that China's not a big problem. Well China is a big problem. We're losing $500 billion a year to China. There's a great hostility. There's a great—China's a big problem. And when somebody says that it shows they don't know what's happening."

---

3   Joe Biden, Vice President from 2009 to 2017 in the Obama Administration, was also a contender for the 2020 Democratic presidential nomination as of the time of this book's preparation.

Response to a question from Catherine Herridge of FOX News, May 2, 2019.

Source: https://www.foxnews.com/politics/transcript-fox-news-interview-with-president-trump

"Well, we are very close to a deal with China. But it's a question of whether or not I want to make it. I mean we're going to make either a real deal, or we're not going to make a deal at all.

"And if we don't make a deal we're going to tariff China, and that'll be fine. We'll frankly, we'll make a lot of money."

Response to a question from Catherine Herridge of FOX News, May 2, 2019.

Source: https://www.foxnews.com/politics/transcript-fox-news-interview-with-president-trump

"Well look, I have a very good relationship with [Chinese] President Xi [Jinping], but as I explained to him, I don't blame them because they ripped off our country and we allowed that to happen. I blame past presidents and representatives for allowing this to happen.

"Representatives of our country, why did they let this happen? Why are we losing $500 billion, for years, $500 billion a year. We, we rebuilt China. They took advantage of us on trade like nobody in history has ever taken advantage of anyone.

"Now we're making either a great deal or we won't make a deal at all. And if we don't make a deal at all, we'll use tariffs and we'll get back to (inaudible)."

Response to a question from Catherine Herridge of FOX News, May 2, 2019.

Source: https://www.foxnews.com/politics/transcript-fox-news-interview-with-president-trump

"You know, eventually we want to be able to get along with countries too, you have to remember that. Whether it's Russia, or China, or anybody else."

Response to a question from Catherine Herridge of FOX News, May 2, 2019.

Source: https://www.foxnews.com/politics/transcript-fox-news-interview-with-president-trump

"Oh, he [Joe Biden[4]] is very naive about China. China—Right now, we lose $500 billion. After I sign the deal, there won't be anything like that. China just, during the Obama years in particular, just took advantage of our country so badly. A very, very big competition, China. And I've stopped it, and I am stopping it.

"You know, during the course of the last two and a half years, we've gone up $17 trillion in value. China's gone down $17 trillion. China, as you know, has taken a very, very big hit, because of the tariffs and everything else I've imposed. We'll see whether or not we have a deal.

"We have a very big chance to have a great deal. But for somebody to be naive and say that China's not a problem, if Biden actually said that, that's a very dumb statement to make."

Response to an unidentified reporter's question before Marine One departure, March 20, 2019.

Source: https://www.whitehouse.gov/briefings-statements/
remarks-president-trump-marine-one-departure-34/

"No. We're not talking about removing them. We're talking about leaving them and for a substantial period of time, because we have to make sure that if we do the deal with China, that China lives by the deal. Because they've had a lot of problems living by certain deals and we have to make sure.

"Now, no President has ever done what I've done with China. China had free reign over our country, taking out $500 billion a year for many years. We actually rebuilt China, in the truest sense of the word. We rebuilt China.

"But we're getting along with China very well. President Xi [Jinping] is a friend of mine. The deal is coming along nicely. We have our top

---

4 Joe Biden, Vice President from 2009 to 2017 in the Obama Administration, was also a contender for the 2020 Democratic presidential nomination as of the time of this book's preparation.

representatives going there this weekend to further the deal. But, no, we have—We're taking in billions and billions of dollars right now in tariff money. And for a period of time, that will stay."

Response to an unidentified reporter's question at the signing of H.R. 3401, July 1, 2019.
Source: https://www.whitehouse.gov/briefings-statements/
remarks-president-trump-signing-h-r-3401/

"Whatever it takes. Look, if we don't make a great deal, if we don't make a fair deal—It has to be better for us than for them because they had such a big advantage for so many years. In other words, you can't make a 50/50 deal when somebody else has been absolutely—I've been talking about this for years.

"China made—We had a surplus, meaning they did, on us, of $507 billion. It's been hundreds of billions of dollars a year for many, many years. So, obviously, we can't make a 50/50 deal. It has to be a deal that is somewhat tilted to our advantage. And if we're not going to do that, we're taking in a fortune from tariffs. And, unfortunately, we're hurting China by doing that because many of their companies are leaving and going to a non-tariff state, so they don't have to pay the tariffs.

"And the other misconception about China, and I think you read an article today in *The Wall Street Journal* about it: Our people aren't paying for those tariffs, in that case, certainly. China is paying for them, and those companies are paying for them.

"China devalued their currency very substantially, and they also put a lot of money into their economy. They're pouring money. It's fake money, but it's money. And they're pouring money into their economy to take care of the tariffs. Some people aren't—You don't have increased inflation. You have no increased inflation. But I'll tell you what is happening: Our Treasury is taking in billions and billions of dollars of money that normally would be for China.

"So we'll see what happens. We hope that we can make a deal, but it's got to be a fair deal. We had a deal, as far as I was concerned. And then, at the last moment, China decided they didn't like that deal, and they

26

changed it. It's all right. Then I said, 'You're going to pay 25% tariffs on $250 billion.'"

Response to an unidentified reporter's question at the signing of H.R. 3401, July 1, 2019.
Source: https://www.whitehouse.gov/briefings-statements/
remarks-president-trump-signing-h-r-3401/

"Yeah, sure, I'd expect him [President Xi Jinping of China] to move. And if he doesn't move, that's okay too. I'm very happy either way. But I think we have a good chance of making a deal. I think they want to make a deal. Because they're losing many companies that are leaving because of the tariffs, because they don't want to pay the tariffs. So they're losing many companies. They're moving to Vietnam. And, by the way, some are moving back to the United States, where they belong."

Response to an unidentified reporter's question after Marine One arrival, September 1, 2019.
Source: https://www.whitehouse.gov/briefings-statements/
remarks-president-trump-marine-one-arrival-5/

"So China is moving along. We're doing very well. It was brought out very strongly today by a number of great economists that, because China has devalued their currency so much, that, in fact, they are actually paying for all of the tariffs. We have—In addition to that, as you know, they're pouring money into their economy. So those two things, they are paying for their tariffs.

"As you know, some new tariffs get on. We're taking in tens of billions of dollars. We're giving some of the money to the farmers. I'm making the farmers more than whole. The farmers are doing better than if China, frankly, were buying. I'm taking a piece of the massive amount of tariffs, and we're giving them to the farmers who have been targeted unfairly by China.

"We are talking to China. The meeting is still on, as you know, in September. That hasn't changed. They haven't changed and we haven't. We'll see what happens.

"But we can't allow China to rip us off anymore as a country. We can't allow China to take $500 billion a year out of our country. We can't do that."

Response to a question from an unidentified reporter before Marine One departure, September 9, 2019.
Source: https://www.whitehouse.gov/briefings-statements/
remarks-president-trump-marine-one-departure-63/

"We have to stop forced technology, international technology theft. If you look at what's going on: intellectual property theft with China—Just so you understand, our country is doing phenomenally well. You know, there's a chance—I don't want to talk about it—But over a very short period of time that we'll hit a yet new record. I think we have 118 records for hitting the top stock market.

"Two weeks ago, the fake news was trying to convince people that maybe there's a possibility for a recession. Well, a lot of things have happened, very positive. We're doing very well against China and we could very well have a new high in our stock market. We have gained trillions of dollars of worth, and China has lost many, many trillions of dollars, including 3 million jobs, including companies that are leaving China. Yes, they want to negotiate very badly."

China/Tariff/Trade—2019 Tweets

January 3, 2019

9:52 am: The United States Treasury has taken in MANY billions of dollars from the Tariffs we are charging China and other countries that have not treated us fairly. In the meantime we are doing well in various Trade Negotiations currently going on. At some point this had to be done!

January 21, 2019

4:57 pm: China posts slowest economic numbers since 1990 due to U.S. trade tensions and new policies. Makes so much sense for China to finally do a Real Deal, and stop playing around!

January 28, 2019

8:16 am: Tariffs on the "dumping" of Steel in the United States have totally revived our Steel Industry. New and expanded plants are happening all over the U.S. We have not only saved this important industry, but created many jobs. Also, billions paid to our treasury. A BIG WIN FOR U.S.

January 31, 2019

7:41 am: China's top trade negotiators are in the U.S. meeting with our representatives. Meetings are going well with good intent and spirit on both sides. China does not want an increase in Tariffs and feels they will do much better if they make a deal. They are correct. I will be...

7:48 am: ...meeting with their top leaders and representatives today in the Oval Office. No final deal will be made until my friend President Xi, and I, meet in the near future to discuss and agree on some of the long standing and more difficult points. Very comprehensive transaction...

7:56 am: ...China's representatives and I are trying to do a complete deal, leaving NOTHING unresolved on the table. All of the many problems are being discussed and will be hopefully resolved. Tariffs on China increase to 25% on March 1st, so all working hard to complete by that date!

9:56 am: Looking for China to open their Markets not only to Financial Services, which they are now doing, but also to our Manufacturing, Farmers and other U.S. businesses and industries. Without this a deal would be unacceptable!

February 16, 2019

7:17 pm: Trade negotiators have just returned from China where the meetings on Trade were very productive. Now at meetings with me at Mar-a-Lago giving the details. In the meantime, Billions of Dollars are being paid to the United States by China in the form of Trade Tariffs!

February 24, 2019

8:05 am: President Xi of China has been very helpful in his support of my meeting with Kim Jong Un. The last thing China wants are large scale nuclear weapons right next door. Sanctions placed on the border by China and Russia have been very helpful. Great relationship with Chairman Kim!

5:39 pm to 5:50 pm: I am pleased to report that the U.S. has made substantial progress in our trade talks with China on important structural issues including intellectual property protection, technology transfer, agriculture, services, currency, and many other issues. As a result of these very...

5:50 pm: ...productive talks, I will be delaying the U.S. increase in tariffs now scheduled for March 1. Assuming both sides make additional progress, we will be planning a Summit for President Xi and myself, at Mar-a-Lago, to conclude an agreement. A very good weekend for U.S. & China!

February 25, 2019

3:12 pm: China Trade Deal (and more) in advanced stages. Relationship between our two Countries is very strong. I have therefore agreed to delay U.S. tariff hikes. Let's see what happens?

7:04 pm: If a deal is made with China, our great American Farmers will be treated better than they have ever been treated before!

March 1, 2019

6:08 pm: I have asked China to immediately remove all Tariffs on our agricultural products (including beef, pork, etc.) based on the fact that we are moving along nicely with Trade discussions…

…and I did not increase their second traunch of Tariffs to 25% on March 1st. This is very important for our great farmers—and me!

May 5, 2019

11:08 am: For 10 months, China has been paying Tariffs to the USA of 25% on 50 Billion Dollars of High Tech, and 10% on 200 Billion Dollars of other goods. These payments are partially responsible for our great economic results. The 10% will go up to 25% on Friday. 325 Billions Dollars…

…of additional goods sent to us by China remain untaxed, but will be shortly, at a rate of 25%. The Tariffs paid to the USA have had little impact on product cost, mostly borne by China. The Trade Deal with China continues, but too slowly, as they attempt to renegotiate. No!

May 6, 2019

6:08 am: The United States has been losing, for many years, 600 to 800 Billion Dollars a year on Trade. With China we lose 500 Billion Dollars. Sorry, we're not going to be doing that anymore!

May 8, 2019

7:48 am: The reason for the China pullback & attempted renegotiation of the Trade Deal is the sincere HOPE that they will be able to "negotiate" with Joe Biden or one of the very weak Democrats, and thereby continue to ripoff the United States (($500 Billion a year)) for years to come…

…Guess what, that's not going to happen! China has just informed us that they (Vice-Premier) are now coming to the U.S. to make a deal.

We'll see, but I am very happy with over $100 Billion a year in Tariffs filling U.S. coffers…great for U.S., not good for China!

May 10, 2019

6:24 am: We have lost 500 Billion Dollars a year, for many years, on Crazy Trade with China. NO MORE!

6:43 am: …The process has begun to place additional Tariffs at 25% on the remaining 325 Billion Dollars. The U.S. only sells China approximately 100 Billion Dollars of goods & products, a very big imbalance. With the over 100 Billion Dollars in Tariffs that we take in, we will buy…

…agricultural products from our Great Farmers, in larger amounts than China ever did, and ship it to poor & starving countries in the form of humanitarian assistance. In the meantime we will continue to negotiate with China in the hopes that they do not again try to redo deal!

Talks with China continue in a very congenial manner—there is absolutely no need to rush—as Tariffs are NOW being paid to the United States by China of 25% on 250 Billion Dollars worth of goods & products. These massive payments go directly to the Treasury of the U.S…

6:46 am: Tariffs will bring in FAR MORE wealth to our Country than even a phenomenal deal of the traditional kind. Also, much easier & quicker to do. Our Farmers will do better, faster, and starving nations can now be helped. Waivers on some products will be granted, or go to new source!

6:48 am: Tariffs will make our Country MUCH STRONGER, not weaker. Just sit back and watch! In the meantime, China should not renegotiate deals with the U.S. at the last minute. This is not the Obama Administration, or the Administration of Sleepy Joe, who let China get away with "murder!"

7:07 am: If we bought 15 Billion Dollars of Agriculture from our Farmers, far more than China buys now, we would have more than

85 Billion Dollars left over for new Infrastructure, Healthcare, or anything else. China would greatly slow down, and we would automatically speed up!

7:08 am: Build your products in the United States and there are NO TARIFFS!

May 11, 2019

8:55 am: Such an easy way to avoid Tariffs? Make or produce your goods and products in the good old USA. It's very simple!

May 12, 2019

6:22 pm: China is DREAMING that Sleepy Joe Biden, or any of the others, gets elected in 2020. They LOVE ripping off America!

May 13, 2019

10:55 am: There is no reason for the U.S. Consumer to pay the Tariffs, which take effect on China today. This has been proven recently when only 4 points were paid by the U.S., 21 points by China because China subsidizes product to such a large degree. Also, the Tariffs can be…

…completely avoided if you buy from a non-Tariffed Country, or you buy the product inside the USA (the best idea). That's Zero Tariffs. Many Tariffed companies will be leaving China for Vietnam and other such countries in Asia. That's why China wants to make a deal so badly!…

There will be nobody left in China to do business with. Very bad for China, very good for USA! But China has taken so advantage of the U.S. for so many years, that they are way ahead (Our Presidents did not do the job). Therefore, China should not retaliate-will only get worse!

May 14, 2019

5:15 am: In one year Tariffs have rebuilt our Steel Industry—it is booming! We placed a 25% Tariff on "dumped" steel from China &

other countries, and we now have a big and growing industry. We had to save Steel for our defense and auto industries, both of which are coming back strong!

5:31 am: China buys MUCH less from us than we buy from them, by almost 500 Billion Dollars, so we are in a fantastic position. Make your product at home in the USA and there is no Tariff. You can also buy from a non-Tariffed country instead of China. Many companies are leaving China…

…so that they will be more competitive for USA buyers. We are now a much bigger economy than China, and have substantially increased in size since the great 2016 Election. We are the "piggy bank" that everyone wants to raid and take advantage of. NO MORE!

5:51 am: We can make a deal with China tomorrow, before their companies start leaving so as not to lose USA business, but the last time we were close they wanted to renegotiate the deal. No way! We are in a much better position now than any deal we could have made. Will be taking in…

…Billions of Dollars, and moving jobs back to the USA where they belong. Other countries are already negotiating with us because they don't want this to happen to them. They must be a part of USA action. This should have been done by our leaders many years ago. Enjoy!

6:16 am: When the time is right we will make a deal with China. My respect and friendship with President Xi is unlimited but, as I have told him many times before, this must be a great deal for the United States or it just doesn't make any sense. We have to be allowed to make up some…

…of the tremendous ground we have lost to China on Trade since the ridiculous one sided formation of the WTO. It will all happen, and much faster than people think!

6:29 am: Our great Patriot Farmers will be one of the biggest beneficiaries of what is happening now. Hopefully China will do us the honor of continuing to buy our great farm product, the best, but if not your Country will be making up the difference based on a very high China buy…

…This money will come from the massive Tariffs being paid to the United States for allowing China, and others, to do business with us. The Farmers have been "forgotten" for many years. Their time is now!

7:35 am: China will be pumping money into their system and probably reducing interest rates, as always, in order to make up for the business they are, and will be, losing. If the Federal Reserve ever did a "match," it would be game over, we win! In any event, China wants a deal!

May 25, 2019

1:57 am: The real trade war began 30 years ago, and we lost. This is a bright new Age, the Age of Enlightenment. We don't lose anymore!

June 1, 2019

3:37 pm: Washington Post got it wrong, as usual. The U.S. is charging 25% against 250 Billion Dollars of goods shipped from China, not 200 BD. Also, China is paying a heavy cost in that they will subsidize goods to keep them coming, devalue their currency, yet companies are moving to…

…U.S. in order to avoid paying the 25% Tariff. Like Mexican companies will move back to the United States once the Tariff reaches the higher levels. They took many of our companies & jobs, the foolish Pols let it happen, and now they will come back unless Mexico stops the…

June 18, 2019

8:39 am: Had a very good telephone conversation with President Xi of China. We will be having an extended meeting next week at the G-20 in Japan. Our respective teams will begin talks prior to our meeting.

June 29, 2019

5:32 pm: I had a great meeting with President Xi of China yesterday, far better than expected. I agreed not to increase the already existing Tariffs that we charge China while we continue to negotiate. China has agreed that, during the negotiation, they will begin purchasing large..

…amounts of agricultural product from our great Farmers. At the request of our High Tech companies, and President Xi, I agreed to allow Chinese company Huawei to buy product from them which will not impact our National Security. Importantly, we have opened up negotiations.

…again with China as our relationship with them continues to be a very good one. The quality of the transaction is far more important to me than speed. I am in no hurry, but things look very good! There will be no reduction in the Tariffs currently being charged to China.

July 3, 2019

9:21 am: China and Europe playing big currency manipulation game and pumping money into their system in order to compete with USA. We should MATCH, or continue being the dummies who sit back and politely watch as other countries continue to play their games—as they have for many years!

July 9, 2019

7:44 am: India has long had a field day putting Tariffs on American products. No longer acceptable!

July 12, 2019

7:48 am: When you are the big "piggy bank" that other countries have been ripping off for years (to a level that is not to be believed), Tariffs are a great negotiating tool, a great revenue producer and, most importantly, a powerful way to get…

…companies to come to the USA and to get companies that have left us for other lands to COME BACK HOME. We stupidly lost 30% of our auto business to Mexico. If the Tariffs went on at the higher level, they would all come back, and fast. But very happy with the deal I made,

…if Mexico produces (which I think they will). Biggest part of deal with Mexico has not yet been revealed! China is similar, except they devalue currency & subsidize companies to lessen effect of 25% Tariffs. So far, little effect to consumers. Companies will relocate to U.S.

July 26, 2019

10:25 am: Apple will not be given Tariff waiver, or relief, for Mac Pro parts that are made in China. Make them in the USA, no Tariffs!

11:32 am: France just put a digital tax on our great American technology companies. If anybody taxes them, it should be their home Country, the USA. We will announce a substantial reciprocal action on Macron's foolishness shortly. I've always said American wine is better than French wine!

July 30, 2019

6:09 am: China is doing very badly, worst year in 27—was supposed to start buying our agricultural product now—no signs that they are doing so. That is the problem with China, they just don't come through. Our Economy has become MUCH larger than the Chinese Economy is last 3 years...

6:10 am: ...My team is negotiating with them now, but they always change the deal in the end to their benefit. They should probably wait out our Election to see if we get one of the Democrat stiffs like Sleepy Joe. Then they could make a GREAT deal, like in past 30 years, and continue

...to ripoff the USA, even bigger and better than ever before. The problem with them waiting, however, is that if & when I win, the deal that they get will be much tougher than what we are negotiating now...or no deal at all. We have all the cards, our past leaders never got it!

August 1, 2019

9:24 am: China, Iran & other foreign countries are looking at the Democrat Candidates and "drooling" over the small prospect that they could be dealing with them in the not too distant future. They would be able to rip off our beloved USA like never before. With President Trump, NO WAY!

12:26 pm: Our representatives have just returned from China where they had constructive talks having to do with a future Trade Deal. We thought we had a deal with China three months ago, but sadly, China decided to re-negotiate the deal prior to signing. More recently, China agreed to…

…buy agricultural product from the U.S. in large quantities, but did not do so. Additionally, my friend President Xi said that he would stop the sale of Fentanyl to the United States—this never happened, and many Americans continue to die! Trade talks are continuing, and…

…during the talks the U.S. will start, on September 1st, putting a small additional Tariff of 10% on the remaining 300 Billion Dollars of goods and products coming from China into our Country. This does not include the 250 Billion Dollars already Tariffed at 25%…

We look forward to continuing our positive dialogue with China on a comprehensive Trade Deal, and feel that the future between our two countries will be a very bright one!

August 3, 2019

7:46 am: Things are going along very well with China. They are paying us Tens of Billions of Dollars, made possible by their monetary devaluations and pumping in massive amounts of cash to keep their system going. So far our consumer is paying nothing—and no inflation. No help from Fed!

August 5, 2019

10:58 am: Based on the historic currency manipulation by China, it is now even more obvious to everyone that Americans are not paying for the Tariffs—they are being paid for compliments of China, and the U.S. is taking in tens of Billions of Dollars! China has always…

…used currency manipulation to steal our businesses and factories, hurt our jobs, depress our workers' wages and harm our farmers' prices. Not anymore!

11:00 am: China is intent on continuing to receive the hundreds of Billions of Dollars they have been taking from the U.S. with unfair trade practices and currency manipulation. So one-sided, it should have been stopped many years ago!

August 6, 2019

7:00 am: Massive amounts of money from China and other parts of the world is pouring into the United States for reasons of safety, investment, and interest rates! We are in a very strong position. Companies are also coming to the U.S. in big numbers. A beautiful thing to watch!

7:36 am: As they have learned in the last two years, our great American Farmers know that China will not be able to hurt them in that their President has stood with them and done what no other president would do—And I'll do it again next year if necessary!

August 10, 2019

4:58 pm: China wants to make a deal so badly. Thousands of companies are leaving because of the Tariffs, they must stem the flow. At the same time China may be hoping for a Democrat to win so they could continue the great ripoff of America, & the theft of hundreds of Billions of $'s

August 13, 2019

12:17 pm: Our Intelligence has informed us that the Chinese Government is moving troops to the Border with Hong Kong. Everyone should be calm and safe!

August 15, 2019

9:04 am: If President Xi would meet directly and personally with the protesters, there would be a happy and enlightened ending to the Hong Kong problem. I have no doubt!

2:29 pm: Biden doesn't have a clue! I will solve the China problem.

August 23, 2019

9:59 am: Our Country has lost, stupidly, Trillions of Dollars with China over many years. They have stolen our Intellectual Property at a rate of Hundreds of Billions of Dollars a year, & they want to continue. I won't let that happen! We don't need China and, frankly, would be far...

...better off without them. The vast amounts of money made and stolen by China from the United States, year after year, for decades, will and must STOP. Our great American companies are hereby ordered to immediately start looking for an alternative to China, including bringing...

...all deliveries of Fentanyl from China (or anywhere else!). Fentanyl kills 100,000 Americans a year. President Xi said this would stop—it didn't. Our Economy, because of our gains in the last 2 1/2 years, is MUCH larger than that of China. We will keep it that way!

August 28, 2019

7:06 am: So interesting to read and see all of the free and interesting advice I am getting on China, from people who have tried to handle it before and failed miserably—In fact, they got taken to the cleaners. We are doing very well with China. This has never happened to them before!

September 1, 2019

7:21 am: Peter Morici, Economist: Tariffs will not impact American consumers that much because the Chinese currency has gone down, which gives our importers a discount. Importers can find suppliers outside of China. Absolutely worth it, we don't want to be servants to the Chinese! This...

...is about American Freedom. Redirect the supply chain. There is no reason to buy everything from China!

September 3, 2019

8:33 am: For all of the "geniuses" out there, many who have been in other administrations and "taken to the cleaners" by China, that want me to get together with the EU and others to go after China Trade practices remember, the EU & all treat us VERY unfairly on Trade also. Will change!

September 4, 2019

8:52 am: "U.S. Winning Trade War With China In Dollars." CNBC

September 6, 2019

10:14 am: "China is eating the Tariffs." Billions pouring into USA. Targeted Patriot Farmers getting massive Dollars from the incoming Tariffs! Good Jobs Numbers, No Inflation(Fed). China having worst year in decades. Talks happening, good for all!

10:05 pm: China just enacted a major stimulus plan. With all the Tariffs THEY are paying to the USA, Billions and Billions of Dollars, they need it! In the meantime, our Federal Reserve sits back and does NOTHING!

September 11, 2019

5:14 am: "China suspends Tariffs on some U.S. products. Being hit very hard, supply chains breaking up as many companies move, or look to move, to other countries. Much more expensive to China than originally thought." @CNBC @JoeSquawk

6:17 pm: At the request of the Vice Premier of China, Liu He, and due to the fact that the People's Republic of China will be celebrating their 70th Anniversary..

on October 1st, we have agreed, as a gesture of good will, to move the increased Tariffs on 250 Billion Dollars worth of goods (25% to 30%), from October 1st to October 15th.

October 11, 2019

8:49 am: Good things are happening at China Trade Talk Meeting. Warmer feelings than in recent past, more like the Old Days. I will be meeting with the Vice Premier today. All would like to see something significant happen!

9:15 am: One of the great things about the China Deal is the fact that, for various reasons, we do not have to go through the very long and politically complex Congressional Approval Process. When the deal is fully negotiated, I sign it myself on behalf of our Country. Fast and Clean!

October 12, 2019

9:09 am: The deal I just made with China is, by far, the greatest and biggest deal ever made for our Great Patriot Farmers in the history of our Country. In fact, there is a question as to whether or not this much product can be produced? Our farmers will figure it out. Thank you China!

Other aspects of the deal are also great—technology, financial services, 16-20 Billion in Boeing Planes etc., but WOW, the Farmers really hit pay dirt! @ChuckGrassley @joniernst @debfisher @BenSasse Thank you to all Republicans in Congress for your invaluable help!

October 13, 2019

4:47 pm: My deal with China is that they will IMMEDIATELY start buying very large quantities of our Agricultural Product, not wait until the deal is signed over the next 3 or 4 weeks. THEY HAVE ALREADY STARTED! Likewise financial services and other deal aspects, start preparing…

…I agreed not to increase Tariffs from 25% to 30% on October 15th. They will remain at 25%. The relationship with China is very good. We will finish out the large Phase One part of the deal, then head directly into Phase Two. The Phase One Deal can be finalized & signed soon!

4:50 pm: CHINA HAS ALREADY BEGUN AGRICULTURAL PURCHASES FROM OUR GREAT PATRIOT FARMERS & RANCHERS!

November 13, 2019

9:32 am: Walmart announces great numbers. No impact from Tariffs (which are contributing $Billions to our Treasury). Inflation low (do you hear that Powell?)!

November 17, 2019

11:08 am: Our great Farmers will recieve another major round of "cash," compliments of China Tariffs, prior to Thanksgiving. The smaller farms and farmers will be big beneficiaries. In the meantime, and as you may have noticed, China is starting to buy big again. Japan deal DONE. Enjoy!

December 2, 2019

5:59 am: Brazil and Argentina have been presiding over a massive devaluation of their currencies. which is not good for our farmers. Therefore, effective immediately, I will restore the Tariffs on all Steel & Aluminum that is shipped into the U.S. from those countries. The Federal...

...Reserve should likewise act so that countries, of which there are many, no longer take advantage of our strong dollar by further devaluing their currencies. This makes it very hard for our manufactures & farmers to fairly export their goods. Lower Rates & Loosen—Fed!

6:11 am: U.S. Markets are up as much as 21% since the announcement of Tariffs on 3/1/2018—and the U.S. is taking in massive amounts of money (and giving some to our farmers, who have been targeted by China)!

December 6, 2019

7:28 pm: Why is the World Bank loaning money to China? Can this be possible? China has plenty of money, and if they don't, they create it. STOP!

December 12, 2019

9:35 am: Getting VERY close to a BIG DEAL with China. They want it, and so do we!

December 13, 2019

9:06 am: The Wall Street Journal story on the China Deal is completely wrong, especially their statement on Tariffs. Fake News. They should find a better leaker!

10:25 am: We have agreed to a very large Phase One Deal with China. They have agreed to many structural changes and massive purchases of Agricultural Product, Energy, and Manufactured Goods, plus much more. The 25% Tariffs will remain as is, with 7 1/2% put on much of the remainder…

…The Penalty Tariffs set for December 15th will not be charged because of the fact that we made the deal. We will begin negotiations on the Phase Two Deal immediately, rather than waiting until after the 2020 Election. This is an amazing deal for all. Thank you!

December 14, 2019

2:09 pm: Chuck Schumer sat for years during the Obama Administration and watched as China ripped off the United States. He & the Do Nothing Democrats did NOTHING as this $ carnage took place. Now, without even seeing it, he snipes at our GREAT new deal with China. Too bad Cryin' Chuck!

December 20, 2019

10:24 am: Had a very good talk with President Xi of China concerning our giant Trade Deal. China has already started large scale purchaes of agricultural product & more. Formal signing being arranged. Also talked about North Korea, where we are working with China, & Hong Kong (progress!).

December 31, 2019

9:16 am: I will be signing our very large and comprehensive Phase One Trade Deal with China on January 15. The ceremony will take place at the White House. High level representatives of China will be present. At a later date I will be going to Beijing where talks will begin on Phase Two!

Economy/Jobs/NAFTA—2017 News Quotes

Response to a question from David Muir of ABC News, January 26, 2017.
Source: https://www.telegraph.co.uk/news/2017/01/26/
full-transcript-president-donald-trumps-interview-abc-news/

"And we do have problems in the world. Big problems. The business also hits because the, the size of it. The size.

"I was with the Ford yesterday. And with General Motors yesterday. The top representatives, great people. And they're gonna do some tremendous work in the United States. They're gonna build plants back in the United States. But when you see the size, even as a businessman, the size of the investment that these big companies are gonna make, it hits you even in that regard. But we're gonna bring jobs back to America, like I promised on the campaign trail."

Response to a question from David Muir of ABC News, January 26, 2017.
Source: https://www.telegraph.co.uk/news/2017/01/26/
full-transcript-president-donald-trumps-interview-abc-news/

"Well, I'd say very simply that they are going to pay for it. I never said they're gonna pay from the start. I said Mexico will pay for the wall. But what I will tell my supporters is, 'Would you like me to wait two years or three years before I make this deal?' Because we have to make a deal on NAFTA. We have to make a new trade deal with Mexico because we're getting clobbered.

"We have a $60 billion trade deficit. So, if you want, I can wait two years and then we can do it nice and easily. I wanna start the wall immediately. Every supporter I have, I have had so many people calling and tweeting and, and writing letters saying they're so happy about it. I wanna start the wall. We will be reimbursed for the wall."

At the Signing of Executive Order on Fiduciary Rule, February 3, 2017.

Source: https://www.whitehouse.gov/briefings-statements/
remarks-president-trump-signing-executive-order-fiduciary-rule/

"Today we're signing core principles for regulating the United States financial system. It doesn't get much better than that, right?"

At Strategic Policy and CEO Discussion, April 11, 2017.

Source: https://www.whitehouse.gov/briefings-statements/
remarks-president-trump-strategic-policy-ceo-discussion/

"At the top of our agenda is the creation of great high-paying jobs for American workers. And we've made a lot of process. You see what's going on; you see the numbers. We've created over 600,000 jobs already in a very short period of time, and it's going to really start catching on now, because some of the things that we've done are big league and they are catching on.

"Already, we've created more than almost 600,000 jobs. And yesterday, Toyota just announced that it will invest more than $1.3 billion, it's probably going to be $1.9 billion, into its Georgetown, Kentucky plant, an investment that would not have been made if we didn't win the election.

"We have a lot of work to do. In the last two decades, our nation has lost a third of its manufacturing jobs, and our business tax is one of the highest in the world. It actually is, of developed countries, the single highest tax anywhere in the world.

"For too long, we've punished production in America and rewarded companies for leaving our country. And we're going to reverse that. We would reward companies, give them incentives to leave. NAFTA is a disaster. It's been a disaster from the day it was devised. And we're

47

going to have some very pleasant surprises for you on NAFTA, that I can tell you.

"My administration has already taken historic action to unleash job creation. We've signed dozens of bills and executive actions to reduce federal overreach and expand domestic production.

"On the environment, we're going to be very, very careful on the environment. It's very important to me and the administration. But we've allowed a lot of companies to go back to work. They were being restricted; their jobs were being restricted. We've unleashed a lot of companies, especially right now in the energy sector—You see what's going on there. It was impossible for people to do what they had to do, and now they can do it. It's all done.

"We're also working to modernize our economy and harness the full potential of women in the workforce, which is crucial to our economic success. Economic confidence is sweeping the nation. You saw the new survey that came out. It's at 93, which is the highest it's ever been. Ninety-three percent of manufacturers are optimistic about the future. It was a 27% increase over two months ago when it was also high because of the administration, and much higher than it's ever been, 93%. Highest it's ever been.

"This is just the beginning. We're going to reduce taxes. We're going to eliminate wasteful regulations, which we've already done, probably 25%. You can take a look at Dodd-Frank. For the bankers in the room, they'll be very happy because we're really doing a major streamlining and, perhaps, elimination, and replacing it with something else. But that will be the minimum. But we're doing a major elimination of the horrendous Dodd-Frank regulations, keeping some obviously, but getting rid of many.

"And we're going to put many millions of people back to work. The banks will be able to lend again. So many people come to see me, I see them all the time—Small businesses—They're unable to borrow from banks. They never had a problem 5, 6, 7, 10 years ago. They had great bankers. They had great relationships. Now they can't borrow. And we're going to let the banks loan them money, and they can build their businesses.

"So with your help and insights, we will use the private sector innovation to drive job creation and reform government. A lot of reform. We have a computer system in this country that's 40 years old. So when you hear we're hacked and we're this, that—We're like easy targets. And one of the things we're doing, in fact—We're working with a very, very wonderful woman from IBM, and others—And others, okay? Many others. It's like when I said to Lockheed, 'I like the F-35 fighter jet.' But then I said, 'But I also like the Boeing F-18.' Okay? So I love your computers, but we're also looking at others, all right?

"But we are. We're going to have a massive program to modernize our equipment. Ideally, get brand-new equipment. The cost of maintaining our computers is a number that is so high that it's not even a believable number. Now, I've heard anywhere—Is this possible? From $39 billion to $89 billion a year. Is that even possible? That's for keeping our computers updated and running. And I think we can buy a whole new system for less money than that, wouldn't you say? I mean, I hope so. We'll give you $10 billion right now—Modernize it."

Response to a question from John Dickerson of CBS News, April 30, 2017.
Source: https://www.cbsnews.com/news/face-the-nation-transcript-april-30-2017-president-trump/

"Well, one of the things that I've learned is how dishonest the media is, really. I've done things that are, I think, very good. I have done, I've set great foundations with foreign leaders. We have, you know, NAFTA, as you know, I was going to terminate it, but I got a very nice call from a man I like, the President of Mexico [then-President Enrique Peña Nieto]. I got a very nice call from Justin Trudeau, the Prime Minister of Canada. And they said, 'Please, would you, rather than terminating NAFTA?' I was all set to do it. In fact, I was going to do it today. I was going to do it as we're sitting here. I would've had to delay you. I was going to do it today. I was going to terminate NAFTA. But they called up and they said, 'Would you negotiate?' And I said, 'Yes, I will negotiate.'"

Response to a question from John Dickerson of CBS News, April 30, 2017.
Source: https://www.cbsnews.com/news/face-the-nation-transcript-april-30-2017-president-trump/

"If I'm not able to renegotiate NAFTA, we will terminate NAFTA."

Response to a question from Peter Baker of *The New York Times*, July 19, 2017.

Source: https://www.nytimes.com/2017/07/19/us/politics/trump-interview-transcript.html

"So, the bottom line is this. The country's doing well. We are, we are moving forward with a lot of great things. The unemployment is the lowest it's been in 16 years. The stock market is the highest it's ever been. It's up almost 20% since I took office. And we're working hard on healthcare. Um, the Russian investigation—It's not an investigation; it's not on me—You know, they're looking at a lot of things."

Economy/Jobs/NAFTA—2017 Tweets

January 24, 2017

6:11 am: Will be meeting at 9:00 with top automobile executives concerning jobs in America. I want new plants to be built here for cars sold here!

7:46 pm: Great meeting with Ford CEO Mark Fields and General Motors CEO Mary Barra at the @WhiteHouse today.

February 8, 2017

2:22 pm: Thank you Brian Krzanich, CEO of @Intel. A great investment ($7 BILLION) in American INNOVATION and JOBS!

February 16, 2017

6:34 am: Stock market hits new high with longest winning streak in decades. Great level of confidence and optimism—even before tax plan rollout!

March 15, 2017

6:13 am: Will be going to Detroit, Michigan (love), today for a big meeting on bringing back car production to State & U.S. Already happening!

7:14 am: CEO's most optimistic since 2009. It will only get better as we continue to slash unnecessary regulations and when we begin our big tax cut!

March 16, 2017

5:43 pm: My representatives had a great meeting w/ the Hispanic Chamber of Commerce at the WH today. Look forward to tremendous growth & future mtgs!

March 24, 2017

12:59 pm: Today, I was thrilled to announce a commitment of $25 BILLION & 20K AMERICAN JOBS over the next 4 years. THANK YOU Charter Communications!

March 28, 2017

5:36 am: Big announcement by Ford today. Major investment to be made in three Michigan plants. Car companies coming back to U.S. JOBS! JOBS! JOBS!

March 31, 2017

4:31 pm: We are going to defend our industry & create a level playing field for the American worker. It is time to put #AmericaFirst & #MAGA!

April 12, 2017

6:09 pm: Economic confidence is soaring as we unleash the power of private sector job creation and stand up for the American Workers. #AmericaFirst

April 20, 2017

2:33 pm: We're going to use American steel, we're going to use American labor, we are going to come first in all deals.
→ … https://t.co/QYjWx9K4YY

April 25, 2017

7:30 am: Canada has made business for our dairy farmers in Wisconsin and other border states very difficult. We will not stand for this. Watch!

6:32 pm: 'Presidential Executive Order on Promoting Agriculture and Rural Prosperity in America' Executive Order:…
https://t.co/LVMjZ9Ax0U

April 26, 2017

5:51 am: The U.S. recorded its slowest economic growth in five years (2016). GDP up only 1.6%. Trade deficits hurt the economy very badly.

April 27, 2017

6:12 am: I received calls from the President of Mexico and the Prime Minister of Canada asking to renegotiate NAFTA rather than terminate. I agreed.

June 9, 2017

5:52 pm: It is time to rebuild OUR country, to bring back OUR jobs, to restore OUR dreams, & yes, to put #AmericaFirst! TY Ohio! #InfrastructureWeek… https://t.co/2b2bXwxGkA

June 11, 2017

7:22 am to 7:23 am: The #FakeNews MSM doesn't report the great economic news since Election Day. #DOW up 16%. #NASDAQ up 19.5%. Drilling & energy sector…

way up. Regulations way down. 600,000+ new jobs added. Unemployment down to 4.3%. Business and economic enthusiasm way up-record levels!

June 12, 2017

12:59 pm: Congratulations! 'First New Coal Mine of Trump Era Opens in Pennsylvania'
https://t.co/aIRllxNLQA

June 30, 2017

1:19 pm: I am encouraged by President Moon's assurances that he will work to level the playing field for American workers, businesses, & automakers.

3:55 pm: Retail sales are at record numbers. We've got the economy going better than anyone ever dreamt—and you haven't seen anything yet!

July 2, 2017

6:55 pm: Stock Market at all time high, unemployment at lowest level in years (wages will start going up) and our base has never been stronger!

July 4, 2017

2:55 pm: Gas prices are the lowest in the U.S. in over ten years! I would like to see them go even lower

July 12, 2017

6:06 pm: Stock market hits another high with spirit and enthusiasm so positive. Jobs outlook looking very good! #MAGA
https://t.co/Vwxsb2vWGe

6:12 pm: JOBS, JOBS, JOBS! #MAGA https://t.co/HScS4Y9ZJK

July 15, 2017

11:30 am: Stock Market hit another all-time high yesterday—despite the Russian hoax story! Also, jobs numbers are starting to look very good!

July 20, 2017

10:31 pm: Billions of dollars in investments & thousands of new jobs in America! An initiative via Corning, Merck & Pfizer: https://t.co/5VtMfuY3PM

July 21, 2017

2:19 pm: Manufacturers' record-high optimism reported in the 1st qtr has carried into the 2nd qtr of 2017 via @ShopFloorNAM: https://t.co/WHZtcAxhRQ

July 25, 2017

10:35 am: "America's Labor Market Continues to Boom" JOBS, JOBS, JOBS! https://t.co/LuOaR1Iz2e

July 26, 2017

7:01 pm: Thank you Foxconn, for investing $10 BILLION DOLLARS with the potential for up to 13K new jobs in Wisconsin! MadeIn-TheUSA https://t.co/jJghVeb63s

July 29, 2017

12:04 pm: U.S. Stock Market up almost 20% since Election!

August 1, 2017

8:03 am: "Corporations have NEVER made as much money as they are making now." Thank you Stuart Varney @foxandfriends Jobs are starting to roar, watch!

August 2, 2017

8:38 am: Small business owners are the DREAMERS & INNOVA-TORS who are powering us into the future! Read more and watch here: https://t.co/TJn5x6HrFG

August 3, 2017

7:12 am: I am continuing to get rid of costly and unnecessary regula-tions. Much work left to do but effect will be great! Business & jobs will grow.

August 4, 2017

5:02 am: Toyota & Mazda to build a new $1.6B plant here in the U.S.A. and create 4K new American jobs. A great investment in American manufacturing!

5:21 am: ...and don't forget that Foxconn will be spending up to 10 billion dollars on a top of the line plant/plants in Wisconsin.

August 5, 2017

11:00 am: Prosperity is coming back to our shores because we are put-ting America WORKERS and FAMILIES first. #AmericaFirst

August 11, 2017

4:43 pm: As promised on the campaign trail, we will provide oppor-tunity for Americans to gain skills needed to succeed & thrive as the economy grows!

August 16, 2017

5:12 am: Amazon is doing great damage to tax paying retailers. Towns, cities and states throughout the U.S. are being hurt—many jobs being lost!

August 27, 2017

8:51 am: We are in the NAFTA (worst trade deal ever made) renegotiation process with Mexico & Canada.Both being very difficult,may have to terminate?

September 1, 2017

6:47 pm: Stock Market up 5 months in a row!

September 2, 2017

9:50 pm: The Manufacturing Index rose to 59%, the highest level since early 2011—and we can do much better!

September 28, 2017

9:22 pm: GDP was revised upward to 3.1 for last quarter. Many people thought it would be years before that happened. We have just begun!

September 29, 2017

8:39 am: RECORD HIGH FOR S & P 500!

October 11, 2017

5:21 am to 5:26 am: Stock Market has increased by 5.2 Trillion dollars since the election on November 8th, a 25% increase. Lowest unemployment in 16 years and…

…if Congress gives us the massive tax cuts (and reform) I am asking for, those numbers will grow by leaps and bounds. #MAGA

October 16, 2017

7:57 am: The U.S. has gained more than 5.2 trillion dollars in Stock Market Value since Election Day! Also, record business enthusiasm.

11:16 am: "Dow Passes 23,000 for the First Time, Fueled by Strong Earnings"#Dow23K https://t.co/wnkrddYlb9 https://t.co/wlP0NCNcou

October 21, 2017

8:14 am: Stock Market hits another all time high on Friday. 5.3 trillion dollars up since Election. Fake News doesn't spent much time on this!

5:51 pm: Just out, but lightly reported: "Fewest jobless claims since 1973 show firm U.S. Job Market" Lowest since March 1973. @bpolitics

October 31, 2017

2:41 pm: U.S. COAL PRODUCTION Up 7.8% past year. Down 31.5% last 10 years. #EndingWarOnCoal https://t.co/xr20OBb2DV

November 1, 2017

9:30 pm: It is finally happening for our great clean coal miners! https://t.co/suAnjs6Ccz

November 4, 2017

7:35 am: Unemployment is down to 4.1%, lowest in 17 years. 1.5 million new jobs created since I took office. Highest stock Market ever, up $5.4 trill

7:49 am: Would very much appreciate Saudi Arabia doing their IPO of Aramco with the New York Stock Exchange. Important to the United States!

November 7, 2017

5:37 am: Stock market hit yet another all-time record high yesterday. There is great confidence in the moves that my Administration…

…is making. Working very hard on TAX CUTS for the middle class, companies and jobs!

November 17, 2017

6:00 am: Great numbers on Stocks and the Economy. If we get Tax Cuts and Reform, we'll really see some great results!

November 20, 2017

6:55 pm: Under President Trump unemployment rate will drop below 4%. Analysts predict economic boom for 2018! @foxandfriends and @Varneyco

November 27, 2017

9:48 pm: New home sales reach a 10 year high. Stock Market has more record gains. Hopefully Republican Senators will give us the much needed Tax Cuts to keep it all going! Democrats want big Tax Increases.

November 28, 2017

5:30 pm: Dow, S&P 500 and Nasdaq all finished the day at new RE-CORD HIGHS!

November 30, 2017

10:46 am: The Dow just broke 24,000 for the first time (another all-time Record). If the Dems had won the Presidential Election, the Market would be down 50% from these levels and Consumer Confidence, which is also at an all-time high, would be "low and glum!"

December 3, 2017

8:15 am: People who lost money when the Stock Market went down 350 points based on the False and Dishonest reporting of Brian Ross of @ABC News (he has been suspended), should consider hiring a lawyer and suing ABC for the damages this bad reporting has caused—many millions of dollars!

December 8, 2017

2:02 pm: "The unemployment rate remains at a 17-year low of 4.1%. The unemployment rate in manufacturing dropped to 2.6%, the lowest ever recorded. The unemployment rate among Hispanics dropped to 4.7%, the lowest ever recorded..." @SecretaryAcosta @USDOL

December 12, 2017

9:23 am: Consumer Confidence is at an All-Time High, along with a Record High Stock Market. Unemployment is at a 17 year low. MAKE AMERICA GREAT AGAIN! Working to pass MASSIVE TAX CUTS (looking good).

December 15, 2017

7:00 pm: DOW, S&P 500 and NASDAQ close at record highs! #MAGA https://t.co/hvqwnqSGuG

December 18, 2017

5:25 pm: 70 Record Closes for the Dow so far this year! We have NEVER had 70 Dow Records in a one year period. Wow!

December 19, 2017

6:04 am: DOW RISES 5000 POINTS ON THE YEAR FOR THE FIRST TIME EVER—MAKE AMERICA GREAT AGAIN!

6:23 am: Stocks and the economy have a long way to go after the Tax Cut Bill is totally understood and appreciated in scope and size. Immediate expensing will have a big impact. Biggest Tax Cuts and Reform EVER passed. Enjoy, and create many beautiful JOBS!

December 21, 2017

10:04 am: Home Sales hit BEST numbers in 10 years! MAKE AMERICA GREAT AGAIN

December 28, 2017

11:18 am: Retail sales are at record numbers. We've got the economy going better than anyone ever dreamt—and you haven't seen anything yet!

Economy/Jobs/NAFTA—2018 News Quotes

Remarks at a rally in Tampa, Florida, July 31, 2018
Source: https://www.tampabay.com/florida-politics/buzz/2018/08/01/
heres-a-full-transcript-of-president-trumps-speech-from-his-tampa-rally/

"I tell the story, I was in New York and I shake hands. I love law enforcement. Do we love law enforcement?

"And I was shaking hands with policemen in New York City, and the first one came up to me and said, 'Mr. President, I want to thank you so much.' I said, 'What did I do?' He said, 'My 401(k) is up 44% and my wife thinks I'm, for the first time, a financial genius.'

"She's giving him all the credit.

"She said, she said, 'Darling, I love you so much.' And he said, 'Yes, I'm a great financial wizard.'

"But he said, 'You're looking, you're just making me look so good.' And all of you, who has 401(k)s here?

"I guarantee you one thing. I have your vote. I guarantee it."

Remarks at a rally in Tampa, Florida, July 31, 2018
Source: https://www.tampabay.com/florida-politics/buzz/2018/08/01/
heres-a-full-transcript-of-president-trumps-speech-from-his-tampa-rally/

"Just last week, it was announced that the U.S. economy grew at 4.1% last quarter. It was a number that everybody said was not reachable. And I would never want to say it during the campaign, even though I believed it. I believed it, because they would not have given us the break. Fake news, fake news.

"They are fake. No, I mean, do you believe—Look at this: Every night, it's the same thing. Wouldn't you think they'd get tired of these speeches? Wouldn't you think?

"And here's one thing I'll tell you: If they don't get ratings, those speeches don't go on, doesn't matter. Look how many they have back there. They just can't get enough. They can't get enough. They cannot get enough. And by the way, outside, if you want to go, we set up, for the first time, a tremendous movie screen, because we have thousands and thousands of people outside that couldn't get in.

"So, we have a big screen and big loudspeakers, and I hope you're all happy out there. This is a great place to be. If you've got to be outside, be outside in the great state of Florida, right? Right?

"So, we're setting records like never before. Since the election, we have added 3.7 million new jobs. They would not have believed that.

"We're in the longest positive job growth streak in history. Think of that. Remember, I said, 'What do you have to lose?' Right? What do I—OK? What do you have to lose? And people said, 'I don't know.' Is that a nice thing? No, it's not nice, or not un-nice. What do you have to lose?

"The African-American unemployment rate has reached the lowest level in history, history.

"Thank you. You guys are great. Thank you. Blacks for Trump. They say, 'Blacks for Trump.'

"You knew a long time ago, didn't you, huh? You knew a long time ago. Thank you, folks. Thank you.

"The Hispanic unemployment rate is at the lowest level in history, Hispanic.

"The Asian unemployment rate has reached the lowest level in history.

"Sorry about this, women, but the employment rate has reached the lowest level in only 65 years. It'll be history soon.

"It'll be. It'll be history soon. Give us about two more weeks.

"The veterans' unemployment rate, oh, do we love our veterans, right?

"Has reached the lowest level in 18 years. More than 3.5 million Americans have been lifted off food stamps since the election.

"American oil production is at an all-time high, we have never produced as much.

"And the United States is now a net natural gas exporter for the first time in more than 60 years, 60.

"We will very shortly be the largest in the world in energy, the largest in the world, think of that."

Remarks at a rally in Tampa, Florida, July 31, 2018
Source: https://www.tampabay.com/florida-politics/buzz/2018/08/01/
heres-a-full-transcript-of-president-trumps-speech-from-his-tampa-rally/

"America first. America first. We're also living by two very important rules, buy American and hire American.

"Last week I visited with hundreds of American steel workers, who were laid off years ago because other countries were dumping steel all over our country. They're not dumping so much anymore; you notice? And if they do, they're paying a 25% tariff or tax.

"So, you know what I say to that? Dump all you want. I hope you dump a lot.

"Now thanks to our tariffs, our steel workers are back on the job, American steel mills are back open for business, we are starting to set new records and nobody believed it could happen this quickly.

"U.S. Steel just announced that they're building six new steel mills.

"And that number's soon going to be lifted, but I'm not allowed to say that, so I won't.

"And I'm very proud to report that NuCor is going to build a brand new $240 million steel mill. That's a big one, right here in Florida. The head of NuCor is here. Thank you, thank you. Head of NuCor. That's a big one."

Remarks at an expanded bilateral meeting with President Uhuru Kenyatta of Kenya, August 27, 2018.

Source: https://www.whitehouse.gov/briefings-statements/
remarks-president-trump-president-kenyatta-republic-kenya-expanded-bilateral-meeting/

"We are with President [Uhuru] Kenyatta of a wonderful country that we do a lot of business with, Kenya. One of the most beautiful countries, from what I understand, Mr. President.

"We have lots of pictures and lots of people that tell me how beautiful your country is. And we do a lot of tourism. We do a lot of trade. And we do a lot of defense and security. And we're working very much on security right now. And I appreciate you very much being with us and your staff. This is really great. Your representatives have been dealing with our representatives and making a lot of progress. We're talking about a very major highway/roadway. And that seems to be going along well. That's a very important project, I think, for your country."

Remarks at an expanded bilateral meeting with President Uhuru Kenyatta of Kenya, August 27, 2018.

Source: https://www.whitehouse.gov/briefings-statements/
remarks-president-trump-president-kenyatta-republic-kenya-expanded-bilateral-meeting/

"Well, you are here on a very special day because the stock market is up almost 300 points today. We just signed a trade agreement with Mexico, and it's a terrific agreement for everybody. It's been in the works for a long time. It's an agreement that a lot of people said couldn't be done, and we did something, and it was very special. Great for our farmers, our workers.

"And our stock market just broke 26,000 for the first time ever in the history. So today we have the highest stock price we've ever had. And we're very happy about that. I said that was going to happen and it's happened. Everything I said is going to happen, it ends up happening.

"So, you picked a good day to come. We're in a very good mood."

Remarks at White House dinner with evangelical leaders, August 27, 2018.

Source: https://www.whitehouse.gov/briefings-statements/
remarks-president-trump-dinner-evangelical-leaders/

"Melania and I are thrilled to welcome you. And these are very special friends of mine, Evangelical pastors and leaders from all across the nation. We welcome you to the White House. It's a special place. It's a place we love. We're having a lot of fun; we're having a lot of success.

"Today we reached the highest level in the history of the stock market. We broke 26,000—[Audience applauds.] So, I assume you have some stock. And I view that differently. We're respected all over the world again, and it means jobs. So, it's a lot of good things happening."

Response to a question from Chris Wallace of FOX News, November 18, 2018.

Source: https://www.youtube.com/watch?v=rMgJnnG-Nql

"I think I'm doing a great job. We have the best economy we've ever had."

Economy/Jobs/NAFTA—2018 Tweets

January 2, 2018

8:49 am: Companies are giving big bonuses to their workers because of the Tax Cut Bill. Really great!

January 3, 2018

9:07 pm: "Some 40 U.S. companies have responded to President Trump's tax cut and reform victory in Congress last year by handing out bonuses up to $2,000, increases in 401k matches and

spending on charity, a much higher number than previously known."
https://t.co/bmWrwWzxMR

January 4, 2018

10:48 am: Dow just crashes through 25,000. Congrats! Big cuts in unnecessary regulations continuing.

January 5, 2018

6:35 am: Dow goes from 18,589 on November 9, 2016, to 25,075 today, for a new all-time Record. Jumped 1000 points in last 5 weeks, Record fastest 1000 point move in history. This is all about the Make America Great Again agenda! Jobs, Jobs, Jobs. Six trillion dollars in value created!

January 6, 2018

6:49 am: The African American unemployment rate fell to 6.8%, the lowest rate in 45 years. I am so happy about this News! And, in the Washington Post (of all places), headline states, "Trumps first year jobs numbers were very, very good."

January 8, 2018

5:59 pm: In every decision we make, we are honoring America's PROUD FARMING LEGACY. Years of crushing taxes, crippling regs, & corrupt politics left our communities hurting, our economy stagnant, & millions of hardworking Americans COMPLETELY FORGOTTEN. But they are not forgotten ANYMORE! https://t.co/MdYS7xnukQ

January 10, 2018

6:37 pm: Cutting taxes and simplifying regulations makes America the place to invest! Great news as Toyota and Mazda announce they are bringing 4,000 JOBS and investing $1.6 BILLION in Alabama, helping to further grow our economy! https://t.co/Kcg8IVH6iA

11:29 pm: Good news: Toyota and Mazda announce giant new Huntsville, Alabama, plant which will produce over 300,000 cars and SUV's a year and employ 4000 people. Companies are coming back to the U.S. in a very big way. Congratulations Alabama!

January 11, 2018

10:37 am: Great news, as a result of our TAX CUTS & JOBS ACT! https://t.co/SLvhLxP3Jl

9:49 pm: More great news as a result of historical Tax Cuts and Reform: Fiat Chrysler announces plan to invest more than $1 BILLION in Michigan plant, relocating their heavy-truck production from Mexico to Michigan, adding 2,500 new jobs and paying $2,000 bonus to U.S. employees!

9:53 pm: Chrysler is moving a massive plant from Mexico to Michigan, reversing a years long opposite trend. Thank you Chrysler, a very wise decision. The voters in Michigan are very happy they voted for Trump/Pence. Plenty of more to follow!

January 13, 2018

8:13 am: Yesterday was a big day for the stock market. Jobs are coming back to America. Chrysler is coming back to the USA, from Mexico and many others will follow. Tax cut money to employees is pouring into our economy with many more companies announcing. American business is hot again!

January 14, 2018

8:50 am to 8:59 am: "President Trump is not getting the credit he deserves for the economy. Tax Cut bonuses to more than 2,000,000 workers. Most explosive Stock Market rally that we've seen in modern times. 18,000 to 26,000 from Election, and grounded in profitability and growth. All Trump, not 0…

…big unnecessary regulation cuts made it all possible" (among many other things). "President Trump reversed the policies of President

Obama, and reversed our economic decline."Thank you Stuart Varney. @foxandfriends

January 16, 2018

9:30 am: Unemployment for Black Americans is the lowest ever recorded. Trump approval ratings with Black Americans has doubled. Thank you, and it will get even (much) better! @FoxNews

January 17, 2018

6:28 pm: I promised that my policies would allow companies like Apple to bring massive amounts of money back to the United States. Great to see Apple follow through as a result of TAX CUTS. Huge win for American workers and the USA!

6:32 pm: During the campaign, I promised to MAKE AMERICA GREAT AGAIN by bringing businesses and jobs back to our country. I am very proud to see companies like Chrysler moving operations from Mexico to Michigan where there are so many great American workers!

6:36 pm: Main Street is BACK! Strongest Holiday Sales bump since the Great Recession—beating forecasts by BILLIONS OF DOLLARS.

February 2, 2018

1:05 pm: With 3.5 million Americans receiving bonuses or other benefits from their employers as a result of TAX CUTS, 2018 is off to great start! ✓Unemployment rate at 4.1%. ✓Average earnings up 2.9% in the last year. ✓200,000 new American jobs. ✓#MAGA

February 10, 2018

9:02 am: Jobless claims have dropped to a 45 year low!

February 19, 2018

9:29 pm: The U.S. economy is looking very good, in my opinion, even better than anticipated. Companies are pouring back into our country, reversing the long term trend of leaving. The unemployment numbers are looking great, and Regulations & Taxes have been massively Cut! JOBS, JOBS, JOBS

February 24, 2018

4:07 pm: Unemployment claims are at the lowest level since 1973. Much of this has to do with the massive cutting of unnecessary and job killing Regulations!

March 1, 2018

1:06 pm: Unemployment filings are at their lowest level in over 48 years. Great news for workers and JOBS, JOBS, JOBS! #MAGA

7:52 pm: Manufacturing growing at the fastest pace in almost two decades!

March 5, 2018

6:47 am to 6:53 am: We have large trade deficits with Mexico and Canada. NAFTA, which is under renegotiation right now, has been a bad deal for U.S.A. Massive relocation of companies & jobs. Tariffs on Steel and Aluminum will only come off if new & fair NAFTA agreement is signed. Also, Canada must...

...treat our farmers much better. Highly restrictive. Mexico must do much more on stopping drugs from pouring into the U.S. They have not done what needs to be done. Millions of people addicted and dying.

March 7, 2018

6:40 am: From Bush 1 to present, our Country has lost more than 55,000 factories, 6,000,000 manufacturing jobs and accumulated Trade Deficits of more than 12 Trillion Dollars. Last year we had a Trade Deficit of almost 800 Billion Dollars. Bad Policies & Leadership. Must WIN again! #MAGA

April 6, 2018

3:23 pm: "BET founder: Trump's economy is bringing black workers back into the labor force" https://t.co/TtMDfi4bv0

April 17, 2018

7:24 am: Employment is up, Taxes are DOWN. Enjoy!

May 4, 2018

5:28 am: Because Jobs in the U.S. are doing so well, Americans receiving unemployment aid is the lowest since 1973. Great!

8:27 am: JUST OUT: 3.9% Unemployment. 4% is Broken! In the meantime, WITCH HUNT!

May 17, 2018

5:14 pm: Tomorrow, the House will vote on a strong Farm Bill, which includes work requirements. We must support our Nation's great farmers!

May 24, 2018

12:54 pm: Today, it was my honor to sign #S2155, the "Economic Growth, Regulatory Relief, and Consumer Protection Act." Read more: https://t.co/sYZ4PzzxxW https://t.co/gi0qGe6ukX

June 1, 2018

8:18 am: Canada has treated our Agricultural business and Farmers very poorly for a very long period of time. Highly restrictive on Trade! They must open their markets and take down their trade barriers! They report a really high surplus on trade with us. Do Timber & Lumber in U.S.?

June 4, 2018

3:42 pm: In many ways this is the greatest economy in the HISTORY of America and the best time EVER to look for a job!

June 5, 2018

5:51 am: The U.S. has an increased economic value of more than 7 Trillion Dollars since the Election. May be the best economy in the history of our country. Record Jobs numbers. Nice!

June 7, 2018

5:04 pm: Please tell Prime Minister Trudeau and President Macron that they are charging the U.S. massive tariffs and create non-monetary barriers. The EU trade surplus with the U.S. is $151 Billion, and Canada keeps our farmers and others out. Look forward to seeing them tomorrow.

6:44 pm: Prime Minister Trudeau is being so indignant, bringing up the relationship that the U.S. and Canada had over the many years and all sorts of other things...but he doesn't bring up the fact that they charge us up to 300% on dairy—hurting our Farmers, killing our Agriculture!

9:15 pm: Why isn't the European Union and Canada informing the public that for years they have used massive Trade Tariffs and non-monetary Trade Barriers against the U.S. Totally unfair to our farmers, workers & companies. Take down your tariffs & barriers or we will more than match you!

June 8, 2018

5:16 am: Canada charges the U.S. a 270% tariff on Dairy Products! They didn't tell you that, did they? Not fair to our farmers!

5:25 am: Looking forward to straightening out unfair Trade Deals with the G-7 countries. If it doesn't happen, we come out even better!

June 9, 2018

3:56 pm: Just left the @G7 Summit in beautiful Canada. Great meetings and relationships with the six Country Leaders especially since they know I cannot allow them to apply large Tariffs and strong barriers to...

...U.S.A. Trade. They fully understand where I am coming from. After many decades, fair and reciprocal Trade will happen!

3:57 pm: The United States will not allow other countries to impose massive Tariffs and Trade Barriers on its farmers, workers and companies. While sending their product into our country tax free. We have put up with Trade Abuse for many decades—and that is long enough.

6:03 pm: Based on Justin's false statements at his news conference, and the fact that Canada is charging massive Tariffs to our U.S. farmers, workers and companies, I have instructed our U.S. Reps not to endorse the Communique as we look at Tariffs on automobiles flooding the U.S. Market!

6:04 pm: PM Justin Trudeau of Canada acted so meek and mild during our @G7 meetings only to give a news conference after I left saying that, "US Tariffs were kind of insulting" and he "will not be pushed around." Very dishonest & weak. Our Tariffs are in response to his of 270% on dairy!

June 10, 2018

8:05 pm: Fair Trade is now to be called Fool Trade if it is not Reciprocal. According to a Canada release, they make almost 100 Billion Dollars in Trade with U.S. (guess they were bragging and got caught!). Minimum is 17B. Tax Dairy from us at 270%. Then Justin acts hurt when called out!

8:17 pm: Why should I, as President of the United States, allow countries to continue to make Massive Trade Surpluses, as they have for decades, while our Farmers, Workers & Taxpayers have such a big and unfair price to pay? Not fair to the PEOPLE of America! $800 Billion Trade Deficit...

9:41 pm: Sorry, we cannot let our friends, or enemies, take advantage of us on Trade anymore. We must put the American worker first!

June 21, 2018

3:46 pm: Farm Bill just passed in the House. So happy to see work requirements included. Big win for the farmers!

June 23, 2018

6:15 am: Steel is coming back fast! U.S. Steel is adding great capacity also. So are others.

7:38 am: The National Association of Manufacturers just announced that 95.1% of Manufacturers "have a positive outlook for their companies." This is the best number in the Association's history!

June 25, 2018

4:28 pm: Surprised that Harley-Davidson, of all companies, would be the first to wave the White Flag. I fought hard for them and ultimately they will not pay tariffs selling into the E.U., which has hurt us badly on trade, down $151 Billion. Taxes just a Harley excuse—be patient! #MAGA

June 26, 2018

6:16 am to 6:37 am: Early this year Harley-Davidson said they would move much of their plant operations in Kansas City to Thailand. That was long before Tariffs were announced. Hence, they were just using Tariffs/Trade War as an excuse. Shows how unbalanced & unfair trade is, but we will fix it..

...We are getting other countries to reduce and eliminate tariffs and trade barriers that have been unfairly used for years against our farmers, workers and companies. We are opening up closed markets and expanding our footprint. They must play fair or they will pay tariffs!

...When I had Harley-Davidson officials over to the White House, I chided them about tariffs in other countries, like India, being too high. Companies are now coming back to America. Harley must know that they won't be able to sell back into U.S. without paying a big tax!

7:17 am: A Harley-Davidson should never be built in another country- never! Their employees and customers are already very angry at them. If they move, watch, it will be the beginning of the end—they surrendered, they quit! The Aura will be gone and they will be taxed like never before!

June 27, 2018

10:26 am: Harley-Davidson should stay 100% in America, with the people that got you your success. I've done so much for you, and then this. Other companies are coming back where they belong! We won't forget, and neither will your customers or your now very HAPPY competitors!

June 28, 2018

1:57 pm: Today, we broke ground on a plant that will provide jobs for up to 15,000 Wisconsin Workers! As Foxconn has discovered, there is no better place to build, hire and grow than right here in the United States!

June 29, 2018

6:30 pm: The new plant being built by Foxconn in Wisconsin is incredible. Congratulations to the people of Wisconsin and to Governor Scott Walker @GovWalker and his talented representatives for having pulled it off. Great job!

July 3, 2018

9:00 am: Now that Harley-Davidson is moving part of its operation out of the U.S., my Administration is working with other Motor Cycle companies who want to move into the U.S. Harley customers are not happy with their move—sales are down 7% in 2017. The U.S. is where the Action is!

July 14, 2018

4:46 am: The Stock Market hit 25,000 yesterday. Jobs are at an all time record—and that is before we fix some of the worst trade deals and conditions ever seen by any government. It is all happening!

July 24, 2018

8:46 am: Our Country is doing GREAT. Best financial numbers on the Planet. Great to have USA WINNING AGAIN!

July 27, 2018

11:12 am: I am thrilled to announce that in the second quarter of this year, the U.S. Economy grew at the amazing rate of 4.1%!

2:23 pm: Private business investment has surged from 1.8 percent the year BEFORE I came into office to 9.4 percent this year—that means JOBS, JOBS, JOBS!

July 29, 2018

7:42 am: The biggest and best results coming out of the good GDP report was that the quarterly Trade Deficit has been reduced by $52 Billion and, of course, the historically low unemployment numbers, especially for African Americans, Hispanics, Asians and Women.

August 2, 2018

1:59 pm: When the House and Senate meet on the very important Farm Bill—we love our farmers—hopefully they will be able to leave the WORK REQUIREMENTS FOR FOOD STAMPS PROVISION that the House approved. Senate should go to 51 votes!

August 3, 2018

5:10 pm: July is just the ninth month since 1970 that unemployment has fallen below 4%. Our economy has added 3.7 million jobs since I won the Election. 4.1 GDP. More than 4 million people have received a pay raise due to tax reform. $400 Billion brought back from "overseas." @FoxNews

5:59 pm: Almost 500,000 Manufacturing Jobs created since I won the Election. Remember when my opponents were saying that we couldn't create this type of job anymore. Wrong, in fact these are among our best and most important jobs!

August 16, 2018

7:43 am: Our Economy is doing better than ever. Money is pouring into our cherished DOLLAR like rarely before, companies earnings are higher than ever, inflation is low & business optimism is higher than it has ever been. For the first time in many decades, we are protecting our workers!

August 17, 2018

6:30 am: In speaking with some of the world's top business leaders I asked what it is that would make business (jobs) even better in the U.S. "Stop quarterly reporting & go to a six month system," said one. That would allow greater flexibility & save money. I have asked the SEC to study!

August 18, 2018

8:39 am: The Economy is stronger and better than ever before. Importantly, there remains tremendous potential—it will only get better with time!

August 22, 2018

3:07 pm: Longest bull run in the history of the stock market, congratulations America!

August 24, 2018

5:04 am: Our Economy is setting records on virtually every front— Probably the best our country has ever done. Tremendous value created since the Election. The World is respecting us again! Companies are moving back to the U.S.A.

August 25, 2018

6:45 pm: Stock Market hit all time high on Friday. Congratulations U.S.A.!

August 26, 2018

9:31 am: Fantastic numbers on consumer spending released on Friday. Stock Market hits all time high!

August 28, 2018

4:57 am: NASDAQ has just gone above 8000 for the first time in history!

August 29, 2018

9:56 am: Consumer Confidence Index, just out, is the HIGHEST IN 18 YEARS! Also, GDP revised upward to 4.2 from 4.1. Our country is doing great!

August 30, 2018

6:20 am: The news from the Financial Markets is even better than anticipated. For all of you that have made a fortune in the markets, or seen your 401k's rise beyond your wildest expectations, more good news is coming!

September 1, 2018

10:00 am to 10:12 am: There is no political necessity to keep Canada in the new NAFTA deal. If we don't make a fair deal for the U.S. after decade of abuse, Canada will be out. Congress should not interfere with these negotiations or I will simply terminate NAFTA entirely & we will be far better off...

...Remember, NAFTA was one of the WORST Trade Deals ever made. The U.S. lost thousands of businesses and millions of jobs. We were far better off before NAFTA—should never have been signed. Even the Vat Tax was not accounted for. We make new deal or go back to pre-NAFTA!

5:55 pm: We shouldn't have to buy our friends with bad Trade Deals and Free Military Protection!

September 3, 2018

7:23 am: The Worker in America is doing better than ever before. Celebrate Labor Day!

September 5, 2018

8:21 am: The Trump Economy is booming with help of House and Senate GOP. #FarmBill with SNAP work requirements will bolster farmers and get America back to work. Pass the Farm Bill with SNAP work requirements!

September 9, 2018

9:12 am: "Trump has set Economic Growth on fire. During his time in office, the economy has achieved feats most experts thought impossible. GDP is growing at a 3 percent-plus rate. The unemployment rate is near a 50 year low." CNBC...Also, the Stock Market is up almost 50% since Election!

September 10, 2018

6:03 am: The GDP Rate (4.2%) is higher than the Unemployment Rate (3.9%) for the first time in over 100 years!

8:57 am: The Economy is soooo good, perhaps the best in our country's history (remember, it's the economy stupid!), that the Democrats are flailing & lying like CRAZY! Phony books, articles and T.V. "hits" like no other pol has had to endure-and they are losing big. Very dishonest people!

September 16, 2018

8:06 pm: Consumer Sentiment hit its highest level in 17 years this year. Sentiment fell 11% in 2015, an Obama year, and rose 16% since the Election, #TrumpTime

September 17, 2018

5:15 am: Consumer Sentiment hit its highest level in 17 years this year. Sentiment fell 11% in 2015, an Obama year, and rose 16% since the Election, #TrumpTime

September 20, 2018

8:34 am: S&P 500 HITS ALL-TIME HIGH Congratulations USA!

September 26, 2018

5:57 am: Jobless Claims fell to their lowest level in 49 years!

October 1, 2018

5:30 am to 5:53 am: Late last night, our deadline, we reached a wonderful new Trade Deal with Canada, to be added into the deal already reached with Mexico. The new name will be The United States Mexico Canada Agreement, or USMCA. It is a great deal for all three countries, solves the many…

…deficiencies and mistakes in NAFTA, greatly opens markets to our Farmers and Manufacturers, reduces Trade Barriers to the U.S. and will bring all three Great Nations together in competition with the rest of the world. The USMCA is a historic transaction!

5:56 am: Congratulations to Mexico and Canada!

7:08 am: News conference on the USMCA this morning at 11:00— Rose Garden of White House.

October 3, 2018

8:04 am: The Stock Market just reached an All-Time High during my Administration for the 102nd Time, a presidential record, by far, for less than two years. So much potential as Trade and Military Deals are completed.

9:13 am: Mexico, Canada and the United States are a great partnership and will be a very formidable trading force. We will now, because of the USMCA, work very well together. Great Spirit!

October 5, 2018

8:06 am: Just out: 3.7% Unemployment is the lowest number since 1969!

October 12, 2018

2:37 pm: Happy #NationalFarmersDay! With the recent #USMCA our GREAT FARMERS will do better than ever before!!

October 16, 2018

9:12 am: Incredible number just out, 7,036,000 job openings. Astonishing—it's all working! Stock Market up big on tremendous potential of USA. Also, Strong Profits. We are Number One in World, by far!

9:39 pm: Stock Market up 548 points today. Also, GREAT jobs numbers!

October 17, 2018

7:31 am: August job openings hit a record 7.14 million. Congratulations USA!

October 18, 2018

6:49 pm: Prime Minister @AbeShinzo of Japan has been working with me to help balance out the one-sided Trade with Japan. These are some of the investments they are making in our Country—just the beginning!

October 21, 2018

2:26 pm: Best Jobs Numbers in the history of our great Country! Many other things likewise. So why wouldn't we win the Midterms? Dems can never do even nearly as well! Think of what will happen to your now beautiful 401-k's!

October 30, 2018

7:33 am: The Stock Market is up massively since the Election, but is now taking a little pause—people want to see what happens with the Midterms. If you want your Stocks to go down, I strongly suggest voting Democrat. They like the Venezuela financial model, High Taxes & Open Borders

10:00 am: Just out: Consumer Confidence hits highest level since 2000.

October 31, 2018

8:04 am: Stock Market up more than 400 points yesterday. Today looks to be another good one. Companies earnings are great!

November 2, 2018

8:46 am: Wow! The U.S. added 250,000 Jobs in October—and this was despite the hurricanes. Unemployment at 3.7%. Wages UP! These are incredible numbers. Keep it going, Vote Republican!

November 14, 2018

2:28 pm: Not seen in many years, America's steelworkers get a hard-earned raise because of my Administration's policies to help bring back the U.S. steel industry, which is critical to our National Security. I will always protect America and its workers!

November 27, 2018

2:05 pm: Very disappointed with General Motors and their CEO, Mary Barra, for closing plants in Ohio, Michigan and Maryland. Nothing being closed in Mexico & China. The U.S. saved General Motors, and this is the THANKS we get! We are now looking at cutting all @GM subsidies, including…

…for electric cars. General Motors made a big China bet years ago when they built plants there (and in Mexico)—don't think that bet is going to pay off. I am here to protect America's Workers!

November 28, 2018

9:43 am to 9:49 am: The reason that the small truck business in the U.S. is such a go to favorite is that, for many years, Tariffs of 25% have been put on small trucks coming into our country. It is called the "chicken tax." If we did that with cars coming in, many more cars would be built here...

...and G.M. would not be closing their plants in Ohio, Michigan & Maryland. Get smart Congress. Also, the countries that send us cars have taken advantage of the U.S. for decades. The President has great power on this issue—Because of the G.M. event, it is being studied now!

11:09 am: Steel Dynamics announced that it will build a brand new 3 million ton steel mill in the Southwest that will create 600 good-paying U.S. JOBS. Steel JOBS are coming back to America, just like I predicted. Congratulations to Steel Dynamics!

November 30, 2018

9:45 am: Just signed one of the most important, and largest, Trade Deals in U.S. and World History. The United States, Mexico and Canada worked so well together in crafting this great document. The terrible NAFTA will soon be gone. The USMCA will be fantastic for all!

3:23 pm: Great reviews on the USMCA—sooo much better than NAFTA!

December 17, 2018

8:27 am: It is incredible that with a very strong dollar and virtually no inflation, the outside world blowing up around us, Paris is burning and China way down, the Fed is even considering yet another interest rate hike. Take the Victory

4:14 pm: Today I am making good on my promise to defend our Farmers & Ranchers from unjustified trade retaliation by foreign nations. I have authorized Secretary Perdue to implement the 2nd round of Market Facilitation Payments. Our economy is stronger than ever—we stand with our Farmers!

81

Economy/Jobs/NAFTA—2019 News Quotes

From State of the Union address, February 5, 2019.

Source: https://www.whitehouse.gov/briefings-statements/
president-donald-j-trumps-state-union-address-2/

"In just over two years since the election, we have launched an unprecedented economic boom, a boom that has rarely been seen before. We have created 5.3 million new jobs and importantly added 600,000 new manufacturing jobs; something which almost everyone said was impossible to do, but the fact is, we are just getting started.

"Wages are rising at the fastest pace in decades, and growing for blue collar workers, who I promised to fight for, faster than anyone else. Nearly 5 million Americans have been lifted off food stamps. The United States economy is growing almost twice as fast today as when I took office, and we are considered far and away the hottest economy anywhere in the world. Unemployment has reached the lowest rate in half a century. African-American, Hispanic-American, and Asian-American unemployment have all reached their lowest levels ever recorded. Unemployment for Americans with disabilities has also reached an all-time low. More people are working now than at any time in our history: 157 million."

From State of the Union address, February 5, 2019.

Source: https://www.whitehouse.gov/briefings-statements/
president-donald-j-trumps-state-union-address-2/

"We have unleashed a revolution in American energy: the United States is now the number one producer of oil and natural gas in the world. And now, for the first time in 65 years, we are a net exporter of energy.

"After 24 months of rapid progress, our economy is the envy of the world, our military is the most powerful on earth, and America is winning each and every day. Members of Congress: the State of our Union is strong. Our country is vibrant and our economy is thriving like never before."

From State of the Union address, February 5, 2019.

Source: https://www.whitehouse.gov/briefings-statements/
president-donald-j-trumps-state-union-address-2/

"As we work to defend our people's safety, we must also ensure our economic resurgence continues at a rapid pace.

"No one has benefitted more from our thriving economy than women, who have filled 58% of the new jobs created in the last year. All Americans can be proud that we have more women in the workforce than ever before, and exactly one century after the Congress passed the Constitutional amendment giving women the right to vote, we also have more women serving in the Congress than ever before.

"As part of our commitment to improving opportunity for women everywhere, this Thursday we are launching the first ever Government-wide initiative focused on economic empowerment for women in developing countries."

From State of the Union address, February 5, 2019.

Source: https://www.whitehouse.gov/briefings-statements/
president-donald-j-trumps-state-union-address-2/

"Another historic trade blunder was the catastrophe known as NAFTA.

"I have met the men and women of Michigan, Ohio, Pennsylvania, Indiana, New Hampshire, and many other states whose dreams were shattered by NAFTA. For years, politicians promised them they would negotiate for a better deal. But no one ever tried until now.

"Our new U.S.-Mexico-Canada Agreement, or USMCA, will replace NAFTA and deliver for American workers: bringing back our manufacturing jobs, expanding American agriculture, protecting intellectual property, and ensuring that more cars are proudly stamped with four beautiful words: Made in the USA.

"Tonight, I am also asking you to pass the United States Reciprocal Trade Act, so that if another country places an unfair tariff on an American product, we can charge them the exact same tariff on the same product that they sell to us."

Remarks during a visit to the Lima Army Tank Plant in Ohio, March 20, 2019.
Source: https://www.c-span.org/video/?458966-1/
president-trump-delivers-remarks-lima-army-tank-plant-ohio

"Well, you better love me; I kept this place open, that I can tell you. They said, 'We're closing it.' And I said, 'No, we're not.' And now you're doing record business. The job you do is incredible. And I'm thrilled to be here in Ohio with the hardworking men and women of Lima.

"And this is some tank plant. There's nothing like it in the world. You make the finest equipment in the world. You really know what you're doing. They just gave me a little briefing on a couple of those tanks."

Remarks during a visit to the Lima Army Tank Plant in Ohio, March 20, 2019.
Source: https://www.c-span.org/video/?458966-1/
president-trump-delivers-remarks-lima-army-tank-plant-ohio

"After so many years of budget cuts and layoffs, today, jobs are coming back and pouring back, frankly, like never before. Companies are coming back into our country; they want the action. Production is ramping up in the biggest way. And the awesome M1 Abrams tank is once again thundering down the assembly line. A1."

Remarks during a visit to the Lima Army Tank Plant in Ohio, March 20, 2019.
Source: https://www.c-span.org/video/?458966-1/
president-trump-delivers-remarks-lima-army-tank-plant-ohio

"And you look at some of the economic numbers; nobody thought we'd ever see numbers like that in our country, not a for a long time, not for ever. And what we're doing has been incredible. What you're doing has been more incredible. You stuck it out and now you've got one of the most successful military plants anywhere in the world. It's great."

Response to an unidentified reporter's question before Marine One departure, March 20, 2019.
Source: https://www.whitehouse.gov/briefings-statements/
remarks-president-trump-marine-one-departure-34/

"But I want to see the [Special Counsel Robert Mueller] report. And you know who will want to see it? The tens of millions of people that love the fact that we have the greatest economy we've ever had."

Response to an unidentified reporter's question before Marine One departure, March 20, 2019.
Source: https://www.whitehouse.gov/briefings-statements/ remarks-president-trump-marine-one-departure-34/

"No recommendation. It's up for review, and the European Union has been very tough on the United States for many years but nobody talked about it. And so we're looking at something to combat it.

"Not only do they charge our companies—If you look, it was 1.6 billion to Google; it just happened yesterday. And a lot of other things. A lot of litigation.

"But I say the European Union has been as tough on the United States as China, just not as much money involved."

Response to a question from Catherine Herridge of FOX News, May 2, 2019.
Source: https://www.foxnews.com/politics/transcript-fox-news-interview-with-president-trump

"You know you saw the deficit going down. You see the 3.2, which was highly—You know the GDP was 3.2 first quarter. Always the worst quarter, and we had a tremendous first quarter.

"This country is doing well. This country is doing probably better economically than it's ever done before. We have the best unemployment numbers we've had in 51 years, soon to be historic."

Response to a question from Catherine Herridge of FOX News, May 2, 2019.
Source: https://www.foxnews.com/politics/transcript-fox-news-interview-with-president-trump

"We have the strongest economy that we've ever had, we're doing phenomenally. "We have the best unemployment numbers, African American, Asians, Hispanics, best numbers we've ever had. Women: the best in 61 years, unemployment numbers, job numbers, wealth numbers— We have the best numbers. We—I think we have the best economy we've ever had and we have more people, Catherine [Herridge of FOX

News], working right now than ever in the history of our country. So I don't know why somebody beats that."

Remarks at the signing of H.R. 3401, July 1, 2019.
Source: https://www.whitehouse.gov/briefings-statements/remarks-president-trump-signing-h-r-3401/

"I just got back, as you know, from Japan and from South Korea. Met with many of the countries: the G20. So you had the biggest countries. And it was incredible. Everybody greeted me with congratulations on how well we're doing with our economy. We have the number one economy in the world. And a lot of that is tax cuts. A lot of it is regulation cuts."

Remarks at the signing of H.R. 3401, July 1, 2019.
Source: https://www.whitehouse.gov/briefings-statements/remarks-president-trump-signing-h-r-3401/

"But we have many, many companies that left our country and they're now coming back. Especially the automobile business. We have auto plants being built all over the country. We went decades and no plant was built. No plant was even expanded.

"And in leaving Japan, I was with Prime Minister [Shinzō] Abe and he was telling me they have many more companies now that are moving to the United States and building plants in Michigan and Ohio, and North Carolina, South Carolina, Florida: different states all over the country. And it's pretty amazing because we didn't have any. I mean, we had no expansions, and now we have a lot of expansion."

Remarks at the signing of an executive order protecting and improving Medicare for senior citizens, Ocala, Florida, October 3, 2019.
Source: https://www.whitehouse.gov/briefings-statements/remarks-president-trump-signing-executive-order-protecting-improving-medicare-nations-seniors-ocala-fl/

"We've created over 6 million new jobs since the election. The unemployment rate has reached a 51-year low. Two point, think of that. Think of that. Then, soon, it's going to be a historic number, like so many of the other numbers.

"2.5 million people have been lifted out of poverty. That means more Americans that now have, and that's what it's all about—They have a great way of life. They have affordable healthcare options and millions of seniors are enjoying better, healthier, and more prosperous retirements. I should be retiring with you. I should be in this audience, clapping. But I didn't trust anybody to be standing here, because I know what you have."

Economy/Jobs/NAFTA—2019 Tweets

January 1, 2019

6:39 pm: Do you think it's just luck that gas prices are so low, and falling? Low gas prices are like another Tax Cut!

January 8, 2019

8:01 am: Economic numbers looking REALLY good. Can you imagine if I had long term ZERO interest rates to play with like the past administration, rather than the rapidly raised normalized rates we have today. That would have been SO EASY! Still, markets up BIG since 2016 Election!

8:13 am: "The President is the biggest and best supporter of the Steel Industry in many years. We are now doing really well. The Tariffs let us compete. Was unfair that the Steel Industry lost its jobs to unfair trade laws. Very positive outcome." Mark Glyptis, United Steelworkers

January 15, 2019

7:25 am: Volkswagen will be spending 800 million dollars in Chattanooga, Tennessee. They will be making Electric Cars. Congratulations to Chattanooga and Tennessee on a job well done. A big win!

January 20, 2019

7:40 am: Always heard that as President, "it's all about the economy!" Well, we have one of the best economies in the history of our Country. Big GDP, lowest unemployment, companies coming back to the U.S. in BIG numbers, great new trade deals happening, & more. But LITTLE media mention!

January 21, 2019

10:22 am: Last year was the best year for American Manufacturing job growth since 1997, or 21 years. The previous administration said manufacturing will not come back to the U.S., "you would need a magic wand." I guess I found the MAGIC WAND—and it is only getting better!

January 22, 2019

10:01 am: The United States has a great economic story to tell. Number one in the World, by far!

January 24, 2019

6:56 am: The economy is doing great. More people working in U.S.A. today than at any time in our HISTORY. Media barely covers! @ foxandfriends

January 30, 2019

4:54 pm: Dow just broke 25,000. Tremendous news!

February 1, 2019

9:15 am: Best January for the DOW in over 30 years. We have, by far, the strongest economy in the world!

10:48 am: JOBS, JOBS, JOBS!

1:44 pm: Great news on Foxconn in Wisconsin after my conversation with Terry Gou!

February 9, 2019

9:36 am: We have a great economy DESPITE the Obama Administration and all of its job killing Regulations and Roadblocks. If that thinking prevailed in the 2016 Election, the U.S. would be in a Depression right now! We were heading down, and don't let the Democrats sound bites fool you!

February 13, 2019

10:01 am: The Gallup Poll just announced that 69% of our great citizens expect their finances to improve next year, a 16 year high. Nice!

February 25, 2019

10:12 am: Since my election as President the Dow Jones is up 43% and the NASDAQ Composite almost 50%. Great news for your 401(k)s as they continue to grow. We are bringing back America faster than anyone thought possible!

February 27, 2019

4:20 am: Fiat Chrysler will be adding more than 6,500 JOBS in Michigan (Detroit area), doubling its hourly workforce as part of a 4.5 Billion Dollar investment. Thank you Fiat Chrysler. They are all coming back to the USA, it's where the action is!

March 8, 2019

8:58 am: Women's unemployment rate is down to 3.6%—was 7.9% in January, 2011. Things are looking good!

March 12, 2019

11:27 pm: So many records being set with respect to our Economy. Unemployment numbers among BEST EVER. A beautiful thing to watch!

March 14, 2019

11:18 am: Congratulations @Toyota! BIG NEWS for U.S. Auto Workers! The USMCA is already fixing the broken NAFTA deal.

March 17, 2019

5:27 pm: Just spoke to Mary Barra, CEO of General Motors about the Lordstown Ohio plant. I am not happy that it is closed when everything else in our Country is BOOMING. I asked her to sell it or do something quickly. She blamed the UAW Union—I don't care, I just want it open!

March 18, 2019

6:37 am: General Motors and the UAW are going to start "talks" in September/October. Why wait, start them now! I want jobs to stay in the U.S.A. and want Lordstown (Ohio), in one of the best economies in our history, opened or sold to a company who will open it up fast! Car companies...

6:45 am: ...are all coming back to the U.S. So is everyone else. We now have the best Economy in the World, the envy of all. Get that big, beautiful plant in Ohio open now. Close a plant in China or Mexico, where you invested so heavily pre-Trump, but not in the U.S.A. Bring jobs home!

March 19, 2019

4:28 pm: Amazingly, CNN just released a poll at 71%, saying that the economy is in the best shape since 2001, 18 years! WOW, is CNN becoming a believer?

March 20, 2019

3:51 pm: Great news from @Ford! They are investing nearly $1 BILLION in Flat Rock, Michigan for auto production on top of a $1 BILLION investment last month in a facility outside of Chicago.

Companies are pouring back into the United States—they want to be where the action is!

March 22, 2019

5:52 am: 3.1 GDP FOR THE YEAR, BEST NUMBER IN 14 YEARS!

April 14, 2019

9:04 am: If the Fed had done its job properly, which it has not, the Stock Market would have been up 5000 to 10,000 additional points, and GDP would have been well over 4% instead of 3%…with almost no inflation. Quantitative tightening was a killer, should have done the exact opposite!

April 21, 2019

8:55 am: Jobless claims in the United States have reached their lowest (BEST) level in over 50 years!

April 23, 2019

5:43 pm: You mean the Stock Market hit an all-time record high today and they're actually talking impeachment!? Will I ever be given credit for anything by the Fake News Media or Radical Liberal Dems? NO COLLUSION!

April 26, 2019

9:25 am: Just out: Real GDP for First Quarter grew 3.2% at an annual rate. This is far above expectations or projections. Importantly, inflation VERY LOW. MAKE AMERICA GREAT AGAIN!

April 30, 2019

12:56 pm: China is adding great stimulus to its economy while at the same time keeping interest rates low. Our Federal Reserve has incessantly lifted interest rates, even though inflation is very low, and instituted a very big dose of quantitative tightening. We have the potential to go...

1:05 pm: ...up like a rocket if we did some lowering of rates, like one point, and some quantitative easing. Yes, we are doing very well at 3.2% GDP, but with our wonderfully low inflation, we could be setting major records &, at the same time, make our National Debt start to look small!

May 1, 2019

6:01 am: Gallup Poll: 56% of Americans rate their financial situation as excellent or good. This is the highest number since 2002, and up 10 points since 2016.

May 8, 2019

10:18 am: GREAT NEWS FOR OHIO! Just spoke to Mary Barra, CEO of General Motors, who informed me that, subject to a UAW agreement etc., GM will be selling their beautiful Lordstown Plant to Workhorse, where they plan to build Electric Trucks. GM will also be spending $700,000,000 in Ohio...

...in 3 separate locations, creating another 450 jobs. I have been working nicely with GM to get this done. Thank you to Mary B, your GREAT Governor, and Senator Rob Portman. With all the car companies coming back, and much more, THE USA IS BOOMING!

May 10, 2019

6:54 am: The average 401(k) balance has SOARED since the bottom of the market—466%. Wow!

May 13, 2019

6:02 am: The unexpectedly good first quarter 3.2% GDP was greatly helped by Tariffs from China. Some people just don't get it!

8:59 am: Bernie Sanders, "The Economy is doing well, and I'm sure I don't have to give Trump any credit—I'm sure he'll take all the credit that he wants." Wrong Bernie, the Economy is doing GREAT, and would have CRASHED if my opponent (and yours), Crooked Hillary Clinton, had ever won!

May 19, 2019

2:54 pm: Our Economy and Jobs Market is BOOMING, the best in the World and in our Country's history—and we have just started!

9:29 pm: Starting Monday, our great Farmers can begin doing business again with Mexico and Canada. They have both taken the tariff penalties off of your great agricultural product. Please be sure that you are treated fairly. Any complaints should immediately go to @SecretarySonny Perdue!

May 22, 2019

12:01 pm: ...In the meantime, my Administration is achieving things that have never been done before, including unleashing perhaps the Greatest Economy in our Country's history..

May 23, 2019

8:19 pm: 71% of Voters rate the Economy as Excellent or Good. The highest number in more than 18 years! @QuinnipiacPoll

May 27, 2019

4:10 am: Impeach for what, having created perhaps the greatest Economy in our Country's history, rebuilding our Military, taking care of our Vets (Choice), Judges, Best Jobs Numbers Ever, and much more? Dems are Obstructionists!

June 2, 2019

8:44 pm: BIG NEWS! As I promised two weeks ago, the first shipment of LNG has just left the Cameron LNG Export Facility in Louisiana.

Not only have thousands of JOBS been created in USA, we're shipping freedom and opportunity abroad!

June 7, 2019

4:43 pm: Dow Jones has best week of the year!

June 11, 2019

7:10 am: The United States has VERY LOW INFLATION, a beautiful thing!

7:47 am: This is because the Euro and other currencies are devalued against the dollar, putting the U.S. at a big disadvantage. The Fed Interest rate way too high, added to ridiculous quantitative tightening! They don't have a clue!

8:55 am: Good day in the Stock Market. People have no idea the tremendous potential our Country has for GROWTH—and many other things!

June 14, 2019

5:37 pm: Just spoke to Marillyn Hewson, CEO of @LockheedMartin, about continuing operations for the @Sikorsky in Coatesville, Pennsylvania. She will be taking it under advisement and will be making a decision soon.

…While Pennsylvania is BOOMING, I don't want there to be even a little glitch in Coatesville—every job counts. I want Lockhead to BOOM along with it!

June 15, 2019

8:44 am: The Trump Economy is setting records, and has a long way up to go…However, if anyone but me takes over in 2020 (I know the competition very well), there will be a Market Crash the likes of which has not been seen before! KEEP AMERICA GREAT

June 19, 2019

7:12 pm: Since Election Day 2016, Stocks up almost 50%, Stocks gained 9.2 Trillion Dollars in value, and more than 5,000,000 new jobs added to the Economy. @LouDobbs If our opponent had won, there would have been a market crash, plain and simple! @TuckerCarlson @seanhannity @IngrahamAngle

June 20, 2019

8:58 am: S&P opens at Record High!

5:22 pm: S&P closes at Record High!

June 22, 2019

9:13 am: Stock Market is on track to have the best June in over 50 years! Thank you Mr. President! @WSJ

June 23, 2019

9:46 am: When our Country had no debt and built everything from Highways to the Military with CASH, we had a big system of Tariffs. Now we allow other countries to steal our wealth, treasure, and jobs—But no more! The USA is doing great, with unlimited upside into the future!

June 29, 2019

7:29 pm: The leaders of virtually every country that I met at the G-20 congratulated me on our great economy. Many countries are having difficulties on that score. We have the best economy anywhere in the world, with GREAT & UNLIMITED potential looking into the future!

July 2, 2019

6:50 am: The Economy is the BEST IT HAS EVER BEEN! Even much of the Fake News is giving me credit for that!

95

July 3, 2019

9:12 am: S&P 500 hits new record high. Up 19% for the year. Congratulations!

July 5, 2019

10:24 pm: Strong jobs report, low inflation, and other countries around the world doing anything possible to take advantage of the United States, knowing that our Federal Reserve doesn't have a clue! They raised rates too soon, too often, & tightened, while others did just the opposite.

…As well as we are doing from the day after the great Election, when the Market shot right up, it could have been even better—massive additional wealth would have been created, & used very well. Our most difficult problem is not our competitors, it is the Federal Reserve!

July 6, 2019

7:11 am: Our Country is the envy of the World. Thank you, Mr. President!

July 10, 2019

7:06 pm: I was just informed by Marillyn Hewson, CEO of Lockheed Martin, of her decision to keep the Sikorsky Helicopter Plant in Coatesville, Pennsylvania, open and humming! We are very proud of Pennsylvania and the people who work there…

…Thank you to Lockheed Martin, one of the USA's truly great companies!

July 11, 2019

6:39 am: "Nearly one million more blacks and two million more Hispanics are employed than when Barrack Obama left office, and minorities account for more than half of all new jobs created during the Trump Presidency. Unemployment among black women has hovered near 5% for the last six…

...months, the lowest since 1972." The Wall Street Journal Editorial Board, A Tale of Two Economies. @IngrahamAngle

6:42 am: Robert Johnson, B.E.T. "I give the President a lot of credit for moving the Economy in a positive direction that's benefiting a large number of Americans. I think the Tax Cuts clearly helped stimulate the Economy. Overall, if you look at the U.S. Economy, and you look at...

..the number of people who are no longer looking for jobs but who are now seeing the opportunity for job growth, you've got to give the President an A Plus for that." Thank you Robert, one of our great business leaders!

9:52 am: Dow just hit 27,000 for first time EVER!

7:15 pm: I am not a fan of Bitcoin and other Cryptocurrencies, which are not money, and whose value is highly volatile and based on thin air. Unregulated Crypto Assets can facilitate unlawful behavior, including drug trade and other illegal activity...

...Similarly, Facebook Libra's "virtual currency" will have little standing or dependability. If Facebook and other companies want to become a bank, they must seek a new Banking Charter and become subject to all Banking Regulations, just like other Banks, both National...

...and International. We have only one real currency in the USA, and it is stronger than ever, both dependable and reliable. It is by far the most dominant currency anywhere in the World, and it will always stay that way. It is called the United States Dollar!

July 14, 2019

9:17 pm: We are doing great Economically as a Country, Number One, despite the Fed's antiquated policy on rates and tightening. Much room to grow!

July 20, 2019

6:18 am: You can add 10% or 15% to this number. Economy doing better than EVER before! https://t.co/o59vI5tzXn

July 21, 2019

5:54 am: The Great State of West Virginia is producing record setting numbers and doing really well. When I became President, it was practically shut down and closed for business. Not anymore!

July 22, 2019

7:02 am: With almost no inflation, our Country is needlessly being forced to pay a MUCH higher interest rate than other countries only because of a very misguided Federal Reserve. In addition, Quantitative Tightening is continuing, making it harder for our Country to compete. As good…

…as we have done, it could have been soooo much better. Interest rate costs should have been much lower, & GDP & our Country's wealth accumulation much higher. Such a waste of time & money. Also, very unfair that other countries manipulate their currencies and pump money in!

7:05 am: It is far more costly for the Federal Reserve to cut deeper if the economy actually does, in the future, turn down! Very inexpensive, in fact productive, to move now. The Fed raised & tightened far too much & too fast. In other words, they missed it (Big!). Don't miss it again!

July 23, 2019

6:54 am: Farmers are starting to do great again, after 15 years of a downward spiral. The 16 Billion Dollar China "replacement" money didn't exactly hurt!

July 31, 2019

4:37 pm: "The 99% Get a Bigger Raise" https://t.co/negNLaSwMt

August 3, 2019

7:41 am: Countries are coming to us wanting to negotiate REAL trade deals, not the one sided horror show deals made by past administrations. They don't want to be targeted for Tariffs by the U.S.

August 7, 2019

7:46 am: "Three more Central Banks cut rates." Our problem is not China—We are stronger than ever, money is pouring into the U.S. while China is losing companies by the thousands to other countries, and their currency is under siege—Our problem is a Federal Reserve that is too...

...proud to admit their mistake of acting too fast and tightening too much (and that I was right!). They must Cut Rates bigger and faster, and stop their ridiculous quantitative tightening NOW. Yield curve is at too wide a margin, and no inflation! Incompetence is a...

...terrible thing to watch, especially when things could be taken care of sooo easily. We will WIN anyway, but it would be much easier if the Fed understood, which they don't, that we are competing against other countries, all of whom want to do well at our expense!

August 8, 2019

9:38 am: As your President, one would think that I would be thrilled with our very strong dollar. I am not! The Fed's high interest rate level, in comparison to other countries, is keeping the dollar high, making it more difficult for our great manufacturers like Caterpillar, Boeing,...

...John Deere, our car companies, & others, to compete on a level play-ing field. With substantial Fed Cuts (there is no inflation) and no quantitative tightening, the dollar will make it possible for our compa-nies to win against any competition. We have the greatest companies...

...in the world, there is nobody even close, but unfortunately the same cannot be said about our Federal Reserve. They have called it wrong at every step of the way, and we are still winning. Can you imagine what would happen if they actually called it right?

August 11, 2019

4:42 pm: Many incredible things are happening right now for our Country. After years of being ripped off by other nations on both

Trade Deals and the Military, things are changing fast. Big progress is being made. America is respected again. KEEP AMERICA GREAT!

August 13, 2019

8:23 pm: Great day in the incredible Commonwealth of Pennsylvania today, with the amazing energy workers, construction workers, and craft workers who make America run—and who make America PROUD. No one in the world does it better than YOU!

August 16, 2019

6:04 pm: Having dinner tonight with Tim Cook of Apple. They will be spending vast sums of money in the U.S. Great!

August 18, 2019

2:24 pm: Our economy is the best in the world, by far. Lowest unemployment ever within almost all categories. Poised for big growth after trade deals are completed. Import prices down, China eating Tariffs. Helping targeted Farmers from big Tariff money coming in. Great future for USA!

August 21, 2019

7:52 am: Doing great with China and other Trade Deals. The only problem we have is Jay Powell and the Fed. He's like a golfer who can't putt, has no touch. Big U.S. growth if he does the right thing, BIG CUT—but don't count on him! So far he has called it wrong, and only let us down…

…We are competing with many countries that have a far lower interest rate, and we should be lower than them. Yesterday, "highest Dollar in U.S. History." No inflation. Wake up Federal Reserve. Such growth potential, almost like never before!

8:38 am: My proposal to the politically correct Automobile Companies would lower the average price of a car to consumers by more than $3000, while at the same time making the cars substantially safer.

Engines would run smoother. Very little impact on the environment! Foolish executives!

8:56 am: So Germany is paying Zero interest and is actually being paid to borrow money, while the U.S., a far stronger and more important credit, is paying interest and just stopped (I hope!) Quantitative Tightening. Strongest Dollar in History, very tough on exports. No Inflation!...

6:01 pm: Henry Ford would be very disappointed if he saw his modern-day descendants wanting to build a much more expensive car, that is far less safe and doesn't work as well, because execs don't want to fight California regulators. Car companies should know.

...that when this Administration's alternative is no longer available, California will squeeze them to a point of business ruin. Only reason California is now talking to them is because the Feds are giving a far better alternative, which is much better for consumers!

August 23, 2019

6:24 am: The Economy is strong and good, whereas the rest of the world is not doing so well. Despite this the Fake News Media, together with their Partner, the Democrat Party, are working overtime to convince people that we are in, or will soon be going into, a Recession. They are...

...willing to lose their wealth, or a big part of it, just for the possibility of winning the Election. But it won't work because I always find a way to win, especially for the people! The greatest political movement in the history of our Country will have another big win in 2020!

2:01 pm: The Dow is down 573 points perhaps on the news that Representative Seth Moulton, whoever that may be, has dropped out of the 2020 Presidential Race!

August 25, 2019

6:30 pm: My Stock Market gains must be judged from the day after the Election, November 9, 2016, where the Market went up big after the win, and because of the win. Had my opponent won, CRASH!

101

August 30, 2019

7:06 am: General Motors, which was once the Giant of Detroit, is now one of the smallest auto manufacturers there. They moved major plants to China, BEFORE I CAME INTO OFFICE. This was done despite the saving help given them by the USA. Now they should start moving back to America again?

8:55 am: The Euro is dropping against the Dollar "like crazy," giving them a big export and manufacturing advantage…and the Fed does NOTHING! Our Dollar is now the strongest in history. Sounds good, doesn't it? Except to those (manufacturers) that make product for sale outside the U.S.

September 2, 2019

6:38 am: Since my election, many trillions of dollars of worth has been created for our Country, and the Stock Market is up over 50%. If you followed the advice of the Failing New York Times columnist, Paul Krugman, you'd be doing VERY poorly—you'd be angry and hurt. He never got it!

September 11, 2019

5:42 am: The Federal Reserve should get our interest rates down to ZERO, or less, and we should then start to refinance our debt. IN-TEREST COST COULD BE BROUGHT WAY DOWN, while at the same time substantially lengthening the term. We have the great currency, power, and balance sheet.

…The USA should always be paying the the lowest rate. No Infla-tion! It is only the naïveté of Jay Powell and the Federal Reserve that doesn't allow us to do what other countries are already doing. A once in a lifetime opportunity that we are missing because of "Boneheads."

September 15, 2019

5:54 pm: Here we go again with General Motors and the United Auto Workers. Get together and make a deal!

September 18, 2019

7:45 am: So nice that our Country is now Energy Independent. The USA is in better shape than ever before. Strongest Military by far, biggest Economy (no longer even close), number one in Energy! MAGA = KAG

September 30, 2019

1:55 pm: Navistar will be building a new 250 MILLION DOLLAR truck factory in San Antonio with 600 new jobs. Congratulations San Antonio and Texas! America makes the GREATEST trucks in the world!

2:04 pm: Great news! @Apple announced that it is building its new Mac Pro in Texas. This means hundreds of American jobs in Austin and for suppliers across the Country. Congratulations to the Apple team and their workers!

2:08 pm: BIG NEWS by @Hyundai, @Kia, and @Aptiv on a 4 BILLION DOLLAR joint venture to develop autonomous driving technologies in the USA. That's a lot of $$ and JOBS! Great jobs coming back to America!!

October 1, 2019

9:34 am: As I predicted, Jay Powell and the Federal Reserve have allowed the Dollar to get so strong, especially relative to ALL other currencies, that our manufacturers are being negatively affected. Fed Rate too high. They are their own worst enemies, they don't have a clue. Pathetic!

October 3, 2019

5:00 am: The U.S. won a $7.5 Billion award from the World Trade Organization against the European Union, who has for many years treated the USA very badly on Trade due to Tariffs, Trade Barriers, and more. This case going on for years, a nice victory!

103

October 4, 2019

7:47 am: Breaking News: Unemployment Rate, at 3.5%, drops to a 50 YEAR LOW. Wow America, lets impeach your President (even though he did nothing wrong!).

October 6, 2019

6:39 pm: Unemployment Rate just dropped to 3.5%, the lowest in more that 50 years. Is that an impeachable event for your President?

October 15, 2019

10:32 am: Just out: MEDIAN HOUSEHOLD INCOME IS AT THE HIGHEST POINT EVER, EVER, EVER! How about saying it this way, IN THE HISTORY OF OUR COUNTRY! Also, MORE PEO-PLE WORKING TODAY IN THE USA THAN AT ANY TIME IN HISTORY! Tough numbers for the Radical Left Democrats to beat! Impeach the Pres.

October 16, 2019

6:29 am: Our record Economy would CRASH, just like in 1929, if any of those clowns became President!

October 23, 2019

4:19 pm: PROMISES MADE, PROMISES KEPT!
#SHALEINSIGHT2019

October 28, 2019

8:41 am: The S&P just hit an ALL TIME HIGH. This is a big win for jobs, 401-K's, and, frankly, EVERYONE! Our Country is doing great. Even killed long sought ISIS murderer, Al-Baghdadi. We are stronger than ever before, with GREAT upward potential. Enjoy!

October 30, 2019

6:38 am: The Greatest Economy in American History!

October 31, 2019

9:37 am: People are VERY disappointed in Jay Powell and the Federal Reserve. The Fed has called it wrong from the beginning, too fast, too slow. They even tightened in the beginning. Others are running circles around them and laughing all the way to the bank. Dollar & Rates are hurting…

…our manufacturers. We should have lower interest rates than Germany, Japan and all others. We are now, by far, the biggest and strongest Country, but the Fed puts us at a competitive disadvantage. China is not our problem, the Federal Reserve is! We will win anyway

November 1, 2019

7:52 am: Wow, a blowout JOBS number just out, adjusted for revisions and the General Motors strike, 303,000. This is far greater than expectations. USA ROCKS!

9:08 am: Stock Market up BIG! Record highs for S&P 500 and NASDAQ. Enjoy!

November 4, 2019

8:45 am: Stock Market hits RECORD HIGH. Spend your money well!

10:09 am: All-Time High for Stock Market and all the Fake News wants to talk about is the Impeachment Hoax!

November 6, 2019

8:30 am: Stock Markets (all three) hit another ALL TIME & HISTORIC HIGH yesterday! You are sooo lucky to have me as your President (just kidding!). Spend your money well!

November 7, 2019

10:43 am: Stock Market up big today. A New Record. Enjoy!

November 12, 2019

6:32 am: Economy is BOOMING. Seems set to have yet another record day!

November 13, 2019

8:44 am: Hit New Stock Market record again yesterday, the 20th time this year, with GREAT potential for the future. USA is where the action is. Companies and jobs are coming back like never before!

9:32 am: Walmart announces great numbers. No impact from Tariffs (which are contributing $Billions to our Treasury). Inflation low (do you hear that Powell?)!

November 15, 2019

11:34 am: Stock Market up big. New and Historic Record. Job, jobs, jobs!

November 16, 2019

10:18 am: Dow hits 28,000—FIRST TIME EVER, HIGHEST EVER! Gee, Pelosi & Schitt have a good idea, "lets Impeach the President." If something like that ever happened, it would lead to the biggest FALL in Market History. It's called a Depression, not a Recession! So much for 401-K's & Jobs!

November 18, 2019

10:49 am: Just finished a very good & cordial meeting at the White House with Jay Powell of the Federal Reserve. Everything was discused including interest rates, negative interest, low inflation, easing, Dollar strength & its effect on manufacturing, trade with China, E.U. & others, etc.

10:34 pm: At my meeting with Jay Powell this morning, I protested fact that our Fed Rate is set too high relative to the interest rates of other competitor countries. In fact, our rates should be lower than all others (we are the U.S.). Too strong a Dollar hurting manufacturers & growth!

November 19, 2019

9:03 am: NASDAQ UP 27% THIS YEAR ALONE!

November 20, 2019

6:18 pm: Today I opened a major Apple Manufacturing plant in Texas that will bring high paying jobs back to America. Today Nancy Pelosi closed Congress because she doesn't care about American Workers!

November 21, 2019

7:31 am: During my visit yesterday to Austin, Texas, for the startup of the new Mac Pro, & the discussion of a new one $billion campus, also in Texas, I asked Tim Cook to see if he could get Apple involved in building 5G in the U.S. They have it all—Money, Technology, Vision & Cook!

November 23, 2019

11:53 pm: Pushed hard to have Apple build in USA!

November 25, 2019

9:05 am: Another new Stock Market Record. Enjoy!

November 27, 2019

5:09 pm: New Stock Market Record today, AGAIN. Congratulations USA!

November 30, 2019

6:27 pm: Robert Johnson knows business & politics. He also understands lowest African American Unemployment in U.S. history!

December 2, 2019

5:59 am: Brazil and Argentina have been presiding over a massive devaluation of their currencies. which is not good for our farmers. Therefore, effective immediately, I will restore the Tariffs on all Steel & Aluminum that is shipped into the U.S. from those countries. The Federal…

…Reserve should likewise act so that countries, of which there are many, no longer take advantage of our strong dollar by further devaluing their currencies. This makes it very hard for our manufactures & farmers to fairly export their goods. Lower Rates & Loosen—Fed!

4:19 pm: Manufacturers are being held back by the strong Dollar, which is being propped up by the ridiculous policies of the Federal Reserve—Which has called interest rates and quantitative tightening wrong from the first days of Jay Powell!

5:21 pm: The Fed should lower rates (there is almost no inflation) and loosen, making us competitive with other nations, and manufacturing will SOAR! Dollar is very strong relative to others.

December 6, 2019

8:16 am: Stock Markets Up Record Numbers. For this year alone, Dow up 18.65%, S&P up 24.36%, Nasdaq Composite up 29.17%. "It's the economy, stupid."

9:57 am: GREAT JOBS REPORT!

11:00 am: Without the horror show that is the Radical Left, Do Nothing Democrats, the Stock Markets and Economy would be even better, if that is possible, and the Border would be closed to the evil of Drugs, Gangs and all other problems! #2020

December 7, 2019

12:21 pm: While the world is not doing well economically, our Country is doing better, perhaps, than it has ever done before. Jobs, Jobs, Jobs!

1:54 pm: Hard to believe, but if Nancy Pelosi had put our great Trade Deal with Mexico and Canada, USMCA, up for a vote long ago, our economy would be even better. If she doesn't move quickly, it will collapse!

1:55 pm: Our Economy is the envy of the World!

December 9, 2019

10:15 am: The best Economy ever!

December 10, 2019

9:32 am: America's great USMCA Trade Bill is looking good. It will be the best and most important trade deal ever made by the USA. Good for everybody—Farmers, Manufacturers, Energy, Unions—tremendous support. Importantly, we will finally end our Country's worst Trade Deal, NAFTA!

9:35 am: Looking like very good Democrat support for USMCA. That would be great for our Country!

December 12, 2019

7:27 am: Great deal for USA!

December 13, 2019

8:53 am: Record Stock Market & Jobs!

December 16, 2019

12:41 pm: New Stock Market high! I will never get bored of telling you that—and we will never get tired of winning!

December 17, 2019

9:39 am: The Stock Market hit another Record High yesterday, number 133 in less than three years as your all time favorite President, and the Radical Left, Do Nothing Democrats, want to impeach me. Don't worry, I have done nothing wrong. Actually, they have!

10:12 am: Would be sooo great if the Fed would further lower interest rates and quantitative ease. The Dollar is very strong against other currencies and there is almost no inflation. This is the time to do it. Exports would zoom!

December 19, 2019

6:55 pm: The great USMCA Trade Deal (Mexico & Canada) has been sitting on Nancy Pelosi's desk for 8 months, she doesn't even know what it says, & today, after passing by a wide margin in the House, Pelosi tried to take credit for it. Labor will vote for Trump. Trade deal is great for USA!

December 20, 2019

4:23 pm: Economy is GREAT, Big Stock Market uptick today. Best ranking in 20 years admits CNN!

11:43 pm: Broke all time Stock Market Record again today. 135 times since my 2016 Election Win. Thank you!

December 24, 2019

8:25 am: The ONLY reason we were able to get our great USMCA Trade Deal approved was because the Do Nothing Democrats wanted to show that they could approve something productive in light of the fact that all they even think about is impeachment. She knows nothing about the USMCA Deal!

December 25, 2019

3:32 pm: 2019 HOLIDAY RETAIL SALES WERE UP 3.4% FROM LAST YEAR, THE BIGGEST NUMBER IN U.S. HISTORY. CONGRATULATIONS AMERICA!

December 26, 2019

7:03 pm: I guess Justin T doesn't much like my making him pay up on NATO or Trade!

Immigration/Borders—2017 News Quotes

Response to a question from David Muir of ABC News, January 26, 2017.
Source: https://www.telegraph.co.uk/news/2017/01/26/
full-transcript-president-donald-trumps-interview-abc-news/

"They shouldn't be very worried. They are here illegally. They shouldn't be very worried. I do have a big heart. We're going to take care of everybody. We're going to have a very strong border. We're gonna have a very solid border. Where you have great people that are here that have done a good job, they should be far less worried. We'll be coming out with policy on that over the next period of four weeks."

Response to a question from David Muir of ABC News, January 26, 2017.
Source: https://www.telegraph.co.uk/news/2017/01/26/
full-transcript-president-donald-trumps-interview-abc-news/

"I'm gonna tell you over the next four weeks. But I will tell you, we're looking at this, the whole immigration situation, we're looking at it with great heart. Now we have criminals that are here. We have really bad people that are here. Those people have to be worried 'cause they're getting out. We're gonna get them out. We're gonna get 'em out fast. [Then-White House Chief of Staff] General [John F.] Kelly is, I've given that as his number one priority."

Response to a question from Laura Ingraham of FOX News, November 2, 2017.

Source: https://www.youtube.com/watch?v=yTdDH-o_ICM

"Chain migration is a disaster for this country, and it's going to end. Now I've been talking about it for a while, but I think the public until yesterday probably never heard about chain migration."

Response to a question from Laura Ingraham of FOX News, November 2, 2017.

Source: https://www.youtube.com/watch?v=yTdDH-o_ICM

"DACA is a lot different than Dreamers."

Response to a question from Laura Ingraham of FOX News, November 2, 2017.

Source: https://www.youtube.com/watch?v=yTdDH-o_ICM

"Well, first of all they say the wall is going to cost $40 billion. It's not going to cost anywhere near that."

Response to a question from Laura Ingraham of FOX News, November 2, 2017.

Source: https://www.youtube.com/watch?v=yTdDH-o_ICM

"No, I think for $18 billion or less, we're going to have a great wall."

Response to a question from Laura Ingraham of FOX News, November 2, 2017.

Source: https://www.youtube.com/watch?v=yTdDH-o_ICM

"One of the things that's come up pretty strongly is we want to have vision through the wall, because you want to see what's on the other side of the wall. You know, you think we're going to build a nice simple concrete wall, but it's not that simple. No, we're having the wall. We have to have the wall.

"We need the wall for another reason: drugs. Drugs are pouring into our country. A lot of them are coming in through the southern border,

113

and the wall will be a tremendous tool to help facilitate the ending of the drugs coming in.

"No, the wall is actually coming along pretty well. That will also be a part of DACA or whatever."

Immigration/Borders—2017 Tweets

January 25, 2017

7:03 pm: Beginning today, the United States of America gets back control of its borders. Full speech from today @DHSgov.

9:14 pm: As your President, I have no higher duty than to protect the lives of the American people.

January 26. 2017

6:53 pm: Miami-Dade Mayor drops sanctuary policy. Right decision. Strong!

January 29. 2017

8:08 am: Our country needs strong borders and extreme vetting, NOW. Look what is happening all over Europe and, indeed, the world—a horrible mess!

February 11, 2017

8:18 am to 8:24 am: I am reading that the great border WALL will cost more than the government originally thought, but I have not gotten involved in the…

..design or negotiations yet. When I do, just like with the F-35 FighterJet or the Air Force One Program, price will come WAY DOWN!

February 26, 2017

3:46 pm: 'Americans overwhelmingly oppose sanctuary cities'
https://t.co/s5QvsJWA6u

April 24, 2017

7:28 am to 10:31 am: The Wall is a very important tool in stopping drugs from pouring into our country and poisoning our youth (and many others)! If...

...the wall is not built, which it will be, the drug situation will NEVER be fixed the way it should be! #BuildTheWall

June 16, 2017

8:30 pm: Back from Miami where my Cuban/American friends are very happy with what I signed today. Another campaign promise that I did not forget!

June 26, 2017

1:25 pm: Very grateful for the 9-O decision from the U. S. Supreme Court. We must keep America SAFE!

9:31 pm: Great day for America's future Security and Safety, courtesy of the U.S. Supreme Court. I will keep fighting for the American people, & WIN!

June 28, 2017

8:51 pm: Tomorrow the House votes on #KatesLaw & No Sanctuary For Criminals Act. Lawmakers must vote to put American safety first!

July 12, 2017

6:24 pm: Big WIN today for building the wall. It will secure the border & save lives. Now the full House & Senate must act!

July 27, 2017

1:37 pm: Big progress being made in ridding our country of MS-13 gang members and gang members in general. MAKE AMERICA SAFE AGAIN!

August 2, 2017

1:29 pm: I campaigned on creating a merit-based immigration system that protects U.S. workers & taxpayers.
Watch: https://t.co/lv3ScSKnF6 #RAISEAct https://t.co/zCFK5OfYnB

August 22, 2017

7:20 pm: THANK YOU to all of the great men and women at the U.S. Customs and Border Protection facility in Yuma, Arizona & around the United States!

August 24, 2017

12:13 pm: On Tuesday, I visited with the incredible men & women of @ICEgov & @DHSgov Border Patrol in Yuma, AZ. Thank you. We respect & cherish you!

September 5, 2017

3:45 pm: I look forward to working w/ D's + R's in Congress to address immigration reform in a way that puts hardworking citizens of our country 1st.

7:38 pm: Congress now has 6 months to legalize DACA (something the Obama Administration was unable to do). If they can't, I will revisit this issue!

September 7, 2017

8:42 am: For all of those (DACA) that are concerned about your status during the 6 month period, you have nothing to worry about—No action!

September 14, 2017

5:11 am: No deal was made last night on DACA. Massive border security would have to be agreed to in exchange for consent. Would be subject to vote.

5:20 am: The WALL, which is already under construction in the form of new renovation of old and existing fences and walls, will continue to be built

5:28 am to 5:35 am: Does anybody really want to throw out good, educated and accomplished young people who have jobs, some serving in the military? Really!...

...They have been in our country for many years through no fault of their own—brought in by parents at young age. Plus BIG border security

September 15, 2017

8:00 am: CHAIN MIGRATION cannot be allowed to be part of any legislation on Immigration!

September 24, 2017

5:49 pm: Making America Safe is my number one priority. We will not admit those into our country we cannot safely vet.

October 10, 2017

5:18 am: The problem with agreeing to a policy on immigration is that the Democrats don't want secure borders, they don't care about safety for U.S.A.

October 17, 2017

6:03 pm: BORDER WALL prototypes underway!

November 1, 2017

6:03 pm: CHAIN MIGRATION must end now! Some people come in, and they bring their whole family with them, who can be truly evil. NOT ACCEPTABLE!

9:19 pm: The United States will be immediately implementing much tougher Extreme Vetting Procedures. The safety of our citizens comes first!

November 2, 2017

1:33 pm: I am calling on Congress to TERMINATE the diversity visa lottery program that presents significant vulnerabilities to our national security.

1:43 pm: Congress must end chain migration so that we can have a system that is SECURITY BASED! We need to make AMERICA SAFE! #USA

November 19, 2017

8:29 pm: Border Patrol Officer killed at Southern Border, another badly hurt. We will seek out and bring to justice those responsible. We will, and must, build the Wall!

November 30, 2017

10:30 pm: A disgraceful verdict in the Kate Steinle case! No wonder the people of our Country are so angry with Illegal Immigration.

December 1, 2017

6:03 am: The Kate Steinle killer came back and back over the weakly protected Obama border, always committing crimes and being violent, and yet this info was not used in court. His exoneration is a complete travesty of justice. BUILD THE WALL!

6:13 am: The jury was not told the killer of Kate was a 7 time felon. The Schumer/Pelosi Democrats are so weak on Crime that they will pay a big price in the 2018 and 2020 Elections.

December 9, 2017

9:17pm: No American should be separated from their loved ones because of preventable crime committed by those illegally in our country. Our cities should be Sanctuaries for Americans—not for criminal aliens!

Immigration/Borders—2018 News Quotes

Reply to a question from an unidentified reporter before a dinner with then-House Majority Leader Kevin McCarthy at the Trump International Golf Club in Palm Beach, Florida, January 14, 2018.

Source: https://www.whitehouse.gov/briefings-statements/
remarks-president-trump-dinner-house-majority-leader-kevin-mccarthy-palm-beach-fl/

"Now, we used to say the DACA children, but the children aren't children."

Remarks after reviewing border wall prototypes in San Diego, California, March 13, 2018.

Source: https://www.whitehouse.gov/briefings-statements/
remarks-president-trump-review-border-wall-prototypes-san-diego-ca/

"Every day, criminals and tariffs try to infiltrate our country. You got a good glimpse of it before. We did it together, with the media, frankly. Didn't know we were going to be doing that, but you got, really, maybe a far better glimpse than you're going to get right now.

"But the border wall is truly our first line of defense, and it's probably, if you think about it, our first and last, other than the great ICE agents and other people, moving people out. It will save thousands and thousands of lives, save taxpayers hundreds of billions of dollars by reducing crime, drug flow, welfare fraud, and burdens on schools and hospitals. The wall will save hundreds of billions of dollars, many, many times what it's going to cost.

"We must also close the deadly loopholes exploited by smugglers and traffickers. And we're in that area. We're in one of the many areas along the border where we have that problem. And we have to confront the dangerous sanctuary cities, which you've been all hearing so much about.

"California sanctuary policies put the entire nation at risk. They're the best friend of the criminal. That's what exactly is happening. The criminals take refuge in these sanctuary cities, and it's very dangerous for our police and enforcement folks.

"The smugglers, the traffickers, the gang members, they're all taking refuge, and I think a lot of people in California understand that. A lot of people from a lot of other places understand it, and they don't want sanctuary cities.

"These policies release dangerous criminal offenders to prey on innocent people and nullify the federal law. They're threatening the security and the safety of the people of our country. In the upcoming omnibus budget bill, Congress must fund the border wall and prohibit grants to sanctuary jurisdictions that threaten the security of our country and the people of our country. We must enforce our laws and protect our people.

"And I have to say, law enforcement, ICE, Border Patrol, all of the people that have been so good to me for so long, they're really doing a job. But our job—And I think we all understand the job would be a lot easier if we weren't protecting criminals in the sanctuary cities. We had a great talk about it inside.

"Cooperation with Mexico is another crucial element of border security. DHS coordinates closely with the Mexican law enforcement, and we must absolutely build on that cooperation. Both countries recognize the need to stem the cross-border flow of illegal weapons, drugs, people, and cash.

"I have a great relationship with the President of Mexico, a wonderful guy. Enrique [Peña Nieto][5]. Terrific guy. We're working—We're trying to work things out. We'll see whether or not it happens. I don't know that it's going to happen. He's a very good negotiator. He loves the people of Mexico, and he's working very hard. We'll see what happens.

"But we have to, obviously, have a couple of disagreements before we get there. You'll see over the next month whether or not it takes place in this administration, meaning his administration. They have an election coming up. I hear they have some very good people running, and they have some that maybe aren't so good. In any event, we'll handle it.

"I want to again thank everyone for being here today, and I want to again call on Congress to deliver a budget that protects our homeland and properly funds all of our law enforcement needs. I want to thank the Secretary. I want to thank ICE and the Border Patrol agents for their incredible work and their incredible bravery. I want to thank all of law enforcement on the border. It's a dangerous job. It's a tough job. And if you didn't have even these remnant walls— We call them remnant; they've been here for a long time. People don't say that. But they've been here for a long time. If you didn't have them, you would have crime in numbers that far surpass the numbers that you see today.

"We've cut down, and way down, on crossings, border crossings, because of the job that the Border Patrol does. And the ones that get through, we've gotten out. MS-13, we're taking them out by the thousands. But we don't want them here in the first place. We don't want them to come in.

---

5   At the time of President Trump's remarks, the President of Mexico was Enrique Peña Nieto. Andrés Manuel López Obrador was elected to succeed Peña Nieto in July 2018.

"So, this was really a day where we look at the different prototypes of the wall. You've seen them. The media has seen them. And some work very well; some don't work so well. When we build, we want to build the right thing.

"Interestingly, the ones that work the best aren't necessarily the most expensive. Something I like about that ring.

"So, I want to thank everybody for being here. I want to thank, frankly, the media for being here. And we'll let the people of our country know that we need safety, we need security at the border, and we're getting it like we've never had it before. But we want to make it perfecto."

Response to a question from Lesley Stahl of *60 Minutes*, October 15, 2018.
Source: https://www.theguardian.com/us-news/2018/oct/15/
donald-trumps-60-minutes-interview-eight-takeaways

"You can't say yes or no. What I can say is this: There are consequences from coming into a country, namely our country, illegally."

Response to a question from the Associated Press[6], published October 17, 2018[7].
Source: https://www.cnbc.com/2018/10/17/read-the-transcript-of-aps-interview-with-president-trump.html

"When people enter our country illegally, there are consequences to pay. But despite the consequences, you have many children that, sadly, are there without parents. Then you have people that grab children and use them as a prop and it's a disgrace. And they come in with a child and they don't even know who the child is five hours before. And that's a shame. That's a terrible thing, what they do."

---

6   AP White House reporters Catherine Lucey, Zeke Miller, and Jonathan Lemire conducted this interview. However, the transcript does not indicate which reporter asked President Trump which question.

7   The interview was conducted by the AP before the midterm elections of October 16, 2018. However, it was published by CNBC on October 17, 2018.

Response to a question from the Associated Press[8], published October 17, 2018[9].

Source: https://www.cnbc.com/2018/10/17/read-the-transcript-of-aps-interview-with-president-trump.html

"They take children and they use them to try and come into our country. There are many, many bad things going on, on the border. We have the worst laws in the history of the world on immigration, and we're getting them changed one by one. We've made a lot of progress in the last couple of weeks even, but we're getting them changed one by one. But you have children that we're taking care of, that don't even have parents at least anywhere within hundreds of miles of the border, and we're taking those children, caring for those children, and in many cases sending them back to their parents in countries where their parents didn't even make the journey up with them, incredibly. And some of those children are really young. And we are, actually, in fact, today there was a beautiful statement put out by *The Washington Examiner* congratulating us on the great job we do with children. Now [former U.S.] President [Barack] Obama had the same law; he did the same thing. And, in fact, the picture of children living in cages that was taken in 2014 was a picture of President Obama's administration and the way they handled children. They had the kids living in cages. They thought it was our administration and they used it and then unbeknownst to them and the fake news, they found out, 'Oh my God, this is a terrible situation.' This was during the Obama administration."

---

8   AP White House reporters Catherine Lucey, Zeke Miller, and Jonathan Lemire conducted this interview. However, the transcript does not indicate which reporter asked President Trump which question.

9   The interview was conducted by the AP before the midterm elections of October 16, 2018. However, it was published by CNBC on October 17, 2018.

Response to a question from the Associated Press[10], published October 17, 2018[11].

Source: https://www.cnbc.com/2018/10/17/read-the-transcript-of-aps-interview-with-president-trump.html

"Here's the thing. I think we've done an incredible job with children. As I just said, we've taken children who have no parents with them standing on the border. We've taken many children, and I'm not talking about a small percentage, I'm talking about a very large percentage where they have no people, no parents. In addition to that, we're separating children who are just met by people that are using them coming into the border, not their parents. They are using them coming into the border. The one thing I will also say is that when a person thinks they will not be separated, our border becomes overrun with people coming in. So that's another problem. With all of that being said, we're getting the laws changed so that catch and release, so that visa lottery, so that chain migration and every other form of incredible stupidity can be taken out of our system."

Immigration/Borders—2018 Tweets

January 9, 2018

5:51 pm: Thanks to all of the Republican and Democratic lawmakers for today's very productive meeting on immigration reform. There was strong agreement to negotiate a bill that deals with border security, chain migration, lottery and DACA.

---

10 AP White House reporters Catherine Lucey, Zeke Miller, and Jonathan Lemire conducted this interview. However, the transcript does not indicate which reporter asked President Trump which question.

11 The interview was conducted by the AP before the midterm elections of October 16, 2018. However, it was published by CNBC on October 17, 2018.

January 10, 2018

6:07 pm: The United States needs the security of the Wall on the Southern Border, which must be part of any DACA approval. The safety and security of our country is #1!

January 11, 2018

8:11 am: "45 year low in illegal immigration this year." @foxandfriends

11:42 pm: The Democrats seem intent on having people and drugs pour into our country from the Southern Border, risking thousands of lives in the process. It is my duty to protect the lives and safety of all Americans. We must build a Great Wall, think Merit and end Lottery & Chain. USA!

January 12, 2018

6:59 am to 7:20 am: The so-called bipartisan DACA deal presented yesterday to myself and a group of Republican Senators and Congressmen was a big step backwards. Wall was not properly funded, Chain & Lottery were made worse and USA would be forced to take large numbers of people from high crime...

...countries which are doing badly. I want a merit based system of immigration and people who will help take our country to the next level. I want safety and security for our people. I want to stop the massive inflow of drugs. I want to fund our military, not do a Dem defund...

...Because of the Democrats not being interested in life and safety, DACA has now taken a big step backwards. The Dems will threaten "shutdown," but what they are really doing is shutting down our military, at a time we need it most. Get smart, MAKE AMERICA GREAT AGAIN!

7:28 am: The language used by me at the DACA meeting was tough, but this was not the language used. What was really tough was the outlandish proposal made—a big setback for DACA!

7:50 am: Sadly, Democrats want to stop paying our troops and government workers in order to give a sweetheart deal, not a fair deal, for DACA. Take care of our Military, and our Country, FIRST!

January 14, 2018

8:19 am: I, as President, want people coming into our Country who are going to help us become strong and great again, people coming in through a system based on MERIT. No more Lotteries! #AMERICA FIRST

January 16, 2018

8:54 am: We must have Security at our VERY DANGEROUS SOUTHERN BORDER, and we must have a great WALL to help protect us, and to help stop the massive inflow of drugs pouring into our country!

6:19 pm to 6:20 pm: New report from DOJ & DHS shows that nearly 3 in 4 individuals convicted of terrorism-related charges are foreign-born. We have submitted to Congress a list of resources and reforms…

…we need to keep America safe, including moving away from a random chain migration and lottery system, to one that is merit-based.

January 18, 2018

6:15 am to 6:25 am: The Wall is the Wall, it has never changed or evolved from the first day I conceived of it. Parts will be, of necessity, see through and it was never intended to be built in areas where there is natural protection such as mountains, wastelands or tough rivers or water…

…The Wall will be paid for, directly or indirectly, or through longer term reimbursement, by Mexico, which has a ridiculous $71 billion dollar trade surplus with the U.S. The $20 billion dollar Wall is "peanuts" compared to what Mexico makes from the U.S. NAFTA is a bad joke!

8:16 am: We need the Wall for the safety and security of our country. We need the Wall to help stop the massive inflow of drugs from Mexico, now rated the number one most dangerous country in the world. If there is no Wall, there is no Deal!

January 19, 2018

9:28 pm: Not looking good for our great Military or Safety & Security on the very dangerous Southern Border. Dems want a Shutdown in order to help diminish the great success of the Tax Cuts, and what they are doing for our booming economy.

January 23, 2018

11:07 pm: Cryin' Chuck Schumer fully understands, especially after his humiliating defeat, that if there is no Wall, there is no DACA. We must have safety and security, together with a strong Military, for our great people!

January 27, 2018

10:58 pm: I have offered DACA a wonderful deal, including a doubling in the number of recipients & a twelve year pathway to citizenship, for two reasons: (1) Because the Republicans want to fix a long time terrible problem. (2) To show that Democrats do not want to solve DACA, only use it!

February 6, 2018

8:32 am: So disgraceful that a person illegally in our country killed @ Colts linebacker Edwin Jackson. This is just one of many such preventable tragedies. We must get the Dems to get tough on the Border, and with illegal immigration, FAST!

11:05 am: We need a 21st century MERIT-BASED immigration system. Chain migration and the visa lottery are outdated programs that hurt our economic and national security.

February 13, 2018

5:52 am: Negotiations on DACA have begun. Republicans want to make a deal and Democrats say they want to make a deal. Wouldn't it be great if we could finally, after so many years, solve the DACA puzzle. This will be our last chance, there will never be another opportunity! March 5th.

February 15, 2018

9:57 am: While the Republicans and Democrats in Congress are working hard to come up with a solution to DACA, they should be strongly considering a system of Merit Based Immigration so that we will have the people ready, willing and able to help all of those companies moving into the USA!

February 23, 2018

6:28 am: MS-13 gang members are being removed by our Great ICE and Border Patrol Agents by the thousands, but these killers come back in from El Salvador, and through Mexico, like water. El Salvador just takes our money, and Mexico must help MORE with this problem. We need The Wall!

February 27, 2018

11:28 am: Big legal win today. U.S. judge sided with the Trump Administration and rejected the attempt to stop the government from building a great Border Wall on the Southern Border. Now this important project can go forward!

February 28, 2018

7:29 am: I have decided that sections of the Wall that California wants built NOW will not be built until the whole Wall is approved. Big victory yesterday with ruling from the courts that allows us to proceed. OUR COUNTRY MUST HAVE BORDER SECURITY!

9:08 am: 45 year low on illegal border crossings this year. Ice and Border Patrol Agents are doing a great job for our Country. MS-13 thugs being hit hard.

March 6, 2018

8:46 am: Federal Judge in Maryland has just ruled that "President Trump has the right to end DACA." President Obama had 8 years to fix this problem, and didn't. I am waiting for the Dems, they are running for the hills!

March 13, 2018

9:37 am: Heading to see the BORDER WALL prototypes in California!

10:24 am: "According to the Center for Immigration Studies, the $18 billion wall will pay for itself by curbing the importation of crime, drugs and illegal immigrants who tend to go on the federal dole..."

10:27 am: California's sanctuary policies are illegal and unconstitutional and put the safety and security of our entire nation at risk. Thousands of dangerous & violent criminal aliens are released as a result of sanctuary policies, set free to prey on innocent Americans. THIS MUST STOP!

5:23 pm: If we don't have a wall system, we're not going to have a country. Congress must fund the BORDER WALL & prohibit grants to sanctuary jurisdictions that threaten the security of our country & the people of our country. We must enforce our laws & protect our people! #BuildTheWall

March 23, 2018

7:26 am: DACA was abandoned by the Democrats. Very unfair to them! Would have been tied to desperately needed Wall.

March 25, 2018

5:33 am: Because of the $700 & $716 Billion Dollars gotten to rebuild our Military, many jobs are created and our Military is again rich. Building a great Border Wall, with drugs (poison) and enemy combatants pouring into our Country, is all about National Defense. Build WALL through M!

5:42 am: Much can be done with the $1.6 Billion given to building and fixing the border wall. It is just a down payment. Work will start immediately. The rest of the money will come—and remember DACA, the Democrats abandoned you (but we will not)!

March 31, 2018

7:53 am: Governor Jerry "Moonbeam" Brown pardoned 5 criminal illegal aliens whose crimes include (1) Kidnapping and Robbery (2) Badly beating wife and threatening a crime with intent to terrorize (3) Dealing drugs. Is this really what the great people of California want? @FoxNews

April 1, 2018

8:56 am: Border Patrol Agents are not allowed to properly do their job at the Border because of ridiculous liberal (Democrat) laws like Catch & Release. Getting more dangerous. "Caravans" coming. Republicans must go to Nuclear Option to pass tough laws NOW. NO MORE DACA DEAL!

9:25 am: Mexico is doing very little, if not NOTHING, at stopping people from flowing into Mexico through their Southern Border, and then into the U.S. They laugh at our dumb immigration laws. They must stop the big drug and people flows, or I will stop their cash cow, NAFTA. NEED WALL!

April 2, 2018

6:02 am to 6:10 am: Mexico has the absolute power not to let these large "Caravans" of people enter their country. They must stop them at their Northern Border, which they can do because their border laws work, not allow them to pass through into our country, which has no effective border laws…

...Congress must immediately pass Border Legislation, use Nuclear Option if necessary, to stop the massive inflow of Drugs and People. Border Patrol Agents (and ICE) are GREAT, but the weak Dem laws don't allow them to do their job. Act now Congress, our country is being stolen!

6:17 am: DACA is dead because the Democrats didn't care or act, and now everyone wants to get onto the DACA bandwagon... No longer works. Must build Wall and secure our borders with proper Border legislation. Democrats want No Borders, hence drugs and crime!

April 7, 2018

1:11 pm: We are sealing up our Southern Border. The people of our great country want Safety and Security. The Dems have been a disaster on this very important issue!

April 12, 2018

5:08 am: California Governor Jerry Brown is doing the right thing and sending the National Guard to the Border. Thank you Jerry, good move for the safety of our Country!

April 17, 2018

7:24 am: Looks like Jerry Brown and California are not looking for safety and security along their very porous Border. He cannot come to terms for the National Guard to patrol and protect the Border. The high crime rate will only get higher. Much wanted Wall in San Diego already started!

4:34 pm: Today's Court decision means that Congress must close loopholes that block the removal of dangerous criminal aliens, including aggravated felons. This is a public safety crisis that can only be fixed by...

April 18, 2018

4:59 am: There is a Revolution going on in California. Soooo many Sanctuary areas want OUT of this ridiculous, crime infested &

breeding concept. Jerry Brown is trying to back out of the National Guard at the Border, but the people of the State are not happy. Want Security & Safety NOW!

April 19, 2018

9:23 am: Thank you San Diego County for defending the rule of law and supporting our lawsuit against California's illegal and unconstitutional 'Sanctuary' policies. California's dangerous policies release violent criminals back into our communities, putting all Americans at risk.

10:48 am: Governor Jerry Brown announced he will deploy "up to 400 National Guard Troops" to do nothing. The crime rate in California is high enough, and the Federal Government will not be paying for Governor Brown's charade. We need border security and action, not words!

5:30 pm: Sanctuary Cities released at least 142 Gang Members across the United States, making it easy for them to commit all forms of violent crimes where none would have existed. We are doing a great job of law enforcement, but things such as this make safety in America difficult!

April 23, 2018

8:44 am: Despite the Democrat inspired laws on Sanctuary Cities and the Border being so bad and one sided, I have instructed the Secretary of Homeland Security not to let these large Caravans of people into our Country. It is a disgrace. We are the only Country in the World so naive! WALL

April 30, 2018

5:38 pm: The migrant 'caravan' that is openly defying our border shows how weak & ineffective U.S. immigration laws are. Yet Democrats like Jon Tester continue to support the open borders agenda—Tester even voted to protect Sanctuary Cities. We need lawmakers who will put America First.

May 4, 2018

4:59 pm: We are going to demand Congress secure the border in the upcoming CR. Illegal immigration must end!

May 18, 2018

5:51 am: Fake News Media had me calling Immigrants, or Illegal Immigrants, "Animals." Wrong! They were begrudgingly forced to withdraw their stories. I referred to MS 13 Gang Members as "Animals," a big difference—and so true. Fake News got it purposely wrong, as usual!

May 23, 2018

2:29 pm: Today on Long Island, we were all moved to be joined by families who have suffered unthinkable heartbreak at the hands of MS-13. I was truly honored to be joined again by the courageous families who were my guests at the State of the Union...

2:35 pm: Crippling loopholes in our laws have enabled MS-13 gang members and other criminals to infiltrate our communities—and Democrats in Congress REFUSE to close these loopholes, including the disgraceful practice known as Catch-and-Release. Democrats must abandon their resistance...

May 24, 2018

11:24 am: It was my great honor to host a roundtable re: MS-13 yesterday in Bethpage, New York. Democrats must abandon their resistance to border security so that we can SUPPORT law enforcement and SAVE innocent lives!

May 26, 2018

8:59 am: Put pressure on the Democrats to end the horrible law that separates children from there parents once they cross the Border into the U.S. Catch and Release, Lottery and Chain must also go with it and we MUST continue building the WALL! DEMOCRATS ARE PROTECTING MS-13 THUGS.

May 29, 2018

5:07 am: Democrats mistakenly tweet 2014 pictures from Obama's term showing children from the Border in steel cages. They thought it was recent pictures in order to make us look bad, but backfires. Dems must agree to Wall and new Border Protection for good of country... Bipartisan Bill!

June 15, 2018

12:08 pm: The Democrats are forcing the breakup of families at the Border with their horrible and cruel legislative agenda. Any Immigration Bill MUST HAVE full funding for the Wall, end Catch & Release, Visa Lottery and Chain, and go to Merit Based Immigration. Go for it! WIN!

June 18, 2018

7:46 am: Why don't the Democrats give us the votes to fix the world's worst immigration laws? Where is the outcry for the killings and crime being caused by gangs and thugs, including MS-13, coming into our country illegally?

8:02 am: The people of Germany are turning against their leadership as migration is rocking the already tenuous Berlin coalition. Crime in Germany is way up. Big mistake made all over Europe in allowing millions of people in who have so strongly and violently changed their culture!

8:04 am: We don't want what is happening with immigration in Europe to happen with us!

8:50 am: Children are being used by some of the worst criminals on earth as a means to enter our country. Has anyone been looking at the Crime taking place south of the border. It is historic, with some countries the most dangerous places in the world. Not going to happen in the U.S.

June 19, 2018

8:52 am: Crime in Germany is up 10% plus (officials do not want to report these crimes) since migrants were accepted. Others countries are even worse. Be smart America!

8:06 pm: Homeland Security @SecNielsen did a fabulous job yesterday at the press conference explaining security at the border and for our country, while at the same time recommending changes to obsolete & nasty laws, which force family separation. We want "heart" and security in America!

June 21, 2018

7:12 am: We shouldn't be hiring judges by the thousands, as our ridiculous immigration laws demand, we should be changing our laws, building the Wall, hire Border Agents and Ice and not let people come into our country based on the legal phrase they are told to say as their password.

7:29 am: The Border has been a big mess and problem for many years. At some point Schumer and Pelosi, who are weak on Crime and Border security, will be forced to do a real deal, so easy, that solves this long time problem. Schumer used to want Border security—now he'll take Crime!

12:02 pm: My Administration is acting swiftly to address the illegal immigration crisis on the Southern Border. Loopholes in our immigration laws all supported by extremist open border Democrats…and that's what they are—they're extremist open border Democrats…

5:40 pm: We have to maintain strong borders or we will no longer have a country that we can be proud of—and if we show any weakness, millions of people will journey into our country.

6:07 pm: You cannot pass legislation on immigration whether it be for safety and security or any other reason including "heart," without getting Dem votes. Problem is, they don't care about security and R's do. Zero Dems voted to support the Goodlatte Bill. They won't vote for anything!

June 22, 2018

8:43 am: We must maintain a Strong Southern Border. We cannot allow our Country to be overrun by illegal immigrants as the Democrats tell their phony stories of sadness and grief, hoping it will help them in the elections. Obama and others had the same pictures, and did nothing about it!

2:30 pm: We are gathered today to hear directly from the AMERICAN VICTIMS of ILLEGAL IMMIGRATION. These are the American Citizens permanently separated from their loved ones b/c they were killed by criminal illegal aliens. These are the families the media ignores...https://t.co/ZjXESYAcjY

June 23, 2018

12:35 pm: It's very sad that Nancy Pelosi and her sidekick, Cryin' Chuck Schumer, want to protect illegal immigrants far more than the citizens of our country. The United States cannot stand for this. We wants safety and security at our borders!

June 24, 2018

8:12 am: Democrats, fix the laws. Don't RESIST. We are doing a far better job than Bush and Obama, but we need strength and security at the Border! Cannot accept all of the people trying to break into our Country. Strong Borders, No Crime!

10:02 am: We cannot allow all of these people to invade our Country. When somebody comes in, we must immediately, with no Judges or Court Cases, bring them back from where they came. Our system is a mockery to good immigration policy and Law and Order. Most children come without parents...

June 30, 2018

6:07 am: The Democrats are making a strong push to abolish ICE, one of the smartest, toughest and most spirited law enforcement groups of men and women that I have ever seen. I have watched ICE liberate towns from the grasp of MS-13 & clean out the toughest of situations. They are great

6:22 am: To the great and brave men and women of ICE, do not worry or lose your spirit. You are doing a fantastic job of keeping us safe by eradicating the worst criminal elements. So brave! The radical left Dems want you out. Next it will be all police. Zero chance, It will never happen!

2:44 pm: When people come into our Country illegally, we must IMMEDIATELY escort them back out without going through years of legal maneuvering. Our laws are the dumbest anywhere in the world. Republicans want Strong Borders and no Crime. Dems want Open Borders and are weak on Crime!

July 3, 2018

5:45 am: When we have an "infestation" of MS-13 GANGS in certain parts of our country, who do we send to get them out? ICE! They are tougher and smarter than these rough criminal elelments that bad immigration laws allow into our country. Dems do not appreciate the great job they do! Nov.

July 5, 2018

9:17 am: Congress—FIX OUR INSANE IMMIGRATION LAWS NOW!

July 29, 2018

6:58 am: Please understand, there are consequences when people cross our Border illegally, whether they have children or not—and many are just using children for their own sinister purposes. Congress must act on fixing the DUMBEST & WORST immigration laws anywhere in the world! Vote "R"

July 30, 2018

6:57 am: We must have Border Security, get rid of Chain, Lottery, Catch & Release Sanctuary Cities—go to Merit based Immigration.

Protect ICE and Law Enforcement and, of course, keep building, but much faster, THE WALL!

5:34 pm: Illegal immigration is a top National Security problem. After decades of playing games, with the whole World laughing at the stupidity of our immigration laws, and with Democrats thinking...

...that Open Borders, large scale Crime, and abolishing ICE is good for them, we must get smart and finally do what must be done for the Safety and Security of our Country!

July 31, 2018

12:33 pm: I don't care what the political ramifications are, our immigration laws and border security have been a complete and total disaster for decades, and there is no way that the Democrats will allow it to be fixed without a Government Shutdown.

...Border Security is National Security, and National Security is the long-term viability of our Country. A Government Shutdown is a very small price to pay for a safe and Prosperous America!

August 15, 2018

7:44 am: "People who enter the United States without our permission are illegal aliens and illegal aliens should not be treated the same as people who enters the U.S. legally." Chuck Schumer in 2009, before he went left and haywire! @foxandfriends

September 7, 2018

11:35 am: Under our horrible immigration laws, the Government is frequently blocked from deporting criminal aliens with violent felony convictions. House GOP just passed a bill to increase our ability to deport violent felons (Crazy Dems opposed). Need to get this bill to my desk fast!

September 14, 2018

7:43 pm: My thoughts and prayers are with Evelyn Rodriguez this evening, along with her family and friends. #RIPEvelyn

September 20, 2018

6:43 am: I want to know, where is the money for Border Security and the WALL in this ridiculous Spending Bill, and where will it come from after the Midterms? Dems are obstructing Law Enforcement and Border Security. REPUBLICANS MUST FINALLY GET TOUGH!

October 16, 2018

8:24 pm: Anybody entering the United States illegally will be arrested and detained, prior to being sent back to their country!

October 17, 2018

8:45 am: Hard to believe that with thousands of people from South of the Border, walking unimpeded toward our country in the form of large Caravans, that the Democrats won't approve legislation that will allow laws for the protection of our country. Great Midterm issue for Republicans!

8:48 am: Republicans must make the horrendous, weak and outdated immigration laws, and the Border, a part of the Midterms!

October 18, 2018

6:25 am to 6:45 am: I am watching the Democrat Party led (because they want Open Borders and existing weak laws) assault on our country by Guatemala, Honduras and El Salvador, whose leaders are doing little to stop this large flow of people, INCLUDING MANY CRIMINALS, from entering Mexico to U.S...

...In addition to stopping all payments to these countries, which seem to have almost no control over their population, I must, in the strongest of terms, ask Mexico to stop this onslaught—and if unable to do so I will call up the U.S. Military and CLOSE OUR SOUTHERN BORDER!

...The assault on our country at our Southern Border, including the Criminal elements and DRUGS pouring in, is far more important to me, as President, than Trade or the USMCA. Hopefully Mexico will stop this onslaught at their Northern Border. All Democrats fault for weak laws!

October 21, 2018

2:11 pm: Full efforts are being made to stop the onslaught of illegal aliens from crossing our Souther Border. People have to apply for asylum in Mexico first, and if they fail to do that, the U.S. will turn them away. The courts are asking the U.S. to do things that are not doable!

2:14 pm: The Caravans are a disgrace to the Democrat Party. Change the immigration laws NOW!

October 22, 2018

7:37 am: Sadly, it looks like Mexico's Police and Military are unable to stop the Caravan heading to the Southern Border of the United States. Criminals and unknown Middle Easterners are mixed in. I have alerted Border Patrol and Military that this is a National Emergy. Must change laws!

7:49 am: Every time you see a Caravan, or people illegally coming, or attempting to come, into our Country illegally, think of and blame the Democrats for not giving us the votes to change our pathetic Immigration Laws! Remember the Midterms! So unfair to those who come in legally.

7:57 am: Every time you see a Caravan, or people illegally coming, or attempting to come, into our Country illegally, think of and blame the Democrats for not giving us the votes to change our pathetic Immigration Laws! Remember the Midterms! So unfair to those who come in legally.

October 24, 2018

6:52 am: For those who want and advocate for illegal immigration, just take a good look at what has happened to Europe over the last 5 years. A total mess! They only wish they had that decision to make over again.

October 25, 2018

1:31 pm: To those in the Caravan, turnaround, we are not letting people into the United States illegally. Go back to your Country and if you want, apply for citizenship like millions of others are doing!

October 31, 2018

7:38 am: The Caravans are made up of some very tough fighters and people. Fought back hard and viciously against Mexico at Northern Border before breaking through. Mexican soldiers hurt, were unable, or unwilling to stop Caravan. Should stop them before they reach our Border, but won't!

7:45 am: Our military is being mobilized at the Southern Border. Many more troops coming. We will NOT let these Caravans, which are also made up of some very bad thugs and gang members, into the U.S. Our Border is sacred, must come in legally. TURN AROUND!

8:25 am: So-called Birthright Citizenship, which costs our Country billions of dollars and is very unfair to our citizens, will be ended one way or the other. It is not covered by the 14th Amendment because of the words "subject to the jurisdiction thereof." Many legal scholars agree…

9:19 am: The World is using our laws to our detriment. They laugh at the Stupidity they see!

November 1, 2018

3:54 pm: Illegal immigration affects the lives of all Americans. Illegal Immigration hurts American workers, burdens American taxpayers, undermines public safety, and places enormous strain on local schools, hospitals and communities

November 3, 2018

8:46 pm: If you want to protect criminal aliens—VOTE DEMO-CRAT. If you want to protect Law-Abiding Americans—VOTE REPUBLICAN!

November 16, 2018

7:43 pm: Isn't it ironic that large Caravans of people are marching to our border wanting U.S.A. asylum because they are fearful of being in their country-yet they are proudly waving…

their country's flag. Can this be possible? Yes, because it is all a BIG CON, and the American taxpayer is paying for it!

November 18, 2018

2:55 pm: Catch and Release is an obsolete term. It is now Catch and Detain. Illegal Immigrants trying to come into the U.S.A., often proudly flying the flag of their nation as they ask for U.S. Asylum, will be detained or turned away. Dems must approve Border Security & Wall NOW!

November 21, 2018

4:31 pm: "Thank you to President Trump on the Border. No American President has ever done this before." Hector Garza, National Border Patrol Council

4:42 pm: There are a lot of CRIMINALS in the Caravan. We will stop them. Catch and Detain! Judicial Activism, by people who know nothing about security and the safety of our citizens, is putting our country in great danger. Not good!

November 22, 2018

7:21 am to 7:30 am: Justice Roberts can say what he wants, but the 9th Circuit is a complete & total disaster. It is out of control, has a horrible reputation, is overturned more than any Circuit in the Country,

79%, & is used to get an almost guaranteed result. Judges must not Legislate Security...

...and Safety at the Border, or anywhere else. They know nothing about it and are making our Country unsafe. Our great Law Enforcement professionals MUST BE ALLOWED TO DO THEIR JOB! If not there will be only bedlam, chaos, injury and death. We want the Constitution as written!

6:07 pm: Our highly trained security professionals are not allowed to do their job on the Border because of the Judicial Activism and Interference by the 9th Circuit. Nevertheless, they are working hard to make America a safer place, though hard to do when anybody filing a lawsuit wins!

November 23, 2018

7:21 am: Republicans and Democrats MUST come together, finally, with a major Border Security package, which will include funding for the Wall. After 40 years of talk, it is finally time for action. Fix the Border, for once and for all, NOW!

6:49 pm: Migrants at the Southern Border will not be allowed into the United States until their claims are individually approved in court. We only will allow those who come into our Country legally. Other than that our very strong policy is Catch and Detain. No "Releasing" into the U.S..

November 25, 2018

3:20 pm: General Anthony Tata: "President Trump is a man of his word & he said he was going to be tough on the Border, and he is tough on the Border. He has rightfully strengthened the Border in the face of an unprecedented threat. It's the right move by President Trump." Thanks General!

November 26, 2018

6:19 am: Mexico should move the flag waving Migrants, many of whom are stone cold criminals, back to their countries. Do it by plane, do it by bus, do it anyway you want, but they are NOT coming into the U.S.A. We will close the Border permanently if need be. Congress, fund the WALL!

December 6, 2018

10:15 pm: Arizona, together with our Military and Border Patrol, is bracing for a massive surge at a NON-WALLED area. WE WILL NOT LET THEM THROUGH. Big danger. Nancy and Chuck must approve Boarder Security and the Wall!

December 11, 2018

7:30 am to 7:42 am: ...I look forward to my meeting with Chuck Schumer & Nancy Pelosi. In 2006, Democrats voted for a Wall, and they were right to do so. Today, they no longer want Border Security. They will fight it at all cost, and Nancy must get votes for Speaker. But the Wall will get built...

...People do not yet realize how much of the Wall, including really effective renovation, has already been built. If the Democrats do not give us the votes to secure our Country, the Military will build the remaining sections of the Wall. They know how important it is!

December 18, 2018

7:55 am: Illegal immigration costs the United States more than 200 Billion Dollars a year. How was this allowed to happen?

8:13 pm: The Democrats, are saying loud and clear that they do not want to build a Concrete Wall—but we are not building a Concrete Wall, we are building artistically designed steel slats, so that you can easily see through it...

...It will be beautiful and, at the same time, give our Country the security that our citizens deserve. It will go up fast and save us BILLIONS of dollars a month once completed!

December 21, 2018

6:58 am to 7:10 am: The Democrats are trying to belittle the concept of a Wall, calling it old fashioned. The fact is there is nothing else's that will work, and that has been true for thousands of years. It's like the wheel, there is nothing better. I know tech better than anyone, & technology...

...on a Border is only effective in conjunction with a Wall. Properly designed and built Walls work, and the Democrats are lying when they say they don't. In Israel the Wall is 99.9% successful. Will not be any different on our Southern Border! Hundreds of $Billions saved!

7:19 am: No matter what happens today in the Senate, Republican House Members should be very proud of themselves. They flew back to Washington from all parts of the World in order to vote for Border Security and the Wall. Not one Democrat voted yes, and we won big. I am very proud of you!

7:24 am: The Democrats, whose votes we need in the Senate, will probably vote against Border Security and the Wall even though they know it is DESPERATELY NEEDED. If the Dems vote no, there will be a shutdown that will last for a very long time. People don't want Open Borders and Crime!

7:38 am: Even President Ronald Reagan tried for 8 years to build a Border Wall, or Fence, and was unable to do so. Others also have tried. We will get it done, one way or the other!

9:49 pm: OUR GREAT COUNTRY MUST HAVE BORDER SECURITY! https://t.co/ZGcYygMf3a

December 23, 2018

11:06 am: The most important way to stop gangs, drugs, human trafficking and massive crime is at our Southern Border. We need Border Security, and as EVERYONE knows, you can't have Border Security without a Wall. The Drones & Technology are just bells and whistles. Safety for America!

December 24, 2018

12:10 pm: The Wall is different than the 25 Billion Dollars in Border Security. The complete Wall will be built with the Shutdown money plus funds already in hand. The reporting has been inaccurate on the point. The problem is, without the Wall, much of the rest of Dollars are wasted!

5:24 pm: I am in the Oval Office & just gave out a 115 mile long contract for another large section of the Wall in Texas. We are already building and renovating many miles of Wall, some complete. Democrats must end Shutdown and finish funding. Billions of Dollars, & lives, will be saved!

December 27, 2018

7:06 am: Have the Democrats finally realized that we desperately need Border Security and a Wall on the Southern Border. Need to stop Drugs, Human Trafficking,Gang Members & Criminals from coming into our Country. Do the Dems realize that most of the people not getting paid are Democrats?

2:35 pm: The reason the DACA for Wall deal didn't get done was that a ridiculous court decision from the 9th Circuit allowed DACA to remain, thereby setting up a Supteme Court case. After ruling, Dems dropped deal—and that's where we are today, Democrat obstruction of the needed Wall.

4:04 pm: There is right now a full scale manhunt going on in California for an illegal immigrant accused of shooting and killing a police officer during a traffic stop. Time to get tough on Border Security. Build the Wall!

5:10 pm: This isn't about the Wall, everybody knows that a Wall will work perfectly (In Israel the Wall works 99.9%). This is only about the Dems not letting Donald Trump & the Republicans have a win. They may have the 10 Senate votes, but we have the issue, Border Security. 2020!

December 29, 2018

1:30 pm to 1:36 pm: Any deaths of children or others at the Border are strictly the fault of the Democrats and their pathetic immigration policies that allow people to make the long trek thinking they can enter our country illegally. They can't. If we had a Wall, they wouldn't even try! The two…

…children in question were very sick before they were given over to Border Patrol. The father of the young girl said it was not their fault, he hadn't given her water in days. Border Patrol needs the Wall and it will all end. They are working so hard & getting so little credit!

2:25 pm: For those that naively ask why didn't the Republicans get approval to build the Wall over the last year, it is because IN THE SENATE WE NEED 10 DEMOCRAT VOTES, and they will gives us "NONE" for Border Security! Now we have to do it the hard way, with a Shutdown. Too bad!

December 31, 2018

7:51 am: An all concrete Wall was NEVER ABANDONED, as has been reported by the media. Some areas will be all concrete but the experts at Border Patrol prefer a Wall that is see through (thereby making it possible to see what is happening on both sides). Makes sense to me!

Immigration/Borders—2019 News Quotes

Remarks on border security, January 3, 2019.
Source: https://www.whitehouse.gov/briefings-statements/
remarks-president-trump-border-security/

"I'm going to have them introduce themselves right now and also say a few words about the wall, about—You can call it a barrier. You can call it whatever you want. But essentially, we need protection in our country. We're going to make it good. The people of our country want it. I have never had so much support, as I have in the last week, over my stance for border security, for border control and for, frankly, the wall or the barrier. I have never had anything like it in terms of calls coming in, in terms of people writing in and tweeting, and doing whatever they have to do. I have never had this much support. And we've done some things that, as you know, have been very popular.

"So I'm going to ask [National Border Control Council President] Brandon Judd to just step forward and say a few words. This group has apprehended, last year, 17,000 criminals trying to get across the border. Seventeen thousand. And that's one category. There are plenty of others. The other thing that has been so incredible is what they've done in terms of drugs and stopping drugs. And with that, and with everything else—Plenty, unfortunately, come through our southern border."

Response to a question from Kevin McCarthy of C-SPAN, January 4, 2019.

Source: https://www.c-span.org/video/?c4770863/
presidents-declare-national-emergency-build-border-wall

"No, we can use them. Absolutely, we can call a national emergency because of the security of our country. Absolutely. No, we can do it. I haven't done it. I may do it. I may do it. But we can call a national emergency and build it very quickly. And it's another way of doing it. But if we can do it through a negotiated process, we're giving that a shot."

Address to the nation on the crisis at the border, January 8, 2019.

Source: https://www.whitehouse.gov/briefings-statements/
president-donald-j-trumps-address-nation-crisis-border/

"My fellow Americans: Tonight, I am speaking to you because there is a growing humanitarian and security crisis at our southern border.

"Every day, Customs and Border Patrol agents encounter thousands of illegal immigrants trying to enter our country. We are out of space to hold them, and we have no way to promptly return them back home to their country.

"America proudly welcomes millions of lawful immigrants who enrich our society and contribute to our nation. But all Americans are hurt by uncontrolled, illegal migration. It strains public resources and drives down jobs and wages. Among those hardest hit are African Americans and Hispanic Americans.

"Our southern border is a pipeline for vast quantities of illegal drugs, including meth, heroin, cocaine, and fentanyl. Every week, 300 of our citizens are killed by heroin alone, 90% of which floods across from our southern border. More Americans will die from drugs this year than were killed in the entire Vietnam War.

"In the last two years, ICE officers made 266,000 arrests of aliens with criminal records, including those charged or convicted of 100,000 assaults, 30,000 sex crimes, and 4,000 violent killings. Over the years, thousands of Americans have been brutally killed by those who illegally entered our country, and thousands more lives will be lost if we don't act right now.

"This is a humanitarian crisis: a crisis of the heart and a crisis of the soul.

"Last month, 20,000 migrant children were illegally brought into the United States: a dramatic increase. These children are used as human pawns by vicious coyotes and ruthless gangs. One in three women are sexually assaulted on the dangerous trek up through Mexico. Women and children are the biggest victims, by far, of our broken system.

"This is the tragic reality of illegal immigration on our southern border. This is the cycle of human suffering that I am determined to end.

"My administration has presented Congress with a detailed proposal to secure the border and stop the criminal gangs, drug smugglers, and human traffickers. It's a tremendous problem. Our proposal was developed by law enforcement professionals and border agents at the Department of Homeland Security. These are the resources they have requested to properly perform their mission and keep America safe. In fact, safer than ever before.

"The proposal from Homeland Security includes cutting-edge technology for detecting drugs, weapons, illegal contraband, and many other things. We have requested more agents, immigration judges, and bed space to process the sharp rise in unlawful migration fueled by our very strong economy. Our plan also contains an urgent request for humanitarian assistance and medical support.

"Furthermore, we have asked Congress to close border security loopholes so that illegal immigrant children can be safely and humanely returned back home.

"Finally, as part of an overall approach to border security, law enforcement professionals have requested $5.7 billion for a physical barrier. At the request of Democrats, it will be a steel barrier rather than a concrete wall. This barrier is absolutely critical to border security. It's also what our professionals at the border want and need. This is just common sense.

"The border wall would very quickly pay for itself. The cost of illegal drugs exceeds $500 billion a year, vastly more than the $5.7 billion we have requested from Congress. The wall will also be paid for, indirectly, by the great new trade deal we have made with Mexico.

"Senator Chuck Schumer, who you will be hearing from later tonight, has repeatedly supported a physical barrier in the past, along with many other Democrats. They changed their mind only after I was elected President.

"Democrats in Congress have refused to acknowledge the crisis. And they have refused to provide our brave border agents with the tools they desperately need to protect our families and our nation.

"The federal government remains shut down for one reason and one reason only: because Democrats will not fund border security.

"My administration is doing everything in our power to help those impacted by the situation. But the only solution is for Democrats to pass a spending bill that defends our borders and re-opens the government.

"This situation could be solved in a 45-minute meeting. I have invited Congressional leadership to the White House tomorrow to get this done. Hopefully, we can rise above partisan politics in order to support national security.

"Some have suggested a barrier is immoral. Then why do wealthy politicians build walls, fences, and gates around their homes? They don't build walls because they hate the people on the outside, but because they love the people on the inside. The only thing that is immoral is the politicians to do nothing and continue to allow more innocent people to be so horribly victimized.

"America's heart broke the day after Christmas when a young police officer in California was savagely murdered in cold blood by an illegal alien, who just came across the border. The life of an American hero was stolen by someone who had no right to be in our country.

"Day after day, precious lives are cut short by those who have violated our borders. In California, an Air Force veteran was raped, murdered, and beaten to death with a hammer by an illegal alien with a long criminal history. In Georgia, an illegal alien was recently charged with murder for killing, beheading, and dismembering his neighbor. In Maryland, MS-13 gang members who arrived in the United States as unaccompanied minors were arrested and charged last year after viciously stabbing and beating a 16-year-old girl.

"Over the last several years, I've met with dozens of families whose loved ones were stolen by illegal immigration. I've held the hands of the weeping mothers and embraced the grief-stricken fathers. So sad. So terrible. I will never forget the pain in their eyes, the tremble in their voices, and the sadness gripping their souls.

"How much more American blood must we shed before Congress does its job?

"To those who refuse to compromise in the name of border security, I would ask: imagine if it was your child, your husband, or your wife whose life was so cruelly shattered and totally broken?

"To every member of Congress: pass a bill that ends this crisis.

"To every citizen: call Congress and tell them to finally, after all of these decades, secure our border.

"This is a choice between right and wrong, justice and injustice. This is about whether we fulfill our sacred duty to the American citizens we serve.

"When I took the Oath of Office, I swore to protect our country. And that is what I will always do, so help me God."

Remarks in a meeting with conservative leaders on his immigration proposal, January 23, 2019.
Source: https://www.whitehouse.gov/briefings-statements/
remarks-president-trump-meeting-conservative-leaders-immigration-proposal/

"We're doing a great job on the border, considering we don't have the tools. They don't give us the tools to work with, meaning we have to have a wall. We have to have a barricade of some kind, a steel barricade. It's already designed.

"We're building a lot of wall as we speak, a tremendous amount. And we're renovating a lot of the other wall. Otherwise—By the way, with what's coming up, because of the strong economy that we have, we haven't had an economy like this, I guess, in over 50 years."

Remarks in a meeting with conservative leaders on his immigration proposal, January 23, 2019.
Source: https://www.whitehouse.gov/briefings-statements/
remarks-president-trump-meeting-conservative-leaders-immigration-proposal/

"And because of the strong economy, everyone is pouring up, and we're stopping them. But it's a lot of work. We have incredible people at the border, and you have to thank all of the Border Patrol agents and the ICE agents I see in Long Island. They don't want ICE. The radical Democrats don't want ICE there because they're too good; they're doing too good a job.

"And I always talk about Long Island; that's one of the real hotbeds for the MS-13 gangs. And I just see this morning, where the, really, radical Democrats don't want them there because they don't want to do anything to disturb MS-13. And when you think about it, MS-13 is about the most violent gang, they say; one of the most violent anywhere in the world. And they have done—We're sending them out by the thousands out of our country. So we think it's too bad."

Response to a question from Maggie Haberman of *The New York Times*, January 31, 2019.

Source: https://www.nytimes.com/2019/02/01/us/politics/trump-interview-transcripts.html

"National security is very important and we're fighting over—A very important element is the southern border. When we talk about drugs coming from China, the fentanyl—You look at the heroin and a lot of the other drugs, they come from, 90%, more than 90% from right across the southern border. And unlike what the Democrats say, they don't, you don't bring trucks of drugs through the checkpoints. You bring trucks of drugs by making a right 20 miles, and a left into the country. They're not bringing, you know, they bring massive amounts of drugs, and they do it because there's no barrier, there's no hardened wall that you can't knock down with your breath."

Response to a question from Maggie Haberman of *The New York Times*, January 31, 2019.

Source: https://www.nytimes.com/2019/02/01/us/politics/trump-interview-transcripts.html

"Yeah, I did. I did. I've actually always gotten along with her [Speaker of the House Nancy Pelosi], but now I don't think I will anymore. I think that she's hurting the country very badly. I think she's doing a tremendous disservice to the country. If she doesn't approve a wall, the rest of it's just a waste of money and time and energy because it's, it's desperately needed. People are flowing in.

"I mean, we have caravans coming in right now, 12,000 people. We have three of them lined up. And you know they're lining up from Honduras and Guatemala and El Salvador. And they're coming in.

"With a wall, you don't need very much help. We just had to move more military down there to handle the one that's coming up now: 12,000 people or whatever it might be. But they say it's about 12,000 people.

"No, I think Nancy Pelosi is hurting our country very badly by doing what she's doing. And ultimately I think I've set the table very nicely."

Response to a question from Peter Baker of *The New York Times*, January 31, 2019.

Source: https://www.nytimes.com/2019/02/01/us/politics/trump-interview-transcripts.html

"You know I'm building the wall. You know that. I'm building the wall right now. I'm building—It's been funded, and we're buying it right. And we're renovating large sections of wall. We're building new sections of wall. We're building the wall. The wall is going up as we speak. We'll be up to, by the end of this year, 115 miles."

Response to a question from Peter Baker of *The New York Times*, January 31, 2019.

Source: https://www.nytimes.com/2019/02/01/us/politics/trump-interview-transcripts.html

"And that doesn't include large amounts of wall that we'll be starting before the end of the year. So we'll be up to hundreds of miles of wall between new wall and renovation wall in a fairly short period of time. It's the one thing. So I'm building the wall now, as we speak. And I'll continue to build the wall, and we'll get the wall finished. Now whether or not I declare a national emergency, that you'll see."

Response to a question from Margaret Brennan of CBS News, February 3, 2019

Source: https://www.cbsnews.com/news/
transcript-president-trump-on-face-the-nation-february-3-2019/

"Well, I don't, I don't take anything off the table. I don't like to take things off the table. It's that alternative. It's national emergency, it's other things and you know there have been plenty national emergencies called. And this really is an invasion of our country by human traffickers. These are people that are horrible people bringing in women mostly, but bringing in women and children into our country. Human trafficking. And we're going to have a strong border. And the only way you have a strong border is you need a physical barrier. You need a wall. And anybody that says you don't, they're just playing games."

From State of the Union address, February 5, 2019.

Source: https://www.whitehouse.gov/briefings-statements/
president-donald-j-trumps-state-union-address-2/

"As we have seen, when we are united, we can make astonishing strides for our country. Now, Republicans and Democrats must join forces again to confront an urgent national crisis.

"The Congress has 10 days left to pass a bill that will fund our Government, protect our homeland, and secure our southern border.

"Now is the time for the Congress to show the world that America is committed to ending illegal immigration and putting the ruthless coyotes, cartels, drug dealers, and human traffickers out of business.

"As we speak, large, organized caravans are on the march to the United States. We have just heard that Mexican cities, in order to remove the illegal immigrants from their communities, are getting trucks and buses to bring them up to our country in areas where there is little border protection. I have ordered another 3,750 troops to our southern border to prepare for the tremendous onslaught.

"This is a moral issue. The lawless state of our southern border is a threat to the safety, security, and financial well-being of all Americans. We have a moral duty to create an immigration system that protects the lives and jobs of our citizens. This includes our obligation to the millions of immigrants living here today, who followed the rules and respected our laws. Legal immigrants enrich our nation and strengthen our society in countless ways. I want people to come into our country, but they have to come in legally.

"Tonight, I am asking you to defend our very dangerous southern border out of love and devotion to our fellow citizens and to our country.

"No issue better illustrates the divide between America's working class and America's political class than illegal immigration. Wealthy politicians and donors push for open borders while living their lives behind walls and gates and guards.

"Meanwhile, working class Americans are left to pay the price for mass illegal migration: reduced jobs, lower wages, overburdened schools and hospitals, increased crime, and a depleted social safety net.

"Tolerance for illegal immigration is not compassionate; it is cruel. One in three women is sexually assaulted on the long journey north. Smugglers use migrant children as human pawns to exploit our laws and gain access to our country.

"Human traffickers and sex traffickers take advantage of the wide open areas between our ports of entry to smuggle thousands of young girls and women into the United States and to sell them into prostitution and modern-day slavery.

"Tens of thousands of innocent Americans are killed by lethal drugs that cross our border and flood into our cities, including meth, heroin, cocaine, and fentanyl.

"The savage gang, MS-13, now operates in 20 different American states, and they almost all come through our southern border. Just yesterday, an MS-13 gang member was taken into custody for a fatal shooting on a subway platform in New York City. We are removing these gang members by the thousands, but until we secure our border they're going to keep streaming back in.

"Year after year, countless Americans are murdered by criminal illegal aliens.

"I've gotten to know many wonderful Angel Moms, Dads, and families: no one should ever have to suffer the horrible heartache they have endured.

"Here tonight is Debra Bissell. Just three weeks ago, Debra's parents, Gerald and Sharon, were burglarized and shot to death in their Reno, Nevada, home by an illegal alien. They were in their eighties and are survived by four children, 11 grandchildren, and 20 great-grandchildren. Also here tonight are Gerald and Sharon's granddaughter, Heather, and great-granddaughter, Madison.

"To Debra, Heather, Madison, please stand: few can understand your pain. But I will never forget, and I will fight for the memory of Gerald and Sharon, that it should never happen again.

"Not one more American life should be lost because our nation failed to control its very dangerous border.

"In the last two years, our brave ICE officers made 266,000 arrests of criminal aliens, including those charged or convicted of nearly 100,000 assaults, 30,000 sex crimes, and 4,000 killings.

"We are joined tonight by one of those law enforcement heroes: ICE Special Agent Elvin Hernandez. When Elvin was a boy, he and his family legally immigrated to the United States from the Dominican Republic. At the age of eight, Elvin told his dad he wanted to become a Special Agent. Today, he leads investigations into the scourge of international sex trafficking. Elvin says, 'If I can make sure these young girls get their justice, I've done my job.' Thanks to his work and that of his colleagues, more than 300 women and girls have been rescued from horror and more than 1,500 sadistic traffickers have been put behind bars in the last year.

"Special Agent Hernandez, please stand. We will always support the brave men and women of law enforcement, and I pledge to you tonight that we will never abolish our heroes from ICE.

"My administration has sent to the Congress a commonsense proposal to end the crisis on our southern border.

"It includes humanitarian assistance, more law enforcement, drug detection at our ports, closing loopholes that enable child smuggling, and plans for a new physical barrier, or wall, to secure the vast areas between our ports of entry. In the past, most of the people in this room voted for a wall, but the proper wall never got built. I'll get it built.

"This is a smart, strategic, see-through steel barrier, not just a simple concrete wall. It will be deployed in the areas identified by border agents as having the greatest need, and as these agents will tell you, where walls go up, illegal crossings go way down.

"San Diego used to have the most illegal border crossings in the country. In response, and at the request of San Diego residents and political leaders, a strong security wall was put in place. This powerful barrier almost completely ended illegal crossings.

"The border city of El Paso, Texas, used to have extremely high rates of violent crime, one of the highest in the country, and considered one of our nation's most dangerous cities. Now, with a powerful barrier in place, El Paso is one of our safest cities.

"Simply put, walls work and walls save lives. So let's work together, compromise, and reach a deal that will truly make America safe."

"Sure. It's going to be—Have a negative impact on the economy. It's one of the biggest trade deals in the world that we've just done with the USMCA.

"It's a very big trading partner. But to me, trading is very important, the borders are very important, but security is what is most important to me. I have to have security. This is what this gentleman is all about, to my right. And we're going to have security in this country. That's more important than trade.

"Hey, all you hear me talking about is trade. But let me just give you a little secret: security is more important to me than trade.

"So, we're going to have a strong border or we're going to have a closed border. And you know, when we close that border, we will stop hundreds of millions of dollars of drugs from coming in, because tremendous amounts of drugs come through our southern border. And so that's one of the benefits.

"So, I'm totally prepared to do it. We're going to see what happens over the next few days."

Response to a question from Griff Jenkins of FOX News, April 6, 2019.

Source: https://www.foxnews.com/politics/trump-declares-the-country-full-in-fox-news-interview-says-american-can-no-longer-accept-illegal-immigrants

"No, we're witnessing people that are going to be brought out of the country, the country is full. We have our system full. We can't do it anymore,"

Response to a question from Griff Jenkins of FOX News, April 6, 2019.

Source: https://www.foxnews.com/politics/trump-declares-the-country-full-in-fox-news-interview-says-american-can-no-longer-accept-illegal-immigrants

"We go by this horrible Flores situation. You know that decision is a horror show. We have to release after 20 days and we build big detention areas but they fill up immediately"

Remarks at the signing of H.R. 3401, July 1, 2019.

Source: https://www.whitehouse.gov/briefings-statements/remarks-president-trump-signing-h-r-3401/

"And today, I'm signing a bill to deliver $4.6 billion in humanitarian assistance to our southern border. This includes funding for medical care, shelters, and increased housing for minors through the Department of Health and Human Services."

Remarks at the signing of H.R. 3401, July 1, 2019.

Source: https://www.whitehouse.gov/briefings-statements/remarks-president-trump-signing-h-r-3401/

"For many weeks, Democrats were giving us a hard time. But I tell you, it became a bipartisan bill. We were very happy about it. And now, what we want to do is we have to do a bill for border security, and all of this will go away."

Remarks at the signing of H.R. 3401, July 1, 2019.

Source: https://www.whitehouse.gov/briefings-statements/remarks-president-trump-signing-h-r-3401/

"But we have to do a bill on border security. And we can solve the problem entirely at our border. The wall is being built. But unfortunately, we had a very bad case from the Ninth Circuit, as usual. A Ninth Circuit judge, and I say that loud and clear—It's very hard to win at the Ninth Circuit, if not impossible. He ruled against something that, in my opinion, was a terrible error. And it really affected the construction of part of our wall.

"And much of it is being build. Most of it is being built. But it had an impact. These were contracts that were out. They were being built and now we're supposed to stop because a judge decided, in his own whim, that he wanted to stop it. So we appealed it, and we're asking for an expedited appeal.

"But again, much of the wall is being built. We had it all being built, and the Ninth Circuit, as usual, came through for the other side. And it's an incredible situation we have going. There's something wrong with this. Where something like this can happen, it's not a good situation.

"Anyway, we're asking Congress to step forward on border security and help us with border security. If we do that, it's going to be perfect because the Mexicans have done a fantastic job, and I want to thank the President of Mexico [Andrés Manuel López Obrador]. And they've [Mexico has] done this over the last week and a half. It started at the other border, and now it's at our border and it's had a very big impact. You'll see the numbers come out. You probably have to wait three or four weeks, but you'll see there's a tremendous difference.

"And most importantly, we must eliminate all incentives for smuggling children and for smuggling women. They're smuggling women through borders and the borders that don't have the wall, or the borders where you can't physically have security because it's so many miles. You know, we have 2,000 miles of border.

"So, they're smuggling in women and they're smuggling in children. And they're using the children, in particular, as pawns, who are getting other people into our country. Because when you're with a child, even if the child is not yours, which in itself is ridiculous, then it's much easier to come across and come into our country because the laws are very bad. Our immigration laws are very bad.

"And right now, smugglers coach migrants to travel with minors and to send minors alone to gain easy entry into the United States. Catch-and-release must stop. DHS [The U.S. Department of Homeland Security] must have the authority to humanely return minors to be with their families in their home countries. It's, right now, a situation where nobody knows what they're doing because our laws are so bad and it can be changed in—I always say 15 minutes; make it an hour. It's very simple. These changes are very simple. It's changes to the asylum. If we change asylum, we can have 75% of it done. The rest has to be done on the loopholes.

"Vast migrations out of Central America undermine the future of those countries. And these countries now, they want their children back. They're actually wanting their children back.

"As you know, I stopped hundreds of millions of dollars from going to Guatemala, Honduras, and El Salvador because they haven't been doing what they should be doing. Caravans have been forming, but now the caravans are being stopped by Mexico.

"And again, we want to thank Mexico, but the caravans that formed are being stopped by Mexico, short of our southern border, and in many cases, before they even get out of Guatemala. But I'm hearing that Guatemala is starting to help us a lot. But we're not paying them all of the money. We used to pay them over $500 million a year. I stopped that money from going to them. Some people think it should be the opposite: we should give them money. I don't think they were doing what they could do, and therefore I stopped it. And at some point, maybe if they do a great job and the job they're supposed to, we can be talking. But right now, it's disgraceful what's happening.

"And Congress and the Democrats have to step forward to provide humane solutions to put child smugglers out of business. You have child smugglers by the hundreds, and, actually, probably by the thousands, and they're becoming very rich because our laws are so bad. And they have to restore the integrity of the United States' asylum system.

"Without these changes, more than 1 million immigrants will arrive at the borders this year, many of them lodging frivolous asylum claims. And that's what they do to gain access into the country: they lodge claims on asylum. And they're totally bogus claims.

"We apprehend these people. But because of catch-and-release, we have to apprehend them, take their names, sometimes bring them to court. Sometimes they're criminals; oftentimes they have to be released. But they're all coming out of the country because that's what we do.

After July 4th, a lot of people are going to be brought back out. So people that come up may be here for a short while, but they're going to be going—They're going back to their countries. They go back home.

"ICE is going to be apprehending them and bringing them back. And we have a very big system for that, and it's been very effective and it will be very effective.

"So they may feel, and you may read, that they came across. And because of the ridiculous laws of catch-and-release, which I call not a law; I call it a loophole. You release them, but they go back. They get caught. They come in illegally and they go out legally. Very simple system.

"Most border crossers never show up in court. They never come. About 3% show up. Nobody even knows why they show up. But only 3% show up.

"But we are apprehending them, and we bring them out of the country. In some cases, they're criminals and, ideally, we want them to use the other country's criminal justice system because we don't want to load up our prisoners any—Our prisons any more than they're already loaded up.

"So that's it in a nutshell. It's $4.6 billion. It was bipartisan. It was done in a bipartisan manner. We all got together.

"This is a humane solution to a tremendous problem that's caused because we have bad immigration laws, and we can solve that problem very, very quickly if we could get together with the Democrats. The problem is the Democrats actually like this system because it's open borders.

"Now, we don't allow it to be open borders because we're apprehending and we're doing a great job. Border Patrol has been incredible. Law enforcement has been incredible. And ICE has been incredible.

"But it shouldn't be this way. It shouldn't be this way. We're the only ones in the world that have a system like this. It's absolutely insane, our system of immigration.

"And the reason they come up is because our economy is doing so well."

Remarks at the signing of H.R. 3401, July 1, 2019.

Source: https://www.whitehouse.gov/briefings-statements/
remarks-president-trump-signing-h-r-3401/

"So we are signing this now, and it's an honor to sign it. And if we could do border security along with it, or follow it up shortly, everybody would be extremely happy."

Remarks at the signing of H.R. 3401, July 1, 2019.

Source: https://www.whitehouse.gov/briefings-statements/
remarks-president-trump-signing-h-r-3401/

"You know, we're not in the hospital business. We're in the border security business at the border. And all of a sudden, we're forced to be in the hospital business."

Response to an unidentified reporter's question at the signing of H.R. 3401, July 1, 2019.

Source: https://www.whitehouse.gov/briefings-statements/
remarks-president-trump-signing-h-r-3401/

"Yeah, we're looking at that. We think that a census—Obviously, if you do all of this work and you're talking about—Nobody can believe this, but they spend billions of dollars on the census, and you're not allowed to ask? You don't knock on doors of houses, check houses? You go through all this detail and you're not allowed to ask whether or not somebody is a citizen? So you can ask other things, but you can't ask whether or not somebody is a citizen?

So we are trying to do that. We're looking at that very strongly."

Response to an unidentified reporter's question at the signing of H.R. 3401, July 1, 2019.

Source: https://www.whitehouse.gov/briefings-statements/
remarks-president-trump-signing-h-r-3401/

"I think it's very important to find out if somebody is a citizen as opposed to an illegal? I think there's a big difference, to me, between being a citizen of the United States and being an illegal. And, you know, the Democrats want to treat the illegals, with healthcare and with other things, better than they treat the citizens of our country.

"If you look at a coal miner that has black lung disease, you're talking about people that get treated better than the coal miner. And these people got sick working for the United States. And we treated people that just walked in better.

"If you look at what they're doing in California, how they're treating people, they don't treat their people as well as they treat illegal immigrants. So at what point does it stop? It's crazy what they're doing. It's crazy. And it's mean, and it's very unfair to our citizens. And we're going to stop it, but we may need an election to stop it, and we may need to get back the House.

"And again, they're coming up because they want a piece of what's happening in this country. They want the economy. They want the jobs. They're not coming up, for the most part, for other reasons. They're coming up because they want the jobs.

"And we want them, but we want them to come in legally through a process. And we want them to come in based on merit. So the merit is very important."

Response to a question from an unidentified reporter before Marine One departure, September 9, 2019.
Source: https://www.whitehouse.gov/briefings-statements/remarks-president-trump-marine-one-departure-63/

"So, we're talking to a lot of different people on that. You know, we're recovering from the hurricane also. Florida did get hit, not as hard as we anticipated. And you look at Georgia. You look at South Carolina, North Carolina. I'm going to North Carolina right now, North Carolina, to have a rally for Dan Bishop[12]. But before I go to the rally,

---

12   At the time of President Trump's remarks, Dan Bishop (R-North Carolina) was running for a Congressional seat in a special election. Bishop, a former member of the U.S. House of Representative, won that election and started his term of Congressional office in September 2019.

we're going to be stopping at one of the sites that got hit very hard by the hurricane.

"So we're also recovering from a hurricane. But we have to be very careful. Everybody needs totally proper documentation because the— Look, the Bahamas had some tremendous problems with people going to the Bahamas that weren't supposed to be there. I don't want to allow people that weren't supposed to be in the Bahamas to come into the United States, including some very bad people and some very bad gang members and some very, very bad drug dealers. So we are going to be very, very strong on that.

"Let me, let me just explain. Large sections, believe it or not, of the Bahamas were not hit. And what we're doing is bringing the people to those sections of the Bahamas that have not been hit. We've done a lot of the USAID. We've done a lot of work with our Coast Guard, with our FEMA people, who have been phenomenal. I mean, they have been phenomenal."

Remarks at the signing of an executive order protecting and improving Medicare for senior citizens, Ocala, Florida, October 3, 2019.

Source: https://www.whitehouse.gov/briefings-statements/remarks-president-trump-signing-executive-order-protecting-improving-medicare-nations-seniors-ocala-fl/

"To protect healthcare for our seniors and all Americans, my administration is taking strong actions to ensure that newcomers to our society do not drain our healthcare system, or burden the services that you depend on. You see these people in California, the governor of California: 'Come on in, everybody.' Then you wonder why people are flooding our borders. 'Come on in. You have free education, free healthcare. Everybody gets a Rolls-Royce. Come on in. Come on in.'"

Immigration/Borders—2019 Tweets

January 1, 2019

9:32 am: The Democrats, much as I suspected, have allocated no money for a new Wall. So imaginative! The problem is, without a Wall there can be no real Border Security—and our Country must finally have a Strong and Secure Southern Border!

10:51 am: One thing has now been proven. The Democrats do not care about Open Borders and all of the crime and drugs that Open Borders bring!

January 5, 2019

10:16 am: We are working hard at the Border, but we need a WALL! In 2018, 1.7 million pounds of narcotics seized, 17,000 adults arrested with criminal records, and 6000 gang members, including MS-13, apprehended. A big Human Trafficking problem.

January 6, 2019

4:53 pm: V.P. Mike Pence and group had a productive meeting with the Schumer/Pelosi representatives today. Many details of Border Security were discussed. We are now planning a Steel Barrier rather than concrete. It is both stronger & less obtrusive. Good solution, and made in the U.S.A.

January 9, 2019

3:34 pm: Just left a meeting with Chuck and Nancy, a total waste of time. I asked what is going to happen in 30 days if I quickly open things up, are you going to approve Border Security which includes a Wall or Steel Barrier? Nancy said, NO. I said bye-bye, nothing else works!

January 11, 2019

7:40 am: H1-B holders in the United States can rest assured that changes are soon coming which will bring both simplicity and certainty to your stay, including a potential path to citizenship. We want to encourage talented and highly skilled people to pursue career options in the U.S

11:04 am: Humanitarian Crisis at our Southern Border. I just got back and it is a far worse situation than almost anyone would understand, an invasion! I have been there numerous times—The Democrats, Cryin' Chuck and Nancy don't know how bad and dangerous it is for our ENTIRE COUNTRY...

11:16 am: ...The Steel Barrier, or Wall, should have been built by previous administrations long ago. They never got it done—I will. Without it, our Country cannot be safe. Criminals, Gangs, Human Traffickers, Drugs & so much other big trouble can easily pour in. It can be stopped cold!

January 12, 2019

9:42 am: 23% of Federal inmates are illegal immigrants. Border arrests are up 240%. In the Great State of Texas, between 2011 & 2018, there were a total of 292,000 crimes by illegal aliens, 539 murders, 32,000 assaults, 3,426 sexual assaults and 3000 weapons charges. Democrats come back!

January 13, 2019

10:36 am: The damage done to our Country from a badly broken Border—Drugs, Crime and so much that is bad—is far greater than a Shutdown, which the Dems can easily fix as soon as they come back to Washington!

10:45 am: Thousands of illegal aliens who have committed sexual crimes against children are right now in Texas prisons. Most came through our Southern Border. We can end this easily—We need a

Steel Barrier or Wall. Walls Work! John Jones, Texas Department of Public Safety. @FoxNews

January 14, 2019

5:19 pm: For decades, politicians promised to secure the border, fix our trade deals, bring back our factories, get tough on China, move the Embassy to Jerusalem, make NATO pay their fair share, and so much else—only to do NOTHING (or worse)…

January 15, 2019

7:37 am: A big new Caravan is heading up to our Southern Border from Honduras. Tell Nancy and Chuck that a drone flying around will not stop them. Only a Wall will work. Only a Wall, or Steel Barrier, will keep our Country safe! Stop playing political games and end the Shutdown!

7:49 am: Polls are now showing that people are beginning to understand the Humanitarian Crisis and Crime at the Border. Numbers are going up fast, over 50%. Democrats will soon be known as the Party of Crime. Ridiculous that they don't want Border Security!

January 16, 2019

7:33 am: There are now 77 major or significant Walls built around the world, with 45 countries planning or building Walls. Over 800 miles of Walls have been built in Europe since only 2015. They have all been recognized as close to 100% successful. Stop the crime at our Southern Border!

January 18, 2019

8:22 am: Border rancher: "We've found prayer rugs out here. It's unreal." Washington Examiner People coming across the Southern Border from many countries, some of which would be a big surprise.

9:13 am: Another big Caravan heading our way. Very hard to stop without a Wall!

5:51 pm: I will be making a major announcement concerning the Humanitarian Crisis on our Southern Border, and the Shutdown, tomorrow afternoon at 3 P.M., live from the @WhiteHouse.

January 20, 2019

8:23 am: No, Amnesty is not a part of my offer. It is a 3 year extension of DACA. Amnesty will be used only on a much bigger deal, whether on immigration or something else. Likewise there will be no big push to remove the 11,000,000 plus people who are here illegally-but be careful Nancy!

9:20 am: Don't forget, we are building and renovating big sections of Wall right now. Moving quickly, and will cost far less than previous politicians thought possible. Building, after all, is what I do best, even when money is not readily available!

January 21, 2019

6:37 pm: Four people in Nevada viciously robbed and killed by an illegal immigrant who should not have been in our Country. 26 people killed on the Border in a drug and gang related fight. Two large Caravans from Honduras broke into Mexico and are headed our way. We need a powerful Wall!

9:46 pm: Democrats are kidding themselves (they don't really believe it!) if they say you can stop Crime, Drugs, Human Trafficking and Caravans without a Wall or Steel Barrier. Stop playing games and give America the Security it deserves. A Humanitarian Crisis!

January 22, 2019

7:48 am: Without a Wall our Country can never have Border or National Security. With a powerful Wall or Steel Barrier, Crime Rates (and Drugs) will go substantially down all over the U.S. The Dems know this but want to play political games. Must finally be done correctly. No Cave!

January 25, 2019

7:33 pm: I wish people would read or listen to my words on the Border Wall. This was in no way a concession. It was taking care of millions of people who were getting badly hurt by the Shutdown with the understanding that in 21 days, if no deal is done, it's off to the races!

January 26, 2019

9:06 am: We have turned away, at great expense, two major Caravans, but a big one has now formed and is coming. At least 8000 people! If we had a powerful Wall, they wouldn't even try to make the long and dangerous journey. Build the Wall and Crime will Fall!

3:52 pm: Only fools, or people with a political agenda, don't want a Wall or Steel Barrier to protect our Country from Crime, Drugs and Human Trafficking. It will happen—it always does!

January 27, 2019

8:22 am: 58,000 non-citizens voted in Texas, with 95,000 non-citizens registered to vote. These numbers are just the tip of the iceberg. All over the country, especially in California, voter fraud is rampant. Must be stopped. Strong voter ID! @foxandfriends

10:11 am: We are not even into February and the cost of illegal immigration so far this year is $18,959,495,168. Cost Friday was $603,331,392. There are at least 25,772,342 illegal aliens, not the 11,000,000 that have been reported for years, in our Country. So ridiculous! DHS

January 31, 2019

7:13 am: Large sections of WALL have already been built with much more either under construction or ready to go. Renovation of existing WALLS is also a very big part of the plan to finally, after many decades, properly Secure Our Border. The Wall is getting done one way or the other!

7:16 am: Lets just call them WALLS from now on and stop playing political games! A WALL is a WALL!

9:52 am: More troops being sent to the Southern Border to stop the attempted Invasion of Illegals, through large Caravans, into our Country. We have stopped the previous Caravans, and we will stop these also. With a Wall it would be soooo much easier and less expensive. Being Built!

7:14 pm: Our great U.S. Border Patrol Agents made the biggest Fentanyl bust in our Country's history. Thanks, as always, for a job well done!

February 3, 2019

5:03 pm: With Caravans marching through Mexico and toward our Country, Republicans must be prepared to do whatever is necessary for STRONG Border Security. Dems do nothing. If there is no Wall, there is no Security. Human Trafficking, Drugs and Criminals of all dimensions—KEEP OUT!

February 5, 2019

9:10 am: Tremendous numbers of people are coming up through Mexico in the hopes of flooding our Southern Border. We have sent additional military. We will build a Human Wall if necessary. If we had a real Wall, this would be a non-event!

February 10, 2019

10:24 am: Gallup Poll: "Open Borders will potentially attract 42 million Latin Americans." This would be a disaster for the U.S. We need the Wall now!

February 12, 2019

6:47 pm: Was just presented the concept and parameters of the Border Security Deal by hard working Senator Richard Shelby. Looking over all aspects knowing that this will be hooked up with lots of money from other sources...

...Will be getting almost $23 BILLION for Border Security. Regardless of Wall money, it is being built as we speak!

February 16, 2019

7:10 pm: BUILDING THE WALL!

February 20, 2019

1:56 pm: We have just built this powerful Wall in New Mexico. Completed on January 30, 2019—47 days ahead of schedule! Many miles more now under construction! #FinishTheWall

February 21, 2019

9:17 am: THE WALL IS UNDER CONSTRUCTION RIGHT NOW! https://t.co/exUJCiITsz

March 7, 2019

9:38 am: We are on track to APPREHEND more than one million people coming across the Southern Border this year. Great job by Border Patrol (and others) who are working in a Broken System. Can be fixed by Congress so easily and quickly if only the Democrats would get on board!

March 8, 2019

7:24 am: The Wall is being built and is well under construction. Big impact will be made. Many additional contracts are close to being signed. Far ahead of schedule despite all of the Democrat Obstruction and Fake News!

8:54 am: We are apprehending record numbers of illegal immigrants—but we need the Wall to help our great Border Patrol Agents!

March 9, 2019

9:07 am: Border Patrol and Law Enforcement has apprehended (captured) large numbers of illegal immigrants at the Border. They won't be coming into the U.S. The Wall is being built and will greatly help us in the future, and now!

5:04 pm to 5:13 pm: Wacky Nut Job @AnnCoulter, who still hasn't figured out that, despite all odds and an entire Democrat Party of Far Left Radicals against me (not to mention certain Republicans who are sadly unwilling to fight), I am winning on the Border. Major sections of Wall are being built...

...and renovated, with MUCH MORE to follow shortly. Tens of thousands of illegals are being apprehended (captured) at the Border and NOT allowed into our Country. With another President, millions would be pouring in. I am stopping an invasion as the Wall gets built. #MAGA

March 14, 2019

9:13 am: Prominent legal scholars agree that our actions to address the National Emergency at the Southern Border and to protect the American people are both CONSTITUTIONAL and EXPRESSLY authorized by Congress...

...If, at a later date, Congress wants to update the law, I will support those efforts, but today's issue is BORDER SECURITY and Crime!!! Don't vote with Pelosi!

2:16 pm: VETO!

March 16, 2019

11:16 am: Veto Message to the House of Representatives for H.J. Res. 46: https://t.co/9Z5JHAUv6N https://t.co/lA4RSYTZo0

2:32 pm: This is a National Emergency... https://t.co/AAKBuNW2ro

March 17, 2019

3:58 pm: Those Republican Senators who voted in favor of Strong Border Security (and the Wall) are being uniformly praised as they return to their States. They know there is a National Emergency at the Southern Border, and they had the courage to ACT. Great job!

March 28, 2019

2:51 pm: We have a National Emergency at our Southern Border. The Dems refuse to do what they know is necessary—amend our immigration laws. Would immediately solve the problem! Mexico, with the strongest immigration laws in the World, refuses to help with illegal immigration & drugs!

March 29, 2019

10:23 am: The DEMOCRATS have given us the weakest immigration laws anywhere in the World. Mexico has the strongest, & they make more than $100 Billion a year on the U.S. Therefore, CONGRESS MUST CHANGE OUR WEAK IMMIGRATION LAWS NOW, & Mexico must stop illegals from entering the U.S...

10:37 am: ...through their country and our Southern Border. Mexico has for many years made a fortune off of the U.S., far greater than Border Costs. If Mexico doesn't immediately stop ALL illegal immigration coming into the United States throug our Southern Border, I will be CLOSING...

...the Border, or large sections of the Border, next week. This would be so easy for Mexico to do, but they just take our money and "talk." Besides, we lose so much money with them, especially when you add in drug trafficking etc.), that the Border closing would be a good thing!

March 31, 2019

6:41 pm: The Democrats are allowing a ridiculous asylum system and major loopholes to remain as a mainstay of our immigration system. Mexico is likewise doing NOTHING, a very bad combination for our Country. Homeland Security is being sooo very nice, but not for long!

April 3, 2019

8:35 pm: Congress must get together and immediately eliminate the loopholes at the Border! If no action, Border, or large sections of Border, will close. This is a National Emergency!

April 5, 2019

8:22 am: Heading to the Southern Border to show a section of the new Wall being built! Leaving now!

12:48 pm: Will soon be landing in Calexico, California to look at a portion of the new WALL being built on our Southern Border. Within two years we will have close to 400 miles built or under construction & keeping our Country SAFE—not easy when the Dems are always fighting to stop you!

5:16 pm: Just checked out the new Wall on the Border—GREAT! Leaving now for L.A.

April 6, 2019

6:33 pm: We have redeployed 750 agents at the Southern Border's specific Ports of Entry in order to help with the large scale surge of illegal migrants trying to make their way into the United States. This will cause traffic & commercial delays until such time as Mexico is able to use...

6:36 pm: ...it's powerful common sense Immigration Laws to stop illegals from coming through Mexico into the U.S., and removing them back to their country of origin. Until Mexico cleans up this ridiculous & massive migration, we will be focusing on Border Security, not Ports of Entry...

...In the meantime, the Democrats in Congress must help the Republicans (we need their votes) to end the horrible, costly and foolish loopholes in our Immigration Laws. Once that happens, all will be smooth. We can NEVER allow Open Borders!

April 7, 2019

5:02 pm: Secretary of Homeland Security Kirstjen Nielsen will be leaving her position, and I would like to thank her for her service...

...I am pleased to announce that Kevin McAleenan, the current U.S. Customs and Border Protection Commissioner, will become Acting Secretary for @DHSgov. I have confidence that Kevin will do a great job!

7:45 pm: More apprehensions (captures) at the Southern Border than in many years. Border Patrol amazing! Country is FULL! System has been broken for many years. Democrats in Congress must agree to fix loopholes—No Open Borders (Crimes & Drugs). Will Close Southern Border If necessary...

April 13, 2019

6:51 pm: I never offered Pardons to Homeland Security Officials, never ordered anyone to close our Southern Border (although I have the absolute right to do so, and may if Mexico does not apprehend the illegals coming to our Border), and am not "frustrated." It is all Fake & Corrupt News!

7:01 pm: ...So interesting to see the Mayor of Oakland and other Sanctuary Cities NOT WANT our currently "detained immigrants" after release due to the ridiculous court ordered 20 day rule. If they don't want to serve our Nation by taking care of them, why should other cities & towns?

7:08 pm: Democrats must change the Immigration Laws FAST. If not, Sanctuary Cities must immediately ACT to take care of the Illegal Immigrants—and this includes Gang Members, Drug Dealers, Human Traffickers, and Criminals of all shapes, sizes and kinds. CHANGE THE LAWS NOW!

April 15, 2019

6:28 am: Congress should come back to D.C. now and FIX THE IMMIGRATION LAWS!

11:05 am: Those Illegal Immigrants who can no longer be legally held (Congress must fix the laws and loopholes) will be, subject to Homeland Security, given to Sanctuary Cities and States!

April 24, 2019

6:18 am: The American people deserve to know who is in this Country. Yesterday, the Supreme Court took up the Census

Citizenship question, a really big deal. MAKE AMERICA GREAT AGAIN!

8:34 am: Can anyone comprehend what a GREAT job Border Patrol and Law Enforcement is doing on our Southern Border. So far this year they have APPREHENDED 418,000 plus illegal immigrants, way up from last year. Mexico is doing very little for us. DEMS IN CONGRESS MUST ACT NOW!

May 5, 2019

9:55 am: I am pleased to inform all of those that believe in a strong, fair and sound Immigration Policy that Mark Morgan will be joining the Trump Administration as the head of our hard working men and women of ICE. Mark is a true believer and American Patriot. He will do a great job!

7:08 pm: Pending the confirmation of Mark Morgan as our Nation's new ICE Director, Matt Albence will serve in the role of Acting Director. Matt is tough and dedicated and has my full support to deploy ICE to the maximum extent of the law! #MAGA

May 8, 2019

8:42 am: Big Court win at our Southern Border! We are getting there—and Wall is being built!

May 22, 2019

6:22 am: Much of the Wall being built at the Southern Border is a complete demolition and rebuilding of old and worthless barriers with a brand new Wall and footings. Problem is, the Haters say that is not a new Wall, but rather a renovation. Wrong, and we must build where most needed…

Also, tremendous work is being done on pure renovation—fixing existing Walls that are in bad condition and ineffective, and bringing them to a very high standard!

May 30, 2019

4:16 pm: Yesterday, Border Patrol agents apprehended the largest group of illegal aliens ever: 1,036 people who illegally crossed the border in El Paso around 4am. Democrats need to stand by our incredible Border Patrol and finally fix the loopholes at our Border!

June 2, 2019

6:53 am: The Wall is under construction and moving along quickly, despite all of the Radical Liberal Democrat lawsuits. What are they thinking as our Country is invaded by so many people (illegals) and things (Drugs) that we do not want. Make America Great Again!

June 17, 2019

8:20 pm: Next week ICE will begin the process of removing the millions of illegal aliens who have illicitly found their way into the United States. They will be removed as fast as they come in. Mexico, using their strong immigration laws, is doing a very good job of stopping people...

...long before they get to our Southern Border. Guatemala is getting ready to sign a Safe-Third Agreement. The only ones who won't do anything are the Democrats in Congress. They must vote to get rid of the loopholes, and fix asylum! If so, Border Crisis will end quickly!

June 22, 2019

7:30 am: The people that Ice will apprehend have already been ordered to be deported. This means that they have run from the law and run from the courts. These are people that are supposed to go back to their home country. They broke the law by coming into the country, & now by staying.

7:32 am: When people come into our Country illegally, they will be DEPORTED!

1:56 pm: At the request of Democrats, I have delayed the Illegal Immigration Removal Process (Deportation) for two weeks to see if the Democrats and Republicans can get together and work out a solution to the Asylum and Loophole problems at the Southern Border. If not, Deportations start!

June 23, 2019

7:13 am: I want to give the Democrats every last chance to quickly negotiate simple changes to Asylum and Loopholes. This will fix the Southern Border, together with the help that Mexico is now giving us. Probably won't happen, but worth a try. Two weeks and big Deportation begins!

June 26, 2019

7:02 pm: These flyers depict Australia's policy on Illegal Immigration. Much can be learned! https://t.co/QgGU0gyjRS

June 27, 2019

5:22 pm: Bipartisan Humanitarian Aid Bill for the Southern Border just passed. A great job done by all! Now we must work to get rid of the Loopholes and fix Asylum. Thank you also to Mexico for the work being done on helping with Illegal Immigration—a very big difference!

July 3, 2019

2:31 pm: Our Border Patrol people are not hospital workers, doctors or nurses. The Democrats bad Immigration Laws, which could be easily fixed, are the problem. Great job by Border Patrol, above and beyond. Many of these illegals aliens are living far better now than where they…

…came from, and in far safer conditions. No matter how good things actually look, even if perfect, the Democrat visitors will act shocked & aghast at how terrible things are. Just Pols. If they really want to fix them, change the Immigration Laws and Loopholes. So easy to do!

3:22 pm: If Illegal Immigrants are unhappy with the conditions in the quickly built or refitted detentions centers, just tell them not to come. All problems solved!

July 7, 2019

4:09 pm: We are building the Wall now, but the reason the badly need-ed Wall wasn't approved in the Republican controlled House and Sen-ate was that we had a very slim majority in the Senate, & needed 9 Democrat votes. They were totally unwilling to give Wall votes to us, want Open Borders!

July 14, 2019

8:45 am: Friday's tour showed vividly, to politicians and the media, how well run and clean the children's detention centers are. Great reviews! Failing @nytimes story was FAKE! The adult single men areas were clean but crowded—also loaded up with a big percentage of criminals…

July 15, 2019

4:08 pm: …Detention facilities are not Concentration Camps! Amer-ica has never been stronger than it is now—rebuilt Military, highest Stock Market EVER, lowest unemployment and more people work-ing than ever before. Keep America Great!

4:43 pm: The Obama Administration built the Cages, not the Trump Administration! DEMOCRATS MUST GIVE US THE VOTES TO CHANGE BAD IMMIGRATION LAWS.

July 18, 2019

10:10 am: Most of the MS-13 Gang members indicted & arrested in L.A. were illegal aliens, 19 of 22. They are said to have killed many people in the most brutal fashion. They should never have been al-lowed in our Country for so long, 10 years. We have arrested and deported thousands…

of gang members, in particular MS-13. ICE and Border Patrol are do-ing a great job!

July 21, 2019

9:16 pm: Senator Chuck Schumer has finally gone to the Southern Border with some Democrat Senators. This is a GREAT thing! Nearby, he missed a large group of Illegal Immigrants trying to enter the USA illegally. They wildly rushed Border Patrol. Some Agents were badly injured…

…Based on the comments made by Senator Schumer, he must have seen how dangerous & bad for our Country the Border is. It is not a "manufactured crisis," as the Fake News Media & their Democrat partners tried to portray. He said he wants to meet. I will set up a meeting ASAP!

July 22, 2019

6:16 pm: When we rip down and totally replace a badly broken and dilapidated Barrier on the Southern Border, something which cannot do the job, the Fake News Media gives us zero credit for building a new Wall. We have replaced many miles of old Barrier with powerful new Walls!

July 26, 2019

5:37 pm: Wow! Big VICTORY on the Wall. The United States Supreme Court overturns lower court injunction, allows Southern Border Wall to proceed. Big WIN for Border Security and the Rule of Law!

August 21, 2019

6:44 am: Brandon Judd, President, National Border Patrol Council. "This will effectively end Catch and Release and curb illegal entries."

August 28, 2019

12:48 pm: The Wall is going up very fast despite total Obstruction by Democrats in Congress, and elsewhere! https://t.co/12tIW3aNQP https://t.co/2nFIEFppho

September 6, 2019

7:08 am: The Immigration Law Institute's Christopher Hajec says, "The Supreme Court has to look st whether DACA is lawful. What they are looking at now is whether Trump's recision of DACA is lawful. Must consider lawfulness of DACA itself. Looks very odd that President Trump doesn't…

…have the discretion to end the program that President Obama began in his discretion. That program was unlawful to begin with. I think it's very unlikely that the SCOTUS is going to issue an order reinstating what it believes is an unlawful program. DACA Is unlawful."

…President Obama never had the legal right to sign DACA, and he indicated so at the time of signing. But In any event, how can he have the right to sign and I don't have the right to "unsigned." Totally illegal document which would actually give the President new powers.

7:20 am: DACA will be going before the Supreme Court. It is a document that even President Obama didn't feel he had the legal right to sign—he signed it anyway! Rest assured that if the SC does what all say it must, based on the law, a bipartisan deal will be made to the benefit of all!

September 7, 2019

8:14 am: "In 22 years of patrolling our Southern Border, I have never seen Mexico act like a true Border Security Partner until President Trump got involved, and now they are stepping up to the plate and doing what they need to do." Brandon Judd, National Border Patrol

September 11, 2019

10:26 pm: The Wall is going up very fast despite total Obstruction by Democrats in Congress, and elsewhere!

September 12, 2019

8:05 am: Some really big Court wins on the Border lately!

September 18, 2019

9:05 pm: GREAT progress on the Border Wall!

October 2, 2019

8:06 am: Massive sections of The Wall are being built at our Southern Border. It is going up rapidly, and built to the highest standards and specifications of the Border Patrol experts. It is actually an amazing structure! Our U.S. Military is doing a GREAT job.

October 16, 2019

1:44 pm: Guatemala, Honduras & El Salvador have all signed historic Asylum Cooperation Agreements and are working to end the scourge of human smuggling. To further accelerate this progress, the U.S. will shortly be approving targeted assistance in the areas of law enforcement & security.

8:47 pm: Just out: The USA has the absolute legal right to have apprehended illegal immigrants transferred to Sanctuary Cities. We hereby demand that they be taken care of at the highest level, especially by the State of California, which is well known or its poor management & high taxes!

October 23, 2019

11:20 pm: (Kiddingly) We're building a Wall in Colorado"(then stated, "we're not building a Wall in Kansas but they get the benefit of the Wall we're building on the Border") refered to people in the very packed auditorium, from Colorado & Kansas, getting the benefit of the Border Wall!

November 26, 2019

6:53 am: When the Military rips down an old & badly broken Border Wall in an important location, & replaces it with a brand new 30 ft. high Steel & Concrete Wall, Nancy Pelosi says we are not building a

Wall. Wrong, and it is going up fast. Brandon Judd just gave us great marks! @FoxNews

December 8, 2019

3:02 pm: The Wall is going up fast! https://t.co/8tmUsC9oPq

December 20, 2019

5:41 pm: We are getting MS-13 gang members, and many other people that shouldn't be here, out of our Country!

Intelligence Agencies/Justice System—2017 News Quotes

Response to a question from David Muir of ABC News, January 26, 2017.
Source: https://www.telegraph.co.uk/news/2017/01/26/
full-transcript-president-donald-trumps-interview-abc-news/

"It's carnage. You know, in my speech I got tremendous, from certain people the word carnage. It is carnage. It's horrible carnage. This is Afghanistan, is not like what's happening in Chicago. People are being shot left and right. Thousands of people over a period, over a short period of time.

"This year, which has just started, is worse than last year, which was a catastrophe. They're not doing the job. Now if they want help, I would love to help them. I will send in what we have to send in. Maybe they're not gonna have to be so politically correct. Maybe they're being overly political correct. Maybe there's something going on. But you can't have those killings going on in Chicago. Chicago is like a war zone. Chicago is worse than some of the people that you report in some of the places that you report about every night."

Response to a question from David Muir of ABC News, January 26, 2017.
Source: https://www.telegraph.co.uk/news/2017/01/26/
full-transcript-president-donald-trumps-interview-abc-news/

"I want them to fix the problem. You can't have thousands of people being shot in a city, in a country that I happen to be President of. Maybe it's okay if somebody else is President. I want them to fix the problem. They have a problem that's very easily fixable.

185

"They're gonna have to get tougher and stronger and smarter. But they gotta fix the problem. I don't want to have thousands of people shot in a city where essentially I'm the President. I love Chicago. I know Chicago. And Chicago is a great city, can be a great city."

Response to a question from David Muir of ABC News, January 26, 2017.
Source: https://www.telegraph.co.uk/news/2017/01/26/
full-transcript-president-donald-trumps-interview-abc-news/

"It [Chicago] can't be a great city. Excuse me. It can't be a great city if people are shot walking down the street for a loaf of bread. Can't be a great city."

Response to a question from David Muir of ABC News, January 26, 2017.
Source: https://www.telegraph.co.uk/news/2017/01/26/
full-transcript-president-donald-trumps-interview-abc-news/

"So, look, when [then-U.S.] President [Barack] Obama was there [Chicago] two weeks ago making a speech, very nice speech. Two people were shot and killed during his speech. You can't have that."

Response to a question from David Muir of ABC News, January 26, 2017.
Source: https://www.telegraph.co.uk/news/2017/01/26/
full-transcript-president-donald-trumps-interview-abc-news/

"They weren't shot at the [then-U.S. President Barack Obama] speech. But they were shot in the city of Chicago during his speech. What, what's going on? So, all I'm saying is to the mayor who came up to my office recently—I say, 'You have to smarten up and you have to toughen up, because you can't let that happen. That's a war zone.'"

Response to a question from Laura Ingraham of FOX News, November 2, 2017.
Source: https://www.youtube.com/watch?v=yTdDH-o_ICM

"Now the justice system has to go quicker, and it has to be really stronger and fairer. It probably has to be fairer too."

Response to a question from Laura Ingraham of FOX News, November 2, 2017.

Source: https://www.youtube.com/watch?v=yTdDH-o_ICM

"In the end, what is very nice is we really have, I don't think, I'm not saying this in a braggadocious way, I don't think over a period of 9 or 10 months there's been any president in the beginning of their presidency that's done anywhere close. When you think about regulations, and Supreme Court, and so many different things, things, and stock markets, and the economy—[Ingraham interrupts.]"

Intelligence Agencies/Justice System—2017 Tweets

January 22, 2017

7:35 am: Had a great meeting at CIA Headquarters yesterday, packed house, paid great respect to Wall, long standing ovations, amazing people. WIN!

January 24, 2017

9:25 am: If Chicago doesn't fix the horrible "carnage" going on, 228 shootings in 2017 with 42 killings (up 24% from 2016), I will send in the Feds

February 15, 2017

8:13 am: The real scandal here is that classified information is illegally given out by "intelligence" like candy. Very un-American!

February 17, 2017

8:16 am: General Keith Kellogg, who I have known for a long time, is very much in play for NSA—as are three others.

February 24, 2017

7:31 am to 7:36 am: The FBI is totally unable to stop the national security "leakers" that have permeated our government for a long time. They can't even...

find the leakers within the FBI itself. Classified information is being given to media that could have a devastating effect on U.S. FIND NOW

March 20, 2017

6:02 am: The real story that Congress, the FBI and all others should be looking into is the leaking of Classified information. Must find leaker now!

May 8, 2017

5:41 pm: Director Clapper reiterated what everybody, including the fake media already knows-there is "no evidence" of collusion w/ Russia and Trump.

5:50 pm: Biggest story today between Clapper & Yates is on surveillance. Why doesn't the media report on this? #FakeNews!

May 10, 2017

6:27 am: Comey lost the confidence of almost everyone in Washington, Republican and Democrat alike. When things calm down, they will be thanking me!

May 12, 2017

7:26 am: James Comey better hope that there are no "tapes" of our conversations before he starts leaking to the press!

7:54 am: When James Clapper himself, and virtually everyone else with knowledge of the witch hunt, says there is no collusion, when does it end?

May 16, 2017

7:10 am: I have been asking Director Comey & others, from the beginning of my administration, to find the LEAKERS in the intelligence community...

June 7, 2017

6:44 pm: I will be nominating Christopher A. Wray, a man of impeccable credentials, to be the new Director of the FBI. Details to follow.

June 9, 2017

5:10 am: Despite so many false statements and lies, total and complete vindication...and WOW, Comey is a leaker!

June 11, 2017

7:29 am: I believe the James Comey leaks will be far more prevalent than anyone ever thought possible. Totally illegal? Very 'cowardly!'

June 16, 2017

8:07 am: I am being investigated for firing the FBI Director by the man who told me to fire the FBI Director! Witch Hunt

June 22, 2017

8:18 am: Former Homeland Security Advisor Jeh Johnson is latest top intelligence official to state there was no grand scheme between Trump & Russia.

11:54 am to 11:55 am: I certainly hope the Democrats do not force Nancy P out. That would be very bad for the Republican Party—and please let Cryin' Chuck stay!

4:49 pm: As promised, our campaign against the MS-13 gang continues. "@ICEgov Busts 39 MS-13 Members in New York Operation" https://t.co/ki41GXeCMy

July 25, 2017

5:21 am: Problem is that the acting head of the FBI & the person in charge of the Hillary investigation, Andrew McCabe, got $700,000 from H for wife!

July 26, 2017

8:48 am to 8:52 am: Why didn't A.G. Sessions replace Acting FBI Director Andrew McCabe, a Comey friend who was in charge of Clinton investigation but got...

big dollars ($700,000) for his wife's political run from Hillary Clinton and her representatives. Drain the Swamp!

August 24, 2017

8:10 am: James Clapper, who famously got caught lying to Congress, is now an authority on Donald Trump. Will he show you his beautiful letter to me?

September 1, 2017

6:56 am: Wow, looks like James Comey exonerated Hillary Clinton long before the investigation was over...and so much more. A rigged system!

September 26, 2017

7:30 pm: 70 years ago today, the National Security Council met for the first time. Great history of advising Presidents-then & now! Thanks NSC Staff!

October 18, 2017

5:21 am to 5:27 am: Wow, FBI confirms report that James Comey drafted letter exonerating Crooked Hillary Clinton long before investigation was complete. Many..

...people not interviewed, including Clinton herself. Comey stated under oath that he didn't do this-obviously a fix? Where is Justice Dept?

5:56 am: As it has turned out, James Comey lied and leaked and totally protected Hillary Clinton. He was the best thing that ever happened to her!

December 03, 2017

3:27 pm: How can FBI Deputy Director Andrew McCabe, the man in charge, along with leakin' James Comey, of the Phony Hillary Clinton investigation (including her 33,000 illegally deleted emails) be given $700,000 for wife's campaign by Clinton Puppets during investigation?

3:30 pm: FBI Deputy Director Andrew McCabe is racing the clock to retire with full benefits. 90 days to go?!!!

December 30, 2017

7:42 am: Tainted (no, very dishonest?) FBI "agent's role in Clinton probe under review." Led Clinton Email probe. @foxandfriends Clinton money going to wife of another FBI agent in charge.

8:00 am: After years of Comey, with the phony and dishonest Clinton investigation (and more), running the FBI, its reputation is in Tatters—worst in History! But fear not, we will bring it back to greatness.

Intelligence Agencies/Justice System—2018 News Quotes

Remarks at National Sheriffs' Association Roundtable, February 13, 2018.

Source: https://www.whitehouse.gov/briefings-statements/
remarks-president-trump-national-sheriffs-association-roundtable/

"I'm thrilled to welcome America's great sheriffs back to the White House. We've seen each other often and we're working together very well. Been a great relationship. Always have had a great relationship with the sheriffs.

"My administration stands proudly with America's sheriffs, deputies, and law enforcement officers. And we stand, also, 100% with strong law and order. We want you to just keep doing your job as well as you're doing it.

"We've helped you a lot with military equipment and other things, but we just want you to keep going just the way you have been. You've been fantastic.

"We're participating with local law enforcement through the Project Safe Neighborhoods. We're increasing prosecutions of federal gun crimes. We're taking the fight to the drug dealers and drug pushers which, frankly, I think, is the number one way we're going to stop drugs. We can form all the Blue Ribbon Committees in the world, but the way you're going to stop it is you folks, with the strong, really, law and order, when it comes to the drug, and the drug pushers, the drug dealers. That's the way it's going to stop.

"It's going to—Really, the number one way. I think you probably all agree with that. And you've really done—Especially, some of you have really done a job."

Statement after the shooting at Stone Douglas High School[13] in Parkland, Florida, February 15, 2018.

Source: https://www.whitehouse.gov/briefings-statements/
statement-president-trump-shooting-parkland-florida/

"My fellow Americans, today I speak to a nation in grief. Yesterday, a school filled with innocent children and caring teachers became the scene of terrible violence, hatred, and evil.

"Around 2:30 yesterday afternoon, police responded to reports of gunfire at Marjory Stoneman Douglas High School in Parkland, Florida, a great and safe community. There, a shooter, who is now in custody, opened fire on defenseless students and teachers. He murdered 17 people and badly wounded at least 14 others.

"Our entire nation, with one heavy heart, is praying for the victims and their families. To every parent, teacher, and child who is hurting so badly, we are here for you. Whatever you need, whatever we can do, to ease your pain. We are all joined together as one American family, and your suffering is our burden also. No child, no teacher, should ever be in danger in an American school. No parent should ever have to fear for their sons and daughters when they kiss them goodbye in the morning.

"Each person who was stolen from us yesterday had a full life ahead of them, a life filled with wondrous beauty and unlimited potential and promise. Each one had dreams to pursue, love to give, and talents to share with the world. And each one had a family to whom they meant everything in the world.

"Today, we mourn for all of those who lost their lives. We comfort the grieving and the wounded. And we hurt for the entire community of Parkland, Florida that is now in shock, in pain, and searching for answers.

"To law enforcement, first responders, and teachers who responded so bravely in the face of danger: We thank you for your courage. Soon

---

13   Seventeen people were killed and 17 more injured at this school shooting on February 14, 2018. As of October 17, 2019, per CNN, confessed shooter Nikolas Cruz' death penalty trial was slated to begin in January 2020. Source: https://edition.cnn.com/2019/10/17/us/parkland-florida-shooting-trial/index.html.

after the shooting, I spoke with Governor [Rick] Scott to convey our deepest sympathies to the people of Florida and our determination to assist in any way that we can. I also spoke with Florida Attorney General Pam Bondi and Broward County Sheriff Scott Israel.

"I'm making plans to visit Parkland to meet with families and local officials, and to continue coordinating the federal response.

"In these moments of heartache and darkness, we hold on to God's word in Scripture: 'I have heard your prayer and seen your tears. I will heal you.'

"We trust in that promise, and we hold fast to our fellow Americans in their time of sorrow. I want to speak now directly to America's children, especially those who feel lost, alone, confused, or even scared. I want you to know that you are never alone, and you never will be. You have people who care about you, who love you, and who will do anything at all to protect you. If you need help, turn to a teacher, a family member, a local police officer, or a faith leader. Answer hate with love; answer cruelty with kindness.

"We must also work together to create a culture in our country that embraces the dignity of life, that creates deep and meaningful human connections, and that turns classmates and colleagues into friends and neighbors.

"Our administration is working closely with local authorities to investigate the shooting and learn everything we can. We are committed to working with state and local leaders to help secure our schools and tackle the difficult issue of mental health.

"Later this month, I will be meeting with the nation's governors and attorney generals, where making our schools and our children safer will be our top priority. It is not enough to simply take actions that make us feel like we are making a difference. We must actually make that difference.

"In times of tragedy, the bonds that sustain us are those of family, faith, community, and country. These bonds are stronger than the forces of hatred and evil, and these bonds grow even stronger in the hours of our greatest need.

"And so always, but especially today, let us hold our loved ones close, let us pray for healing and for peace, and let us come together as one nation to wipe away the tears and strive for a much better tomorrow."

Remarks at the Broward County Sheriff's Office[14], February 17, 2018.
Source: https://www.whitehouse.gov/briefings-statements/
remarks-president-trump-broward-county-sheriffs-office/

"Fantastic community here. Thank you. What a great job you've done, and we appreciate it very much. An incredible job, and everybody's talking about it.

"I just got back from the hospital. A young woman was shot. Four bullets, two in her lungs. And they got her over to the hospital in less than 21 minutes. She had no chance, and, between the first responders, your people who got her—You know who I'm talking about, they got her there, [then-Broward County Sheriff] Scott [Israel].

"What a job you've done, and the doctors did a great job over at the hospital. A combination which is incredible. And I hope you're getting the credit for it. Because, believe me, you deserve it. The job you've done is unparalleled."

---

14   President Trump's visit was in response to the February 14, 2018 shooting at Marjory Stoneman Douglas High School in Parkland, Florida. Seventeen people died and an additional 17 were injured. As of October 17, 2019, per CNN, confessed shooter Nikolas Cruz' death penalty trial was slated to begin in January 2020. Source: https://edition.cnn.com/2019/10/17/us/parkland-florida-shooting-trial/index.html.

Remarks at the Broward County Sheriff's Office[15], February 17, 2018.

Source: https://www.whitehouse.gov/briefings-statements/
remarks-president-trump-broward-county-sheriffs-office/

"So, the governor of Florida, we all know. Rick Scott has done a fantastic job. Fantastic governor. Truly a state that's doing well. We know that Rick, right?"

Remarks at White House dinner with evangelical leaders, August 27, 2018.

Source: https://www.whitehouse.gov/briefings-statements/
remarks-president-trump-dinner-evangelical-leaders/

"We're advancing prison reform to give former inmates a second chance. And these incredible unemployment numbers are probably the greatest thing that ever happened to people getting out and wanting a second, and sometimes a third, chance. But they'd come out of prison, and they were not hired, and bad things would happen, and they'd go back. Now they're coming out of prison, they're getting jobs. We're working with them. And they are very, very thankful.

"I'll tell you who else is thankful: the employers. I have a friend who hired numerous people coming out of prison. Something he never thought he'd do, and in a way, he was forced to do it, frankly. He was forced to do it by the fact that he couldn't get people; he needed people. The numbers are so low in that community. He is so happy. He's hired some people that he said he hopes he never loses them. They're happy, and he is thrilled. So that's a great story. A great story."

---

15   President Trump's visit was in response to the February 14, 2018 shooting at Marjory Stoneman Douglas High School in Parkland, Florida. Seventeen people died and an additional 17 were injured. As of October 17, 2019, per CNN, confessed shooter Nikolas Cruz' death penalty trial was slated to begin in January 2020. Source: https://edition.cnn.com/2019/10/17/us/parkland-florida-shooting-trial/index.html.

Intelligence Agencies/Justice System—2018 Tweets

January 4, 2018

6:32 am: There is great anger in our Country caused in part by inaccurate, and even fraudulent, reporting of the news. The Fake News Media, the true Enemy of the People, must stop the open & obvious hostility & report the news accurately & fairly. That will do much to put out the flame...

January 11, 2018

7:33 am: "House votes on controversial FISA ACT today." This is the act that may have been used, with the help of the discredited and phony Dossier, to so badly surveil and abuse the Trump Campaign by the previous administration and others?

9:14 am: With that being said, I have personally directed the fix to the unmasking process since taking office and today's vote is about foreign surveillance of foreign bad guys on foreign land. We need it! Get smart!

January 19, 2018

3:53 pm: Just signed 702 Bill to reauthorize foreign intelligence collection. This is NOT the same FISA law that was so wrongly abused during the election. I will always do the right thing for our country and put the safety of the American people first!

January 23, 2018

6:51 am: In one of the biggest stories in a long time, the FBI says it is now missing five months worth of lovers Strzok—Page texts, perhaps 50,000, all in prime time. Wow!

February 2, 2018

6:33 am: The top Leadership and Investigators of the FBI and the Justice Department have politicized the sacred investigative process in favor of Democrats and against Republicans—something which would have been unthinkable just a short time ago. Rank & File are great people!

February 7, 2018

11:10 am: NEW FBI TEXTS ARE BOMBSHELLS!

February 17, 2018

11:08 am: Very sad that the FBI missed all of the many signals sent out by the Florida school shooter. This is not acceptable. They are spending too much time trying to prove Russian collusion with the Trump campaign—there is no collusion. Get back to the basics and make us all proud!

March 16, 2018

11:08 pm: Andrew McCabe FIRED, a great day for the hard working men and women of the FBI—A great day for Democracy. Sanctimonious James Comey was his boss and made McCabe look like a choirboy. He knew all about the lies and corruption going on at the highest levels of the FBI!

March 17, 2018

12:11 pm: As the House Intelligence Committee has concluded, there was no collusion between Russia and the Trump Campaign. As many are now finding out, however, there was tremendous leaking, lying and corruption at the highest levels of the FBI, Justice & State. #DrainTheSwamp

12:34 pm: The Fake News is beside themselves that McCabe was caught, called out and fired. How many hundreds of thousands of dollars was given to wife's campaign by Crooked H friend, Terry M, who was also under investigation? How many lies? How many leaks? Comey knew it all, and much more!

March 18, 2018

7:02 am: Wow, watch Comey lie under oath to Senator G when asked "have you ever been an anonymous source...or known someone else to be an anonymous source...?" He said strongly "never, no." He lied as shown clearly on @foxandfriends.

7:22 am: Spent very little time with Andrew McCabe, but he never took notes when he was with me. I don't believe he made memos except to help his own agenda, probably at a later date. Same with lying James Comey. Can we call them Fake Memos?

April 7, 2018

4:00 pm: What does the Department of Justice and FBI have to hide? Why aren't they giving the strongly requested documents (unredacted) to the HOUSE JUDICIARY COMMITTEE? Stalling, but for what reason? Not looking good!

April 8, 2018

6:27 am: "The FBI closed the case on Hillary, which was a rigged investigation. They exonerated her even before they ever interviewed her, they never even put her under oath..." and much more. So true Jesse! @WattersWorld

April 11, 2018

8:00 am: Much of the bad blood with Russia is caused by the Fake & Corrupt Russia Investigation, headed up by the all Democrat loyalists, or people that worked for Obama. Mueller is most conflicted of all (except Rosenstein who signed FISA & Comey letter). No Collusion, so they go crazy

April 13, 2018

7:01 am to 7:17 am: James Comey is a proven LEAKER & LIAR. Virtually everyone in Washington thought he should be fired for the terrible job he did-until he was, in fact, fired. He leaked CLASSIFIED information, for which he should be prosecuted. He lied to Congress under OATH. He is a weak and…

…untruthful slime ball who was, as time has proven, a terrible Director of the FBI. His handling of the Crooked Hillary Clinton case, and the events surrounding it, will go down as one of the worst "botch jobs" of history. It was my great honor to fire James Comey!

2:36 pm: DOJ just issued the McCabe report—which is a total disaster. He LIED! LIED! LIED! McCabe was totally controlled by Comey—McCabe is Comey!! No collusion, all made up by this den of thieves and lowlifes!

April 15, 2018

6:42 am: Unbelievably, James Comey states that Polls, where Crooked Hillary was leading, were a factor in the handling (stupidly) of the Clinton Email probe. In other words, he was making decisions based on the fact that he thought she was going to win, and he wanted a job. Slimeball!

7:32 am: I never asked Comey for Personal Loyalty. I hardly even knew this guy. Just another of his many lies. His "memos" are self serving and FAKE!

8:07 am: Slippery James Comey, a man who always ends up badly and out of whack (he is not smart!), will go down as the WORST FBI Director in history, by far!

April 16, 2018

7:25 am: Comey drafted the Crooked Hillary exoneration long before he talked to her (lied in Congress to Senator G), then based his decisions on her poll numbers. Disgruntled, he, McCabe, and the others, committed many crimes!

April 18, 2018

7:05 am: Slippery James Comey, the worst FBI Director in history, was not fired because of the phony Russia investigation where, by the way, there was NO COLLUSION (except by the Dems)!

April 19, 2018

5:46 pm: James Comey just threw Andrew McCabe "under the bus." Inspector General's Report on McCabe is a disaster for both of them! Getting a little (lot) of their own medicine?

10:37 pm: James Comey Memos just out and show clearly that there was NO COLLUSION and NO OBSTRUCTION. Also, he leaked classified information. WOW! Will the Witch Hunt continue?

April 20, 2018

5:34 am: So General Michael Flynn's life can be totally destroyed while Shadey James Comey can Leak and Lie and make lots of money from a third rate book (that should never have been written). Is that really the way life in America is supposed to work? I don't think so!

10:13 pm: James Comey illegally leaked classified documents to the press in order to generate a Special Council? Therefore, the Special Council was established based on an illegal act? Really, does everybody know what that means?

April 21, 2018

2:24 pm: James Comey's Memos are Classified, I did not Declassify them. They belong to our Government! Therefore, he broke the law! Additionally, he totally made up many of the things he said I said, and he is already a proven liar and leaker. Where are Memos on Clinton, Lynch & others?

April 27, 2018

5:26 am: Is everybody believing what is going on. James Comey can't define what a leak is. He illegally leaked CLASSIFIED INFORMATION but doesn't understand what he did or how serious it is. He lied all over the place to cover it up. He's either very sick or very dumb. Remember sailor!

May 7, 2018

8:29 am: James Comey's Memos are Classified, I did not Declassify them. They belong to our Government! Therefore, he broke the law! Additionally, he totally made up many of the things he said I said, and he is already a proven liar and leaker. Where are Memos on Clinton, Lynch & others?

May 17, 2018

6:56 am: Wow, word seems to be coming out that the Obama FBI "SPIED ON THE TRUMP CAMPAIGN WITH AN IMBEDDED INFORMANT." Andrew McCarthy says, "There's probably no doubt that they had at least one confidential informant in the campaign." If so, this is bigger than Watergate!

4:00 pm: Congratulations to our new CIA Director, Gina Haspel!

May 20, 2018

12:37 pm: I hereby demand, and will do so officially tomorrow, that the Department of Justice look into whether or not the FBI/DOJ infiltrated or surveilled the Trump Campaign for Political Purposes—and if any such demands or requests were made by people within the Obama Administration!

May 21, 2018

6:53 am to 7:12 am: "John Brennan is panicking. He has disgraced himself, he has disgraced the Country, he has disgraced the entire Intelligence Community. He is the one man who is largely responsible for the destruction of American's faith in the Intelligence Community and in some people at the...

...top of the FBI. Brennan started this entire debacle about President Trump. We now know that Brennan had detailed knowledge of the (phony) Dossier...he knows about the Dossier, he denies knowledge of the Dossier, he briefs the Gang of 8 on the Hill about the Dossier, which...

..they then used to start an investigation about Trump. It is that simple. This guy is the genesis of this whole Debacle. This was a Political hit job, this was not an Intelligence Investigation. Brennan has disgraced himself, he's worried about staying out of Jail." Dan Bongino

May 24, 2018

7:34 am: Not surprisingly, the GREAT Men & Women of the FBI are starting to speak out against Comey, McCabe and all of the political corruption and poor leadership found within the top ranks of the FBI. Comey was a terrible and corrupt leader who inflicted great pain on the FBI! #SPYGATE

May 31, 2018

7:11 am: Not that it matters but I never fired James Comey because of Russia! The Corrupt Mainstream Media loves to keep pushing that narrative, but they know it is not true!

June 3, 2018

8:25 am: As only one of two people left who could become President, why wouldn't the FBI or Department of "Justice" have told me that they were secretly investigating Paul Manafort (on charges that were 10 years old and had been previously dropped) during my campaign? Should have told me!

June 5, 2018

7:37 pm: Wow, Strzok-Page, the incompetent & corrupt FBI lovers, have texts referring to a counter-intelligence operation into the

Trump Campaign dating way back to December, 2015. SPYGATE is in full force! Is the Mainstream Media interested yet? Big stuff!

June 17, 2018

7:25 pm: Why was the FBI giving so much information to the Fake News Media. They are not supposed to be doing that, and knowing the enemy of the people Fake News, they put their own spin on it—truth doesn't matter to them!

7:42 pm: Why was the FBI's sick loser, Peter Strzok, working on the totally discredited Mueller team of 13 Angry & Conflicted Democrats, when Strzok was giving Crooked Hillary a free pass yet telling his lover, lawyer Lisa Page, that "we'll stop" Trump from becoming President? Witch Hunt!

June 18, 2018

10:27 am: Comey gave Strozk his marching orders. Mueller is Comey's best friend. Witch Hunt!

June 19, 2018

8:52 am: I can't think of something more concerning than a law enforcement officer suggesting that their going to use their powers to affect an election!" Inspector General Horowitz on what was going on with numerous people regarding my election. A Rigged Witch Hunt!

June 25, 2018

6:30 pm: The hearing of Peter Strzok and the other hating frauds at the FBI & DOJ should be shown to the public on live television, not a closed door hearing that nobody will see. We should expose these people for what they are—there should be total transparency!

June 26, 2018

8:30 am: "The most profound question of our era: Was there a conspiracy in the Obama Department of Justice and the FBI to prevent

Donald Trump from becoming President of the U.S., and was Strzok at the core of the conspiracy?" Judge Andrew Napolitano

June 28, 2018

6:02 am: Lover FBI Agent Peter Strzok was given poor marks on yesterday's closed door testimony and, according to most reports, refused to answer many questions. There was no Collusion and the Witch Hunt, headed by 13 Angry Democrats and others who are totally conflicted, is Rigged!

July 3, 2018

9:18 am: Wow! The NSA has deleted 685 million phone calls and text messages. Privacy violations? They blame technical irregularities. Such a disgrace. The Witch Hunt continues!

July 10, 2018

9:40 am: I am on Air Force One flying to NATO and hear reports that the FBI lovers, Peter Strzok and Lisa Page are getting cold feet on testifying about the Rigged Witch Hunt headed by 13 Angry Democrats and people that worked for Obama for 8 years. Total disgrace!

July 11, 2018

4:53 pm: Ex-FBI LAYER Lisa Page today defied a House of Representatives issued Subpoena to testify before Congress! Wow, but is anybody really surprised! Together with her lover, FBI Agent Peter Strzok, she worked on the Rigged Witch Hunt, perhaps the most tainted and corrupt case EVER

5:47 pm: How can the Rigged Witch Hunt proceed when it was started, influenced and worked on, for an extended period of time, by former FBI Agent/Lover Peter Strzok? Read his hate filled and totally biased Emails and the answer is clear!

July 16, 2018

2:40 pm: As I said today and many times before, "I have GREAT confidence in MY intelligence people." However, I also recognize that in order to build a brighter future, we cannot exclusively focus on the past—as the world's two largest nuclear powers, we must get along! #HELSINKI2018

August 11, 2018

7:35 am: Why isn't the FBI giving Andrew McCabe text messages to Judicial Watch or appropriate governmental authorities. FBI said they won't give up even one (I may have to get involved, DO NOT DESTROY). What are they hiding? McCabe wife took big campaign dollars from Hillary people…

7:49 am: …Will the FBI ever recover it's once stellar reputation, so badly damaged by Comey, McCabe, Peter S and his lover, the lovely Lisa Page, and other top officials now dismissed or fired? So many of the great men and women of the FBI have been hurt by these clowns and losers!

August 13, 2018

11:04 am: Agent Peter Strzok was just fired from the FBI—finally. The list of bad players in the FBI & DOJ gets longer & longer. Based on the fact that Strzok was in charge of the Witch Hunt, will it be dropped? It is a total Hoax. No Collusion, No Obstruction—I just fight back!

11:09 am: Just fired Agent Strzok, formerly of the FBI, was in charge of the Crooked Hillary Clinton sham investigation. It was a total fraud on the American public and should be properly redone!

August 14, 2018

8:01 am: Fired FBI Agent Peter Strzok is a fraud, as is the rigged investigation he started. There was no Collusion or Obstruction with Russia, and everybody, including the Democrats, know it. The only

Collusion and Obstruction was by Crooked Hillary, the Democrats and the DNC!

August 15, 2018

9:08 am: The Rigged Russian Witch Hunt goes on and on as the "originators and founders" of this scam continue to be fired and demoted for their corrupt and illegal activity. All credibility is gone from this terrible Hoax, and much more will be lost as it proceeds. No Collusion!

9:15 am: "The action (the Strzok firing) was a decisive step in the right direction in correcting the wrongs committed by what has been described as Comey's skinny inner circle." Chris Swecker, former FBI Assistant Director.

August 16, 2018

6:37 pm: "The FBI received documents from Bruce Ohr (of the Justice Department & whose wife Nelly worked for Fusion GPS)." Disgraced and fired FBI Agent Peter Strzok. This is too crazy to be believed! The Rigged Witch Hunt has zero credibility.

8:49 pm: "…An incredibly corrupt FBI & DOJ trying to steer the outcome of a Presidential Election. Brennan has gone off the deep end, he's disgraced and discredited himself. His conduct has been outrageous." Chris Farrell, Judicial Watch.

August 20, 2018

9:13 am: I hope John Brennan, the worst CIA Director in our country's history, brings a lawsuit. It will then be very easy to get all of his records, texts, emails and documents to show not only the poor job he did, but how he was involved with the Mueller Rigged Witch Hunt. He won't sue!

9:23 am: Everybody wants to keep their Security Clearance, it's worth great prestige and big dollars, even board seats, and that is why certain people are coming forward to protect Brennan. It certainly isn't because of the good job he did! He is a political "hack."

August 21, 2018

5:55 am: Even James Clapper has admonished John Brennan for having gone totally off the rails. Maybe Clapper is being nice to me so he doesn't lose his Security Clearance for lying to Congress!

August 25, 2018

8:11 am: "The FBI only looked at 3000 of 675,000 Crooked Hillary Clinton Emails." They purposely didn't look at the disasters. This news is just out. @FoxNews

8:14 am: "The FBI looked at less than 1%" of Crooked's Emails!

August 28, 2018

9:26 pm: New Poll—A majority of Americans think that John Brennan and James Comey should have their Security Clearances Revoked. Not surprised! @FoxNews

August 30, 2018

6:56 am: The only thing James Comey ever got right was when he said that President Trump was not under investigation!

September 3, 2018

2:21 pm: According to the Failing New York Times, the FBI started a major effort to flip Putin loyalists in 2014-2016. "It wasn't about Trump, he wasn't even close to a candidate yet." Rigged Witch Hunt!

September 17, 2018

9:36 am: Immediately after Comey's firing Peter Strzok texted to his lover, Lisa Page "We need to Open the case we've been waiting on now while Andy (McCabe, also fired) is acting. Page answered, "We need to lock in (redacted). In a formal chargeable way. Soon." Wow, a conspiracy caught?

September 21, 2018

8:29 am: The radical left lawyers want the FBI to get involved NOW. Why didn't someone call the FBI 36 years ago?

September 28, 2018

7:27 pm: Just started, tonight, our 7th FBI investigation of Judge Brett Kavanaugh. He will someday be recognized as a truly great Justice of The United States Supreme Court!

October 4, 2018

9:17 am: This is now the 7th. time the FBI has investigated Judge Kavanaugh. If we made it 100, it would still not be good enough for the Obstructionist Democrats.

October 24, 2018

1:55 pm: The safety of the American People is my highest priority. I have just concluded a briefing with the FBI, Department of Justice, Department of Homeland Security, and the U.S. Secret Service...

October 26, 2018

12:59 pm: I want to applaud the FBI, Secret Service, Department of Justice, the U.S. Attorneys' Office for the Southern District of New York, the NYPD, and all Law Enforcement partners across the Country for their incredible work, skill and determination!

Intelligence Agencies/Justice System—2019 News Quotes

From State of the Union address, February 5, 2019.

Source: https://www.whitehouse.gov/briefings-statements/
president-donald-j-trumps-state-union-address-2/

"And just weeks ago, both parties united for groundbreaking criminal justice reform. Last year, I heard through friends the story of Alice Johnson. I was deeply moved. In 1997, Alice was sentenced to life in prison as a first-time non-violent drug offender. Over the next two decades, she became a prison minister, inspiring others to choose a better path. She had a big impact on that prison population and far beyond.

"Alice's story underscores the disparities and unfairness that can exist in criminal sentencing and the need to remedy this injustice. She served almost 22 years and had expected to be in prison for the rest of her life.

"In June, I commuted Alice's sentence, and she is here with us tonight. Alice, thank you for reminding us that we always have the power to shape our own destiny.

"When I saw Alice's beautiful family greet her at the prison gates, hugging and kissing and crying and laughing, I knew I did the right thing.

"Inspired by stories like Alice's, my administration worked closely with members of both parties to sign the First Step Act into law. This legislation reformed sentencing laws that have wrongly and disproportionately harmed the African-American community. The First Step Act gives non-violent offenders the chance to re-enter society as productive, law-abiding citizens. Now, States across the country are following our lead. America is a Nation that believes in redemption.

"We are also joined tonight by Matthew Charles from Tennessee. In 1996, at age 30, Matthew was sentenced to 35 years for selling drugs and related offenses. Over the next two decades, he completed more than 30 Bible studies, became a law clerk, and mentored fellow inmates. Now, Matthew is the very first person to be released from prison under the First Step Act. Matthew, on behalf of all Americans: welcome home."

Response to an unidentified reporter's question after Marine One arrival, September 1, 2019.
Source: https://www.whitehouse.gov/briefings-statements/
remarks-president-trump-marine-one-arrival-5/

"Well, I think Congress has got a lot of thinking to do, frankly, and they have a lot of—They've been doing a lot of work. I will tell you, on behalf of Republicans and Democrats, they've been doing a lot of work having to do with guns. And I think you're going to see some interesting things coming along."

Response to a question from an unidentified reporter before Marine One departure, September 9, 2019.
Source: https://www.whitehouse.gov/briefings-statements/
remarks-president-trump-marine-one-departure-63/

"We're looking very much at human smuggling. And if you look at 'trafficking,' they call it—If you look at what's going on with the human trafficking, we're bringing it down to a much lower level. This should have been done for years and years. But we're bringing the human trafficking, as you can see by the numbers, we're bringing it down. Mostly affects women and children. It's a terrible thing. It's been going on for many years, and we're bringing it down."

Remarks at rally in Minneapolis, Minnesota, October 10, 2019.
Source: https://www.twincities.com/2019/10/10/
trump-attacks-joe-biden-ilhan-omar-and-jacob-frey-at-minneapolis-rally/

"Cops love Trump. Trump loves cops."

Intelligence Agencies/Justice System—2019 Tweets

January 12, 2019

7:05 am: Wow, just learned in the Failing New York Times that the corrupt former leaders of the FBI, almost all fired or forced to leave the agency for some very bad reasons, opened up an investigation on me, for no reason & with no proof, after I fired Lyin' James Comey, a total sleaze!

7:18 am: …Funny thing about James Comey. Everybody wanted him fired, Republican and Democrat alike. After the rigged & botched Crooked Hillary investigation, where she was interviewed on July 4th Weekend, not recorded or sworn in, and where she said she didn't know anything (a lie),…

7:33 am: …the FBI was in complete turmoil (see N.Y. Post) because of Comey's poor leadership and the way he handled the Clinton mess (not to mention his usurpation of powers from the Justice Department). My firing of James Comey was a great day for America. He was a Crooked Cop…

7:53 am: …who is being totally protected by his best friend, Bob Mueller, & the 13 Angry Democrats—leaking machines who have NO interest in going after the Real Collusion (and much more) by Crooked Hillary Clinton, her Campaign, and the Democratic National Committee. Just Watch!

January 15, 2019

6:58 am: The rank and file of the FBI are great people who are disgusted with what they are learning about Lyin' James Comey and the so-called "leaders" of the FBI. Twelve have been fired or forced to leave. They got caught spying on my campaign and then called it an investigation. Bad!

January 26, 2019

8:42 am: If Roger Stone was indicted for lying to Congress, what about the lying done by Comey, Brennan, Clapper, Lisa Page & lover, Baker and soooo many others? What about Hillary to FBI and her 33,000 deleted Emails? What about Lisa & Peter's deleted texts & Wiener's laptop? Much more!

February 14, 2019

9:39 am: Disgraced FBI Acting Director Andrew McCabe pretends to be a "poor little Angel" when in fact he was a big part of the Crooked Hillary Scandal & the Russia Hoax—a puppet for Leakin' James Comey. I.G. report on McCabe was devastating. Part of "insurance policy" in case I won...

9:55 am: ...Many of the top FBI brass were fired, forced to leave, or left. McCabe's wife received BIG DOLLARS from Clinton people for her campaign—he gave Hillary a pass. McCabe is a disgrace to the FBI and a disgrace to our Country. MAKE AMERICA GREAT AGAIN!

February 18, 2019

7:15 am: Wow, so many lies by now disgraced acting FBI Director Andrew McCabe. He was fired for lying, and now his story gets even more deranged. He and Rod Rosenstein, who was hired by Jeff Sessions (another beauty), look like they were planning a very illegal act, and got caught...

7:29 am: ...There is a lot of explaining to do to the millions of people who had just elected a president who they really like and who has done a great job for them with the Military, Vets, Economy and so much more. This was the illegal and treasonous "insurance policy" in full action!

10:26 pm: Remember this, Andrew McCabe didn't go to the bathroom without the approval of Leakin' James Comey!

February 19, 2019

11:05 am: I never said anything bad about Andrew McCabe's wife other than she (they) should not have taken large amounts of campaign money from a Crooked Hillary source when Clinton was under investigation by the FBI. I never called his wife a loser to him (another McCabe made up lie)!

March 13, 2019

9:14 am: Comey testified (under oath) that it was a "unanimous" decision on Crooked Hillary. Lisa Page transcripts show he LIED.

March 20, 2019

9:04 pm: "The reason we have the Special Counsel investigation is that James Comey (a dirty cop) leaked his memos to a friend, who leaked them to the press, on purpose." @KennedyNation Totally illegal!

March 28, 2019

5:34 am: FBI & DOJ to review the outrageous Jussie Smollett case in Chicago. It is an embarrassment to our Nation!

April 17, 2019

6:34 am: Wow! FBI made 11 payments to Fake Dossier's discredited author, Trump hater Christopher Steele. @OANN @JudicialWatch The Witch Hunt has been a total fraud on your President and the American people! It was brought to you by Dirty Cops, Crooked Hillary and the DNC.

April 25, 2019

6:47 am to 7:09 am: As has been incorrectly reported by the Fake News Media, I never told then White House Counsel Don McGahn to fire Robert Mueller, even though I had the legal right to do so. If I wanted to fire Mueller, I didn't need McGahn to do it, I could have done it myself. Nevertheless,…

...Mueller was NOT fired and was respectfully allowed to finish his work on what I, and many others, say was an illegal investigation (there was no crime), headed by a Trump hater who was highly conflicted, and a group of 18 VERY ANGRY Democrats. DRAIN THE SWAMP!

...Despite the fact that the Mueller Report was "composed" by Trump Haters and Angry Democrats, who had unlimited funds and human resources, the end result was No Collusion, No Obstruction. Amazing!

May 9, 2019

10:00 pm: James Comey is a disgrace to the FBI & will go down as the worst Director in its long and once proud history. He brought the FBI down, almost all Republicans & Democrats thought he should be FIRED, but the FBI will regain greatness because of the great men & women who work there!

May 12, 2019

6:04 am: Think of it. I became President of the United States in one of the most hard fought and consequential elections in the history of our great nation. From long before I ever took office, I was under a sick & unlawful investigation concerning what has become known as the Russian...

..Hoax. My campaign was being seriously spied upon by intel agencies and the Democrats. This never happened before in American history, and it all turned out to be a total scam, a Witch Hunt, that yielded No Collusion, No Obstruction. This must never be allowed to happen again!

May 17, 2019

6:11 am: It now seems the General Flynn was under investigation long before was common knowledge. It would have been impossible for me to know this but, if that was the case, and with me being one of two people who would become president, why was I not told so that I could make a change?

May 25, 2019

2:35 pm: Another activist Obama appointed judge has just ruled against us on a section of the Southern Wall that is already under construction. This is a ruling against Border Security and in favor of crime, drugs and human trafficking. We are asking for an expedited appeal!

May 30, 2019

10:31 am: Robert Mueller came to the Oval Office (along with other potential candidates) seeking to be named the Director of the FBI. He had already been in that position for 12 years, I told him NO. The next day he was named Special Counsel—A total Conflict of Interest. NICE!

June 13, 2019

5:21 am: General Michael Flynn, the 33 year war hero who has served with distinction, has not retained a good lawyer, he has retained a GREAT LAWYER, Sidney Powell. Best Wishes and Good Luck to them both!

June 17, 2019

11:51 pm: Wow! The State Department said it has identified 30 Security Incidents involving current or former employees and their handling of Crooked Hillary Clinton's Emails. @FoxNews This is really big. Never admitted before. Highly Classified Material. Will the Dems investigate this?

June 26, 2019

5:47 pm: Why aren't the Democrats in the House calling Comey, Brennan, Clapper, Page and her FBI lover (whose invaluable phone records were illegally deleted), Crooked Hillary, Podesta, Ohr (and Nellie), the GPS Fusion characters, Christopher Steele, the DNC (& their missing server)...

...and all of the others who have leaked, lied and did so many other terrible things? How is it even possible that these people are not being brought forward? Because it is a Rigged Democrat Con Game, and the Fake and Corrupt Media loves every minute of it!

June 27, 2019

12:37 pm: Seems totally ridiculous that our government, and indeed Country, cannot ask a basic question of Citizenship in a very expensive, detailed and important Census, in this case for 2020. I have asked the lawyers if they can delay the Census, no matter how long, until the...

...United States Supreme Court is given additional information from which it can make a final and decisive decision on this very critical matter. Can anyone really believe that as a great Country, we are not able the ask whether or not someone is a Citizen. Only in America!

July 2, 2019

9:33 pm: A very sad time for America when the Supreme Court of the United States won't allow a question of "Is this person a Citizen of the United States?" to be asked on the #2020 Census! Going on for a long time. I have asked the Department of Commerce and the Department of Justice...

...to do whatever is necessary to bring this most vital of questions, and this very important case, to a successful conclusion. USA! USA! USA!

July 3, 2019

10:06 am: The News Reports about the Department of Commerce dropping its quest to put the Citizenship Question on the Census is incorrect or, to state it differently, FAKE! We are absolutely moving forward, as we must, because of the importance of the answer to this question.

July 4, 2019

6:20 am: So important for our Country that the very simple and basic "Are you a Citizen of the United States?" question be allowed to be

217

asked in the 2020 Census. Department of Commerce and the Department of Justice are working very hard on this, even on the 4th of July!

July 9, 2019

9:31 am: Recent "strained" decisions by the United States Supreme Court, some so simple as allowing the question, "Are you a citizen of the United States" on our very expensive Census Report, or the even more strained decisions (2) allowing the world's most expensive & pathetic…

…healthcare (Obamacare) to stay in place, when it would have been replaced by something far better, shows how incredibly important our upcoming 2020 Election is. I have long heard that the appointment of Supreme Court Justices is a President's most important decision. SO TRUE!

8:44 pm: So now the Obama appointed judge on the Census case (Are you a Citizen of the United States?) won't let the Justice Department use the lawyers that it wants to use. Could this be a first?

July 10, 2019

10:06 am: Word just out that I won a big part of the Deep State and Democrat induced Witch Hunt. Unanimous decision in my favor from The United States Court of Appeals For The Fourth Circuit on the ridiculous Emoluments Case. I don't make money, but lose a fortune for the honor of…

July 13, 2019

6:56 am: Andy McCabe is a major sleazebag. Among many other things, he took massive amounts of money from Crooked Hillary reps, for wife's campaign, while Hillary was under "investigation" by FBI!

7:20 am: This is one of the most horrible abuses of all. Those texts between gaga lovers would have told the whole story. Illegal deletion by Mueller. They gave us "the insurance policy."

July 23, 2019

9:29 pm: So Robert Mueller has now asked for his long time Never Trumper lawyer to sit beside him and help with answers. What's this all about? His lawyer represented the "basement server guy" who got off free in the Crooked Hillary case. This should NOT be allowed. Rigged Witch Hunt!

July 24, 2019

7:18 am: It has been reported that Robert Mueller is saying that he did not apply and interview for the job of FBI Director (and get turned down) the day before he was wrongfully appointed Special Counsel. Hope he doesn't say that under oath in that we have numerous witnesses to the...

...interview, including the Vice President of the United States!

July 26, 2019

9:02 am: There may or may not be National Security concerns with regard to Google and their relationship with China. If there is a problem, we will find out about it. I sincerely hope there is not!!!

5:37 pm: Wow! Big VICTORY on the Wall. The United States Supreme Court overturns lower court injunction, allows Southern Border Wall to proceed. Big WIN for Border Security and the Rule of Law!

July 27, 2019

3:51 pm: Such a big victory of our Country! "Supreme Court approves Trump Administration plan to use Military Funds for the Wall." @ FoxNews We will be fully reimbursed for this expenditure, over time, by other countries.

10:28 pm: ...Robert Mueller's testimony, and the Mueller Report itself, was a disaster for this illegal Democrat inspired Witch Hunt. It is an embarrassment to the USA that they don't know how to stop. They can't help themselves, they are totally lost, they are Clowns!

July 28, 2019

3:45 pm: I am pleased to announce that highly respected Congressman John Ratcliffe of Texas will be nominated by me to be the Director of National Intelligence. A former U.S. Attorney, John will lead and inspire greatness for the Country he loves. Dan Coats, the current Director, will…

…be leaving office on August 15th. I would like to thank Dan for his great service to our Country. The Acting Director will be named shortly.

July 31, 2019

2:58 pm: The Prosecutors who lost the case against SEAL Eddie Gallagher (who I released from solitary confinement so he could fight his case properly), were ridiculously given a Navy Achievement Medal. Not only did they lose the case, they had difficulty with respect…

…to information that may have been obtained from opposing lawyers and for giving immunity in a totally incompetent fashion. I have directed the Secretary of the Navy Richard Spencer & Chief of Naval Operations John Richardson to immediately withdraw and rescind the awards. I am very happy for Eddie Gallagher and his family!

August 4, 2019

7:13 am: The FBI, local and state law enforcement are working together in El Paso and in Dayton, Ohio. Information is rapidly being accumulated in Dayton. Much has already be learned in El Paso. Law enforcement was very rapid in both instances. Updates will be given throughout the day!

August 5, 2019

12:10 pm: Today, I am also directing the Department of Justice to propose legislation ensuring that those who commit hate crimes and mass murders face the DEATH PENALTY—and that this capital punishment be delivered quickly, decisively, and without years of needless delay.

August 29, 2019

1:05 pm: Perhaps never in the history of our Country has someone been more thoroughly disgraced and excoriated than James Comey in the just released Inspector General's Report. He should be ashamed of himself!

August 30, 2019

7:28 am: The disastrous IG Report on James Comey shows, in the strongest of terms, how unfairly I, and tens of millions of great people who support me, were treated. Our rights and liberties were illegally stripped away by this dishonest fool. We should be given our stolen time back?

7:54 am: The fact that James Comey was not prosecuted for the absolutely horrible things he did just shows how fair and reasonable Attorney General Bill Barr is. So many people and experts that I have watched and read would have taken an entirely different course. Comey got Lucky!

1:57 pm: "FALLOUT FROM IG'S SCATHING COMEY REPORT" https://t.co/NrpeBkPbww

August 31, 2019

8:07 am: I was right about Comey, CROOKED COP!

2:06 pm: Being scolded by failed former "Intelligence" officials, like James Clapper, on my condolences to Iran on their failed Rocket launch. Sadly for the United States, guys like him, Comey, and the even dumber John Brennan, don't have a clue. They really set our Country back,…

…but now we are moving forward like never before. We are winning again, and we are respected again!

5:35 pm: Just briefed by Attorney General Barr about the shootings in Texas. FBI and Law Enforcement is fully engaged. More to follow.

September 7, 2019

5:52 am: I want to congratulate @senatemajldr Mitch McConnell and all Republicans. Today I signed the 160th Federal Judge to the Bench. Within a short period of time we will be at over 200 Federal Judges, including many in the Appellate Courts & two great new U.S. Supreme Court Justices!

September 11, 2019

5:47 pm: BIG United States Supreme Court WIN for the Border on Asylum!

September 15, 2019

8:47 am: Brett Kavanaugh should start suing people for libel, or the Justice Department should come to his rescue. The lies being told about him are unbelievable. False Accusations without recrimination. When does it stop? They are trying to influence his opinions. Can't let that happen!

1:08 pm: Can't let Brett Kavanaugh give Radical Left Democrat (Liberal Plus) Opinions based on threats of Impeaching him over made up stories (sound familiar?), false allegations, and lies. This is the game they play. Fake and Corrupt News is working overtime! #ProtectKavanaugh

September 16, 2019

6:21 am: The @nytimes. "This week, the Senate passed a milestone in confirming the 150th Federal Judge of Mr. Trump's Administration to a lifetime appointment, far outstripping Barack Obama's pace and fulfilling pledges by Mr. Trump and Mr. O'Connell to remake the Federal Judiciary…

'These Conservative Judicial appointments will impact our nation for years to come,' said Lindsey Graham, Republican of South Carolina, who leads the Judiciary Committee and who has been speeding through Trump nominees." The entire Court System is changing at a record pace!

7:06 am: "The New York Times walks back report on Kavanaugh assault claim." @foxandfriends The one who is actually being assaulted is Justice Kavanaugh—Assaulted by lies and Fake News! This is all about the LameStream Media working with their partner, the Dems.

7:35 am: Just Out: "Kavanaugh accuser doesn't recall incident." @foxandfriends DO YOU BELIEVE WHAT THESE HORRIBLE PEOPLE WILL DO OR SAY. They are looking to destroy, and influence his opinions—but played the game badly. They should be sued!

September 18, 2019

8:23 am: I am pleased to announce that I will name Robert C. O'Brien, currently serving as the very successful Special Presidential Envoy for Hostage Affairs at the State Department, as our new National Security Advisor. I have worked long & hard with Robert. He will do a great job!

September 22, 2019

9:29 am: "They are trying to destroy and influence Justice Kavanaugh, a very good man." @LindseyGrahamSC 100% correct, and they should be fully exposed for what they are!

September 30, 2019

7:43 am: WHO CHANGED THE LONG STANDING WHISTLEBLOWER RULES JUST BEFORE SUBMITTAL OF THE FAKE WHISTLEBLOWER REPORT? DRAIN THE SWAMP!

October 7, 2019

6:51 am: We just WON the big court case on Net Neutrality Rules! A great win for the future and speed of the internet. Will lead to many big things including 5G. Congratulations to the FCC and its Chairman, Ajit Pai!

7:04 am: "IG: DECLASSIFIED INFORMATION CONTRADICTS THE WHISTLEBLOWER." @foxandfriends But why are people surprised? The "partisan" Whistleblower was very wrong on what was said on my perfect, "no pressure," call with the Ukrainian President. Bring in another Whistleblower from the bench!

October 8, 2019

9:15 pm: "Bob Mueller was pursuing the FBI Director job when he met with President Trump in 2017, Administration officials say." @ FoxNews Bret Baier and Jake Gibson @seanhannity This is true even though Mueller denied it!

October 11, 2019

6:46 pm: Kevin McAleenan has done an outstanding job as Acting Secretary of Homeland Security. We have worked well together with Border Crossings being way down. Kevin now, after many years in Government, wants to spend more time with his family and go to the private sector...

November 1, 2019

7:39 am: Chicago will never stop its crime wave with the current Superintendent of Police. It just won't happen! Thank you to Kevin Graham and all of the GREAT Chicago Police Officers I just had the privilege to meet. Tremendous crime fighting potential if allowed to do your thing!

November 5, 2019

9:05 am: So sad to see what is happening in New York where Governor Cuomo & Mayor DeBlasio are letting out 900 Criminals, some hardened & bad, onto the sidewalks of our rapidly declining, because of them, city. The Radical Left Dems are killing our cities. NYPD Commissioner is resigning!

November 6, 2019

4:54 pm: Thanks to many of you here today, my Administration and Republicans in Congress have now confirmed 157 FEDERAL

JUDGES who will uphold our Constitution AS WRITTEN, a profoundly historic milestone and a truly momentous achievement!

November 10, 2019

1:58 pm: Corrupt politician Adam Schiff wants people from the White House to testify in his and Pelosi's disgraceful Witch Hunt, yet he will not allow a White House lawyer, nor will he allow ANY of our requested witnesses. This is a first in due process and Congressional history!

December 2, 2019

1:07 pm: When Lisa Page, the lover of Peter Strzok, talks about being "crushed", and how innocent she is, ask her to read Peter's "Insurance Policy" text, to her, just in case Hillary loses. Also, why were the lovers text messages scrubbed after he left Mueller. Where are they Lisa?

December 10, 2019

7:02 am: "You have to look at the 17 instances of misconduct cited in the Report, they are very bad. The FISA Court was clearly taken for a ride on this, a failure of the FBI up and fown the chain of command. It's about as strong a medicine as I've seen in a report of this kind…

…in a very long time. The FBI has had some dark day in its past, but nothing like this. This was VERY SERIOUS MISCONDUCT ON THE PART OF THE FBI." @brithume @BretBaier Are you listening Comey, McCabe, lovers Lisa & Peter, the beautiful Ohr family, Brennan, Clapper & many more?

7:16 am: I don't know what report current Director of the FBI Christopher Wray was reading, but it sure wasn't the one given to me. With that kind of attitude, he will never be able to fix the FBI, which is badly broken despite having some of the greatest men & women working there!

December 11, 2019

2:12 pm: They spied on my campaign!

December 12, 2019

7:57 am: Congratulations to JUDGE LAWRENCE VANDYKE on being confirmed to the Ninth Circuit. Great job!

8:49 am: Dirty cops!

December 15, 2019

1:01 pm: As bad as the I.G. Report is for the FBI and others, and it is really bad, remember that I.G. Horowitz was appointed by Obama. There was tremendous bias and guilt exposed, so obvious, but Horowitz couldn't get himself to say it. Big credibility loss. Obama knew everything!

1:34 pm: So now Comey's admitting he was wrong. Wow, but he's only doing so because he got caught red handed. He was actually caught a long time ago. So what are the consequences for his unlawful conduct. Could it be years in jail? Where are the apologies to me and others, Jim?

December 17, 2019

6:14 pm: Wow! "In a stunning rebuke of the FBI, the FISA court severly chastised the FBI for the FISA abuses brought to light in the recent Inspector General's Report. There were at least 17 significant errors." @FoxNews Statement by the Court was long and tough. Means my case was a SCAM!

11:10 pm: So, if Comey & the top people in the FBI were dirty cops and cheated on the FISA Court, wouldn't all of these phony cases have to be overturned or dismissed? They went after me with the Fake Dossier, paid for by Crooked Hillary & the DNC, which they illegally presented to FISA...

...They want to Impeach me (I'm not worried!), and yet they were all breaking the law in so many ways. How can they do that and yet

226

impeach a very successful (Economy Plus) President of the United States, who has done nothing wrong? These people are Crazy!

December 23, 2019

6:58 pm: 187 new Federal Judges have been confirmed under the Trump Administration, including two great new United States Supreme Court Justices. We are shattering every record! Read all about this in "The Long Game," a great new book by @senatemajldr Mitch McConnell. Amazing story!

Mexico—2017 News Quotes

Response to a question from David Muir of ABC News, January 26, 2017.

Source: https://www.telegraph.co.uk/news/2017/01/26/
full-transcript-president-donald-trumps-interview-abc-news/

"All it is, is we'll be reimbursed at a later date from whatever transaction we make from Mexico. Now, I could wait a year and I could hold off the wall. But I wanna build the wall. We have to build the wall. We have to stop drugs from pouring in. We have to stop people from just pouring into our country. We have no idea where they're from. And I campaigned on the wall. And it's very important. But that wall will cost us nothing."

Response to a question from David Muir of ABC News, January 26, 2017.

Source: https://www.telegraph.co.uk/news/2017/01/26/
full-transcript-president-donald-trumps-interview-abc-news/

"But I'm just telling you there will be a payment. It will be in a form, perhaps a complicated form. And you have to understand what I'm doing is good for the United States. It's also going to be good for Mexico.

"We wanna have a very stable, very solid Mexico. Even more solid than it is right now. And they need it also. Lots of things are coming across Mexico that they don't want. I think it's going to be a good thing for both countries. And I think the relationship will be better than ever before.

"You know, when we had a prisoner in Mexico, as you know, two years ago, that we were trying to get out. And Mexico was not helping us, I will tell you, those days are over. I think we're gonna end up with a much better relationship with Mexico. We will have the wall and in a very serious form Mexico will pay for the wall."

Response to a question from Bill O'Reilly of FOX News, February 7, 2017.
Source: https://www.foxnews.com/transcript/bill-oreillys-exclusive-interview-with-president-trump

"Well, it's [Mexico is] a country that has got difficulty. It's certainly has done well with us. We have a trade deficit with Mexico of $60 billion a year. That doesn't include drugs, and it doesn't include the border and all the things that are happening on the border.

"But it is a country that I have great respect for the people. I love the people. I really like this administration. I think he [then-President Enrique Peña Nieto] is a good man. We get along very well. But they have problems controlling aspects of their country. There is no question about it. And I would say that drugs and the drug cartels number one."

Response to a question from Bill O'Reilly of FOX News, February 7, 2017.
Source: https://www.foxnews.com/transcript/bill-oreillys-exclusive-interview-with-president-trump

"We are losing, Bill [O'Reilly of FOX News]. We are losing $60 billion a year in trade deficits with Mexico. We can't do that."

Mexico—2017 Tweets

April 23, 2017

10:44 am: Eventually, but at a later date so we can get started early, Mexico will be paying, in some form, for the badly needed border wall.

June 29, 2017

9:27 am: New Sugar deal negotiated with Mexico is a very good one for both Mexico and the U.S. Had no deal for many years which hurt U.S. badly.

August 27, 2017

8:24 am: With Mexico being one of the highest crime Nations in the world, we must have THE WALL. Mexico will pay for it through reimbursement/other.

September 14, 2017

2:18 pm: Spoke to President of Mexico to give condolences on terrible earthquake. Unable to reach for 3 days b/c of his cell phone reception at site.

September 19, 2017

3:05 pm: God bless the people of Mexico City. We are with you and will be there for you.

Mexico—2018 News Quotes

Remarks during a meeting with Republican senators about immigration, January 4, 2018.
Source: https://www.whitehouse.gov/briefings-statements/remarks-president-trump-vice-president-pence-meeting-immigration-republican-members-senate/

"We need a physical border wall. We're going to have a wall, remember that; we're going to have a wall to keep out deadly drug dealers, dangerous traffickers, and violent criminal cartels. Mexico is having a tremendous problem with crime, and we want to keep it out of our country."

Response to a comment by Congressman Henry Cuellar (D-Texas) in meeting with bipartisan members of Congress on immigration, January 9, 2018.
Source: https://www.whitehouse.gov/briefings-statements/
remarks-president-trump-meeting-bipartisan-members-congress-immigration/

"Henry [Cuellar, Democrat Congressman from Texas], we stopped them. We stopped them. You know why? Mexico told me, the President told me, everybody tells me—Not as many people are coming through their southern border because they don't think they can get through our southern border and therefore they don't come. That's what happened with Mexico. We did Mexico a tremendous favor."

Remarks at Customs and Border Protection roundtable, February 2, 2018.
Source: https://www.whitehouse.gov/briefings-statements/
remarks-president-trump-customs-border-protection-roundtable/

"I mean, I'll just tell you for the media, this doesn't make sense at all for anybody. This was made up by people that don't know what they're doing. And this isn't like this in other countries. You try staying in Mexico. You go and do things in Mexico, they throw you out fast.

"You look at other countries, they have strong controls. We have no controls. And a lot of it is Congress' fault, and we're going to get it changed."

Remarks before an Easter church service in Palm Beach, Florida, April 1, 2018.
Source: https://www.whitehouse.gov/briefings-statements/
remarks-president-trump-easter-church-service/

"Mexico has got to help us at the border. If they're not going to help us at the border, it's a very sad thing between our two countries.

"Mexico has got to help us at the border. And a lot of people are coming in because they want to take advantage of DACA, and we're going to have to really see.

"They had a great chance. The Democrats blew it. They had a great, great chance but we'll have to take a look, because Mexico has got to help us at the border. They flow right through Mexico. They send them into the United States. It can't happen that way anymore."

Mexico—2018 Tweets

March 5, 2018

6:47 am to 6:53 am: We have large trade deficits with Mexico and Canada. NAFTA, which is under renegotiation right now, has been a bad deal for U.S.A. Massive relocation of companies & jobs. Tariffs on Steel and Aluminum will only come off if new & fair NAFTA agreement is signed. Also, Canada must..

...treat our farmers much better. Highly restrictive. Mexico must do much more on stopping drugs from pouring into the U.S. They have not done what needs to be done. Millions of people addicted and dying.

April 2, 2018

8:08 am: Mexico is making a fortune on NAFTA...They have very strong border laws—ours are pathetic. With all of the money they make from the U.S., hopefully they will stop people from coming through their country and into ours, at least until Congress changes our immigration laws!

7:12 pm: Honduras, Mexico and many other countries that the U.S. is very generous to, sends many of their people to our country through our WEAK IMMIGRATION POLICIES. Caravans are heading here. Must pass tough laws and build the WALL. Democrats allow open borders, drugs and crime!

June 18, 2018

8:04 am: Children are being used by some of the worst criminals on earth as a means to enter our country. Has anyone been looking at the Crime taking place south of the border. It is historic, with some countries the most dangerous places in the world. Not going to happen in the U.S.

June 22, 2018

8:30 am: 80% of Mexico's Exports come to the United States. They totally rely on us, which is fine with me. They do have, though, very strong Immigration Laws. The U.S. has pathetically weak and ineffective Immigration Laws that the Democrats refuse to help us fix. Will speak to Mexico!

July 3, 2018

5:49 am: The big Caravan of People from Honduras, now coming across Mexico and heading to our "Weak Laws" Border, had better be stopped before it gets there. Cash cow NAFTA is in play, as is foreign aid to Honduras and the countries that allow this to happen. Congress MUST ACT NOW!

July 31, 2018

6:00 am: One of the reasons we need Great Border Security is that Mexico's murder rate in 2017 increased by 27% to 31,174 people killed, a record! The Democrats want Open Borders. I want Maximum Border Security and respect for ICE and our great Law Enforcement Professionals! @FoxNews

August 10, 2018

6:12 pm: Deal with Mexico is coming along nicely. Autoworkers and farmers must be taken care of or there will be no deal. New President of Mexico has been an absolute gentleman. Canada must wait. Their Tariffs and Trade Barriers are far too high. Will tax cars if we can't make a deal!

August 25, 2018

8:22 am: Our relationship with Mexico is getting closer by the hour. Some really good people within both the new and old government, and all working closely together…A big Trade Agreement with Mexico could be happening soon!

August 27, 2018

8:39 am: A big deal looking good with Mexico!

1:11 pm: United States-Mexico Trade Agreement: https://t.co/E1AzveYPli https://t.co/ZYbHt1pD8a

August 28, 2018

9:19 pm: Our new Trade Deal with Mexico focuses on FARMERS, GROWTH for our country, tearing down TRADE BARRIERS, JOBS and having companies continue to POUR BACK INTO OUR COUNTRY. It will be a big hit!

September 16, 2018

4:28 pm: Congratulations to all of our Mexican friends on National Independence Day. We will be doing great things together!

October 3, 2018

9:35 am: Just spoke to President-Elect Andres Manuel Lopez Obrador of Mexico. Great call, we will work well together!

October 18, 2018

5:51 pm: Thank you Mexico, we look forward to working with you! https://t.co/wf7sE0DHFT

November 18, 2018

1:42 pm: The Mayor of Tijuana, Mexico, just stated that "the City is ill-prepared to handle this many migrants, the backlog could last 6 months." Likewise, the U.S. is ill-prepared for this invasion, and will not stand for it. They are causing crime and big problems in Mexico. Go home!

November 23, 2018

6:49 pm to 6:56 pm: Migrants at the Southern Border will not be allowed into the United States until their claims are individually approved in court. We only will allow those who come into our Country legally.

November 25, 2018

8:28 am: Would be very SMART if Mexico would stop the Caravans long before they get to our Southern Border, or if originating countries would not let them form (it is a way they get certain people out of their country and dump in U.S. No longer). Dems created this problem. No crossings!

November 26, 2018

6:19 am: Mexico should move the flag waving Migrants, many of whom are stone cold criminals, back to their countries. Do it by plane, do it by bus, do it anyway you want, but they are NOT coming into the U.S.A. We will close the Border permanently if need be. Congress, fund the WALL!

December 3, 2018

2:42 pm: Congratulations to newly inaugurated Mexican President @ lopezobrador_. He had a tremendous political victory with the great support of the Mexican People. We will work well together for many years to come!

December 13, 2018

7:38 am: I often stated, "One way or the other, Mexico is going to pay for the Wall." This has never changed. Our new deal with Mexico (and Canada), the USMCA, is so much better than the old, very costly & anti-USA NAFTA deal, that just by the money we save, MEXICO IS PAYING FOR THE WALL!

December 19, 2018

3:43 am: Mexico is paying (indirectly) for the Wall through the new USMCA, the replacement for NAFTA! Far more money coming to the U.S. Because of the tremendous dangers at the Border, including large scale criminal and drug inflow, the United States Military will build the Wall!

December 31, 2018

7:40 pm: MEXICO IS PAYING FOR THE WALL through the many billions of dollars a year that the U.S.A. is saving through the new Trade Deal, the USMCA, that will replace the horrendous NAFTA Trade Deal, which has so badly hurt our Country. Mexico & Canada will also thrive—good for all!

Mexico—2019 News Quotes

Response to an unidentified reporter's question before Trump's bilateral meeting with NATO Secretary General Jens Stoltenberg, April 2, 2019.
Source: https://www.whitehouse.gov/briefings-statements/
remarks-president-trump-nato-secretary-general-jens-stoltenberg-bilateral-meeting/

"Mexico, as you know, as of yesterday, has been starting to apprehend a lot of people at their southern border coming in from Honduras and

Guatemala and El Salvador. And they've—They're really apprehending thousands of people. And it's the first time, really, in decades that this has taken place. And it should have taken place a long time ago.

"You know, Mexico has the strongest immigration laws in the world. There's nobody who has stronger. I guess some have the same, but you can't get any stronger than what Mexico has. And we don't want people coming up making that very dangerous journey and coming in.

"Our system is absolutely maxed out. And Border Patrol has done an incredible job, but the system is absolutely maxed out. And it's a very unfair thing.

"So Mexico has, as of yesterday, made a big difference. You'll see that because few people, if any, are coming up. And they say they're going to stop them. Let's see. They have the power to stop them. They have the laws to stop them.

"And what we have to do is Congress has to meet quickly and make a deal. I could do it in 45 minutes. We need to get rid of chain migration. We need to get rid of catch and release and visa lottery. And we have to do something about asylum. And to be honest with you, you have to get rid of judges.

"Every time, and you won't even believe this, Mr. Secretary General, you catch somebody that's coming illegally into your country, and they bring them to a court. But we can't bring them to a court because you could never have that many judges. So they take their name, they take their information, and they release them. Now, we don't release too many. We keep them. It's called 'catch and keep.' But you don't have facilities for that. But you have to bring them through a court system. If they touch your land, one foot on your land: 'Welcome to being Perry Mason. You now have a big trial.'

"So what they've done over the years is they release them into the United States and they say, 'Come back in four years for a trial.' And nobody comes back. I guess 1%, 1 to 2 percent, on average, come back. And nobody can understand why they come back. They're the only ones that come back.

237

"It is the worst, dumbest immigration system in the world. The Democrats could change it with one meeting. Everybody would agree. But they don't want to change it because they don't want to give the Republicans a victory. They don't want to change it because they want open borders, which means crimes and lots of other things coming in, including drugs.

"So we'll see what happens. I think the Democrats—Today, I spoke to a couple of them and they—All of a sudden, they're changing because they're seeing it really is a crisis. It is a national emergency on the border. And let's see if they can do it.

"But I want to thank—It's a very short period of time, because for years this should have been done. But Mexico is now stopping people coming—Very easy for them to do—Stopping people coming in through Mexico. Let's see if they keep it done, if—If they keep doing that.

"Now, if they don't, or if we don't make a deal with Congress, the border is going to be closed, 100%. And this should have been done by other presidents. So many things should have been done by other presidents.

"But if we don't make a deal with Congress, or if Mexico—And probably you can say 'and/or'—If Mexico doesn't do what they should be doing—They shouldn't have people coming into their country either; this is their southern border that they have to protect—Then we're going to close the border. That's going to be it. Or we're going to close large sections of the border. Maybe not all of it. But it's the only way we're getting a response, and I'm totally ready to do it.

"And I will say this: many people want me to do it, because we're being abused by a bad legal system that was put in by Democrats. And that has to be changed. And it can be changed in 45 minutes, if they want to change it. Let's see what they do."

Remarks to reporters from the White House, April 4, 2019.
Source: https://www.nbcnews.com/politics/donald-trump/
trump-gives-mexico-one-year-warning-stop-drugs-tariffs-border-n991026

"We're going to give them a one year warning, and if the drugs don't stop, or largely stop, we're going to put tariffs on Mexico and products, in particular cars. And if that doesn't work, we're going to close the border."

Remarks to reporters from the White House, April 4, 2019.
Source: https://www.nbcnews.com/politics/donald-trump/
trump-gives-mexico-one-year-warning-stop-drugs-tariffs-border-n991026

"If we don't see people apprehended and brought back to their countries, if we see these massive caravans coming up to our country, right through Mexico, coming right through Mexico like nothing. Buses are even given to them. For the last three days it hasn't happened, since I said we're closing the border. The only thing, frankly, better but less drastic than closing the border is to tariff the cars coming in."

Response to a question from Griff Jenkins of FOX News, April 6, 2019.
Source: https://www.foxnews.com/politics/trump-declares-the-country-full-in-fox-news-
interview-says-american-can-no-longer-accept-illegal-immigrants

"So if we change the laws it would be very easy. But in the meantime, Mexico, if they stop the people from coming in, we won't have a lot of people coming at the border."

Remarks at the signing of H.R. 3401, July 1, 2019.
Source: https://www.whitehouse.gov/briefings-statements/
remarks-president-trump-signing-h-r-3401/

"I want to thank Mexico because Mexico is doing a lot right now. They have almost 20,000 soldiers between the two borders. They have 6,000 on their southern border by Guatemala. And they have about 16,000—15, 16,000 at our southern border. And the numbers are way down for the last week because this just took place over the last few days, over the last week. And it's way down, as you can imagine."

Response to an unidentified reporter's question at the signing of H.R. 3401, July 1, 2019.

Source: https://www.whitehouse.gov/briefings-statements/
remarks-president-trump-signing-h-r-3401/

"Well, now they are, because I think the President [of Mexico] is doing a great job. He [Andrés Manuel López Obrador, President of Mexico] put 16,000 people in this weekend, and they're forming but they're getting to the border, and they're doing a great job. And he has 6,000 people at the border with Guatemala. So—I mean, it's been way down. It's cut way down. You'll start to see the numbers over the next three or four weeks."

Response to an unidentified reporter's question at the signing of H.R. 3401, July 1, 2019.

Source: https://www.whitehouse.gov/briefings-statements/
remarks-president-trump-signing-h-r-3401/

"No, no, that's true. Yeah, if they [the government leaders of Mexico] don't do it. But they're doing a good job. Right now, they're doing a very good job. We're very happy with the job they're doing.

"No, it was because of tariffs that they're doing it. But the point is they're doing a very good job. And he's [Andrés Manuel López Obrador, President of Mexico is] very smart to do it, because that's a tiny fraction. It sounds like a lot of soldiers, but that's a fraction of what tariffs would cost Mexico.

"But I very much appreciate it. And he's [Obrador is] doing a great job for Mexico because the Mexican people were very upset with all of these tens of thousands of people, hundreds of thousands of people walking through Mexico. And the people of Mexico are just as happy as I am with what they're doing."

Response to a question from an unidentified reporter before Marine One departure, September 9, 2019.

Source: https://www.whitehouse.gov/briefings-statements/
remarks-president-trump-marine-one-departure-63/

"Well, right now, Mexico has been doing a great job for us. And, frankly, we're very appreciative. But we've also been very—Pretty rapidly changing the regulations, the rules, winning in court. We've had a lot of wins.

"We did it early on, but we're having a lot of wins in court right now. The courts are backing us up, and that has a lot to do with our success on the southern border.

"In addition, a lot of wall is being built. And every time we put up a mile of wall, that helps us a lot."

Response to a question from an unidentified reporter before Marine One departure, September 9, 2019.
Source: https://www.whitehouse.gov/briefings-statements/
remarks-president-trump-marine-one-departure-63/

"We're starting to do well all over. We won the lawsuit on the wall. We won the lawsuit on a lot of different things having to do with illegal immigration. That's why a lot of our very strong points are coming out.

"And in addition to Mexico helping us, we're ending up with some great legal victories now on illegal immigration. That's one of the reasons we're doing so well."

Remarks at the signing of an executive order protecting and improving Medicare for senior citizens, Ocala, Florida, October 3, 2019.
Source: https://www.whitehouse.gov/briefings-statements/remarks-president-trump-signing-
executive-order-protecting-improving-medicare-nations-seniors-ocala-fl/

"But, you know, when these countries—And now we're getting along great with the countries. Mexico gave us 27,000 soldiers guarding our border and the numbers are way down. Twenty-seven thousand. I want to thank Mexico: the government and the President."

Mexico—2019 Tweets

January 2, 2019

8:35 am: Mexico is paying for the Wall through the new USMCA Trade Deal. Much of the Wall has already been fully renovated or built. We have done a lot of work. $5.6 Billion Dollars that House has approved is very little in comparison to the benefits of National Security. Quick payback!

January 11, 2019

7:05 am: I often said during rallies, with little variation, that "Mexico will pay for the Wall." We have just signed a great new Trade Deal with Mexico. It is Billions of Dollars a year better than the very bad NAFTA deal which it replaces. The difference pays for Wall many times over!

January 19, 2019

9:09 am: Mexico is doing NOTHING to stop the Caravan which is now fully formed and heading to the United States. We stopped the last two—many are still in Mexico but can't get through our Wall, but it takes a lot of Border Agents if there is no Wall. Not easy!

January 31, 2019

7:32 am: With Murders up 33% in Mexico, a record, why wouldn't any sane person want to build a Wall! Construction has started and will not stop until it is finished. @LouDobbs @foxandfriends

March 30, 2019

3:36 pm: Mexico must use its very strong immigration laws to stop the many thousands of people trying to get into the USA. Our detention areas are maxed out & we will take no more illegals. Next step is to close the Border! This will also help us with stopping the Drug flow from Mexico!

March 31, 2019

6:31 pm: The Democrats are allowing a ridiculous asylum system and major loopholes to remain as a mainstay of our immigration system. Mexico is likewise doing NOTHING, a very bad combination for our Country. Homeland Security is being sooo very nice, but not for long!

April 2, 2019

9:41 am: After many years (decades), Mexico is apprehending large numbers of people at their Southern Border, mostly from Guatemala, Honduras and El Salvador. They have ALL been taking U.S. money for years, and doing ABSOLUTELY NOTHING for us, just like the Democrats in Congress!

April 5, 2019

8:11 am: …However, if for any reason Mexico stops apprehending and bringing the illegals back to where they came from, the U.S. will be forced to Tariff at 25% all cars made in Mexico and shipped over the Border to us. If that doesn't work, which it will, I will close the Border…

8:19 am: …This will supersede USMCA. Likewise I am looking at an economic penalty for the 500 Billion Dollars in illegal DRUGS that are shipped and smuggled through Mexico and across our Southern Border. Over 100,00 Americans die each year, sooo many families destroyed!

April 7, 2019

8:03 pm: …Mexico must apprehend all illegals and not let them make the long march up to the United States, or we will have no other choice than to Close the Border and/or institute Tariffs. Our Country is FULL!

April 8, 2019

10:10 pm: A 9th Circuit Judge just ruled that Mexico is too dangerous for migrants. So unfair to the U.S. OUT OF CONTROL!

April 24, 2019

6:25 am: A very big Caravan of over 20,000 people started up through Mexico. It has been reduced in size by Mexico but is still coming. Mexico must apprehend the remainder or we will be forced to close that section of the Border & call up the Military. The Coyotes & Cartels have weapons!

7:00 am: Mexico's Soldiers recently pulled guns on our National Guard Soldiers, probably as a diversionary tactic for drug smugglers on the Border. Better not happen again! We are now sending ARMED SOLDIERS to the Border. Mexico is not doing nearly enough in apprehending & returning!

April 29, 2019

8:17 pm: The Coyotes and Drug Cartels are in total control of the Mexico side of the Southern Border. They have labs nearby where they make drugs to sell into the U.S. Mexico, one of the most dangerous country's in the world, must eradicate this problem now. Also, stop the MARCH to U.S.

May 21, 2019

11:16 am: I am very disappointed that Mexico is doing virtually nothing to stop illegal immigrants from coming to our Southern Border where everyone knows that because of the Democrats, our Immigration Laws are totally flawed & broken...

...Mexico's attitude is that people from other countries, including Mexico, should have the right to flow into the U.S. & that U.S. taxpayers should be responsible for the tremendous costs associated w/this illegal migration. Mexico is wrong and I will soon be giving a response!

May 30, 2019

6:30 pm: On June 10th, the United States will impose a 5% Tariff on all goods coming into our Country from Mexico, until such time as illegal migrants coming through Mexico, and into our Country, STOP. The Tariff will gradually increase until the Illegal Immigration problem is remedied,

...at which time the Tariffs will be removed. Details from the White House to follow.

May 31, 2019

8:30 am: Mexico has taken advantage of the United States for decades. Because of the Dems, our Immigration Laws are BAD. Mexico makes a FORTUNE from the U.S., have for decades, they can easily fix this problem. Time for them to finally do what must be done!

9:27 am: In order not to pay Tariffs, if they start rising, companies will leave Mexico, which has taken 30% of our Auto Industry, and come back home to the USA. Mexico must take back their country from the drug lords and cartels. The Tariff is about stopping drugs as well as illegals!

9:41 am: 90% of the Drugs coming into the United States come through Mexico & our Southern Border. 80,000 people died last year, 1,000,000 people ruined. This has gone on for many years & nothing has been done about it. We have a 100 Billion Dollar Trade Deficit with Mexico. It's time!

June 7, 2019

1:19 pm: Mexico is sending a big delegation to talk about the Border. Problem is, they've been "talking" for 25 years. We want action, not talk. They could solve the Border Crisis in one day if they so desired. Otherwise, our companies and jobs are coming back to the USA!

June 7, 2019

12:16 pm: If we are able to make the deal with Mexico, & there is a good chance that we will, they will begin purchasing Farm & Agricultural products at very high levels, starting immediately. If we are unable to make the deal, Mexico will begin paying Tariffs at the 5% level on Monday!

7:31 pm: I am pleased to inform you that The United States of America has reached a signed agreement with Mexico. The Tariffs scheduled to be implemented by the U.S. on Monday, against Mexico, are hereby indefinitely suspended. Mexico, in turn, has agreed to take strong measures to…

…stem the tide of Migration through Mexico, and to our Southern Border. This is being done to greatly reduce, or eliminate, Illegal Immigration coming from Mexico and into the United States. Details of the agreement will be released shortly by the State Department. Thank you!

June 8, 2019

8:47 am: Everyone very excited about the new deal with Mexico!

9:20 am: I would like to thank the President of Mexico, Andres Manuel Lopez Obrador, and his foreign minister, Marcelo Ebrard, together with all of the many representatives of both the United States and Mexico, for working so long and hard to get our agreement on immigration completed!

June 11, 2019

7:50 am: Maria, Dagan, Steve, Stuart V—When you are the big "piggy bank" that other countries have been ripping off for years (to a level that is not to be believed), Tariffs are a great negotiating tool, a great revenue producers and, most importantly, a powerful way to get…

8:12 am: …Companies to come to the U.S.A and to get companies that have left us for other lands to come back home. We stupidly lost 30% of our auto business to Mexico. If the Tariffs went on at the higher level, they would all come back, and pass. But very happy with the deal I made,..

8:14 am: …If Mexico produces (which I think they will). Biggest part of deal with Mexico has not yet been revealed! China is similar, except they devalue currency and subsidize companies to lessen effect of 25% Tariff. So far, little effect to consumer. Companies will relocate to U.S.

June 9, 2019

5:57 pm: The Failing @nytimes story on Mexico and Illegal Immigration through our Southern Border has now been proven shockingly false and untrue, bad reporting, and the paper is embarrassed by it. The only problem is that they knew it was Fake News before it went out. Corrupt Media!

June 10, 2019

5:31 am: We have fully signed and documented another very important part of the Immigration and Security deal with Mexico, one that the U.S. has been asking about getting for many years. It will be revealed in the not too distant future and will need a vote by Mexico's Legislative body!…

…We do not anticipate a problem with the vote but, if for any reason the approval is not forthcoming, Tariffs will be reinstated!

June 11, 2019

6:54 am: Sad when you think about it, but Mexico right now is doing more for the United States at the Border than the Democrats in Congress! @foxandfriends

June 19, 2019

6:01 pm: Congratulations to President Lopez Obrador—Mexico voted to ratify the USMCA today by a huge margin. Time for Congress to do the same here!

July 3, 2019

3:23 pm: Mexico is doing a far better job than the Democrats on the Border. Thank you Mexico!

September 11, 2019

7:23 pm: I had an excellent telephone conversation with Andrés Manuel López Obrador, President of Mexico, talking about Southern Border Security, and various other things of mutual interest for the people of our respective countries.

Middle East—2017 News Quotes

Response to a question from David Muir of ABC News, January 26, 2017.

Source: https://www.telegraph.co.uk/news/2017/01/26/
full-transcript-president-donald-trumps-interview-abc-news/

"Our roads, excuse me. Our roads, our bridges, our schools, it's falling apart. We have spent as of one month ago $6 trillion in the Middle East. And in our country, we can't afford to build a school in Brooklyn or we can't afford to build a school in Los Angeles. And we can't afford to fix up our inner cities. We can't afford to do anything. Look, it's time. It's been our longest war. We've been in there for 15, 16 years. Nobody even knows what the date is because they don't really know when did we start. But it's time. It's time."

Response to a question from Bill O'Reilly of FOX News, February 7, 2017.

Source: https://www.foxnews.com/transcript/bill-oreillys-exclusive-interview-with-president-trump

"Take a look at what we have done too. We've made a lot of mistakes. I've been against the war in Iraq from the beginning."

Remarks before a bilateral meeting with Palestinian Authority President Mahmoud Abbas, September 20, 2017.

Source: https://www.whitehouse.gov/briefings-statements/
remarks-president-trump-president-abbas-palestinian-authority-bilateral-meeting/

"It's a great honor to have President [Mahmoud] Abbas from the Palestinian Authority with us and his representatives, who have been

249

working very hard with everybody involved toward peace. I mean, we're looking seriously at peace, and maybe, ultimately, peace in the whole of the Middle East. And I think we have a pretty good shot, maybe the best shot ever, and that's what we're looking to do.

"And I just want to thank you for all of the time, all of the meetings, all of the work. It's a complex subject; always been considered the toughest deal of all. Peace between Israel and the Palestinians: the toughest of all.

"But I think we have a very, very good chance, and I certainly will devote everything within my heart and within my soul to get that deal made. Our team is expert; your team is expert. Israel is working very hard toward the same goal, and I must tell you, Saudi Arabia and many of the different nations are working also hard.

"So we'll see if we can put it together. Who knows? Stranger things have happened. But I think we have a good chance, and it's a great honor to have you with us."

Middle East—2017 Tweets

April 5, 2017

4:18 pm: I am deeply committed to preserving our strong relation-ship & to strengthening America's long-standing support for Jordan. @KingAbdullahII.

April 9, 2017

10:20 am to 10:21 am: So sad to hear of the terrorist attack in Egypt. U.S. strongly condemns. I have great…

confidence that President Al Sisi will handle situation properly.

May 23, 2017

10:47 am: Israel, Saudi Arabia and the Middle East were great. Trying hard for PEACE. Doing well. Heading to Vatican & Pope, then #G7 and #NATO.

May 27, 2017

12:19 pm: Bringing hundreds of billions of dollars back to the U.S.A. from the Middle East—which will mean JOBS, JOBS, JOBS!

June 6, 2017

7:06 am: During my recent trip to the Middle East I stated that there can no longer be funding of Radical Ideology. Leaders pointed to Qatar—look!

8:36 am to 8:44 am: So good to see the Saudi Arabia visit with the King and 50 countries already paying off. They said they would take a hard line on funding…

..extremism, and all reference was pointing to Qatar. Perhaps this will be the beginning of the end to the horror of terrorism!

July 3, 2017

6:19 am: Spoke yesterday with the King of Saudi Arabia about peace in the Middle-East. Interesting things are happening!

July 9, 2017

6:37 am: …We negotiated a ceasefire in parts of Syria which will save lives. Now it is time to move forward in working constructively with Russia!

3:09 pm: Syrian ceasefire seems to be holding. Many lives can be saved. Came out of meeting. Good!

July 25, 2017

2:07 pm: Joint Press Conference with Prime Minister Saad Hariri of Lebanon beginning shortly. Join us live!

September 7, 2017

1:13 pm: Welcome to the @WhiteHouse, Amir Sabah al-Ahmed al-Jaber al-Sabah of Kuwait! Joint press conference coming up soon: https://t.co/lfRa4AATaM

2:48 pm: Together, we will show the world that the forces of destruction and extremism are NO MATCH for the BLESSINGS of PROSPERITY and PEACE!

3:18 pm: During my trip to Saudi Arabia, I spoke to the leaders of more than 50 Arab & Muslim nations about the need to confront our shared enemies.. https://t.co/8oeAQfIeX8

September 18, 2017

6:32 pm: Such an honor to have my good friend, Israel PM @Netanyahu, join us w/ his delegation in NYC this afternoon. #UNGA

September 20, 2017

10:23 am: It was a great honor to be with King Abdullah II of Jordan and his delegation this morning. We had a GREAT bilateral meeting!

12:08 pm: Honored to meet w/ Pres Abbas from the Palestinian Authority & his delegation, who have been working hard w/everybody involved toward peace.

September 21, 2017

10:15 am: It was a pleasure to have President Ashraf Ghani of Afghanistan with us this morning! #USAatUNGA

September 23, 2017

4:59 pm: Iran just test-fired a Ballistic Missile capable of reaching Israel. They are also working with North Korea. Not much of an agreement we have!

October 13, 2017

1:09 pm: Today, I announced our strategy to confront the Iranian regime's hostile actions and to ensure that they never acquire a nuclear weapon.

7:53 pm: Starting to develop a much better relationship with Pakistan and its leaders. I want to thank them for their cooperation on many fronts.

8:02 pm: Many people talking, with much agreement, on my Iran speech today. Participants in the deal are making lots of money on trade with Iran!

October 18, 2017

2:27 pm: "Iran hides behind its assertion of technical compliance w/ the nuclear deal, while it brazenly violates the other limits.." Amb. @ NikkiHaley

November 6, 2017

6:03 pm to 6:05 pm: I have great confidence in King Salman and the Crown Prince of Saudi Arabia, they know exactly what they are doing...

Some of those they are harshly treating have been "milking" their country for years!

November 24, 2017

7:04 am: Will be speaking to President Recep Tayyip Erdogan of Turkey this morning about bringing peace to the mess that I inherited in the Middle East. I will get it all done, but what a mistake, in lives and dollars (6 trillion), to be there in the first place!

November 30, 2017

4:00 pm: Today, it was my great honor to meet with the Crown Prince of Bahrain at the @WhiteHouse. Bahrain and the United States are important partners. During the Crown Prince's visit, he is advancing $9 BILLION in commercial deals, including finalizing the purchase of F-16's...

December 6, 2017

4:14 pm: I have determined that it is time to officially recognize Jerusalem as the capital of Israel. I am also directing the State Department to begin preparation to move the American Embassy from Tel Aviv to Jerusalem...

December 27, 2017

5:49 pm: "On 1/20—the day Trump was inaugurated—an estimated 35,000 ISIS fighters held approx 17,500 square miles of territory in both Iraq and Syria. As of 12/21, the U.S. military estimates the remaining 1,000 or so fighters occupy roughly 1,900 square miles..." via @jamiejmcintyre

December 29, 2017

10:42 pm: Many reports of peaceful protests by Iranian citizens fed up with regime's corruption & its squandering of the nation's wealth to fund terrorism abroad. Iranian govt should respect their people's rights, including right to express themselves. The world is watching! #IranProtests

December 30, 2017

2:00 pm: The entire world understands that the good people of Iran want change, and, other than the vast military power of the United States, that Iran's people are what their leaders fear the most... https://t.co/W8rKN9B6RT

2:02 pm: Oppressive regimes cannot endure forever, and the day will come when the Iranian people will face a choice. The world is watching! https://t.co/kvv1uAqcZ9

December 31, 2017

5:00 pm: Iran, the Number One State of Sponsored Terror with numerous violations of Human Rights occurring on an hourly basis, has now closed down the Internet so that peaceful demonstrators cannot communicate. Not good!

Middle East—2018 News Quotes

Remarks before a bilateral meeting with Prime Minister Benjamin Netanyahu of Israel. The meeting was held in Davos, Switzerland on January 25, 2018.

Source: https://www.whitehouse.gov/briefings-statements/
remarks-president-trump-prime-minister-netanyahu-israel-bilateral-meeting-davos-switzerland/

"Israel has always supported the United States. So, what I did with Jerusalem was my honor. And hopefully, we can do something with peace. I would love to see it.

"You know, if you look back at the various peace proposals, and they are endless, and I spoke to some of the people involved, and I said, 'Did you ever talk about the vast amounts of funds, money that we give to the Palestinians?' We give, you know, hundreds of millions of dollars. And they said, 'We never talk.' Well, we do talk about it.

"And when they disrespected us a week ago by not allowing our great Vice President to see them, and we give them hundreds of millions of dollars in aid and support, tremendous numbers; numbers that

255

nobody understands. That money is on the table, and that money is not going to them unless they sit down and negotiate peace. Because I can tell you that Israel does want to make peace. And they're going to have to want to make peace too, or we're going to have nothing to do with it any longer.

"This was never brought up by other negotiators, but it's brought up by me. So, I will say that the hardest subject they had to talk about was Jerusalem. We took Jerusalem off the table, so we don't have to talk about it anymore. They never got past Jerusalem. We took it off the table. We don't have to talk about it anymore. You won one point, and you'll give up some points later on in the negotiation, if it ever takes place. I don't know that it ever will take place.

"But they have to respect the process also, and they have to respect the fact that the U.S. has given tremendous support to them over the years, in terms of monetary support and other support.

"So, we'll see what happens with the peace process, but respect has to be shown to the U.S. or we're just not going any further."

Response to an unidentified reporter's question before a bilateral meeting with Prime Minister Benjamin Netanyahu of Israel. The meeting was held in Davos, Switzerland on January 25, 2018.
Source: https://www.whitehouse.gov/briefings-statements/
remarks-president-trump-prime-minister-netanyahu-israel-bilateral-meeting-davos-switzerland/

"Yes, we have a proposal for peace. It's a great proposal for the Palestinians. I think it's a very good proposal for Israel. It covers a lot of the things that were, over the years, discussed and agreed on. But the fact is, and I think you know this better than anybody, there were never any deals that came close, because Jerusalem—You could never get past Jerusalem.

"So, when people said, 'Oh, I set it back.' I didn't set it back; I helped it. Because by taking it off the table, that was the toughest issue. And Israel will pay for that. Look, Israel—Something is going to happen. They'll do something that's going to be a very good thing. But they want to make peace, and I hope the Palestinians want to make peace. And if they do, everybody is going to be very happy in the end."

Response to an unidentified reporter's question before a bilateral meeting with Prime Minister Benjamin Netanyahu of Israel. The meeting was held in Davos, Switzerland on January 25, 2018.

Source: https://www.whitehouse.gov/briefings-statements/
remarks-president-trump-prime-minister-netanyahu-israel-bilateral-meeting-davos-switzerland/

"You know what, it's many years of killing people. It's many years of killing each other. They [The Palestinians] have to be tired and disgusted of it. So, let's see what happens. I think, eventually, very sound minds—I hope sound minds are going to prevail. And it would be a great achievement of mine. I've said it from day one, if we could make peace between Israel and the Palestinians—If we do that, I would consider that one of our truly great achievements.

"But the money is on the table. The money was never on the table. I'll tell you up front, we give them tremendous amounts, hundreds of millions of dollars a year. That money is on the table. Because why should we do that, as a country, if they're doing nothing for us? And what we want to do for them is help them. We want to create peace and save lives. And we'll see what happens. We'll see what happens. But the money is on the table."

Remarks before a luncheon with Crown Prince Mohammad Bin Salman of Saudi Arabia, March 20, 2018.

Source: https://www.whitehouse.gov/briefings-statements/remarks-president-trump-crown-prince-mohammed-bin-salman-kingdom-saudi-arabia-luncheon/

"It's an honor to have the Crown Prince [Mohammad Bin Salman] of Saudi Arabia with us, and his representatives, many of whom I know and I met in May when we were over there, where a promise of $400 billion was made by Saudi Arabia for the purchase of our equipment and other things.

"And the relationship is probably the strongest it's ever been. We understand each other. Saudi Arabia is a very wealthy nation, and they're going to give the United States some of that wealth, hopefully, in the form of jobs, in the form of the purchase of the finest military equipment anywhere in the world. There's nobody even close.

"As I said before, when it comes to the missiles and the planes and all of the military equipment, there's nobody that even comes close to us in terms of technology and the quality of the equipment. And Saudi Arabia appreciates that. They've done tests of everything, and they appreciate it, and they understand it very well, probably better than most.

"So, I just want to welcome you. It's a great honor to have you back again. Some tremendous things have happened for you since your last visit to the White House, when you were, when you were the Crown Prince, and now you're beyond the Crown Prince. So, I want to just congratulate you. I thought your father [Salman bin Abdulaziz Al Saud, King of Saudi Arabia] made a very wise decision. And I miss your father. A special man. And I know he's coming over soon. But we do miss him. And that was a very incredible two days, and we appreciate the investment in our country."

Statement on Syria, April 13, 2018.

Source: https://www.whitehouse.gov/briefings-statements/statement-president-trump-syria/

"My fellow Americans, a short time ago, I ordered the United States Armed Forces to launch precision strikes on targets associated with the chemical weapons capabilities of Syrian dictator Bashar al-Assad. A combined operation with the armed forces of France and the United Kingdom is now underway. We thank them both.

"Tonight, I want to speak with you about why we have taken this action.

"One year ago, Assad launched a savage chemical weapons attack against his own innocent people. The United States responded with 58 missile strikes that destroyed 20% of the Syrian Air Force.

"Last Saturday, the Assad regime again deployed chemical weapons to slaughter innocent civilians. This time, in the town of Douma, near the Syrian capital of Damascus. This massacre was a significant escalation in a pattern of chemical weapons use by that very terrible regime.

"The evil and the despicable attack left mothers and fathers, infants and children, thrashing in pain and gasping for air. These are not the actions of a man; they are crimes of a monster instead.

"Following the horrors of World War I a century ago, civilized nations joined together to ban chemical warfare. Chemical weapons are uniquely dangerous not only because they inflict gruesome suffering, but because even small amounts can unleash widespread devastation.

"The purpose of our actions tonight is to establish a strong deterrent against the production, spread, and use of chemical weapons. Establishing this deterrent is a vital national security interest of the United States. The combined American, British, and French response to these atrocities will integrate all instruments of our national power: military, economic, and diplomatic. We are prepared to sustain this response until the Syrian regime stops its use of prohibited chemical agents.

"I also have a message tonight for the two governments most responsible for supporting, equipping, and financing the criminal Assad regime.

"To Iran and to Russia, I ask: what kind of a nation wants to be associated with the mass murder of innocent men, women, and children?

"The nations of the world can be judged by the friends they keep. No nation can succeed in the long run by promoting rogue states, brutal tyrants, and murderous dictators.

"In 2013, [Russian] President [Vladimir] Putin and his government promised the world that they would guarantee the elimination of Syria's chemical weapons. Assad's recent attack and today's response are the direct result of Russia's failure to keep that promise.

"Russia must decide if it will continue down this dark path, or if it will join with civilized nations as a force for stability and peace. Hopefully, someday we'll get along with Russia, and maybe even Iran, but maybe not.

"I will say this: the United States has a lot to offer, with the greatest and most powerful economy in the history of the world.

"In Syria, the United States, with but a small force being used to eliminate what is left of ISIS, is doing what is necessary to protect the American people. Over the last year, nearly 100 percent of the territory once controlled by the so-called ISIS caliphate in Syria and Iraq has been liberated and eliminated.

"The United States has also rebuilt our friendships across the Middle East. We have asked our partners to take greater responsibility for securing their home region, including contributing large amounts of money for the resources, equipment, and all of the anti-ISIS effort. Increased engagement from our friends, including Saudi Arabia, the United Arab Emirates, Qatar, Egypt, and others can ensure that Iran does not profit from the eradication of ISIS.

"America does not seek an indefinite presence in Syria under no circumstances. As other nations step up their contributions, we look forward to the day when we can bring our warriors home. And great warriors they are.

"Looking around our very troubled world, Americans have no illusions. We cannot purge the world of evil, or act everywhere there is tyranny.

"No amount of American blood or treasure can produce lasting peace and security in the Middle East. It's a troubled place. We will try to make it better, but it is a troubled place. The United States will be a partner and a friend, but the fate of the region lies in the hands of its own people.

"In the last century, we looked straight into the darkest places of the human soul. We saw the anguish that can be unleashed and the evil that can take hold. By the end of the World War I, more than one million people had been killed or injured by chemical weapons. We never want to see that ghastly specter return.

"So today, the nations of Britain, France, and the United States of America have marshaled their righteous power against barbarism and brutality.

"Tonight, I ask all Americans to say a prayer for our noble warriors and our allies as they carry out their missions.

"We pray that God will bring comfort to those suffering in Syria. We pray that God will guide the whole region toward a future of dignity and of peace.

"And we pray that God will continue to watch over and bless the United States of America."

Remarks before a bilateral meeting with His Majesty King Abdullah II bin Al-Hussein of the Hashemite Kingdom of Jordan, June 25, 2018.
Source: https://www.whitehouse.gov/briefings-statements/remarks-president-trump-majesty-king-abdullah-ii-bin-al-hussein-hashemite-kingdom-jordan-bilateral-meeting/

"It's a great honor to have the King and Queen of Jordan with us. They're friends. We've known each other now for quite a while. Long before this.

"But you have done an incredible job on the refugees and the camps and taking care of people. And I just want to say while our nations have a very good relationship, we now have a great relationship. But the job you do on a humanitarian basis is fantastic. And I would like to thank you very much."

Response to His Majesty King Abdullah II bin Al-Hussein of the Hashemite Kingdom of Jordan before their bilateral meeting, June 25, 2018.
Source: https://www.whitehouse.gov/briefings-statements/remarks-president-trump-majesty-king-abdullah-ii-bin-al-hussein-hashemite-kingdom-jordan-bilateral-meeting/

"Remember, he [His Majesty King Abdullah II bin Al-Hussein of the Hashemite Kingdom of Jordan] used the word 'humility' with respect to me, so I am very happy with that word. That's probably the nicest compliment I've been given in a long time.

"No, the job you do is fantastic. And yes, we do, we spend a lot of money, but we spend a lot of money in a lot of places. And people don't do the job that you do, so I want to thank you very much."

Response to an unidentified reporter's question before a bilateral meeting with His Majesty King Abdullah II bin Al-Hussein of the Hashemite Kingdom of Jordan, June 25, 2018.
Source: https://www.whitehouse.gov/briefings-statements/remarks-president-trump-majesty-king-abdullah-ii-bin-al-hussein-hashemite-kingdom-jordan-bilateral-meeting/

"We're doing very well in the Middle East. We're doing very well in the Middle East, yes."

Response to an unidentified reporter's question before a bilateral meeting with His Majesty King Abdullah II bin Al-Hussein of the Hashemite Kingdom of Jordan, June 25, 2018.

Source: https://www.whitehouse.gov/briefings-statements/remarks-president-trump-majesty-king-abdullah-ii-bin-al-hussein-hashemite-kingdom-jordan-bilateral-meeting/

"I can only say this—And His Majesty [King Abdullah II bin Al-Hussein of the Hashemite Kingdom of Jordan] knows we're doing very well in the Middle East. A lot of progress has been made in the Middle East. A lot. And it really started with the end of the horrible Iran deal. That deal was a disaster, and things are a lot different since we ended that. A lot different."

Remarks at a rally in Tampa, Florida, July 31, 2018.

Source: https://www.tampabay.com/florida-politics/buzz/2018/08/01/heres-a-full-transcript-of-president-trumps-speech-from-his-tampa-rally/

"I also withdrew the United States from the horrible one-sided, $150 billion was paid, $1.8 billion in cash. The Iran nuclear deal, it's a horror show. I hope it works out well with Iran, they're having a lot of difficulty right now. I hope it works out well. And I have a feeling they'll be talking to us pretty soon. And maybe not. And that's okay, too."

Remarks at a rally in Tampa, Florida, July 31, 2018.

Source: https://www.tampabay.com/florida-politics/buzz/2018/08/01/heres-a-full-transcript-of-president-trumps-speech-from-his-tampa-rally/

"In December, I recognized Israel's true capital, Jerusalem.

"And in about five months we opened already the American Embassy in Jerusalem. And people had that scheduled for anywhere from 5 to 10 years, and you all know the story. We took an existing building. We played around with it. We renovated it. We fixed it up. We use Jerusalem stone, one of the finest stones actually in the world, Jerusalem stone. So, instead of spending $1 billion and the papers were right in front of me—'Sir, would you please approve this?' 'What is it?' 'This is for the embassy in Israel, American, sir.' I said, 'How much?' '$1 billion, sir.' '$1 billion!'

"I immediately called our great ambassador to Israel, David Friedman, very successful man, great lawyer, one of the most successful lawyers in the country before he decided to do what he's doing. I said, 'David, they want us to pay a billion dollars for the embassy. I don't want to pay a billion dollars.' I said, 'Study it. Do you have any buildings that we own? We own so much we don't even know what the hell we own. Find some building in a great location. Call me back.'

"Called me back two days later. He said, 'Mr. President, sir, we own the best site in Jerusalem. It's big. It's beautiful and it's got a building on it. I can take that building and renovate it. I can do it for $140,000.'

"I said, 'David, how good is the site?' 'We could never buy a better site.' They were willing to spend tens of millions for a site. They wanted to buy a site which was so bad. It was totally inferior to what we already had. Don't forget, we get there first, right? You know, we have good sites.

"And I said, 'David, do me a favor, don't make it $140,000. Sounds too cheap. Make it like $400,000. That's okay too, David.' So, we saved almost a billion dollars. I could tell you these stories all day long, airplane purchases. I could tell you all day long.

"And we started working, and for $400,000, we actually have a very beautiful American Embassy in Jerusalem, really beautiful. Now, that's one I guarantee no other President is doing. Can you imagine Crooked Hillary doing that? Can you, honestly? Can you imagine? In all fairness, in all fairness to her, could you imagine anybody else doing that? Nobody else. Nobody else is going to do that."

Response to a question from Lesley Stahl of *60 Minutes*, October 15, 2018.
Source: https://www.theguardian.com/us-news/2018/oct/15/
donald-trumps-60-minutes-interview-eight-takeaways

"I tell you what I don't want to do. Boeing, Lockheed, Raytheon, all these com—I don't want to hurt jobs. I don't want to lose an order like that. There are other ways of punishing."

Response to a question from Chris Wallace of FOX News, November 18, 2018.

Source: https://www.youtube.com/watch?v=rMgJnnG-Nql

"Well, I want to see Yemen end, but it takes two to tango. Iran has to end it also. And Iran is a different country than it was when I took over, it's far weakened because of what I did with the Iran, so-called Iran deal, Iran nuclear deal, which was one of the great rip offs of, of all time. But I want Saudi to stop, but I want Iran to stop also."

Middle East—2018 Tweets

January 1, 2018

7:12 am: The United States has foolishly given Pakistan more than 33 billion dollars in aid over the last 15 years, and they have given us nothing but lies & deceit, thinking of our leaders as fools. They give safe haven to the terrorists we hunt in Afghanistan, with little help. No more!

7:44 am: Iran is failing at every level despite the terrible deal made with them by the Obama Administration. The great Iranian people have been repressed for many years. They are hungry for food & for freedom. Along with human rights, the wealth of Iran is being looted. TIME FOR CHANGE!

January 2, 2018

7:09 am: The people of Iran are finally acting against the brutal and corrupt Iranian regime. All of the money that President Obama so foolishly gave them went into terrorism and into their "pockets." The people have little food, big inflation and no human rights. The U.S. is watching!

5:37 pm: It's not only Pakistan that we pay billions of dollars to for nothing, but also many other countries, and others. As an example, we pay the Palestinians HUNDRED OF MILLIONS OF DOLLARS a year and get no appreciation or respect. They don't even want to negotiate a long overdue...

...peace treaty with Israel. We have taken Jerusalem, the toughest part of the negotiation, off the table, but Israel, for that, would have had to pay more. But with the Palestinians no longer willing to talk peace, why should we make any of these massive future payments to them?

January 3, 2018

8:37 am: Such respect for the people of Iran as they try to take back their corrupt government. You will see great support from the United States at the appropriate time!

January 25, 2018

1:03 pm: Very productive bilateral meeting with Prime Minister Benjamin @Netanyahu of Israel—in Davos, Switzerland! #WEF18

January 27, 2018

5:59 pm: Taliban targeted innocent Afghans, brave police in Kabul today. Our thoughts and prayers go to the victims, and first responders. We will not allow the Taliban to win!

April 8, 2018

8:00 am to 8:04 am: Many dead, including women and children, in mindless CHEMICAL attack in Syria. Area of atrocity is in lockdown and encircled by Syrian Army, making it completely inaccessible to outside world. President Putin, Russia and Iran are responsible for backing Animal Assad. Big price...

...to pay. Open area immediately for medical help and verification. Another humanitarian disaster for no reason whatsoever. SICK!

8:12 am: If President Obama had crossed his stated Red Line In The Sand, the Syrian disaster would have ended long ago! Animal Assad would have been history!

April 11, 2018

5:57 am: Russia vows to shoot down any and all missiles fired at Syria. Get ready Russia, because they will be coming, nice and new and "smart!" You shouldn't be partners with a Gas Killing Animal who kills his people and enjoys it!

April 12, 2018

5:15 am: Never said when an attack on Syria would take place. Could be very soon or not so soon at all! In any event, the United States, under my Administration, has done a great job of ridding the region of ISIS. Where is our "Thank you America?"

April 15, 2018

7:19 am: The Syrian raid was so perfectly carried out, with such precision, that the only way the Fake News Media could demean was by my use of the term "Mission Accomplished." I knew they would seize on this but felt it is such a great Military term, it should be brought back. Use often!

May 7, 2018

1:44 pm: I will be announcing my decision on the Iran Deal tomorrow from the White House at 2:00pm.

May 10, 2018

9:30 am: Senator Cryin' Chuck Schumer fought hard against the Bad Iran Deal, even going at it with President Obama, & then Voted AGAINST it! Now he says I should not have terminated the deal—but he doesn't really believe that! Same with Comey. Thought he was terrible until I fired him!

9:33 am: Five Most Wanted Leaders of ISIS just captured!

May 11, 2018

6:39 pm: Big week next week when the American Embassy in Israel will be moved to Jerusalem. Congratulations to all!

May 12, 2018

5:02 pm: Iran's Military Budget is up more than 40% since the Obama negotiated Nuclear Deal was reached…just another indicator that it was all a big lie. But not anymore!

May 13, 2018

3:11 pm: Remember how badly Iran was behaving with the Iran Deal in place. They were trying to take over the Middle East by whatever means necessary. Now, that will not happen!

May 14, 2018

8:36 am: Big day for Israel. Congratulations!

June 13, 2018

6:52 am: Oil prices are too high. OPEC is at it again. Not good!

June 20. 2018

6:37 am: Just spoke to King Salman of Saudi Arabia and explained to him that, because of the turmoil & disfunction in Iran and Venezuela, I am asking that Saudi Arabia increase oil production, maybe up to 2,000,000 barrels, to make up the difference…Prices to high! He has agreed!

June 22, 2018

9:10 am: Hope OPEC will increase output substantially. Need to keep prices down!

July 3, 2018

7:03 am: Just out that the Obama Administration granted citizenship, during the terrible Iran Deal negotiation, to 2,500 Iranians—including to government officials. How big (and bad) is that?

July 4, 2018

3:46 pm: The OPEC Monopoly must remember that gas prices are up & they are doing little to help. If anything, they are driving prices higher as the United States defends many of their members for very little $'s. This must be a two way street. REDUCE PRICING NOW!

July 8, 2018

3:29 pm: Iranian Harassment of U.S. Warships: 2015: 22 2016: 36 2017: 14 2018: 0 Source: @USNavy

July 22, 2018

10:24 pm: To Iranian President Rouhani: NEVER, EVER THREATEN THE UNITED STATES AGAIN OR YOU WILL SUFFER CONSEQUENCES THE LIKES OF WHICH FEW THROUGHOUT HISTORY HAVE EVER SUFFERED BEFORE. WE ARE NO LONGER A COUNTRY THAT WILL STAND FOR YOUR DEMENTED WORDS OF VIOLENCE & DEATH. BE CAUTIOUS!

August 4, 2018

3:53 pm: Iran, and it's economy, is going very bad, and fast! I will meet, or not meet, it doesn't matter—it is up to them!

August 7, 2018

4:31 am: The Iran sanctions have officially been cast. These are the most biting sanctions ever imposed, and in November they ratchet up to yet another level. Anyone doing business with Iran will NOT be doing business with the United States. I am asking for WORLD PEACE, nothing less!

August 18, 2018

4:51 pm: The United States has ended the ridiculous 230 Million Dollar yearly development payment to Syria. Saudi Arabia and other rich countries in the Middle East will start making payments instead of the U.S. I want to develop the U.S., our military and countries that help us!

September 3, 2018

5:20 pm: President Bashar al-Assad of Syria must not recklessly attack Idlib Province. The Russians and Iranians would be making a grave humanitarian mistake to take part in this potential human tragedy. Hundreds of thousands of people could be killed. Don't let that happen!

September 20, 2018

6:13 am: We protect the countries of the Middle East, they would not be safe for very long without us, and yet they continue to push for higher and higher oil prices! We will remember. The OPEC monopoly must get prices down now!

September 21, 2018

8:23 am: I will Chair the United Nations Security Council meeting on Iran next week!

October 13, 2018

9:06 am: Pastor Andrew Brunson, released by Turkey, will be with me in the Oval Office at 2:30 P.M. (this afternoon). It will be wonderful to see and meet him. He is a great Christian who has been through such a tough experience. I would like to thank President @RT_Erdogan for his help!

9:17 am: There was NO DEAL made with Turkey for the release and return of Pastor Andrew Brunson. I don't make deals for hostages. There was, however, great appreciation on behalf of the United States, which will lead to good, perhaps great, relations between the United States & Turkey!

10:42 pm: Big day! Pastor Andrew Brunson, who could have spent 35 years in a Turkish prison, was returned safely home to his family today. Met in Oval Office, great people! Then off to Kentucky for a Rally for Congressman Andy Barr. Tremendous crowd & spirit! Just returned to White House.

October 15, 2018

7:37 am: Just spoke to the King of Saudi Arabia who denies any knowledge of whatever may have happened "to our Saudi Arabian citizen." He said that they are working closely with Turkey to find answer. I am immediately sending our Secretary of State to meet with King!

October 16, 2018

8:15 am: For the record, I have no financial interests in Saudi Arabia (or Russia, for that matter). Any suggestion that I have is just more FAKE NEWS (of which there is plenty)!

October 16, 2018

1:40 pm: Just spoke with the Crown Prince of Saudi Arabia who totally denied any knowledge of what took place in their Turkish Consulate. He was with Secretary of State Mike Pompeo...

...during the call, and told me that he has already started, and will rapidly expand, a full and complete investigation into this matter. Answers will be forthcoming shortly

October 18, 2018

10:40 am: Secretary of State Mike Pompeo returned last night from Saudi Arabia and Turkey. I met with him this morning wherein the Saudi situation was discussed in great detail, including his meeting with…

…the Crown Prince. He is waiting for the results of the investigations being done by the Saudis and Turkey, and just gave a news conference to that effect.

October 19, 2018

12:26 pm: Secretary of State Mike Pompeo was never given or shown a Transcript or Video of the Saudi Consulate event. FAKE NEWS!

November 12, 2018

1:21 pm: Hopefully, Saudi Arabia and OPEC will not be cutting oil production. Oil prices should be much lower based on supply!

November 21, 2018

7:49 am: Oil prices getting lower. Great! Like a big Tax Cut for America and the World. Enjoy! $54, was just $82. Thank you to Saudi Arabia, but let's go lower!

December 19, 2018

9:29 am: We have defeated ISIS in Syria, my only reason for being there during the Trump Presidency.

December 20, 2018

12:04 am: Col. Jim Carafano on @IngrahamAngle "Trump has made the Middle East a better place. When Trump came into office, ISIS was running amuck in the Middle East. Over a million refugees poured into Western Europe—none of that is happening today. That's all due to Trump."

12:17 am: "Trump gets no credit for what he's done in the Middle East." @IngrahamAngle So true, thank you Laura!

6:25 am: "I'm proud of the President today to hear that he is declaring victory in Syria." Senator Rand Paul. "I couldn't agree more with the presidents decision. By definition, this is the opposite of an Obama decision. Senator Mike Lee

6:42 am: Getting out of Syria was no surprise. I've been campaigning on it for years, and six months ago, when I very publicly wanted to do it, I agreed to stay longer. Russia, Iran, Syria & others are the local enemy of ISIS. We were doing there work. Time to come home & rebuild. #MAGA

6:56 am to 7:16 am: Does the USA want to be the Policeman of the Middle East, getting NOTHING but spending precious lives and trillions of dollars protecting others who, in almost all cases, do not appreciate what we are doing? Do we want to be there forever? Time for others to finally fight...

...Russia, Iran, Syria & many others are not happy about the U.S. leaving, despite what the Fake News says, because now they will have to fight ISIS and others, who they hate, without us. I am building by far the most powerful military in the world. ISIS hits us they are doomed!

2:22 pm: So hard to believe that Lindsey Graham would be against saving soldier lives & billions of $$$. Why are we fighting for our enemy, Syria, by staying & killing ISIS for them, Russia, Iran & other locals? Time to focus on our Country & bring our youth back home where they belong!

December 22, 2018

11:18 am to 11:30 am: I am in the White House, working hard. News reports concerning the Shutdown and Syria are mostly FAKE. We are negotiating with the Democrats on desperately needed Border Security (Gangs, Drugs, Human Trafficking & more) but it could be a long stay. On Syria, we were originally...

...going to be there for three months, and that was seven years ago—we never left. When I became President, ISIS was going wild. Now ISIS is largely defeated and other local countries, including

Turkey, should be able to easily take care of whatever remains. We're coming home!

8:59 pm: If anybody but your favorite President, Donald J. Trump, announced that, after decimating ISIS in Syria, we were going to bring our troops back home (happy & healthy), that person would be the most popular hero in America. With me, hit hard instead by the Fake News Media. Crazy!

December 23, 2018

10:32 pm: "It should not be the job of America to replace regimes around the world. This is what President Trump recognized in Iraq, that it was the biggest foreign policy disaster of the last several decades, and he's right…The generals still don't get the mistake." @ RandPaul

December 24, 2018

12:23 pm: Saudi Arabia has now agreed to spend the necessary money needed to help rebuild Syria, instead of the United States. See? Isn't it nice when immensely wealthy countries help rebuild their neighbors rather than a Great Country, the U.S., that is 5000 miles away. Thanks to Saudi A!

December 31, 2018

8:03 am: If anybody but Donald Trump did what I did in Syria, which was an ISIS loaded mess when I became President, they would be a national hero. ISIS is mostly gone, we're slowly sending our troops back home to be with their families, while at the same time fighting ISIS remnants…

8:12 am: .I campaigned on getting out of Syria and other places. Now when I start getting out the Fake News Media, or some failed Generals who were unable to do the job before I arrived, like to complain about me & my tactics, which are working. Just doing what I said I was going to do!

8:19 am: ...Except the results are FAR BETTER than I ever said they were going to be! I campaigned against the NEVER ENDING WARS, remember!

Middle East—2019 News Quotes

Response to a question from Margaret Brennan of CBS News, February 3, 2019
Source: https://www.cbsnews.com/news/
transcript-president-trump-on-face-the-nation-february-3-2019/

"I have intel people, but that doesn't mean I have to agree. President Bush had intel people that said Saddam Hussein in Iraq had nuclear weapons, had all sorts of weapons of mass destruction. Guess what? Those intel people didn't know what the hell they were doing, and they got us tied up in a war that we should have never been in. And we've spent seven trillion dollars in the Middle East and we have lost lives—[Brennan interrupts.]"

From State of the Union address, February 5, 2019.
Source: https://www.whitehouse.gov/briefings-statements/
president-donald-j-trumps-state-union-address-2/

"One of the most complex set of challenges we face is in the Middle East.

"Our approach is based on principled realism, not discredited theories that have failed for decades to yield progress. For this reason, my administration recognized the true capital of Israel and proudly opened the American Embassy in Jerusalem.

"Our brave troops have now been fighting in the Middle East for almost 19 years. In Afghanistan and Iraq, nearly 7,000 American heroes have given their lives. More than 52,000 Americans have been badly wounded. We have spent more than $7 trillion in the Middle East.

"As a candidate for President, I pledged a new approach. Great nations do not fight endless wars."

From State of the Union address, February 5, 2019.
Source: https://www.whitehouse.gov/briefings-statements/
president-donald-j-trumps-state-union-address-2/

"My administration has acted decisively to confront the world's leading state sponsor of terror: the radical regime in Iran.

"To ensure this corrupt dictatorship never acquires nuclear weapons, I withdrew the United States from the disastrous Iran nuclear deal. And last fall, we put in place the toughest sanctions ever imposed on a country.

"We will not avert our eyes from a regime that chants death to America and threatens genocide against the Jewish people. We must never ignore the vile poison of anti-Semitism, or those who spread its venomous creed. With one voice, we must confront this hatred anywhere and everywhere it occurs."

Remarks during a visit to the Lima Army Tank Plant in Ohio, March 20, 2019.
Source: https://www.c-span.org/video/?458966-1/
president-trump-delivers-remarks-lima-army-tank-plant-ohio

"And the other thing is we're in a war in the Middle East that [the late U.S. Senator John] McCain pushed so hard. He was calling Bush, President Bush, all the time, 'Get into the Middle East. Get into the Middle East.'"

Response to an unidentified reporter's question at the signing of H.R. 3401, July 1, 2019.
Source: https://www.whitehouse.gov/briefings-statements/
remarks-president-trump-signing-h-r-3401/

"No. No message to Iran. They know what they're doing. They know what they're playing with. And I think they're playing with fire. So, no message to Iran whatsoever."

Response to a question from an unidentified reporter before Marine One departure, September 9, 2019.
Source: https://www.whitehouse.gov/briefings-statements/
remarks-president-trump-marine-one-departure-63/

"It could happen. It could happen. Yeah. No problem with meeting. Iran should straighten out because, frankly, they're in very bad position right now and they should straighten it out, because they could straighten it out very easily."

Remarks at a rally in Minneapolis, Minnesota, October 10, 2019.
Source: https://www.twincities.com/2019/10/10/
trump-attacks-joe-biden-ilhan-omar-and-jacob-frey-at-minneapolis-rally/

"The single greatest single mistake our country made, in its history, was going into the quicksand of the Middle East."

Remarks before a bilateral meeting with Turkish President Recep Tayyip Erdoğan, November 13, 2019.
Source: https://www.whitehouse.gov/briefings-statements/
remarks-president-trump-president-erdogan-turkey-bilateral-meeting-2/

"The border is holding very well. The ceasefire is holding very well. We've been speaking to the Kurds, and they seem to be very satisfied.

"As you know, we've pulled back our troops quite a while ago, because I think it's time for us not to be worried about other people's borders. I want to worry about our borders. We've got plenty of borders to worry about.

"I want to thank the [Turkish] President [Recep Tayyip Erdoğan] for the job they've done. Again, this has been thousands of years in the process, between borders, between these countries and other countries that we're involved with, 7,000 miles away. So, we want to worry about our things.

"We're keeping the oil. We have the oil. The oil is secure. We left troops behind, only for the oil.

"And I have to just finish by saying that the President [Erdoğan} and I have been—We've been very good friends. We've been friends for a long time, almost from day one. And we understand each other's country. We understand where we're coming from. I understand the problems that they've had, including many people from Turkey being killed in the area that we're talking about. And he has to do something about that, also. It's not a one-way street."

Remarks before a bilateral meeting with Turkish President Recep Tayyip Erdoğan, November 13, 2019.

Source: https://www.whitehouse.gov/briefings-statements/
remarks-president-trump-president-erdogan-turkey-bilateral-meeting-2/

"Turkey is watching the ISIS fighters. When I became President, ISIS was all over the place. I had no idea to the extent. In fact, it was shown to me about a month ago. We came in. It was a mess. And we took over 100% of the caliphate.

"And, last week, as you know, we killed its leader and its founder. And we're very proud of that fact. And we've also knocked out number two. And we have our eye out on number three, who was supposed to become number one, but he's running right now. He's running for his life, but we have our sights right on him.

"So, we are—We're doing very well. ISIS is very much, very much a factor that's different than it was when I took over. When I took over, thousands and thousands of ISIS fighters were all over. Now they're mostly imprisoned."

Remarks to French President Emmanuel Macron during NATO Summit press conference in London, December 3, 2019.

Source: https://www.realclearpolitics.com/video/2019/12/03/trump_asks_macron_if_he_
wants_some_nice_isis_fighters_at_nato_summit.html

"We have a tremendous amount of captured fighters, ISIS fighters over in Syria. And they're all under lock and key, but many are from France, many are from Germany. Many are from UK. They are mostly from Europe. And some of the countries are agreeing—I have not spoken to the President [of France] about that.

"Would you like some nice ISIS fighters? I can give them to you."

Middle East—2019 Tweets

January 7, 2019

10:50 pm: Endless Wars, especially those which are fought out of judgement mistakes that were made many years ago, & those where we are getting little financial or military help from the rich countries that so greatly benefit from what we are doing, will eventually come to a glorious end!

January 13, 2019

5:53 pm: Starting the long overdue pullout from Syria while hitting the little remaining ISIS territorial caliphate hard, and from many directions. Will attack again from existing nearby base if it reforms. Will devastate Turkey economically if they hit Kurds. Create 20 mile safe zone…

6:02 pm: ..Likewise, do not want the Kurds to provoke Turkey. Russia, Iran and Syria have been the biggest beneficiaries of the long term U.S. policy of destroying ISIS in Syria—natural enemies. We also benefit but it is now time to bring our troops back home. Stop the ENDLESS WARS!

January 14, 2019

5:12 pm: Spoke w/ President Erdogan of Turkey to advise where we stand on all matters including our last two weeks of success in fighting the remnants of ISIS, and 20 mile safe zone. Also spoke about economic development between the U.S. & Turkey—great potential to substantially expand!

January 30, 2019

6:25 am: When I became President, ISIS was out of control in Syria & running rampant. Since then tremendous progress made, especially over last 5 weeks. Caliphate will soon be destroyed, unthinkable two years ago. Negotiating are proceeding well in Afghanistan after 18 years of fighting.

6:34 am: ...Fighting continues but the people of Afghanistan want peace in this never ending war. We will soon see if talks will be successful? North Korea relationship is best it has ever been with U.S. No testing, getting remains, hostages returned. Decent chance of Denuclearization...

February 1, 2019

8:23 am: I inherited a total mess in Syria and Afghanistan, the "Endless Wars" of unlimited spending and death. During my campaign I said, very strongly, that these wars must finally end. We spend $50 Billion a year in Afghanistan and have hit them so hard that we are now talking peace.

February 11, 2019

2:58 pm: 40 years of corruption. 40 years of repression. 40 years of terror. The regime in Iran has produced only #40YearsofFailure. The long-suffering Iranian people deserve a much brighter future.

March 28, 2019

7:30 am: Very important that OPEC increase the flow of Oil. World Markets are fragile, price of Oil getting too high. Thank you!

April 10, 2019

9:48 am: Trump flags being waived at the Bibi @Netanyahu VICTORY celebration last night!

2:17 pm: Spoke to Bibi @Netanyahu to congratulate him on a great and hard-fought win. The United States is with him and the People of Israel all the way!

April 22, 2019

8:37 am: Saudi Arabia and others in OPEC will more than make up the Oil Flow difference in our now Full Sanctions on Iranian Oil. Iran is being given VERY BAD advice by @JohnKerry and people who helped him lead the U.S. into the very bad Iran Nuclear Deal. Big violation of Logan Act?

May 19, 2019

3:25 pm: If Iran wants to fight, that will be the official end of Iran. Never threaten the United States again!

May 20, 2019

12:30 pm: ..Iran will call us if and when they are ever ready. In the meantime, their economy continues to collapse—very sad for the Iranian people!

June 2, 2019

6:49 pm: Hearing word that Russia, Syria and, to a lesser extent, Iran, are bombing the hell out of Idlib Province in Syria, and indiscriminately killing many innocent civilians. The World is watching this butchery. What is the purpose, what will it get you? STOP!

June 16, 2019

2:00 pm: Thank you PM @Netanyahu and the State of Israel for this great honor! https://t.co/OUcf6s98UX

June 17, 2019

10:49 am: "Iran to defy Uranium Stockpile Limits"

June 20, 2019

9:15 am: Iran made a very big mistake!

June 21, 2019

8:03 pm: President Obama made a desperate and terrible deal with Iran—Gave them 150 Billion Dollars plus 1.8 Billion Dollars in CASH! Iran was in big trouble and he bailed them out. Gave them a free path to Nuclear Weapons, and SOON. Instead of saying thank you, Iran yelled...

.Death to America. I terminated deal, which was not even ratified by Congress, and imposed strong sanctions. They are a much weakened nation today than at the beginning of my Presidency, when they were causing major problems throughout the Middle East. Now they are Bust!...

...On Monday they shot down an unmanned drone flying in International Waters. We were cocked & loaded to retaliate last night on 3 different sights when I asked, how many will die. 150 people, sir, was the answer from a General. 10 minutes before the strike I stopped it, not.

...proportionate to shooting down an unmanned drone. I am in no hurry, our Military is rebuilt, new, and ready to go, by far the best in the world. Sanctions are biting & more added last night. Iran can NEVER have Nuclear Weapons, not against the USA, and not against the WORLD!

June 22, 2019

1:56 pm: Iran cannot have Nuclear Weapons! Under the terrible Obama plan, they would have been on their way to Nuclear in a short number of years, and existing verification is not acceptable. We are putting major additional Sanctions on Iran on Monday. I look forward to the day that...

...Sanctions come off Iran, and they become a productive and prosperous nation again—The sooner the better!

5:58 pm: I never called the strike against Iran "BACK," as people are incorrectly reporting, I just stopped it from going forward at this time!

June 24, 2019

7:08 am: China gets 91% of its Oil from the Straight, Japan 62%, & many other countries likewise. So why are we protecting the shipping lanes for other countries (many years) for zero compensation. All of these countries should be protecting their own ships on what has always been…

…a dangerous journey. We don't even need to be there in that the U.S. has just become (by far) the largest producer of Energy anywhere in the world! The U.S. request for Iran is very simple—No Nuclear Weapons and No Further Sponsoring of Terror!

June 25, 2019

9:42 am: …a dangerous journey. We don't even need to be there in that the U.S. has just become (by far) the largest producer of Energy anywhere in the world! The U.S. request for Iran is very simple—No Nuclear Weapons and No Further Sponsoring of Terror!

…The wonderful Iranian people are suffering, and for no reason at all. Their leadership spends all of its money on Terror, and little on anything else. The U.S. has not forgotten Iran's use of IED's & EFP's (bombs), which killed 2000 Americans, and wounded many more..

July 2, 2019

11:06 pm: Iran was violating the 150 Billion Dollar (plus 1.8 Billion Dollar in CASH) Nuclear Deal with the United States, and others who paid NOTHING, long before I became President—and they have now breached their stockpile limit. Not good!

July 3, 2019

3:33 pm: Iran has just issued a New Warning. Rouhani says that they will Enrich Uranium to "any amount we want" if there is no new Nuclear Deal. Be careful with the threats, Iran. They can come back to bite you like nobody has been bitten before!

July 10, 2019

9:14 am: Iran has long been secretly "enriching," in total violation of the terrible 150 Billion Dollar deal made by John Kerry and the Obama Administration. Remember, that deal was to expire in a short number of years. Sanctions will soon be increased, substantially!

July 21, 2019

3:33 pm: Congratulations to Bibi @Netanyahu on becoming the longest serving PM in the history of Israel. Under your leadership, Israel has become a technology powerhouse and a world class economy...

...Most importantly you have led Israel with a commitment to the values of democracy, freedom, and equal opportunity that both our nations cherish and share!

July 22, 2019

8:08 am: The Report of Iran capturing CIA spies is totally false. Zero truth. Just more lies and propaganda (like their shot down drone) put out by a Religious Regime that is Badly Failing and has no idea what to do. Their Economy is dead, and will get much worse. Iran is a total mess!

July 29, 2019

3:40 pm: Just remember, the Iranians never won a war, but never lost a negotiation!

August 8, 2019

12:51 pm: Iran is in serious financial trouble. They want desperately to talk to the U.S., but are given mixed signals from all of those purporting to represent us, including President Macron of France...

...I know Emmanuel means well, as do all others, but nobody speaks for the United States but the United States itself. No one is authorized in any way, shape, or form, to represent us!

August 15, 2019

8:57 am: It would show great weakness if Israel allowed Rep. Omar and Rep. Tlaib to visit. They hate Israel & all Jewish people, & there is nothing that can be said or done to change their minds. Minnesota and Michigan will have a hard time putting them back in office. They are a disgrace!

11:38 am: Representatives Omar and Tlaib are the face of the Democrat Party, and they HATE Israel!

August 16, 2019

5:26 pm: Israel was very respectful & nice to Rep. Rashida Tlaib, allowing her permission to visit her "grandmother." As soon as she was granted permission, she grandstanded & loudly proclaimed she would not visit Israel. Could this possibly have been a setup? Israel acted appropriately!

5:58 pm: Just completed a very good meeting on Afghanistan. Many on the opposite side of this 19 year war, and us, are looking to make a deal—if possible!

August 30, 2019

12:44 pm: The United States of America was not involved in the catastrophic accident during final launch preparations for the Safir SLV Launch at Semnan Launch Site One in Iran. I wish Iran best wishes and good luck in determining what happened at Site One.

September 14, 2019

9:57 am: I had a call today with Prime Minister Netanyahu to discuss the possibility of moving forward with a Mutual Defense Treaty, between the United States and Israel, that would further anchor the tremendous alliance.

...between our two countries. I look forward to continuing those discussions after the Israeli Elections when we meet at the United Nations later this month!

September 15, 2019

5:50 pm: Saudi Arabia oil supply was attacked. There is reason to believe that we know the culprit, are locked and loaded depending on verification, but are waiting to hear from the Kingdom as to who they believe was the cause of this attack, and under what terms we would proceed!

PLENTY OF OIL!

September 16, 2019

8:16 am: Remember when Iran shot down a drone, saying knowingly that it was in their "airspace" when, in fact, it was nowhere close. They stuck strongly to that story knowing that it was a very big lie. Now they say that they had nothing to do with the attack on Saudi Arabia. We'll see?

September 18, 2019

7:53 am: I have just instructed the Secretary of the Treasury to substantially increase Sanctions on the country of Iran!

September 27, 2019

8:23 am: Iran wanted me to lift the sanctions imposed on them in order to meet. I said, of course, NO!

October 8, 2019

7:30 am: So many people conveniently forget that Turkey is a big trading partner of the United States, in fact they make the structural steel frame for our F-35 Fighter Jet. They have also been good to deal with, helping me to save many lives at Idlib Province, and returning, in very...

...good health, at my request, Pastor Brunson, who had many years of a long prison term remaining. Also remember, and importantly, that Turkey is an important member in good standing of NATO. He is coming to the U.S. as my guest on November 13th. #ENDENDLESSWARS

7:55 am: We may be in the process of leaving Syria, but in no way have we Abandoned the Kurds, who are special people and wonderful fighters. Likewise our relationship with Turkey, a NATO and Trading partner, has been very good. Turkey already has a large Kurdish population and fully…

..understands that while we only had 50 soldiers remaining in that section of Syria, and they have been removed, any unforced or unnecessary fighting by Turkey will be devastating to their economy and to their very fragile currency. We are helping the Kurds financially/weapons!

October 9, 2019

11:16 am: In case the Kurds or Turkey lose control, the United States has already taken the 2 ISIS militants tied to beheadings in Syria, known as the Beetles, out of that country and into a secure location controlled by the U.S. They are the worst of the worst!

October 10, 2019

8:27 am: Turkey has been planning to attack the Kurds for a long time. They have been fighting forever. We have no soldiers or Military anywhere near the attack area. I am trying to end the ENDLESS WARS. Talking to both sides. Some want us to send tens of thousands of soldiers to…

…the area and start a new war all over again. Turkey is a member of NATO. Others say STAY OUT, let the Kurds fight their own battles (even with our financial help). I say hit Turkey very hard financially & with sanctions if they don't play by the rules! I am watching closely.

3:07 pm: We defeated 100% of the ISIS Caliphate and no longer have any troops in the area under attack by Turkey, in Syria. We did our job perfectly! Now Turkey is attacking the Kurds, who have been fighting each other for 200 years…

…We have one of three choices: Send in thousands of troops and win Militarily, hit Turkey very hard Financially and with Sanctions, or mediate a deal between Turkey and the Kurds!

October 12, 2019

4:20 pm: The Endless Wars Must End!

11:06 pm: The same people that got us into the Middle East Quicksand, 8 Trillion Dollars and many thousands of lives (and millions of lives when you count the other side), are now fighting to keep us there. Don't listen to people that haven't got a clue. They have proven to be inept!

October 13, 2019

7:57 am: Very smart not to be involved in the intense fighting along the Turkish Border, for a change. Those that mistakenly got us into the Middle East Wars are still pushing to fight. They have no idea what a bad decision they have made. Why are they not asking for a Declaration of War?

8:09 am: Do you remember two years ago when Iraq was going to fight the Kurds in a different part of Syria. Many people wanted us to fight with the Kurds against Iraq, who we just fought for. I said no, and the Kurds left the fight, twice. Now the same thing is happening with Turkey.

The Kurds and Turkey have been fighting for many years. Turkey considers the PKK the worst terrorists of all. Others may want to come in and fight for one side or the other. Let them! We are monitoring the situation closely. Endless Wars!

October 14, 2019

6:14 am: Brian Kilmeade over at @foxandfriends got it all wrong. We are not going into another war between people who have been fighting with each other for 200 years. Europe had a chance to get their ISIS prisoners, but didn't want the cost. "Let the USA pay," they said

…Kurds may be releasing some to get us involved. Easily recaptured by Turkey or European Nations from where many came, but they should move quickly. Big sanctions on Turkey coming! Do people really think we should go to war with NATO Member Turkey? Never ending wars will end!

6:40 am: The same people who got us into the Middle East mess are the people who most want to stay there!

2:10 pm: After defeating 100% of the ISIS Caliphate, I largely moved our troops out of Syria. Let Syria and Assad protect the Kurds and fight Turkey for their own land. I said to my Generals, why should we be fighting for Syria…

and Assad to protect the land of our enemy? Anyone who wants to assist Syria in protecting the Kurds is good with me, whether it is Russia, China, or Napoleon Bonaparte. I hope they all do great, we are 7,000 miles away!

October 17, 2019

1:03 pm: This deal could NEVER have been made 3 days ago. There needed to be some "tough" love in order to get it done. Great for everybody. Proud of all!

1:13 pm: This is a great day for civilization. I am proud of the United States for sticking by me in following a necessary, but somewhat unconventional, path. People have been trying to make this "Deal" for many years. Millions of lives will be saved. Congratulations to ALL!

October 18, 2019

10:42 pm: Just spoke to President @RTErdogan of Turkey. He told me there was minor sniper and mortar fire that was quickly eliminated. He very much wants the ceasefire, or pause, to work. Likewise, the Kurds want it, and the ultimate solution, to happen. Too bad there wasn't…

…this thinking years ago. Instead, it was always held together with very weak bandaids, & in an artificial manner. There is good will on both sides & a really good chance for success. The U.S. has secured the Oil, & the ISIS Fighters are double secured by Kurds & Turkey…

...I have just been notified that some European Nations are now willing, for the first time, to take the ISIS Fighters that came from their nations. This is good news, but should have been done after WE captured them. Anyway, big progress being made!!!!

6:25 pm: Think of how many lives we saved in Syria and Turkey by getting a ceasefire yesterday. Thousands and thousands, and maybe many more!

October 20, 2019

10:03 am: "The ceasefire is holding up very nicely. There are some minor skirmishes that have ended quickly. New areas being resettled with Kurds. U.S. soldiers are not in combat or ceasefire zone. We have secured the Oil." Mark Esper, Secretary of Defense. Ending endless wars!

3:20 pm: Pelosi is now leading a delegation of 9, including Corrupt Adam Schiff, to Jordan to check out Syria. She should find out why Obama drew The Red Line In the Sand, & then did NOTHING, losing Syria & all respect. I did something, 58 missiles. One million died under Obama's mistake!

October 22, 2019

5:18 pm: Good news seems to be happening with respect to Turkey, Syria and the Middle East. Further reports to come later!

7:39 am: Big success on the Turkey/Syria Border. Safe Zone created! Ceasefire has held and combat missions have ended. Kurds are safe and have worked very nicely with us. Captured ISIS prisoners secured. I will be making a statement at 11:00 A.M. from the White House. Thank you!

October 24, 2019

10:25 am: The Oil Fields discussed in my speech on Turkey/Kurds yesterday were held by ISIS until the United States took them over with the help of the Kurds. We will NEVER let a reconstituted ISIS have those fields!

October 25, 2019

7:32 am: Turkey fully understands not to fire on the Kurds as they leave what will be known as the Safe Zone for other fairly nearby areas. I don't have to repeat that large scale Sanctions will be imposed for violations. Going well! ISIS secured by Kurds with Turkey ready as backup.

...USA has gained Trillions of Dollars in wealth since November 2016. All others way down. Our power is Economic before having to use our newly rebuilt Military, a much better alternative. Oil is secured. Our soldiers have left and are leaving Syria for other places, then...

..COMING HOME! We were supposed to be there for 30 days—That was 10 years ago. When these pundit fools who have called the Middle East wrong for 20 years ask what we are getting out of the deal, I simply say, THE OIL, AND WE ARE BRINGING OUR SOLDIERS BACK HOME, ISIS SECURED!

October 26, 2019

8:23 pm: Something very big has just happened!

October 28, 2019

3:02 pm: We have declassified a picture of the wonderful dog (name not declassified) that did such a GREAT JOB in capturing and killing the Leader of ISIS, Abu Bakr al-Baghdadi!

4:22 pm: Can you believe that Shifty Adam Schiff, the biggest leaker in D.C., and a corrupt politician, is upset that we didn't inform him before we raided and killed the #1 terrorist in the WORLD!? Wouldn't be surprised if the Do Nothing Democrats Impeach me over that! DRAIN THE SWAMP!!

11:06 pm: "This is a big win for America, and also for President Trump." @nypost

October 29, 2019

8:29 am: Just confirmed that Abu Bakr al-Baghdadi's number one replacement has been terminated by American troops. Most likely would have taken the top spot—Now he is also Dead!

November 5, 2019

12:00 pm: A very good start! Please all work hard to get a final deal. https://t.co/IYGeBqQIQ9

November 6, 2019

3:15 pm: Just had a very good call with President @RTErdogan of Turkey. He informed me that they have captured numerous ISIS fighters that were reported to have escaped during the conflict—including a wife and sister of terrorist killer al Baghdadi...

...Also talked about their Border with Syria, the eradication of terrorism, the ending of hostilities with the Kurds, and many other topics. Look forward to seeing President Erdogan next Wednesday, November 13th at the @WhiteHouse!

November 10, 2019

9:25 pm: If Iran is able to turn over to the U.S. kidnapped former FBI Agent Robert A. Levinson, who has been missing in Iran for 12 years, it would be a very positive step. At the same time, upon information & belief, Iran is, & has been, enriching uranium. THAT WOULD BE A VERY BAD STEP!

November 21, 2019

12:54 pm: Iran has become so unstable that the regime has shut down their entire Internet System so that the Great Iranian people cannot talk about the tremendous violence taking place within the country...

...They want ZERO transparency, thinking the world will not find out the death and tragedy that the Iranian Regime is causing!

December 3, 2019

10:33 am: The United States of America supports the brave people of Iran who are protesting for their FREEDOM. We have under the Trump Administration, and always will!

December 6, 2019

2:18 pm: King Salman of Saudi Arabia just called to express his sincere condolences and give his sympathies to the families and friends of the warriors who were killed and wounded in the attack that took place in Pensacola, Florida…

…The King said that the Saudi people are greatly angered by the barbaric actions of the shooter, and that this person in no way shape or form represents the feelings of the Saudi people who love the American people.

December 7, 2019

12:32 pm: Taken during the Obama Administration (despite $150 Billion gift), returned during the Trump Administration. Thank you to Iran on a very fair negotiation. See, we can make a deal together!

1:51 pm: The United States will not rest until we bring every American wrongfully detained in Iran and around the world back home to their loved ones!

December 26, 2019

10:25 am: Russia, Syria, and Iran are killing, or on their way to killing, thousands of innocent civilians in Idlib Province. Don't do it! Turkey is working hard to stop this carnage.

December 31, 2019

7:02 am: Iran killed an American contractor, wounding many. We strongly responded, and always will. Now Iran is orchestrating an attack on the U.S. Embassy in Iraq. They will be held fully responsible.

In addition, we expect Iraq to use its forces to protect the Embassy, and so notified!

10:44 am: To those many millions of people in Iraq who want freedom and who don't want to be dominated and controlled by Iran, this is your time!

4:19 pm: The U.S. Embassy in Iraq is, & has been for hours, SAFE! Many of our great Warfighters, together with the most lethal military equipment in the world, was immediately rushed to the site. Thank you to the President & Prime Minister of Iraq for their rapid response upon request...

...Iran will be held fully responsible for lives lost, or damage incurred, at any of our facilities. They will pay a very BIG PRICE! This is not a Warning, it is a Threat. Happy New Year!

4:38 pm: The Anti-Benghazi!

6:19 pm: Wonderful account of U.S. Embassy (Iraq) vs. the Benghazi disaster! https://t.co/qDQtgkjr1S

NATO/Allies/Europe—2017 News Quotes

Response to a question from Tucker Carlson of FOX News, March 15, 2017.
Source: https://www.youtube.com/watch?v=RYGH6ejacN0

"Well, it's not easy and it certainly has not been easy. You look at Germany. You know, I took a lot of heat over Sweden. And then the next day, they have this massive riot, now nobody talks about it. It certainly has not proven to be easy. At the same time—Well, they've been trying, and we'll let you know. The assimilation has been very, very hard. It's been a very, very difficult process.

"I want this country to be safe. I want this country to be great. It's called make America great again. That's why I got elected. I want people that love our country and many Muslims do. Many, many Muslims do. But it has been a hard process.

"If you look at Germany, what's happened. If you look at Sweden, what's happened. If you look at Brussels, take a look at Brussels. I mean, look what's going on. Take a look at so many other places. It has been a very hard process. We are going to try very, very hard to make it work."

Response to a question from Maggie Haberman of *The New York Times*, July 19, 2017.
Source: https://www.nytimes.com/2017/07/19/us/politics/trump-interview-transcript.html

"I have had the best reviews on foreign land. So, I go to Poland and make a speech. Enemies of mine in the media, enemies of mine are saying it was the greatest speech ever made on foreign soil by a President. I'm saying, man, they cover [garbled]. You saw the reviews I got on that speech. Poland was beautiful and wonderful, and the reception was incredible."

Response to a question from Maggie Haberman of *The New York Times*, July 19, 2017.
Source: https://www.nytimes.com/2017/07/19/us/politics/trump-interview-transcript.html

"He [Emmanuel Macron, President of France] called me and said, 'I'd love to have you there and honor you in France,' having to do with Bastille Day. Plus, it's the 100th year of the First World War. That's big. And I said yes. I mean, I have a great relationship with him. He's a great guy."

Response to a question from Maggie Haberman of *The New York Times*, July 19, 2017.
Source: https://www.nytimes.com/2017/07/19/us/politics/trump-interview-transcript.html

"He's [Emmanuel Macron, President of France] a great guy. Smart. Strong. Loves holding my hand."

Response to a question from Maggie Haberman of *The New York Times*, July 19, 2017.
Source: https://www.nytimes.com/2017/07/19/us/politics/trump-interview-transcript.html

"People don't realize he [Emmanuel Macron, President of France] loves holding my hand. And that's good, as far as that goes. I mean, really. He's a very good person. And a tough guy, but look, he has to be. I think he is going to be a terrific president of France. But he does love holding my hand."

Response to a question from Maggie Haberman of *The New York Times*, July 19, 2017.
Source: https://www.nytimes.com/2017/07/19/us/politics/trump-interview-transcript.html

"What was interesting—So, when [Emmanuel Macron, President of France] asked, I said, 'Do you think it's a good thing for me to go to

Paris? I just ended the Paris Accord last week. Is this a good thing?' He said, 'They love you in France.' I said, 'OK, I just don't want to hurt you.'

"We had dinner at the Eiffel Tower, and the bottom of the Eiffel Tower looked like they could have never had a bigger celebration ever in the history of the Eiffel Tower. I mean, there were thousands and thousands of people, 'cause they heard we were having dinner."

Remarks before a meeting with President Sauli Niinistö of Finland, August 28, 2017.

Source: https://www.whitehouse.gov/briefings-statements/
remarks-president-trump-president-niinisto-finland-bilateral-meeting/

"It's my honor to have President [Sauli] Niinistö of Finland, a country that we have had a wonderful relationship. We're working with them very strongly right now. We have trading relationships. Sadly, they have a trade surplus against the United States, but maybe we can do something to change that.

"But it's a great honor to have you. Your country has done very well. It's doing extremely well under your leadership. And an honor to have you at the Oval Office."

Remarks before a bilateral meeting with Greek Prime Minister Alexis Tsipras, October 17, 2017.

Source: https://www.whitehouse.gov/briefings-statements/
remarks-president-trump-prime-minister-tsipras-greece-bilateral-meeting/

"It's an honor to have Prime Minister [Alexis] Tsipras of Greece with us.

"As you know, Greece has gone through a lot over the last number of years, but they are doing a terrific job of coming back. And they will be back. We're working with them on many different things. They're upgrading their fleets of airplanes. The F-16 plane, which is a terrific plane. They're doing big upgrades. And we're doing trade with Greece, and we're going to have some meetings right after this.

"We're having meetings with the staff. We're having a luncheon with the staff also. And we'll be talking about additional ways where Greece

will help us, and we will help Greece. But we've had a long-time relationship with Greece. They have been great friends and loyal friends
and allies."

Remarks at a working luncheon with Greek Prime Minister Alexis Tsip-ras, October 17, 2017.

Source: https://www.whitehouse.gov/briefings-statements/
remarks-president-trump-prime-minister-tsipras-greece-working-luncheon/

"Mr. Prime Minister [Alexis Tsipras of Greece], it's great to have you
in the United States. This is the Cabinet Room, a very well-known
place. A lot of things happen here.

"And we will continue our discussions with respect to Greece and the
relationship that we have. It's been an outstanding one, a long-term
relationship. You've gone through a lot.

"I commend you on what you've been able to do in a short period of
time. I know your tourism is coming back very strongly. You had a
record number of tourists, which we have to give you a lot of credit for
that. But it's a beautiful place. Many, many friends from Greece. And
we are with you. We are with you."

Response to a question from Laura Ingraham of FOX News, November 2, 2017.

Source: https://www.youtube.com/watch?v=yTdDH-o_ICM

"Look they're [Japan is] an ally. They're an ally. The Prime Minister is a
very good friend of mine. Prime Minister [Shinzō] Abe—I've become
very close."

From the Proclamation of November 9, 2017 as World Freedom Day.

Source: https://www.whitehouse.gov/presidential-actions/
president-donald-j-trump-proclaims-november-9-2017-world-freedom-day/

"For 28 years, the Berlin Wall divided families, friends, and communities, barricading oppressed Germans living on the Eastern side from
seeking the freedom they deserved in the West. This World Freedom
Day, 28 years after the fall of the Berlin Wall, we celebrate the day

on November 9, 1989, when people of East and West Germany tore down the Berlin Wall and freedom triumphed over Communism. We laud the courage of all people who insist on a better future for themselves, their families, and their country, as we reflect on the state of freedom in our world today and those who have made the ultimate sacrifice defending it.

"The fall of the Berlin Wall spurred the reunification of Germany and the spread of democratic values across Central and Eastern Europe. Through democratic elections, and a strong commitment to human rights, these determined men and women ensured that their fellow and future citizens could live their lives in freedom. Today, we are reminded that the primary function of government is precisely this, to secure precious individual liberties.

"While we live in a time of unprecedented freedom, terrorism and extremism around the world continue to threaten us. The ultimate triumph of freedom, peace, and security over repressive totalitarianism depends on our ability to work side-by-side with our friends and allies. When nations work together, we have and we will secure and advance freedom and stability throughout our world.

"On World Freedom Day, we recommit to the advancement of freedom over the forces of repression and radicalism. We continue to make clear that oppressive regimes should trust their people and grant their citizens the liberty they deserve. The world will be better for it.

"NOW, THEREFORE, I, DONALD J. TRUMP, President of the United States of America, by virtue of the authority vested in me by the Constitution and the laws of the United States, do hereby proclaim November 9, 2017, as World Freedom Day. I call upon the people of the United States to observe this day with appropriate ceremonies and activities, reaffirming our dedication to freedom and democracy."

NATO/Allies/Europe—2017 Tweets

March 18, 2017

8:15 am to 8:23 am: Despite what you have heard from the FAKE NEWS, I had a GREAT meeting with German Chancellor Angela Merkel. Nevertheless, Germany owes…

…vast sums of money to NATO & the United States must be paid more for the powerful, and very expensive, defense it provides to Germany!

April 12, 2017

4:48 pm: Great meeting w/ NATO Sec. Gen. We agreed on the importance of getting countries to pay their fair share & focus on the threat of terrorism.

May 23, 2017

7:04 am: We stand in absolute solidarity with the people of the United Kingdom. https://t.co/X6fUUxxYXE

May 25, 2017

12:54 pm: Today's ceremony is a day for both remembrance and resolve. #NATOMeeting #NATO https://t.co/YNZV3bTekB

May 26, 2017

5:13 am: Just arrived in Italy for the G7. Trip has been very successful. We made and saved the USA many billions of dollars and millions of jobs.

May 27, 2017

5:03 am: Many NATO countries have agreed to step up payments considerably, as they should. Money is beginning to pour in-NATO will be much stronger

7:17 am: I will make my final decision on the Paris Accord next week!

11:16 am to 11:17 am: Just left the #G7Summit. Had great meetings on everything, especially on trade where…

…"we push for the removal of all trade-distorting practices…to foster a truly level playing field."

May 30, 2017

5:40 am: We have a MASSIVE trade deficit with Germany, plus they pay FAR LESS than they should on NATO & military. Very bad for U.S. This will change

June 3, 2017

6:24 pm: Whatever the United States can do to help out in London and the U. K., we will be there—WE ARE WITH YOU. GOD BLESS!

July 3, 2017

6:00 am: Will be speaking with Germany and France this morning.

6:38 am: Will be speaking with Italy this morning!

July 6, 2017

11:02 am: America is proud to stand shoulder-to-shoulder with Poland in the fight to eradicate the evils of terrorism and extremism. #POTUSinPoland

12:21 pm: THE WEST WILL NEVER BE BROKEN. Our values will PREVAIL. Our people will THRIVE and our civilization will TRIUMPH!

3:45 pm: A strong Poland is a blessing to the nations of Europe, and a strong Europe is a blessing to the West, and to the world.

July 7, 2017

2:07 am: After Poland had a great meeting with Chancellor Merkel and then with PM Shinzō Abe of Japan & President Moon of South Korea.

July 13, 2017

1:45 pm: President @EmmanuelMacron, Thank you for the beautiful welcome ceremony at Les Invalides today!

2:20 pm: Great bilateral meetings at Élysée Palace w/ President @ EmmanuelMacron. The friendship between our two nations and ourselves is unbreakable.

July 14, 2017

8:39 am: The United States mourns for the victims of Nice, France. We pledge our solidarity with France against terror.

8:47 am: Great conversations with President @EmmanuelMacron and his representatives on trade, military and security.

5:39 pm: President @EmmanuelMacron, Thank you for inviting Melania and myself to such a historic celebration in France. #BastilleDay #14juillet

July 25, 2017

7:19 am: Working on major Trade Deal with the United Kingdom. Could be very big & exciting. JOBS! The E.U. is very protectionist with the U.S. STOP!

September 17, 2017

10:01 pm: It was a great honor to be with President @Emmanuel-Macron of France this afternoon with his delegation. Great bilateral meeting! #UNGA

September 26, 2017

5:43 pm: It was an honor to welcome President @MarianoraJoy of Spain. Thank you for standing w/ us in our efforts to isolate the brutal #NoKo regime.

November 29, 2017

7:43 pm: Theresa @theresamay, don't focus on me, focus on the destructive Radical Islamic Terrorism that is taking place within the United Kingdom. We are doing just fine!

NATO/Allies/Europe—2018 News Quotes

Remarks before a bilateral meeting with Prime Minister Erna Solberg of Norway, January 10, 2018.

Source: https://www.whitehouse.gov/briefings-statements/
remarks-president-trump-prime-minister-solberg-norway-bilateral-meeting/

"It's a great honor to have Prime Minister [Erna] Solberg of Norway. Just had a very resounding election victory, so it's another four years at least. And very respected by her country. Very liked by her country. We do a lot of business with Norway, and I know you just bought some additional military equipment in the form of F-35s and other things, and so I congratulate you. We make the best in the world, we make. And Norway is a great customer and a great ally, and a great friend."

Remarks as part of a joint press statement with then-President Nursultan Nazarbayev[16] of Kazakhstan, January 16, 2018.

Source: https://www.whitehouse.gov/briefings-statements/
remarks-president-trump-president-nursultan-nazarbayev-kazakhstan-joint-press-statements/

"Thank you. And I'm pleased to welcome President [Nursultan] Nazarbayev who has done a tremendous job in Kazakhstan. And having you at the White House is an honor. Mr. President, thank you for visiting with us, and we have very important discussions going on.

"For more than a quarter century, the United States has seen the strong, sovereign, and independent nation of Kazakhstan as a valued friend and a strategic partner in Central Asia. And we're honored, and we are truly honored to be the first country to recognize Kazakhstani independence on Christmas Day 1991. That's a long time ago, but not that long. You've made incredible strides.

"Since that time, the United States and Kazakhstan have worked together to advance peace and security in the region and far beyond the region.

"Together, we dismantled Kazakhstan's nuclear weapons infrastructure and ensured a safer and healthier future for the children of Kazakhstan and for the world at large. We've pursued opportunities to increase investment in Kazakhstan and the energy sector in particular.

"And today, our strategic partnership with Kazakhstan has advanced my South Asia strategy, which is working, and working far more rapidly than anybody would understand, and providing crucial support for our forces in Afghanistan and denying safe haven for terrorists.

"This cooperation has grown even stronger this month during Kazakhstan's presidency of the United Nations Security Council. And I will say, that's a great honor.

"Today, the President and I have a series of discussions on how our relationship can further the safety, prosperity, and wellbeing of our

---

16   Nazarbayev resigned in 2019 after nearly 30 years in office.
     Source: https://www.reuters.com/article/us-kazakhstan-president/
     president-of-kazakhstan-nursultan-nazarbayev-resigns-idUSKCN1R01N1

people. Kazakhstan is a valued partner in our efforts to rid the Korean Peninsula of nuclear weapons. Together, we are determined to prevent the North Korean regime from threatening the world with nuclear devastation.

"I also want to thank the President for his full support for our South Asia strategy, including our efforts in Afghanistan. I greatly appreciate the President's personal assurances that Kazakhstan will continue to provide critical logistical support and access for our troops fighting ISIS and the Taliban, where we have made tremendous strides.

"We also appreciate Kazakhstan's work to train and educate Afghan civilian specialists, and I'm grateful for the President's pledge of additional support to bolster Afghan security. The United States seeks partners who are strong, prosperous, respectful of their neighbors, and in control of their own destinies.

"I'm pleased that the President has shared his plan for Kazakhstan to become a top 30 global economy by 2015, and he's on his way, very rapidly. He's also working to improve Kazakhstan's business environment, which will create new opportunities for American companies who are over there, and lots of jobs are being provided to both countries.

"American businesses are currently among the largest investors in Kazakhstan. And tonight, the President will attend a roundtable with American business executives at the U.S. Chamber of Commerce to further advance our commercial ties.

"We also agree that fair and reciprocal, such an important word: 'reciprocal,' trade benefits both of our countries.

"I greatly appreciate Kazakhstan's participation in our Central Asia Trade Forum and in our Central Asia Trade and Investment Framework Agreement. The President and I are working together to bring high-quality U.S. products and services to the Kazakhstani people, so important. And it's really happening, and it's happening rapidly all across a range of industries, including commercial aircraft, railways, medical services, technology, and energy.

"Working in common cause, we can advance greater opportunity for citizens in both of our countries. Mr. President, thank you for visiting the White House today. Our nations have a long history of cooperation to promote a safer, healthier, more prosperous, and brighter tomorrow. I look forward to seeing the great advances of the Kazakhstani people under your incredible leadership. And that's what it is, it's incredible leadership.

"We want a strong, sovereign, and thriving future for Kazakhstan and for the peace-loving nations of the world, all of them."

Remarks after a bilateral meeting with then-Prime Minister Theresa May[17] of the United Kingdom, January 25, 2018.

Source: https://www.whitehouse.gov/briefings-statements/remarks-president-trump-prime-minister-may-united-kingdom-bilateral-meeting-davos-switzerland/

"It's an honor to be with Prime Minister [Theresa] May [of the United Kingdom]. We've had a great discussion. We're on the same wavelength in, I think, every respect.

"The Prime Minister and myself have had a really great relationship, although some people don't necessarily believe that. But I can tell you it's true. I have tremendous respect for the Prime Minister and the job she's doing.

"And I think the feeling is mutual from the standpoint of liking each other a lot. And so that was a little bit of a false rumor out there. I just wanted to correct it, frankly, because we have great respect for everything you're doing. And we love your country because it's truly great.

"And we're working on transactions, in terms of economic development, trade, maybe most importantly, military. And we are very much joined at the hip when it comes to the military. We have the same ideas, the same ideals, and there's nothing that would happen to you that we won't be there to fight for you. You know that."

---

17   May resigned in 2019. Source: https://www.nytimes.com/2019/05/24/world/europe/theresa-may-resignation.html

Remarks after a bilateral meeting with then-Prime Minister Theresa May[18] of the United Kingdom, January 25, 2018.

Source: https://www.whitehouse.gov/briefings-statements/remarks-president-trump-prime-minister-may-united-kingdom-bilateral-meeting-davos-switzerland/

"One thing that will be taking place over a number of years will be trade. The trade is going to increase many times, and we look forward to that. But the trade concepts and discussions—And the discussions, really, I think can say, most importantly that will be taking place are going to lead to tremendous increases in trade between our two countries, which is great for both in terms of jobs.

"And we look forward to that, and we are starting that process pretty much as we speak."

Response to a question from Piers Morgan of ITV, January 29, 2018.

Source: https://www.theguardian.com/us-news/2018/jan/29/donald-trump-interview-piers-morgan-im-very-popular-in-britain-get-a-lot-of-fan-mail

"I get so much fan mail from people in your country [the United Kingdom]. They love my sense of security; they love what I'm saying about many different things. We get tremendous support from people in the UK."

Response to a question from Piers Morgan of ITV, January 29, 2018.

Source: https://www.theguardian.com/us-news/2018/jan/29/donald-trump-interview-piers-morgan-im-very-popular-in-britain-get-a-lot-of-fan-mail

"The real me is somebody that loves Britain, loves the UK. I love Scotland. One of the biggest problems I have in winning, I won't be able to get back there so often. I would love to go there."

Response to a question from Piers Morgan of ITV, January 29, 2018.

Source: https://www.theguardian.com/us-news/2018/jan/29/donald-trump-interview-piers-morgan-im-very-popular-in-britain-get-a-lot-of-fan-mail

"He's [President Emmanuel Macron of France is] a great guy. His wife is fantastic. I like them a lot. You know, we had dinner at the top of the Eiffel Tower, and everything was closed."

---

18   May resigned in 2019. Source: https://www.nytimes.com/2019/05/24/world/europe/theresa-may-resignation.html

Remarks before a bilateral meeting with then-Prime Minister Malcolm Turnbull[19] of Australia, February 23, 2018.

Source: https://www.whitehouse.gov/briefings-statements/
remarks-president-trump-prime-minister-turnbull-australia-bilateral-meeting/

"It's an honor to have [Australian] Prime Minister [Malcolm] Turnbull, Mrs. Turnbull, friends of mine and friends of Melania for, actually, quite some time.

"The relationship we have with Australia is a terrific relationship, and probably stronger now than ever before. Maybe because of our relationship, our friendship. But we're working on trade deals, we're working on military and protection, and all of the things that you would think we would be discussing today.

"We have a big meeting set up in a little while, and we have a luncheon set up, also. And we have all of our representatives surrounding us and a lot of good things will come out of this visit."

Remarks before a bilateral meeting with Prime Minister Benjamin Netanyahu of Israel, March 5, 2018.

Source: https://www.whitehouse.gov/briefings-statements/
remarks-president-trump-prime-minister-netanyahu-israel-bilateral-meeting-2/

"It's a great honor to have Prime Minister [Benjamin] Netanyahu [of Israel] and Mrs. Netanyahu with us. They've been friends for a long time. We have, I would say, probably the best relationships right now with Israel that we ever had. I think we're as close now as, maybe, ever before.

"Jerusalem was a wonderful thing, and I know it was very much appreciated in a big part of the world, not just in Israel—In a very big part. So that was a decision that I had to make. Many presidents were discussing whether or not to make that decision, and they promised it in their campaigns, but they never were able to do what they should have done. So, I was able to do it, and I think it's something that's very much appreciated in Israel, but far beyond Israel.

---

19 Turnbull resigned in 2018. Source: https://www.aljazeera.com/news/2018/08/
pm-malcolm-turnbull-resigns-australian-parliament-180831080258361.html

"We are very close on trade deals. We are very, very close on military and terrorism and all of the things that we have to work together on.

"So, the relationship has never been better. And, Mr. Prime Minister and Mrs. Netanyahu, it's a great honor to have you."

Remarks before a bilateral meeting with Prime Minister Benjamin Netanyahu of Israel, March 5, 2018.
Source: https://www.whitehouse.gov/briefings-statements/
remarks-president-trump-prime-minister-netanyahu-israel-bilateral-meeting-2/

"Israel is very special to me. Special country. Special people. And I look forward to being there, and I'm very proud of that decision."

Response to a question from an unidentified reporter before a bilateral meeting with Prime Minister Benjamin Netanyahu of Israel, March 5, 2018.
Source: https://www.whitehouse.gov/briefings-statements/
remarks-president-trump-prime-minister-netanyahu-israel-bilateral-meeting-2/

"We're working on it very hard, and we'd like to—Look, it would be a great achievement, and even from a humanitarian standpoint, what better if we could make peace between Israel and the Palestinians? And I can tell you, we're working very hard on doing that. And I think we have a very good chance.

"And the biggest difficulty that anybody has had, you look over 25 years, nobody could get past number one: Jerusalem. They couldn't get past it. We've taken it off the table. So, this gives us a real opportunity to peace. We'll see how it works out. The Palestinians, I think, are wanting to come back to the table very badly."

Response to a question from an unidentified reporter before a bilateral meeting with Prime Minister Benjamin Netanyahu of Israel, March 5, 2018.
Source: https://www.whitehouse.gov/briefings-statements/
remarks-president-trump-prime-minister-netanyahu-israel-bilateral-meeting-2/

"If they [the Palestinians] don't, you don't have peace, and that's a possibility also. I'm not saying it's going to happen. Everybody said this is the hardest deal to make of any deal. Whenever you have a hard deal, like in business, you say, 'Oh, this is almost as bad as Israel and the Palestinians.' You use it like as an example.

"This is the hardest deal. This is years and years of opposition and, frankly, hatred, and a lot of things involved in this deal beyond the land. And I will tell you that if we could do, if we could do peace between Israel and the Palestinians, that would be a great thing for the world. It would be a great thing for this country and for everybody.

"So, we're working very hard on it, and we have a shot at doing it."

Remarks before a bilateral meeting with Prime Minister Stefan Löfven of Sweden, March 6, 2018.

Source: https://www.whitehouse.gov/briefings-statements/
remarks-president-trump-prime-minister-lofven-sweden-bilateral-meeting/

"It's a great honor to have Prime Minister [Stefan] Löfven [of Sweden] with us. He's a highly respected man and done a great job in Sweden. They are doing, really, record numbers, I guess very much like we're doing record numbers.

"We've had a tremendous run in the United States. We're doing well, and we work well together. Our relationship is a very strong one. We have trade deals; we have military deals. We have—We are working very closely with respect to terrorism and many other things."

Response to a question from an unidentified reporter before a bilateral meeting with Prime Minister Stefan Löfven of Sweden, March 6, 2018.

Source: https://www.whitehouse.gov/briefings-statements/
remarks-president-trump-prime-minister-lofven-sweden-bilateral-meeting/

"Great country, great ally. They've [Sweden has] been with us for a long time. In fact, I think we're together for about 200 years, to be exact. This is an anniversary.

"But we've had very special relationships for many, many years. Two hundred, to be exact. So, it's very important."

Response to a question from an unidentified reporter before a bilateral meeting with Prime Minister Stefan Löfven of Sweden, March 6, 2018.

Source: https://www.whitehouse.gov/briefings-statements/
remarks-president-trump-prime-minister-lofven-sweden-bilateral-meeting/

"Sweden will always be helpful. Sweden has been helpful in the past. They were very helpful, recently, with respect to something else. They are a great friend and a very competent friend."

Remarks before a bilateral meeting with Prime Minister Leo Varadkar of Ireland, March 15, 2018.

Source: https://www.whitehouse.gov/briefings-statements/
remarks-president-trump-prime-minister-varadkar-ireland-bilateral-meeting/

"It's my great honor to have the very popular Prime Minister [Leo Varadkar] of Ireland with us. And we're having some good talks about trade and about military and about cyber and all of the other things that we're talking about. The relationship is outstanding and only getting better."

Remarks at State Dinner at the White House with President Emmanuel Macron of France, April 25, 2018.

Source: https://www.whitehouse.gov/briefings-statements/
remarks-president-trump-president-macron-france-state-dinner/

"[French] President [Emmanuel] Macron, Brigitte [Macron], Melania and I are profoundly honored to host you and your entire French delegation for our first official State Dinner. And to America's absolutely incredible First Lady, thank you for making this an evening we will always cherish and remember. Thank you, Melania.

"Tonight, we celebrate nearly two-and-half centuries of friendship between the United States and France."

Remarks at State Dinner at the White House with President Emmanuel Macron of France, April 25, 2018.

Source: https://www.whitehouse.gov/briefings-statements/
remarks-president-trump-president-macron-france-state-dinner/

"So tonight, I ask that we raise our glasses as I offer this toast to President [Emmanuel] Macron and Brigitte, to the French delegation, and to every proud citizen of France. May our friendship grow even deeper, may our kinship grow even stronger, and may our sacred liberty never die.

"God bless you. God bless France. God bless our alliance. And God bless America."

Remarks before a bilateral meeting with President Shavkat Mirziyoyev of Uzbekistan, May 16, 2018.
Source: https://www.whitehouse.gov/briefings-statements/
remarks-president-trump-president-mirziyoyev-uzbekistan-bilateral-meeting/

"It's a great honor to have the President of Uzbekistan [Shavkat Mirziyoyev] with us. He's a highly respected man in his country and throughout. We've been working very closely together on different things, including trade. They've actually made investments here. We make investments there.

"We're working together from the standpoint of the military, including his purchase of equipment and military equipment from the United States."

Remarks before a bilateral meeting with Prime Minister Justin Trudeau of Canada, June 8, 2018.
Source: https://www.whitehouse.gov/briefings-statements/
remarks-president-trump-prime-minister-trudeau-canada-bilateral-meeting/

"But our [Canada and the United States'] relationship is very good. We are actually working on cutting tariffs and making it all very fair for both countries. And we've made a lot of progress today. We'll see how it all works out. But we've made a lot of progress.

"It could be that NAFTA will be a different form. It could be with Canada, with Mexico, one-on-one. A much simpler agreement. Much easier to do. I think better for both countries. But we're talking about that, among other things.

"But the relationship is probably better—As good or better than it's ever been. And I think we'll get to something very beneficial to Canada and to the United States."

Response to a question from Bret Baier of FOX News, June 12, 2018.
Source: https://www.youtube.com/watch?v=zogD8bnGJu4

"And a reporter asked me, 'Do you think you would be better off with Russia?' And I said, 'Absolutely.' You know, we spend probably 25% of our time talking about Russia. I said to myself, 'Wouldn't it be better if they were here?' Now, I'm not for Russia. I'm for the United States. But as an example, if Vladimir Putin [President of Russia] were sitting next to me today instead of one of the others and we were having dinner the other night in Canada I could say, 'Would you do me a favor? Would you get out of Syria? Would you do me a favor? Would you get out of Ukraine? Get out of Ukraine, you should be there. Just come on.' Now, I think I'd probably have a good relationship with him, or I'd be able to talk to him better than if you call somebody on the telephone and talk. If I'm sitting like I was with the others—For instance the new Prime Minister of Italy [Giuseppe Conte]. He is a great guy. We had a great relationship. He agrees with me on Putin, by the way, I have to tell you."

Response to a question from Bret Baier of FOX News, June 12, 2018.
Source: https://www.youtube.com/watch?v=zogD8bnGJu4

"Yes, but he [Vladimir Putin, President of Russia] didn't—I'm not sticking up for anybody. I'm just saying this, he [Putin] didn't respect our leadership previously. He walked all over them. Look what he did to [former U.S. President Barack] Obama with Crimea. He [Putin] took Crimea. He took Ukraine, I mean sections of Ukraine—"

Response to a question from George Stephanopoulos of ABC News, June 12, 2018.
Source: https://abcnews.go.com/Politics/
president-trump-sits-george-stephanopoulos-transcript/story?id=55831055

"But here's what the story is: we have been taken advantage of as a country for decades by friends and enemies both. We have been, our trade is a disaster, our trade deals. We lose $817 billion was the last count on a yearly basis. Think of it, George [Stephanopoulos of ABC News]. In other words, when you add China and all of the other places, Germany, the European Union is a disaster for us. We lost $151 billion last year. Billion, not, not million. We lost $151 billion. They don't take our product. They won't take our agriculture. They won't. We lost a 151. Now they were at the meeting. The European Union. I can't be thrilled. I let 'em know. And I said, 'Fellas, we gotta change it. And if you don't change it, we're not going to do trading.'"

Remarks before a bilateral meeting with His Majesty King Felipe VI of Spain, June 19, 2018.
Source: https://www.whitehouse.gov/briefings-statements/
remarks-president-trump-majesty-king-felipe-vi-spain-bilateral-meeting/

"It's a great honor to have the King and Queen of Spain, a beautiful country. We were in Spain not so long ago, and we love it. Very special people and a beautiful place.

"And our relationship has been outstanding over the years and, I think, especially right now. Excellent trade relationship, military relationship. Just about everything you can have. So, we love Spain. And it's really a tremendous honor to have you both at the Oval Office."

Remarks at a rally in Tampa, Florida, July 31, 2018.
Source: https://www.tampabay.com/florida-politics/buzz/2018/08/01/
heres-a-full-transcript-of-president-trumps-speech-from-his-tampa-rally/

"And most importantly, America is being respected again. We're respected again.

"And I told the story the other day, I get to meet all these world leaders. Virtually everyone comes into the Oval Office or wherever we're meeting and they don't know me. I'm meeting them in many cases for the first time.

"I'm not sure they like me, like in the case of NATO. I said you got to pay your bills, folks, got to pay up, got to pay up.

"But they liked it, they liked it. But everyone that reached me says, 'Hello, Mr. President, congratulations on what you've done for the economy.' It's the talk of the world, talk of the world. Now that we have the best economy in the history of our country, this is the time to straighten out the worst trade deals ever made by any country on Earth, they are the worst.

"For decades, United States was the piggy bank that everybody was robbing. All of these other countries, our friends, our enemies, our allies—

"The foe, foe."

NATO/Allies/Europe—2018 Tweets

January 26, 2018

6:23 am: Great bilateral meeting with President @Alain_Berset of the Swiss Confederation—as we continue to strengthen our great friendship. Such an honor to be in Switzerland! #WEF18

March 9, 2018

5:48 pm: Spoke to PM @TurnbullMalcolm of Australia. He is committed to having a very fair and reciprocal military and trade relationship. Working very quickly on a security agreement so we don't have to impose steel or aluminum tariffs on our ally, the great nation of Australia!

March 14, 2018

8:29 am: We do have a Trade Deficit with Canada, as we do with almost all countries (some of them massive). P.M. Justin Trudeau of Canada, a very good guy, doesn't like saying that Canada has a Surplus vs. the U.S.(negotiating), but they do…they almost all do…and that's how I know!

April 12, 2018

10:15 pm: Would only join TPP if the deal were substantially better than the deal offered to Pres. Obama. We already have BILATERAL deals with six of the eleven nations in TPP, and are working to make a deal with the biggest of those nations, Japan, who has hit us hard on trade for years!

April 14, 2018

7:21 am: A perfectly executed strike last night. Thank you to France and the United Kingdom for their wisdom and the power of their fine Military. Could not have had a better result. Mission Accomplished!

April 19, 2018

9:45 am: Great meeting with Prime Minister Abe of Japan, who has just left Florida. Talked in depth about North Korea, Military and Trade. Good things will happen!

April 24, 2018

11:43 am: Having great meetings and discussions with my friend, President @EmmanuelMacron of France. We are in the midst of meetings on Iran, Syria and Trade. We will be holding a joint press conference shortly, here at the @WhiteHouse.

12:56 pm: Americans stand with you and all of Canada, Prime Minister @JustinTrudeau. Our thoughts and prayers are with you all. #TorontoStrong

April 27, 2018

8:28 am: Look forward to meeting with Chancellor Angela Merkel of Germany today. So much to discuss, so little time! It will be good for both of our great countries!

June 10, 2018

8:17 pm to 8:42 pm: Look forward to meeting with Chancellor Angela Merkel of Germany today. So much to discuss, so little time! It will be good for both of our great countries!

July 9, 2018

6:55 am: The United States is spending far more on NATO than any other Country. This is not fair, nor is it acceptable. While these countries have been increasing their contributions since I took office, they must do much more. Germany is at 1%, the U.S. is at 4%, and NATO benefits…

July 10, 2018

4:35 am: Getting ready to leave for Europe. First meeting—NATO. The U.S. is spending many times more than any other country in order to protect them. Not fair to the U.S. taxpayer. On top of that we lose $151 Billion on Trade with the European Union. Charge us big Tariffs (& Barriers)!

5:42 am: NATO countries must pay MORE, the United States must pay LESS. Very Unfair!

12:01 pm: Many countries in NATO, which we are expected to defend, are not only short of their current commitment of 2% (which is low), but are also delinquent for many years in payments that have not been made. Will they reimburse the U.S.?

1:52 pm: The European Union makes it impossible for our farmers and workers and companies to do business in Europe (U.S. has a $151 Billion trade deficit), and then they want us to happily defend them through NATO, and nicely pay for it. Just doesn't work!

July 11, 2018

7:40 am: I am in Brussels, but always thinking about our farmers. Soy beans fell 50% from 2012 to my election. Farmers have done poorly for

15 years. Other countries' trade barriers and tariffs have been destroying their businesses. I will open...

...things up, better than ever before, but it can't go too quickly. I am fighting for a level playing field for our farmers, and will win!

11:50 am: What good is NATO if Germany is paying Russia billions of dollars for gas and energy? Why are their only 5 out of 29 countries that have met their commitment? The U.S. is paying for Europe's protection, then loses billions on Trade. Must pay 2% of GDP IMMEDIATELY, not by 2025.

6:33 pm: Billions of additional dollars are being spent by NATO countries since my visit last year, at my request, but it isn't nearly enough. U.S. spends too much. Europe's borders are BAD! Pipeline dollars to Russia are not acceptable!

July 12, 2018

1:03 am: Presidents have been trying unsuccessfully for years to get Germany and other rich NATO Nations to pay more toward their protection from Russia. They pay only a fraction of their cost. The U.S. pays tens of Billions of Dollars too much to subsidize Europe, and loses Big on Trade!

1:12 am: ...On top of it all, Germany just started paying Russia, the country they want protection from, Billions of Dollars for their Energy needs coming out of a new pipeline from Russia. Not acceptable! All NATO Nations must meet their 2% commitment, and that must ultimately go to 4%

12:52 pm: Great success today at NATO! Billions of additional dollars paid by members since my election. Great spirit!

July 16, 2018

12:23 am: Received many calls from leaders of NATO countries thanking me for helping to bring them together and to get them focused on financial obligations, both present & future. We had a truly great

317

Summit that was inaccurately covered by much of the media. NATO is now strong & rich!

July 17, 2018

8:52 pm: I had a great meeting with NATO. They have paid $33 Billion more and will pay hundreds of Billions of Dollars more in the future, only because of me. NATO was weak, but now it is strong again (bad for Russia). The media only says I was rude to leaders, never mentions the money!

9:22 am: While I had a great meeting with NATO, raising vast amounts of money, I had an even better meeting with Vladimir Putin of Russia. Sadly, it is not being reported that way—the Fake News is going Crazy!

September 1, 2018

6:21 am: I love Canada, but they've taken advantage of our Country for many years!

September 23, 2018

5:48 pm: Prime Minster @AbeShinzo is coming up to Trump Tower for dinner but, most importantly, he just had a great landslide victory in Japan. I will congratulate him on behalf of the American people!

October 25, 2018

1:42 pm: Spoke with French President @EmmanuelMacron this morning. Discussed many topics including the very exciting upcoming visit to Paris where @FLOTUS Melania and I will attend the Armistice Day Centennial Commemoration!

November 11, 2018

9:52 am: Beautiful ceremony today in Paris commemorating the end of World War One. Many World leaders in attendance. Thank you to @EmmanuelMacron, President of France! Now off to Suresnes American Cemetery to make speech in honor of our great heroes! Then back to the U.S.A.

11:03 am: Poland, a great country—Congratulations on the 100th Anniversary of your Independence. I will never forget my time there!

11:38 pm: Exactly 100 years ago today, on November 11th, 1918, World War I came to an end. We are gathered together, at this hallowed resting place, to pay tribute to the brave Americans who gave their last breath in that mighty struggle...

December 24, 2018

9:59 am: .We are substantially subsidizing the Militaries of many VERY rich countries all over the world, while at the same time these countries take total advantage of the U.S., and our TAXPAYERS, on Trade. General Mattis did not see this as a problem. I DO, and it is being fixed!

NATO/Allies/Europe—2019 News Quotes

Remarks before a bilateral meeting with NATO Secretary General Jens Stoltenberg, April 2, 2019.

Source: https://www.whitehouse.gov/briefings-statements/
remarks-president-trump-nato-secretary-general-jens-stoltenberg-bilateral-meeting/

"We've worked together on getting some of our allies to pay their fair share. It's called burden sharing. And as you know, when I came, it wasn't so good, and now it's—They're catching up.

"We have 7 of the 28 countries are currently current and the rest are trying to catch up, and they will catch up. And some of them have no problems because they haven't been paying and they're very rich. But we're looking at the 2% of GDP level. And at some point, I think it's going to have to go higher than that. I think probably it should be higher. But we're at a level of 7 out of the 28.

"The United States pays for a very big share of NATO, a disproportionate share. But the relationship with NATO has been very good. The relationship with the Secretary General has been outstanding. And I think tremendous progress has been made.

"If you look, in fact, you showed me this originally, yourself, if you look at the charts and the different things, if you go back 10 and 15 years, and it's a roller coaster ride down, in terms of payment.

"And since I came to office, it's a rocket ship up. We've picked up over $140 billion of additional money, and we look like we're going to have at least another $100 billion more in spending by the nations, the 28 nations. We're going to have—And that's exclusive of the United States. We'll have another $100 billion more by 2020 or a little bit into 2020.

"So, tremendous progress has been made, and NATO is much stronger because of that progress."

Response to comments made by NATO Secretary General Jens Stoltenberg before their bilateral meeting, April 2, 2019.

Source: https://www.whitehouse.gov/briefings-statements/
remarks-president-trump-nato-secretary-general-jens-stoltenberg-bilateral-meeting/

"Well, thank you. And it has been an honor. And we're very proud of what's happened over the last couple of years with respect to the relationship and to NATO.

"A lot of the media doesn't understand what took place, but a tremendous amount of additional money was invested by other nations, which was a fair thing from the United States; you know, from our standpoint, the standpoint of the United States. And a lot more money will be invested.

"But we've been picking up a tremendous and disproportionate share, and we just want fairness. I have to have fairness for our taxpayer too. And I think that's what's happening, and I very much appreciate it."

Response to an unidentified reporter's question after Marine One arrival, September 1, 2019.

Source: https://www.whitehouse.gov/briefings-statements/
remarks-president-trump-marine-one-arrival-5/

"I do have a great message for Poland. And we have Mike Pence, our Vice President, is just about landing right now. And he is representing me. I look forward to being there soon.

"But I just want to congratulate Poland. It's a great country with great people. We also have many Polish people in our country; it could be 8 million. We love our Polish friends. And I will be there soon."

Remarks from video made on the White House lawn as published by *The Guardian*, November 3, 2019.

Source: https://www.theguardian.com/us-news/2019/nov/03/
trump-johnson-farage-come-together-general-election

"I like them both. I'm with—Look, I think [UK Prime Minister] Boris Johnson is the right man for the times. He's really for the times—He's a great gentleman, he's a wonderful guy. He's tough, he's smart, and I think he's going to do something.

"We're far and away the Number One economy in the world, and if you do it a certain way, we're prohibited from trading with the UK. That would be very bad for the UK, because we can do much more business than the European Union.

"So, I think Boris will get it right—They're both friends of mine. What I'd like to see is for [Brexit Party Leader] Nigel [Farage] and Boris to come together. I think that's a possibility."

Remarks before Marine One departure, December 2, 2019.

Source: https://www.whitehouse.gov/briefings-statements/
remarks-president-trump-marine-one-departure-78/

"So, I'm going to London, to NATO. We're fighting for the American people. It has not been a fair situation for us because we pay far too much. As you know, Secretary Stoltenberg said that we were responsible, I was responsible, for getting over $130 billion extra from other countries that we protect, that weren't paying. They were delinquent. So we'll be talking about that. We'll be talking about a lot of things.

"We are leading the world now on the economy, and we have been almost since I became President. But we're substantially ahead of anybody else; nobody is even close. You know that very well. And I look forward to having a number of very, very productive days for our country. We'll be working hard."

NATO/Allies/Europe—2019 Tweets

January 27, 2019

10:11 am: Jens Stoltenberg, NATO Secretary General, just stated that because of me NATO has been able to raise far more money than ever before from its members after many years of decline. It's called burden sharing. Also, more united. Dems & Fake News like to portray the opposite!

10:27 am: Thank you to Brit. This is a very big deal in Europe. Fake News is the Enemy of the People! https://t.co/WX0o8gaiMC

February 16, 2019

10:51 pm: The United States is asking Britain, France, Germany and other European allies to take back over 800 ISIS fighters that we captured in Syria and put them on trial. The Caliphate is ready to fall. The alternative is not a good one in that we will be forced to release them…

11:01 pm: …The U.S. does not want to watch as these ISIS fighters permeate Europe, which is where they are expected to go. We do so much, and spend so much—Time for others to step up and do the job that they are so capable of doing. We are pulling back after 100% Caliphate victory!

March 14, 2019

6:22 am: My Administration looks forward to negotiating a large scale Trade Deal with the United Kingdom. The potential is unlimited!

March 15, 2019

6:41 am: My warmest sympathy and best wishes goes out to the people of New Zealand after the horrible massacre in the Mosques. 49 innocent people have so senselessly died, with so many more seriously injured. The U.S. stands by New Zealand for anything we can do. God bless all!

2:14 pm: Just spoke with Jacinda Ardern, the Prime Minister of New Zealand, regarding the horrific events that have taken place over the past 24 hours. I informed the Prime Minister...

...that we stand in solidarity with New Zealand—and that any assistance the U.S.A. can give, we stand by ready to help. We love you New Zealand!

March 16, 2019

4:22 pm: How is the Paris Environmental Accord working out for France? After 18 weeks of rioting by the Yellow Vest Protesters, I guess not so well! In the meantime, the United States has gone to the top of all lists on the Environment.

April 2, 2019

2:59 pm: Today, it was my great honor to welcome @NATO Secretary General @JensStoltenberg to the @WhiteHouse! https://t.co/4drPHXZBWH

April 9, 2019

6:34 am: The World Trade Organization finds that the European Union subsidies to Airbus has adversely impacted the United States, which will now put Tariffs on $11 Billion of EU products! The EU has taken advantage of the U.S. on trade for many years. It will soon stop!

April 10, 2019

9:48 am: Trump flags being waived at the Bibi @Netanyahu VICTO-RY celebration last night! https://t.co/SX8RVAALYW

2:17 pm: Spoke to Bibi @Netanyahu to congratulate him on a great and hard-fought win. The United States is with him and the People of Israel all the way!

9:52 pm: Too bad that the European Union is being so tough on the United Kingdom and Brexit. The E.U. is likewise a brutal trading partner with the United States, which will change. Sometimes in life you have to let people breathe before it all comes back to bite you!

April 15, 2019

12:39 pm: So horrible to watch the massive fire at Notre Dame Cathedral in Paris. Perhaps flying water tankers could be used to put it out. Must act quickly!

4:58 pm: God bless the people of France!

April 17, 2019

11:14 am: Just had a wonderful conversation with @Pontifex Francis offering condolences from the People of the United States for the horrible and destructive fire at Notre Dame Cathedral. I offered the help of our great experts on renovation and construction as I did…

…in my conversation yesterday with President @EmmanuelMacron of France. I also wished both Pope Francis and President Macron a very Happy Easter!

April 22, 2019

1:26 pm: Spoke to the Prime Minister of Italy, Giuseppe Conte, mostly concerning Immigration, Taxes, Trade, and the Economy of both of our countries. Very good call!

April 23, 2019

6:04 am: "Harley Davidson has struggled with Tariffs with the EU, currently paying 31%. They've had to move production overseas to try and offset some of that Tariff that they've been hit with which will rise to 66% in June of 2021." @MariaBartiromo So unfair to U.S. We will Reciprocate!

April 27, 2019

5:14 pm: Great day with Prime Minister @AbeShinzo of Japan. We played a quick round of golf by the beautiful Potomac River while talking Trade and many other subjects. He has now left for Japan and I am on my way to Wisconsin where a very large crowd of friends await!

April 30, 2019

11:31 am: European countries are not helping at all, even though this was very much done for their benefit. They are refusing to take back prisoners from their specific countries. Not good!

May 5, 2019

7:13 pm: Once again, Israel faces a barrage of deadly rocket attacks by terrorist groups Hamas and Islamic Jihad. We support Israel 100% in its defense of its citizens…

To the Gazan people—these terrorist acts against Israel will bring you nothing but more misery. END the violence and work towards peace—it can happen!

May 6, 2019

8:51 am: Just spoke to Prime Minister Abe of Japan concerning North Korea and Trade. Very good conversation!

May 14, 2019

11:27 am: Today marks the one-year anniversary of the opening of the United States Embassy in Jerusalem, Israel. Our beautiful embassy stands as a proud reminder of our strong relationship with Israel and of the importance of keeping a promise and standing for the truth.

May 23, 2019

12:13 pm: Congratulations to Prime Minister @NarendraModi and his BJP party on their BIG election victory! Great things are in store for the US-India partnership with the return of PM Modi at the helm. I look forward to continuing our important work together!

May 25, 2019

11:07 pm: Great morning of golf with Prime Minister @AbeShinzo at Mobara Country Club in Chiba, Japan!

May 27, 2019

10:24 am: Hoping things will work out with Israel's coalition formation and Bibi and I can continue to make the alliance between America and Israel stronger than ever. A lot more to do!

June 3, 2019

2:51 am: .@SadiqKhan, who by all accounts has done a terrible job as Mayor of London, has been foolishly "nasty" to the visiting President of the United States, by far the most important ally of the United Kingdom. He is a stone cold loser who should focus on crime in London, not me...

...Kahn reminds me very much of our very dumb and incompetent Mayor of NYC, de Blasio, who has also done a terrible job—only half his height. In any event, I look forward to being a great friend to the United Kingdom, and am looking very much forward to my visit. Landing now!

12:41 pm: London part of trip is going really well. The Queen and the entire Royal family have been fantastic. The relationship with the United Kingdom is very strong. Tremendous crowds of well wishers and people that love our Country. Haven't seen any protests yet, but I'm sure the...

...Fake News will be working hard to find them. Great love all around. Also, big Trade Deal is possible once U.K. gets rid of the shackles. Already starting to talk!

June 5, 2019

3:02 am: Could not have been treated more warmly in the United Kingdom by the Royal Family or the people. Our relationship has never been better, and I see a very big Trade Deal down the road. "This trip has been an incredible success for the President." @IngrahamAngle

June 6, 2019

2:38 am: Heading over to Normandy to celebrate some of the bravest that ever lived. We are eternally grateful! #DDay75thAnniversary #DDay75

June 12, 2019

7:34 am: It was a pleasure to host my friends President Andrzej Duda and Mrs. Agata Kornhauser-Duda of Poland at the @WhiteHouse today. U.S.-Poland ties are at an all-time high. Thank you for being such an exemplary Ally!

June 15, 2019

1:47 pm: LONDON needs a new mayor ASAP. Khan is a disaster—will only get worse!

6:17 pm: He is a national disgrace who is destroying the City of London!

June 29, 2019

5:35 pm: I am in South Korea now. President Moon and I have "toasted" our new Trade Deal, a far better one for us than that which it replaced. Today I will visit with, and speak to, our Troops—and also go to the the DMZ (long planned). My meeting with President Moon went very well!

July 1, 2019

10:02 am: Congratulations to Prime Minister Abe of Japan for hosting such a fantastic and well run G-20. There wasn't a thing that was missing or a mistake that was made. PERFECT! The people of Japan must be very proud of their Prime Minister.

July 3, 2019

9:21 am: China and Europe playing big currency manipulation game and pumping money into their system in order to compete with USA. We should MATCH, or continue being the dummies who sit back and politely watch as other countries continue to play their games—as they have for many years!

July 8, 2019

1:31 pm: I have been very critical about the way the U.K. and Prime Minister Theresa May handled Brexit. What a mess she and her representatives have created. I told her how it should be done, but she decided to go another way. I do not know the Ambassador, but he is not liked or well…

...thought of within the U.S. We will no longer deal with him. The good news for the wonderful United Kingdom is that they will soon have a new Prime Minister. While I thoroughly enjoyed the magnificent State Visit last month, it was the Queen who I was most impressed with!

July 9, 2019

6:48 am: The wacky Ambassador that the U.K. foisted upon the United States is not someone we are thrilled with, a very stupid guy. He should speak to his country, and Prime Minister May, about their failed Brexit negotiation, and not be upset with my criticism of how badly it was...

...handled. I told @theresa_may how to do that deal, but she went her own foolish way-was unable to get it done. A disaster! I don't know the Ambassador but have been told he is a pompous fool. Tell him the USA now has the best Economy & Military anywhere in the World, by far...

and they are both only getting bigger, better and stronger... Thank you, Mr. President!

July 20, 2019

5:41 am: With the incompetent Mayor of London, you will never have safe streets!

8:52 am: Just had a very good call with @SwedishPM Stefan Löfven who assured me that American citizen A$AP Rocky will be treated fairly. Likewise, I assured him that A$AP was not a flight risk and offered to personally vouch for his bail, or an alternative...

Our teams will be talking further, and we agreed to speak again in the next 48 hours!

July 23, 2019

6:29 am: Congratulations to Boris Johnson on becoming the new Prime Minister of the United Kingdom. He will be great!

July 25, 2019

4:24 am: Give A$AP Rocky his FREEDOM. We do so much for Sweden but it doesn't seem to work the other way around. Sweden should focus on its real crime problem! #FreeRocky

July 26, 2019

11:32 am: France just put a digital tax on our great American technology companies. If anybody taxes them, it should be their home Country, the USA. We will announce a substantial reciprocal action on Macron's foolishness shortly. I've always said American wine is better than French wine!

August 8, 2019

12:51 pm: …I know Emmanuel means well, as do all others, but nobody speaks for the United States but the United States itself. No one is authorized in any way, shape, or form, to represent us!

August 19, 2019

6:43 am: Spoke to my two good friends, Prime Minister Modi of India, and Prime Minister Khan of Pakistan, regarding Trade, Strategic Partnerships and, most importantly, for India and Pakistan to work towards reducing tensions in Kashmir. A tough situation, but good conversations!

6:55 pm: Great discussion with Prime Minister @BorisJohnson today. We talked about Brexit and how we can move rapidly on a US-UK free trade deal. I look forward to meeting with Boris this weekend, at the @G7, in France!

7:07 pm: I promise not to do this to Greenland! https://t.co/03DdyVU6HA

August 20, 2019

6:51 pm: Denmark is a very special country with incredible people, but based on Prime Minister Mette Frederiksen's comments, that she would have no interest in discussing the purchase of Greenland, I will be postponing our meeting scheduled in two weeks for another time...

The Prime Minister was able to save a great deal of expense and effort for both the United States and Denmark by being so direct. I thank her for that and look forward to rescheduling sometime in the future!

August 21, 2019

12:32 pm: For the record, Denmark is only at 1.35% of GDP for NATO spending. They are a wealthy country and should be at 2%. We protect Europe and yet, only 8 of the 28 NATO countries are at the 2% mark. The United States is at a much, much higher level than that...

...Because of me, these countries have agreed to pay ONE HUNDRED BILLION DOLLARS more—but still way short of what they should pay for the incredible military protection provided. Sorry!

12:43 pm: .@NATO, very unfair to the United States!

August 24, 2019

10:22 am: Just had lunch with French President @EmmanuelMacron. Many good things are happening for both of our countries. Big weekend with other world leaders!

5:52 pm: France and President @EmmanuelMacron have done a really great job thus far with a very important G-7. Lunch with Emmanuel was the best meeting we have yet had. Likewise, evening meeting with World Leaders went very well. Progress being made!

August 25, 2019

3:05 am: Great working breakfast this morning with Prime Minister @BorisJohnson at the Hôtel du Palais in Biarritz, France! #G7Biarritz

11:38 am: Big Trade Deal just agreed to with Prime Minister Abe of Japan. Will be great for our Farmers, Ranchers and more. Really big Corn purchase!

12:30 pm: The question I was asked most today by fellow World Leaders, who think the USA is doing so well and is stronger than ever before, happens to be, "Mr. President, why does the American media hate your Country so much? Why are they rooting for it to fail?"

August 26, 2019

7:13 am: Very productive meeting with Angela Merkel, the Chancellor of the Federal Republic of Germany, at the #G7Summit in Biarritz, France

7:26 am: Just wrapped up a great meeting with my friend Prime Minister @NarendraModi of India at the #G7Summit in Biarritz, France!

September 3, 2019

8:33 am: For all of the "geniuses" out there, many who have been in other administrations and "taken to the cleaners" by China, that want me to get together with the EU and others to go after China Trade practices remember, the EU & all treat us VERY unfairly on Trade also. Will change!

8:45 am: Germany, and so many other countries, have negative interest rates, "they get paid for loaning money," and our Federal Reserve fails to act! Remember, these are also our weak currency competitors!

9:48 am: The incompetent Mayor of London, Sadiq Khan, was bothered that I played a very fast round of golf yesterday. Many Pols exercise for hours, or travel for weeks. Me, I run through one of my courses (very inexpensive). President Obama would fly to Hawaii. Kahn should focus on...

"knife crime," which is totally out of control in London. People are afraid to even walk the streets. He is a terrible mayor who should stay out of our business!

September 22, 2019

10:28 am: Look forward to being with our great India loving community!

2:03 pm: The USA Loves India!

December 2, 2019

11:02 am: Heading to Europe to represent our Country and fight hard for the American People while the Do Nothing Democrats purposely scheduled an Impeachment Hoax hearing on the same date as NATO. Not nice!

1:17 pm: In the 3 decades before my election, NATO spending declined by two-thirds, and only 3 other NATO members were meeting their financial obligations. Since I took office, the number of NATO allies fulfilling their obligations more than DOUBLED, and NATO spending increased by $130B!

5:30 pm: Just landed in the United Kingdom, heading to London for NATO meetings tomorrow. Prior to landing I read the Republicans Report on the Impeachment Hoax. Great job! Radical Left has NO CASE. Read the Transcripts. Shouldn't even be allowed. Can we go to Supreme Court to stop?

December 4, 2019

4:22 am: Enjoyed my meeting with Prime Minister @BorisJohnson of the United Kingdom at @10DowningStreet last night. Talked about numerous subjects including @NATO and Trade.

9:26 am: Great progress has been made by NATO over the last three years. Countries other than the U.S. have agreed to pay 130 Billion Dollars more per year, and by 2024, that number will be 400 Billion Dollars. NATO will be richer and stronger than ever before…

…When today's meetings are over, I will be heading back to Washington. We won't be doing a press conference at the close of NATO because we did so many over the past two days. Safe travels to all!

11:46 am: Thank you @NATO! #NATOLondon

5:26 pm: The Fake News Media is doing everything possible to belittle my VERY successful trip to London for NATO. I got along great with the NATO leaders, even getting them to pay $130 Billion a year more, & $400 Billion a year more in 3 years. No increase for U.S., only deep respect!

5:43 pm: .@NATO has now recognized SPACE as an operational domain and the alliance is STRONGER for it. U.S. leadership ensures peace through strength and we must continue to show strength and WIN on all fronts—land, air, sea, and SPACE!

December 5, 2019

7:20 am: Tremendous things achieved for U.S. on my NATO trip. Proudly for our Country, no President has ever achieved so much in so little time. Without a U.S. increase, other countries have already increased by $130 Billion-with $400 Billion soon. Such a thing has never been done before!

December 8, 2019

2:59 pm: I got NATO countries to pay 530 Billion Dollars a year more, and the U.S. less, and came home to a Fake News Media that mocked me. Didn't think that was possible!

December 11, 2019

9:19 am: They were just upset that I demanded they pay their fair share for NATO. Their countries are delinquent. I raised $530 Billion more from NATO countries! Thank you Charles.

December 12, 2019

11:06 pm: Looking like a big win for Boris in the U.K.!

December 13, 2019

1:08 am: Congratulations to Boris Johnson on his great WIN! Britain and the United States will now be free to strike a massive new Trade Deal after BREXIT. This deal has the potential to be far bigger and more lucrative than any deal that could be made with the E.U. Celebrate Boris!

December 17, 2019

2:09 pm: We support @JeanineAnez in Bolivia as she works to ensure a peaceful democratic transition through free elections. We denounce the ongoing violence and those that provoke it both in Bolivia and from afar. The U.S. stands with the people of the region for peace and democracy!

December 26, 2019

7:03 pm: I guess Justin T doesn't much like my making him pay up on NATO or Trade!

December 31, 2019

6:25 pm: How is the Paris Accord doing? Don't ask!
https://t.co/9N0yibmDkj

North Korea—2017 News Quotes

Response to a question from John Dickerson of CBS News, April 30, 2017.
Source: https://www.cbsnews.com/news/face-the-nation-transcript-april-30-2017-president-trump/

"Well, I didn't say, don't test a missile.

"He's [Chairman Kim Jong Un of North Korea is] going to have to do what he has to do. But he understands we're not going to be very happy. And I will tell you, a man that I've gotten to like and respect, the president of China, President Xi [Jinping], I believe, has been putting pressure on him also.

"But, so far, perhaps nothing's happened. And perhaps it has. This was a small missile. This was not a big missile. This was not a nuclear test, which he was expected to do three days ago. We'll see what happens."

Response to a question from John Dickerson of CBS News, April 30, 2017.
Source: https://www.cbsnews.com/news/face-the-nation-transcript-april-30-2017-president-trump/

"I would not be happy. If he [Chairman Kim Jong Un of North Korea] does a nuclear test, I will not be happy. And I can tell you also, I don't believe that the president of China, who is a very respected man, will be happy either."

Response to a question from John Dickerson of CBS News, April 30, 2017.
Source: https://www.cbsnews.com/news/face-the-nation-transcript-april-30-2017-president-trump/

"Well, I'd rather not discuss it. But perhaps they're just not very good missiles. But, eventually, he'll [Chairman Kim Jong Un of North Korea will] have good missiles."

Response to a question from John Dickerson of CBS News, April 30, 2017.
Source: https://www.cbsnews.com/news/face-the-nation-transcript-april-30-2017-president-trump/

"I just don't want to discuss it. And I think you know me very well, where you've asked me many times over the last couple of years about military. I said, we shouldn't be announcing we're going into Mosul. I said, we shouldn't be announcing all our moves. It is a chess game. I just don't want people to know what my thinking is. So, eventually, [Chairman Kim Jong Un of North Korea] will have a better delivery system. And if that happens, we can't allow it to happen."

Response to a question from John Dickerson of CBS News, April 30, 2017.
Source: https://www.cbsnews.com/news/face-the-nation-transcript-april-30-2017-president-trump/

"I have, I really, you know, have no comment on him [Chairman Kim Jong Un of North Korea]. People are saying, 'Is he sane?' I have no idea. I can tell you this. And a lot of people don't like when I say it, but he was a young man of 26 or 27 when he took over from his father, when his father died. He's dealing with obviously very tough people, in particular the generals and others. And, at a very young age, he was able to assume power. A lot of people, I'm sure, tried to take that power away, whether it was his uncle or anybody else. And he was able to do it. So, obviously, he's a pretty smart cookie. But we have a situation that we just cannot let, we cannot let what's been going on for a long period of years continue. And, frankly, this should've been done and taken care of by the Obama administration. Should've been taken care of by the Bush administration. Should've been taken care of by [former U.S. President Bill] Clinton."

Response to a question from John Dickerson of CBS News, April 30, 2017.

Source: https://www.cbsnews.com/news/face-the-nation-transcript-april-30-2017-president-trump/

"No. I think that, frankly, North Korea is maybe more important than trade. Trade is very important. But massive warfare with millions, potentially millions of people being killed? That, as we would say, trumps trade."

Response to a question from Laura Ingraham of FOX News, November 2, 2017.

Source: https://www.youtube.com/watch?v=yTdDH-o_ICM

"You have to understand something very important. We have a problem called North Korea."

Response to a question from Laura Ingraham of FOX News, November 2, 2017.

Source: https://www.youtube.com/watch?v=yTdDH-o_ICM

"Well, of course, they're [Japan is] worried. They should be worried. You know, they're very close to North Korea."

Response to a question from Laura Ingraham of FOX News, November 2, 2017.

Source: https://www.youtube.com/watch?v=yTdDH-o_ICM

"Well, you know, Japan, Japan is a warrior nation. And I tell China, and I tell everyone else that listens, I mean, you're going to have yourself a big problem with Japan pretty soon if you allow this to continue with North Korea."

Response to a question from Laura Ingraham of FOX News, November 2, 2017.

Source: https://www.youtube.com/watch?v=yTdDH-o_ICM

"And we may have a meeting with [Russian President Vladimir] Putin. We may—And again, Putin is very important because they can help us with North Korea."

North Korea—2017 Tweets

March 17, 2017

8:07 am: North Korea is behaving very badly. They have been "playing" the United States for years. China has done little to help!

April 11, 2017

7:03 am: North Korea is looking for trouble. If China decides to help, that would be great. If not, we will solve the problem without them! U.S.A.

April 28, 2017

6:26 pm: North Korea disrespected the wishes of China & its highly respected President when it launched, though unsuccessfully, a missile today. Bad!

May 29, 2017

7:18 am: North Korea has shown great disrespect for their neighbor, China, by shooting off yet another ballistic missile…but China is trying hard!

June 19, 2017

6:44 pm: Melania and I offer our deepest condolences to the family of Otto Warmbier.

June 20, 2017

11:41 am: The U.S. once again condemns the brutality of the North Korean regime as we mourn its latest victim.
Video: https://t.co/Rvm11ZbPk7

1:38 pm: While I greatly appreciate the efforts of President Xi & China to help with North Korea, it has not worked out. At least I know China tried!

June 29, 2017

8:44 pm: Just finished a very good meeting with the President of South Korea. Many subjects discussed including North Korea and new trade deal!

June 30, 2017

3:55 pm: The era of strategic patience with the North Korea regime has failed. That patience is over. We are working closely...
https://t.co/MxN04V2Yn4

July 3, 2017

9:19 pm to 9:24 pm: North Korea has just launched another missile. Does this guy have anything better to do with his life? Hard to believe that South Korea...

...and Japan will put up with this much longer. Perhaps China will put a heavy move on North Korea and end this nonsense once and for all!

July 5, 2017

6:21 am: Trade between China and North Korea grew almost 40% in the first quarter. So much for China working with us—but we had to give it a try!

July 29, 2017

6:29 pm to 6:35 pm: I am very disappointed in China. Our foolish past leaders have allowed them to make hundreds of billions of dollars a year in trade, yet...

...they do NOTHING for us with North Korea, just talk. We will no longer allow this to continue. China could easily solve this problem!

August 5, 2017

5:44 pm: The United Nations Security Council just voted 15-0 to sanction North Korea. China and Russia voted with us. Very big financial impact

6:14 pm: United Nations Resolution is the single largest economic sanctions package ever on North Korea. Over one billion dollars in cost to N.K.

August 6, 2017

8:22 pm: Just completed call with President Moon of South Korea. Very happy and impressed with 15-0 United Nations vote on North Korea sanctions.

August 7, 2017

3:15 pm: The Fake News Media will not talk about the importance of the United Nations Security Council's 15-0 vote in favor of sanctions on N. Korea!

August 8, 2017

6:17 am: After many years of failure, countries are coming together to finally address the dangers posed by North Korea. We must be tough & decisive!

August 11, 2017

6:29 am: Military solutions are now fully in place,locked and loaded,should North Korea act unwisely. Hopefully Kim Jong Un will find another path!

August 16, 2017

6:39 am: Kim Jong Un of North Korea made a very wise and well reasoned decision. The alternative would have been both catastrophic and unacceptable!

August 30, 2017

7:47 am: The U.S. has been talking to North Korea, and paying them extortion money, for 25 years. Talking is not the answer!

September 3, 2017

6:30 am to 6:30 am: North Korea has conducted a major Nuclear Test. Their words and actions continue to be very hostile and dangerous to the United States…

..North Korea is a rogue nation which has become a great threat and embarrassment to China, which is trying to help but with little success.

6:46 am: South Korea is finding, as I have told them, that their talk of appeasement with North Korea will not work, they only understand one thing!

11:07 am: I will be meeting General Kelly, General Mattis and other military leaders at the White House to discuss North Korea. Thank you.

11:14 am: The United States is considering, in addition to other options, stopping all trade with any country doing business with North Korea.

September 15, 2017

5:58 pm: We will defend our people, our nations and our civilization from all who dare to threaten our way of life…
cont: https://t.co/SYBRshx89b https://t.co/sIiAuxL3OE

September 17, 2017

6:53 am: I spoke with President Moon of South Korea last night. Asked him how Rocket Man is doing. Long gas lines forming in North Korea. Too bad!

September 20, 2017

5:40 am: After allowing North Korea to research and build Nukes while Secretary of State (Bill C also), Crooked Hillary now criticizes.

September 21, 2017

12:58 pm: Today, I announced a new Executive Order with re: to North Korea. We must all do our part to ensure the complete denuclearization of #NoKo. https://t.co/igjOSM7N7h

September 22, 2017

5:28 am: Kim Jong Un of North Korea, who is obviously a madman who doesn't mind starving or killing his people, will be tested like never before!

September 23, 2017

10:08 pm: Just heard Foreign Minister of North Korea speak at U.N. If he echoes thoughts of Little Rocket Man, they won't be around much longer!

October 1, 2017

9:30 am to 9:31 am: I told Rex Tillerson, our wonderful Secretary of State, that he is wasting his time trying to negotiate with Little Rocket Man...

...Save your energy Rex, we'll do what has to be done!

2:01 pm: Being nice to Rocket Man hasn't worked in 25 years, why would it work now? Clinton failed, Bush failed, and Obama failed. I won't fail.

October 7, 2017

2:40 pm to 2:45 pm: Presidents and their administrations have been talking to North Korea for 25 years, agreements made and massive amounts of money paid...

...hasn't worked, agreements violated before the ink was dry, makings fools of U.S. negotiators. Sorry, but only one thing will work!

October 9, 2017

5:50 am: Our country has been unsuccessfully dealing with North Korea for 25 years, giving billions of dollars & getting nothing. Policy didn't work!

November 6, 2017

4:28 pm: Getting ready to leave for South Korea and meetings with President Moon, a fine gentleman. We will figure it all out!

November 7, 2017

10:12 pm: The North Korean regime has pursued its nuclear & ballistic missile programs in defiance of every assurance, agreement, & commmitment it has made to the U.S. and its allies. It's broken all of those commitments… https://t.co/xJ4jUpA8d8

10:14 pm: Anyone who doubts the strength or determination of the U.S. should look to our past…and you will doubt it no longer. https://t.co/zyuYcofIH6

10:43 pm: Together, we dream of a Korea that is free, a peninsula that is safe, and families that are reunited once again! https://t.co/9tsZRCC83j

November 8, 2017

10:15 am: NoKo has interpreted America's past restraint as weakness. This would be a fatal miscalculation. Do not underestimate us. AND DO NOT TRY US. https://t.co/4llqLrNpK3

November 11, 2017

6:32 pm: President Xi of China has stated that he is upping the sanctions against #NoKo. Said he wants them to denuclearize. Progress is being made.

7:16 pm: Met with President Putin of Russia who was at #APEC meetings. Good discussions on Syria. Hope for his help to solve, along with China the dangerous North Korea crisis. Progress being made.

7:48 pm: Why would Kim Jong-un insult me by calling me "old," when I would NEVER call him "short and fat?" Oh well, I try so hard to be his friend—and maybe someday that will happen!

November 16, 2017

7:43 am: China is sending an Envoy and Delegation to North Korea—A big move, we'll see what happens!

November 28, 2017

8:45 pm: After North Korea missile launch, it's more important than ever to fund our gov't & military! Dems shouldn't hold troop funding hostage for amnesty & illegal immigration. I ran on stopping illegal immigration and won big. They can't now threaten a shutdown to get their demands.

November 29, 2017

9:40 am: Just spoke to President XI JINPING of China concerning the provocative actions of North Korea. Additional major sanctions will be imposed on North Korea today. This situation will be handled!

November 30, 2017

7:25 am: The Chinese Envoy, who just returned from North Korea, seems to have had no impact on Little Rocket Man. Hard to believe his people, and the military, put up with living in such horrible conditions. Russia and China condemned the launch.

December 22, 2017

3:47 pm: The United Nations Security Council just voted 15-0 in favor of additional Sanctions on North Korea. The World wants Peace, not Death!

December 28, 2017

11:24 am: Caught RED HANDED—very disappointed that China is allowing oil to go into North Korea. There will never be a friendly solution to the North Korea problem if this continues to happen!

North Korea—2018 News Quotes

Remarks at meeting with defectors from North Korea, February 2, 2018.

Source: https://www.whitehouse.gov/briefings-statements/
remarks-president-trump-meeting-north-korean-defectors/

"We have a very special group of people with us today. These are es-
capees from North Korea. There have been many of them over the last
year, and there seems to be more and more. It's a tough place to live,
and people aren't liking it. There's great danger, great risk."

Response to a question from an unidentified reporter before a bilateral meeting with Prime Minister Stefan Löfven of Sweden, March 6, 2018.

Source: https://www.whitehouse.gov/briefings-statements/
remarks-president-trump-prime-minister-lofven-sweden-bilateral-meeting/

"We have come, certainly, a long way, at least rhetorically, with North
Korea. It would be a great thing for the world. It would be a great
thing for North Korea. It would be a great thing for the Peninsula.

"But we'll see what happens. We have, we've been in a situation that
should have been handled for a long time. For many, many years, this
should have been taken care of. It shouldn't have been waited. But
we'll get it done."

Response to a question from an unidentified reporter before a bilateral meeting with Prime Minister Stefan Löfven of Sweden, March 6, 2018.

Source: https://www.whitehouse.gov/briefings-statements/
remarks-president-trump-prime-minister-lofven-sweden-bilateral-meeting/

"I think that their statement and the statements coming out of South
Korea and North Korea have been very positive. That would be a great
thing for the world. A great thing for the world. So, we'll see how it
all comes about.

"I will say this—And we've been given tremendous credit, because the
Olympics was not going well. And when they came in out of the blue

and they said, 'We'd love to participate in the Olympics,' it made the Olympics very successful. President Moon [Jae-In] of South Korea was very generous in his statements, as to the fact that we had a lot to do with that, if not everything. We had a lot to do with it.

"The Olympics were beautiful. There were, really, very successful. And as you know, they weren't looking that way prior to. So, I thought North Korea was terrific. They came out—They went into the Olympics, they went in with good spirit, they did well. Let's see if we can carry it over.

"We may carry it over. It may not. It's a very tenuous situation. It's going to be very interesting to see what happens."

Remarks at a dinner reception hosted at Mar-a-Lago with Prime Minister Shinzō Abe of Japan, April 18, 2018.

Source: https://www.whitehouse.gov/briefings-statements/
remarks-president-trump-prime-minister-abe-japan-dinner-reception/

"It's been a great honor to have the Prime Minister of Japan [Shinzō Abe] and his extraordinary wife with us tonight at Mar-a-Lago. We call this the Southern White House. It was originally built, as you probably have heard, as the Southern White House. And it's turned out to be the Southern White House. So, it's really an honor.

"We've have had two very productive days on trade, on military, on North Korea. And we will continue, and we will also continue into the weeks ahead. And we're coming up with what will be a very fair trade deal for both countries. And we look forward to it. Plus, we have some very big meetings, as we all know, on North Korea."

Response to a question from Brian Kilmeade of FOX News, April 26, 2018.

Source: https://www.bbc.com/news/world-us-canada-43913798

"We're doing very well with North Korea. We'll see how it all works out."

Response to a question from Bret Baier of FOX News, June 12, 2018.

Source: https://www.youtube.com/watch?v=zogD8bnGJu4

"People are really happy about it, and even I would say non-Trump fans, people are really happy. It's something that I'm very proud of.

Now, with that being said, I want to get it done, but I believe that Chairman Kim [Jong Un of North Korea] wants to get it done."

Response to a question from Bret Baier of FOX News, June 12, 2018.
Source: https://www.youtube.com/watch?v=zogD8bnGJu4

"But we have 32,000 soldiers in South Korea. I would like to get them home. I would like to. But it is not on the table right now. At the appropriate time, it will be."

Response to a question from Bret Baier of FOX News, June 12, 2018.
Source: https://www.youtube.com/watch?v=zogD8bnGJu4

"No, I think China really would like to see no nuclear weapons if you want to know the truth because look, whether you are semi-friendly with a nation or not when they have nuclear weapons and you're that close, it can't be a positive feeling. It just can't be.

"So, China has been very helpful. I think over the last two months, maybe less so. I think the border got a little bit more open. Now, it didn't affect today's negotiation, but I think the border opened up a little bit more because China could be a little bit upset about trade because we are very strongly clamping down on trade."

Response to a question from Bret Baier of FOX News, June 12, 2018.
Source: https://www.youtube.com/watch?v=zogD8bnGJu4

"Yes. But that's with a different President and nobody has taken it this far. And presidents have never met with anybody from North Korea. It's been, you know, delegated to other people. And even if they did meet, they wouldn't have been able to pull it off.

"But this is something that should have been done years ago. I mean you've heard me say it many times. This should have been done 10 years, 15, 20 years ago. This shouldn't be done now where they have an arsenal of nuclear weapons. It should have never allowed to get to this point.

"With that being said, Chairman Kim [Jong Un of North Korea] wants to resolve the problem because he knew that we weren't playing around. I wasn't playing around. He's not playing around. We have a very—I really say for, you know, for a fairly short-term relationship because it was unbelievably hostile, the rhetoric."

Response to a question from Bret Baier of FOX News, June 12, 2018.
Source: https://www.youtube.com/watch?v=zogD8bnGJu4

"He's [Chairman Kim Jong Un of North Korea is] a tough guy. Hey, when you take over a country, tough country, tough people and you take it over from your father, I don't care who you are, what you are, how much of an advantage you have. If you can do that at 27 years old, I mean that's one in 10,000 that could do that. So, he's a very smart guy. He's a great negotiator, but I think we understand each other."

Response to a question from Bret Baier of FOX News, June 12, 2018.
Source: https://www.youtube.com/watch?v=zogD8bnGJu4

"Yes. But so have a lot of other people done some really bad things. I mean I could go through a lot of nations where a lot of bad things were done.

"Now look, with all of that being said, the answer is yes, I'm going from today. I'm going from maybe 90 days ago because we really started this—We got a call that he [Chairman Kim Jong Un of North Korea] was going to the Olympics. He would like to go to the Olympics and that was sort of the beginning of what we have right now. And we are very far down the line. You saw the agreement. Nobody thought we were going to have an agreement like that.

"And things were given to me as you know from the news conference, things were given to me, Bret [Baier of FOX News],that were not even part of the agreement. I got them after we had signed the agreement."

Response to a question from George Stephanopoulos of ABC News, June 12, 2018.
Source: https://abcnews.go.com/Politics/
president-trump-sits-george-stephanopoulos-transcript/story?id=55831055

"Yeah, I have spoken, yes, I have spoken to him [Chairman Kim Jong Un of North Korea]. I have spoken to a lot of his people, his, as you know, his, I would say very top person was at the White House last week. And so, we've developed a pretty good relationship in terms of getting something done. It got done. I think it's a terrific document. It's a starter, but it's a terrific document. I think far more—And there are things that we negotiated after that document that are also very important."

Response to a question from George Stephanopoulos of ABC News, June 12, 2018.
Source: https://abcnews.go.com/Politics/
president-trump-sits-george-stephanopoulos-transcript/story?id=55831055

"They're [North Korea is] going to get rid of certain ballistic missile sites and various other things. We're gonna put that out later. But we have the framework of getting ready to denuclearize North Korea."

Response to a question from George Stephanopoulos of ABC News, June 12, 2018.
Source: https://abcnews.go.com/Politics/
president-trump-sits-george-stephanopoulos-transcript/story?id=55831055

"They're [North Korea is] going to get rid of their nuclear weapons, George [Stephanopoulos of ABC News], and I think they want to do it relatively quickly. Now, we're going to see. I mean, they're going to start working on it immediately. We're going to work with South Korea. We're going to work with Japan. We're going to work with China. But it really has been an incredible exercise."

Response to a question from George Stephanopoulos of ABC News, June 12, 2018.
Source: https://abcnews.go.com/Politics/
president-trump-sits-george-stephanopoulos-transcript/story?id=55831055

"I don't think a deal could be softer. First of all, we're not paying $150 billion, OK, we're paying nothing from that standpoint other than, you will see what happens. I think there's going to be a great partnership with Japan and South Korea. President Moon [Jae-In of South Korea] has been terrific."

Response to a question from George Stephanopoulos of ABC News, June 12, 2018.

Source: https://abcnews.go.com/Politics/
president-trump-sits-george-stephanopoulos-transcript/story?id=55831055

"I've gotten to know him [Chairman Kim Jong Un of North Korea] well in a short period of time."

Response to a question from George Stephanopoulos of ABC News, June 12, 2018.

Source: https://abcnews.go.com/Politics/
president-trump-sits-george-stephanopoulos-transcript/story?id=55831055

"Yeah, he's [Chairman Kim Jong Un of North Korea is] de-nuking, I mean he's de-nuking the whole place. It's going to start very quickly. I think he's going to start now. They'll be announcing things over the next few days talking about other missile sites because they were, as you know, they were sending out a lot of missiles. It was a period of time where I was saying, what are they doing? Every week it seems another missile going up. I mean, they're going to be getting rid of sites."

Response to a question from George Stephanopoulos of ABC News, June 12, 2018.

Source: https://abcnews.go.com/Politics/
president-trump-sits-george-stephanopoulos-transcript/story?id=55831055

"It [Denuclearization] takes a period of time. Some say 15 years, if you go rapidly. But when you're in the process of doing it, you're really dismantling, in other words, you can't do anything during that period of time. But they have a process for getting rid of nukes that does take, it's not like, 'Oh gee, we'll get rid of them tomorrow.' It just can't be done scientifically. But they're [North Korea is] gonna do it. They're gonna start immediately. They really already started. They blew up a site, which was the real deal site that was their big site; they've blown it up. They're getting rid of things that haven't been mentioned in the document, they're getting rid of certain missile areas, and they're not going to be sending missiles up. They're not doing research—[Stephanopoulos interrupts.]"

351

Response to a question from George Stephanopoulos of ABC News, June 12, 2018.

Source: https://abcnews.go.com/Politics/
president-trump-sits-george-stephanopoulos-transcript/story?id=55831055

"And I'm doing something that I've wanted to do from the beginning. We stopped playing those war games that cost us a fortune. You know, we're spending a fortune, every couple of months we're doing war games with South Korea, and I said, 'What's this costing?' We're flying planes in from Guam; we're bombing empty mountains for practice. I said, 'I want to stop that.' And I will stop that, and I think it's very provocative—[Stephanopoulos interrupts.]"

Response to a question from George Stephanopoulos of ABC News, June 12, 2018.

Source: https://abcnews.go.com/Politics/
president-trump-sits-george-stephanopoulos-transcript/story?id=55831055

"Well, we've given him [Chairman Kim Jong Un of North Korea]—I don't wanna talk about it specifically, but we've given him—He's going to be happy. His country does love him. His people, you see the fervor. They have a great fervor. They're gonna put it together, and I think they're going to end up with a very strong country, and a country which has people—That they're so hard working, so industrious. I think if you look at South Korea, someday, maybe in the not too distant future, it will be something that—"

Response to a question from George Stephanopoulos of ABC News, June 12, 2018.

Source: https://abcnews.go.com/Politics/
president-trump-sits-george-stephanopoulos-transcript/story?id=55831055

"George [Stephanopoulos of ABC News], I'm given what I'm given, okay? I mean, this is what we have, and this is where we are, and I can only tell you from my experience, and I met him [Chairman Kim Jong Un of North Korea]. I've spoken with him, and I've met him. And this was, as you know, started very early and it's been very intense. I think that he really wants to do a great job for North Korea. I think he wants to denuke; it's very important. Without that, there's nothing to discuss. That was on the table at the beginning, and you see a total denuclearization of North Korea—So important. And, he [Kim Jong Un] wants to do the right thing. Now, with all of that being said, I can't talk about—It doesn't matter. We're starting from scratch. We're starting right now, and we have to get rid of those nuclear weapons."

Response to a question from George Stephanopoulos of ABC News, June 12, 2018.
Source: https://abcnews.go.com/Politics/
president-trump-sits-george-stephanopoulos-transcript/story?id=55831055

"Well, you know, over my lifetime I've done a lot of deals with a lot of people, and sometimes the people that you most distrust turn out to be the most honorable ones, and the people that you do trust they are not the honorable ones, so we [Chairman Kim Jong Un of North Korea and I] are starting from a very high plane; we're starting from a very good relationship. This has been a very big day in terms of the world. I think it's been, maybe I—A lot of people have been saying it's historic."

Response to a question from George Stephanopoulos of ABC News, June 12, 2018.
Source: https://abcnews.go.com/Politics/
president-trump-sits-george-stephanopoulos-transcript/story?id=55831055

"He [Chairman Kim Jong Un of North Korea] said that, you know, there are reasons he didn't because he was let down by the United States, but that's irrelevant. What he's doing, and, and he very much said that, he said you know over the years—First of all, they've never gone this far, you know, they've never been at a level like this, and his father never dealt with a President, and a lot of other things. But he [Kim Jong Un] said, it's very much on his mind. He said, 'We are going to get this done.' In the past we've tried, but it never worked out and it never did work out. And it was embarrassing actually to the United States and to our leadership. This is different, I believe you'll find in the years to come, George [Stephanopoulos of ABC News]. I think you're going to find this different."

Response to a question from George Stephanopoulos of ABC News, June 12, 2018.
Source: https://abcnews.go.com/Politics/
president-trump-sits-george-stephanopoulos-transcript/story?id=55831055

"Well, we're going to be following things. We're going to be monitoring things. We're dealing with him [Chairman Kim Jong Un of North Korea] very—On a constant basis. [U.S.] Secretary of State Mike Pompeo did a very, very good job; great energy. And they have a great relationship, his counterpart. They have a really good relationship. They're moving along; they're getting it done. I mean, I've been up 24 hours now straight between phone calls and working it. This is a very—Look, this is 72 years we're talking about, and we put it into one very intensive day and some meetings beforehand."

Response to a question from George Stephanopoulos of ABC News, June 12, 2018.
Source: https://abcnews.go.com/Politics/
president-trump-sits-george-stephanopoulos-transcript/story?id=55831055

"Well, I think we have to disagree. Otherwise I wouldn't be here, or I would have respectfully, you know, I would have shaken his [Chairman of North Korea Kim Jong Un's] hand. I would have said, 'Listen, I'll see you sometime.' But I wouldn't have had any interest. No, this was very important, it's in the first paragraph and it says complete total denuclearization. Without that I wouldn't have been interested. I believe that he [Kim Jong Un] wants to get it done."

Response to a question from George Stephanopoulos of ABC News, June 12, 2018.
Source: https://abcnews.go.com/Politics/
president-trump-sits-george-stephanopoulos-transcript/story?id=55831055

"I do trust him [Chairman Kim Jong Un of North Korea], yeah. Now, will I come back to you [George Stephanopoulos of ABC News} in a year and you'll be interviewing, and I'll say, 'Gee, I made a mistake?' That's always possible. You know, we're dealing at a very high level, a lot of things can change, a lot of things are possible. He [Kim Jong Un] trusts me, I believe—I really do. I mean, he said openly, and he said it to a couple of reporters that were with him that he knows that no other President ever could have done this, I mean no other Pre— He knows the presidents; he knows who we had in front of me. He said no other President could have done this. I think he trusts me, and I trust him."

Response to a question from George Stephanopoulos of ABC News, June 12, 2018.
Source: https://abcnews.go.com/Politics/
president-trump-sits-george-stephanopoulos-transcript/story?id=55831055

"Well, we're going to be verifying and we're going to be working with them [North Korea]. And it's going to be much more open than it is right now. Right now, it's obviously very closed, it's a very closed society we know very little about. You know, if you ask intelligence, they will tell you probably they know less about this area of the world than they do any place, anywhere in the world.

"We're going to be working very closely with him [Chairman Kim Jong Un of North Korea]. We've developed great relationships at different levels. [U.S. Secretary of State] Mike Pompeo has got really, very good, strong relationships and others have also. Today, we introduced him [Kim Jong Un] to [former U.S. Ambassador to the United Nations] John Bolton, which was a very interesting thing, and—[Stephanopoulos interrupts.]"

Response to a question from George Stephanopoulos of ABC News, June 12, 2018.
Source: https://abcnews.go.com/Politics/
president-trump-sits-george-stephanopoulos-transcript/story?id=55831055

"Well, no, I have great friendships. If you speak to Prime Minister [Shinzō] Abe, who I'm helping a lot, because, you know, Japan, three or four times they had missiles going right over the middle of Japan. I have a very good relationship with Prime Minister Abe. I have great relationship with the new man [Prime Minister Giuseppe Conte] who I like a lot as you know from Italy. He just won and you know, we had very good—And frankly really good with [Chancellor Angela] Merkel [of Germany]. Really good pretty much with all of them. I was very surprised because we actually were getting ready to sign a document, I made them make various changes. And you know, the so-called semi-famous picture of—[Stephanopoulos interrupts.]"

Response to a question from George Stephanopoulos of ABC News, June 12, 2018.

Source: https://abcnews.go.com/Politics/
president-trump-sits-george-stephanopoulos-transcript/story?id=55831055

"I want to see some real work going on, which I believe I will, and I would love to have him [Chairman Kim Jong Un of North Korea] at the White House. Whatever it takes, and I would love to have him at the White House, and I think he'd love to be there. And at a certain point when it's all complete, I'd love to be there."

Remarks at a rally in Tampa, Florida, July 31, 2018.

Source: https://www.tampabay.com/florida-politics/buzz/2018/08/01/
heres-a-full-transcript-of-president-trumps-speech-from-his-tampa-rally/

"And we're doing well in North Korea, although I happen to think that we're doing so well with China that China maybe is getting in our way. But we're going to figure that one out before you can even think about it.

"But we're doing well in North Korea. We have our, as you know, we have our hostages back. There's been no nuclear testing. There's been no missiles or rockets flying beautifully over Japan. I think our relationship is very good with Chairman Kim [Jong Un of North Korea], and we'll all see how it all works out. But there's nothing like talking, and we'll see how it is. You remember when I first took office? It really looked like big trouble.

"In the past administration, they thought that was by far their biggest problem. So, I think it's going to work out very well. But a lot of good things are happening. No tests. No rockets flying. But we'll see what happens.

"And our Vice President, Mike Pence, is going to Hawaii to bring back the remains and to greet the families of our great heroes who gave their lives in Korea. Our fallen warriors are finally coming home to lay at rest in American soil."

Remarks at White House dinner with evangelical leaders, August 27, 2018.

Source: https://www.whitehouse.gov/briefings-statements/
remarks-president-trump-dinner-evangelical-leaders/

"We brought home hostages from North Korea, including an American pastor."

Response to a question from Chris Wallace of FOX News, November 18, 2018.

Source: https://www.youtube.com/watch?v=rMgJnnG-NqI

"We're doing really well. We would have been at war with North Korea if, let's say, that administration continued forward. I would give myself, I would—Look, I hate to do it, but I will do it, I would give myself an A+, is that enough? Can I go higher than that?"

Response to a question from Chris Wallace of FOX News, November 18, 2018.

Source: https://www.youtube.com/watch?v=rMgJnnG-NqI

"Well, I think North Korea's been very tough because, you know, we were very close. When I took that over, [U.S.] President [Barack] Obama, right in those two chairs, we sat and talked and he said that's by far the biggest problem that this country has. And I think we had real decision as to which way to go on North Korea and certainly, at least so far, I'm very happy with the way we went."

North Korea—2018 Tweets

January 2, 2018

9:08 am: Sanctions and "other" pressures are beginning to have a big impact on North Korea. Soldiers are dangerously fleeing to South Korea. Rocket man now wants to talk to South Korea for first time. Perhaps that is good news, perhaps not—we will see!

7:49 pm: North Korean Leader Kim Jong Un just stated that the "Nuclear Button is on his desk at all times." Will someone from his depleted and food starved regime please inform him that I too have a Nuclear Button, but it is a much bigger & more powerful one than his, and my Button works!

February 8, 2018

1:44 pm: I will be meeting with Henry Kissinger at 1:45pm. Will be discussing North Korea, China and the Middle East.

March 6, 2018

9:11 am: Possible progress being made in talks with North Korea. For the first time in many years, a serious effort is being made by all parties concerned. The World is watching and waiting! May be false hope, but the U.S. is ready to go hard in either direction!

March 8, 2018

8:08 pm: Kim Jong Un talked about denuclearization with the South Korean Representatives, not just a freeze. Also, no missile testing by North Korea during this period of time. Great progress being made but sanctions will remain until an agreement is reached. Meeting being planned

March 9, 2018

7:42 pm: The deal with North Korea is very much in the making and will be, if completed, a very good one for the World. Time and place to be determined.

March 10, 2018

10:22 am: Chinese President XI XINPING and I spoke at length about the meeting with KIM JONG UN of North Korea. President XI told me he appreciates that the U.S. is working to solve the problem diplomatically rather than going with the ominous alternative. China continues to be helpful!

12:33 pm: Spoke to Prime Minister Abe of Japan, who is very enthusiastic about talks with North Korea. Also discussing opening up Japan to much better trade with the U.S. Currently have a massive $100 Billion Trade Deficit. Not fair or sustainable. It will all work out!

1:38 pm: North Korea has not conducted a Missile Test since November 28, 2017 and has promised not to do so through our meetings. I believe they will honor that commitment!

3:02 pm: In the first hours after hearing that North Korea's leader wanted to meet with me to talk denuclearization and that missile launches will end, the press was startled & amazed. They couldn't believe it. But by the following morning the news became FAKE. They said so what, who cares!

March 28, 2018

5:05 am: For years and through many administrations, everyone said that peace and the denuclearization of the Korean Peninsula was not even a small possibility. Now there is a good chance that Kim Jong Un will do what is right for his people and for humanity. Look forward to our meeting!

5:16 am: Received message last night from XI JINPING of China that his meeting with KIM JONG UN went very well and that KIM looks forward to his meeting with me. In the meantime, and unfortunately, maximum sanctions and pressure must be maintained at all cost!

April 18, 2018

5:42 am: Mike Pompeo met with Kim Jong Un in North Korea last week. Meeting went very smoothly and a good relationship was formed. Details of Summit are being worked out now. Denucleariza-tion will be a great thing for World, but also for North Korea!

April 20, 2018

5:50 pm: North Korea has agreed to suspend all Nuclear Tests and close up a major test site. This is very good news for North Korea and the World—big progress! Look forward to our Summit.

10:22 pm: A message from Kim Jong Un: "North Korea will stop nu-clear tests and launches of intercontinental ballistic missiles." Also will "Shut down a nuclear test site in the country's Northern Side to prove the vow to suspend nuclear tests." Progress being made for all!

April 22, 2018

7:50 am: Sleepy Eyes Chuck Todd of Fake News NBC just stated that we have given up so much in our negotiations with North Korea, and they have given up nothing. Wow, we haven't given up anything & they have agreed to denuclearization (so great for World), site closure, & no more testing!

8:02 am: …We are a long way from conclusion on North Korea, may-be things will work out, and maybe they won't—only time will tell… But the work I am doing now should have been done a long time ago!

1:43 pm: Funny how all of the Pundits that couldn't come close to making a deal on North Korea are now all over the place telling me how to make a deal!

April 27, 2018

5:41 am: After a furious year of missile launches and Nuclear testing, a historic meeting between North and South Korea is now taking place. Good things are happening, but only time will tell!

5:55 am: KOREAN WAR TO END! The United States, and all of its GREAT people, should be very proud of what is now taking place in Korea!

6:50 am: Please do not forget the great help that my good friend, President Xi of China, has given to the United States, particularly at the Border of North Korea. Without him it would have been a much longer, tougher, process!

April 28, 2018

8:45 am: Just had a long and very good talk with President Moon of South Korea. Things are going very well, time and location of meeting with North Korea is being set. Also spoke to Prime Minister Abe of Japan to inform him of the ongoing negotiations.

April 29, 2018

9:59 pm: Headline: "Kim Prepared to Cede Nuclear Weapons if U.S. Pledges Not to Invade"—from the Failing New York Times. Also, will shut down Nuclear Test Site in May.

April 30, 2018

7:19 am: Numerous countries are being considered for the MEETING, but would Peace House/Freedom House, on the Border of North & South Korea, be a more Representative, Important and Lasting site than a third party country? Just asking!

May 2, 2018

7:53 pm: As everybody is aware, the past Administration has long been asking for three hostages to be released from a North Korean Labor camp, but to no avail. Stay tuned!

May 9, 2018

7:30 am: I am pleased to inform you that Secretary of State Mike Pompeo is in the air and on his way back from North Korea with the 3 wonderful gentlemen that everyone is looking so forward to meeting. They seem to be in good health. Also, good meeting with Kim Jong Un. Date & Place set.

7:35 am: Secretary Pompeo and his "guests" will be landing at Andrews Air Force Base at 2:00 A.M. in the morning. I will be there to greet them. Very exciting!

5:41 pm: Looking forward to greeting the Hostages (no longer) at 2:00 A.M.

May 10, 2018

5:01 am: On behalf of the American people, WELCOME HOME! https://t.co/hISaCI95CB

9:37 am: The highly anticipated meeting between Kim Jong Un and myself will take place in Singapore on June 12th. We will both try to make it a very special moment for World Peace!

May 12, 2018

4:08 pm: North Korea has announced that they will dismantle Nuclear Test Site this month, ahead of the big Summit Meeting on June 12th. Thank you, a very smart and gracious gesture!

May 24, 2018

11:18 am: Sadly, I was forced to cancel the Summit Meeting in Singapore with Kim Jung Un. https://t.co/qEoi9ymUEz

11:57 am: I have decided to terminate the planned Summit in Singapore on June 12th. While many things can happen and a great opportunity lies ahead potentially, I believe that this is a tremendous setback for North Korea and indeed a setback for the world...

May 25, 2018

7:37 pm: We are having very productive talks with North Korea about reinstating the Summit which, if it does happen, will likely remain in Singapore on the same date, June 12th., and, if necessary, will be extended beyond that date.

May 27, 2018

3:09 pm: Our United States team has arrived in North Korea to make arrangements for the Summit between Kim Jong Un and myself. I truly believe North Korea has brilliant potential and will be a great economic and financial Nation one day. Kim Jong Un agrees with me on this. It will happen!

May 31, 2018

8:15 am: Very good meetings with North Korea.

June 9, 2018

3:58 pm: I am on my way to Singapore where we have a chance to achieve a truly wonderful result for North Korea and the World. It will certainly be an exciting day and I know that Kim Jong-un will work very hard to do something that has rarely been done before...

...Create peace and great prosperity for his land. I look forward to meeting him and have a feeling that this one-time opportunity will not be wasted!

June 11, 2018

5:04 pm: The fact that I am having a meeting is a major loss for the U.S., say the haters & losers. We have our hostages, testing, research and all missle launches have stoped, and these pundits, who have called me wrong from the beginning, have nothing else they can say! We will be fine!

June 12, 2018

3:40 pm: Heading back home from Singapore after a truly amazing visit. Great progress was made on the denuclearization of North Korea. Hostages are back home, will be getting the remains of our great heroes back to their families, no missiles shot, no research happening, sites closing…

…Got along great with Kim Jong-un who wants to see wonderful things for his country. As I said earlier today: Anyone can make war, but only the most courageous can make peace! #SingaporeSummit

7:02 pm: There is no limit to what NoKo can achieve when it gives up its nuclear weapons and embraces commerce & engagement w/ the world. Chairman Kim has before him the opportunity to be remembered as the leader who ushered in a glorious new era of security & prosperity for his citizens!

7:11 pm: I want to thank Chairman Kim for taking the first bold step toward a bright new future for his people. Our unprecedented meeting—the first between an American President and a leader of North Korea—proves that real change is possible!

7:27 pm: The World has taken a big step back from potential Nuclear catastrophe! No more rocket launches, nuclear testing or research! The hostages are back home with their families. Thank you to Chairman Kim, our day together was historic!

8:14 pm: A year ago the pundits & talking heads, people that couldn't do the job before, were begging for conciliation and peace—"please meet, don't go to war." Now that we meet and have a great relationship with Kim Jong Un, the same haters shout out, "you shouldn't meet, do not meet!"

June 13, 2018

4:56 am: Just landed—a long trip, but everybody can now feel much safer than the day I took office. There is no longer a Nuclear Threat from North Korea. Meeting with Kim Jong Un was an interesting and very positive experience. North Korea has great potential for the future!

5:01 am: Before taking office people were assuming that we were going to War with North Korea. President Obama said that North Korea was our biggest and most dangerous problem. No longer—sleep well tonight!

6:10 am: We save a fortune by not doing war games, as long as we are negotiating in good faith—which both sides are!

June 14, 2018

10:08 am: Now that I am back from Singapore, where we had a great result with respect to North Korea, the thought process must sadly go back to the Witch Hunt, always remembering that there was No Collusion and No Obstruction of the fabricated No Crime.

June 17, 2018

7:48 am: Holding back the "war games" during the negotiations was my request because they are VERY EXPENSIVE and set a bad light during a good faith negotiation. Also, quite provocative. Can start up immediately if talks break down, which I hope will not happen!

8:01 am: The denuclearization deal with North Korea is being praised and celebrated all over Asia. They are so happy! Over here, in our country, some people would rather see this historic deal fail than give Trump a win, even if it does save potentially millions & millions of lives!

July 3, 2018

6:16 am: Many good conversations with North Korea-it is going well! In the meantime, no Rocket Launches or Nuclear Testing in 8 months. All of Asia is thrilled. Only the Opposition Party, which includes the Fake News, is complaining. If not for me, we would now be at War with North Korea!

July 9, 2018

9:25 am: I have confidence that Kim Jong Un will honor the contract we signed &, even more importantly, our handshake. We agreed to the denuclearization of North Korea. China, on the other hand, may be exerting negative pressure on a deal because of our posture on Chinese Trade-Hope Not!

July 12, 2018

1:12 am: A very nice note from Chairman Kim of North Korea. Great progress being made! https://t.co/6NI6AqL0xt

July 15, 2018

11:11 am: There hasn't been a missile or rocket fired in 9 months in North Korea, there have been no nuclear tests and we got back our hostages. Who knows how it will all turn out in the end, but why isn't the Fake News talking about these wonderful facts? Because it is FAKE NEWS!

July 18, 2018

5:16 am: …Russia has agreed to help with North Korea, where relationships with us are very good and the process is moving along. There is no rush, the sanctions remain! Big benefits and exciting future for North Korea at end of process!

July 23, 2018

8:06 am: A Rocket has not been launched by North Korea in 9 months. Likewise, no Nuclear Tests. Japan is happy, all of Asia is happy. But the Fake News is saying, without ever asking me (always anonymous sources), that I am angry because it is not going fast enough. Wrong, very happy!

July 26, 2018

10:52 pm: The Remains of American Servicemen will soon be leaving North Korea and heading to the United States! After so many years, this will be a great moment for so many families. Thank you to Kim Jong Un.

August 1, 2018

10:32pm: Incredibly beautiful ceremony as U.S. Korean War remains are returned to American soil. Thank you to Honolulu and all of our great Military participants on a job well done. A special thanks to Vice President Mike Pence on delivering a truly magnificent tribute!

11:47 pm: Thank you to Chairman Kim Jong Un for keeping your word & starting the process of sending home the remains of our great and beloved missing fallen! I am not at all surprised that you took this kind action. Also, thank you for your nice letter—l look forward to seeing you soon!

August 24, 2018

12:36 pm: I have asked Secretary of State Mike Pompeo not to go to North Korea, at this time, because I feel we are not making sufficient progress with respect to the denuclearization of the Korean Peninsula...

...Additionally, because of our much tougher Trading stance with China, I do not believe they are helping with the process of denuclearization as they once were (despite the UN Sanctions which are in place)...

...Secretary Pompeo looks forward to going to North Korea in the near future, most likely after our Trading relationship with China is resolved. In the meantime I would like to send my warmest regards and respect to Chairman Kim. I look forward to seeing him soon!

September 6, 2018

5:58 am: Kim Jong Un of North Korea proclaims "unwavering faith in President Trump." Thank you to Chairman Kim. We will get it done together!

September 18, 2018

11:04 to 11:11 pm: Kim Jong Un has agreed to allow Nuclear inspections, subject to final negotiations, and to permanently dismantle a test site and launch pad in the presence of international experts. In the meantime there will be no Rocket or Nuclear testing. Hero remains to continue being…

…returned home to the United States. Also, North and South Korea will file a joint bid to host the 2032 Olympics. Very exciting!

September 20, 2018

1:10 pm: Army Master Sgt. Charles H. McDaniel, 32, of Vernon, Indiana, and Army Pfc. William H. Jones, 19, of Nash County, North Carolina, are the first American remains from…

…North Korea to be identified as a result of my Summit with Chairman Kim. These HEROES are home, they may Rest In Peace, and hopefully their families can have closure.

December 14, 2018

1:17 pm: Many people have asked how we are doing in our negotiations with North Korea—I always reply by saying we are in no hurry, there is wonderful potential for great economic success for that country…

..Kim Jong Un sees it better than anyone and will fully take advantage of it for his people. We are doing just fine!

North Korea—2019 News Quotes

Response to a question from Margaret Brennan of CBS News, February 3, 2019

Source: https://www.cbsnews.com/news/
transcript-president-trump-on-face-the-nation-february-3-2019/

"I won't tell you yet, but you'll be finding out probably State of the Union or shortly before. But the meeting [with Chairman Kim Jong Un of North Korea] is set. He's looking forward to it. I'm looking forward to it. We've made tremendous progress. If you remember, before I became president, it looked like we were going to war with North Korea. Now we have a very good relationship. The hostages are back. Okay, the remains are starting to come back. The remains of our Korean War veterans—[Brennan interrupts.]"

From State of the Union address, February 5, 2019.

Source: https://www.whitehouse.gov/briefings-statements/
president-donald-j-trumps-state-union-address-2/

"As part of a bold new diplomacy, we continue our historic push for peace on the Korean Peninsula. Our hostages have come home, nuclear testing has stopped, and there has not been a missile launch in 15 months. If I had not been elected President of the United States, we would right now, in my opinion, be in a major war with North Korea with potentially millions of people killed. Much work remains to be done, but my relationship with [Chairman] Kim Jong Un [of North Korea] is a good one. And Chairman Kim and I will meet again on February 27 and 28 in Vietnam."

Remarks at a press conference in Hanoi, Vietnam, February 28, 2019.

Source: https://www.vox.com/2019/2/28/18241334/
trump-north-korea-press-conference-full-text

"On North Korea we just left Chairman Kim [Jong Un] who had a really I think a very productive time. We thought and I thought and

369

Secretary [Mike] Pompeo felt that it wasn't a good thing to be signing anything. I'm going to let Mike speak about it, but we literally
just we spent pretty much all day with Kim Jong Un, who is—He's
quite a guy and quite a character. And I think our relationship is
very strong.

"But at this time we had some options, and at this time we decided not
to do any of the options, and we'll see where that goes. But it was—It
was a very interesting two days. And I think actually it was a very
productive two days. But sometimes you have to walk. And this was
just one of those times, and I'll let Mike speak to that for a couple of
minutes, please."

Remarks at a press conference in Hanoi, Vietnam, February 28, 2019.

Source: https://www.vox.com/2019/2/28/18241334/
trump-north-korea-press-conference-full-text

"Basically they [North Korea] wanted the sanctions lifted in their entirety, and we couldn't do that. They were willing to denuke a large
portion of the areas that we wanted, but we couldn't give up all of the
sanctions for that, so we'll continue to work and we'll see. But we had
to walk away from that particular suggestion. We had to walk away
from that."

Remarks at a press conference in Hanoi, Vietnam, February 28, 2019.

Source: https://www.vox.com/2019/2/28/18241334/
trump-north-korea-press-conference-full-text

"They're in place. I was watching as a lot of you folks over the weeks
have said, oh, we've given up—We haven't given up anything. And
I think frankly we'll be good friends with Chairman Kim [Jong
Un] and North Korea, and I think they have tremendous potential.
I've been telling everybody they have tremendous potential, unbelievable potential, and we're going to see. But it was about sanctions. They wanted sanctions lifted but they weren't willing to do
an area we wanted. They were willing to give us areas but not the
ones we wanted."

Remarks at a press conference in Hanoi, Vietnam, February 28, 2019.

Source: https://www.vox.com/2019/2/28/18241334/
trump-north-korea-press-conference-full-text

"I want to keep the relationship, and we will keep the relationship. We'll see what happens over the next period of time. But as you know we've got our hostages back. There's no more testing.

"And one of the things importantly that Chairman Kim [Jong Un of North Korea] promised me last night is regardless he's not going to do testing of rockets and nuclear—Not going to do testing. So, you know, I trust him, and I take him at his word. I hope that's true. But in the meantime we'll be talking. [U.S. Secretary of State] Mike [Pompeo] will be speaking with his people.

"He's [Pompeo has] also developed a very good relationship with the people—Really the people representing North Korea. I haven't spoken to Prime Minister [Shinzō] Abe [of Japan] yet.

"I haven't spoken to President Moon [Jae-In], South Korea. But we will, and we'll tell them it's a process and it's moving along, but we felt it wasn't appropriate to sign an agreement today. We could have, I just felt it wasn't appropriate."

Remarks at a press conference in Hanoi, Vietnam, February 28, 2019.

Source: https://www.vox.com/2019/2/28/18241334/
trump-north-korea-press-conference-full-text

"We discussed many ways and the denuclearization is a very important word, has become a very well-used word. And a lot of people don't know what it means, but to me it's pretty obvious we have to get rid of the nukes. I think he's [Chairman Kim Jong Un of North Korea is] going to have a chance to have one of most successful countries rapidly on Earth, too. If you think of it you have on one side Russia and China and on the other you have South Korea and you're surrounded by water.

"And among the most beautiful shorelines in the world. It's tremendous potential in North Korea, and I think he's [Kim Jong Un is] going to lead it to a very important thing economically. I think it's going to be an absolute economic power."

Response to a question from an unidentified reporter before Marine One departure, September 9, 2019.

Source: https://www.whitehouse.gov/briefings-statements/remarks-president-trump-marine-one-departure-63/

"Well, I saw a statement was just put out having to do with North Korea, and that'll be interesting. We'll see. It just came out over the wires a little while ago. So, we'll see what happens.

"In the meantime, in the meantime, we have our hostages back, we're getting the remains of our great heroes back, and we've had no nuclear testing for a long time."

Response to a question from an unidentified reporter before Marine One departure, September 9, 2019.

Source: https://www.whitehouse.gov/briefings-statements/remarks-president-trump-marine-one-departure-63/

"Well, it just came out over the wires that he'd like to have a meeting. I have a very good relationship with [North Korean] Chairman Kim, Kim Jong Un. And it just came out; I just saw it as I'm coming out here, it just came out that they would like to meet. We'll see what happens. But I always say having meetings is a good thing, not a bad thing."

Response to a question from an unidentified reporter at President Trump's remarks before a New Year's Eve celebration at Mar-a-Lago in Palm Beach, Florida, December 31, 2019.

Source: https://www.whitehouse.gov/briefings-statements/remarks-president-trump-new-years-eve-celebration/

"Well, we'll see. I have a very good relationship with [North Korean Chairman] Kim Jong Un. I know he's sending out certain messages about Christmas presents, and I hope his Christmas present is a beautiful vase. That's what I'd like, a vase, as opposed to something else. I don't know. I—Look, he likes me; I like him. We get along. He's representing his country. I'm representing my country. We have to do what we have to do.

"But he did sign a contract. He did sign an agreement, talking about denuclearization. And that was signed. Number-one sentence: denuclearization. That was done in Singapore. And I think he's a man of his word. So we're going to find out, but I think he's a man of his word."

North Korea—2019 Tweets

January 20, 2019

1:16 pm: The Media is not giving us credit for the tremendous progress we have made with North Korea. Think of where we were at the end of the Obama Administration compared to now. Great meeting this week with top Reps. Looking forward to meeting with Chairman Kim at end of February!

January 24, 2019

8:21 am: The Fake News Media loves saying "so little happened at my first summit with Kim Jong Un." Wrong! After 40 years of doing nothing with North Korea but being taken to the cleaners, & with a major war ready to start, in a short 15 months, relationships built, hostages & remains…

8:34 am: …back home where they belong, no more Rockets or M's being fired over Japan or anywhere else and, most importantly, no Nuclear Testing. This is more than has ever been accomplished with North Korea, and the Fake News knows it. I expect another good meeting soon, much potential!

January 30, 2019

6:34 am: ...Fighting continues but the people of Afghanistan want peace in this never ending war. We will soon see if talks will be successful? North Korea relationship is best it has ever been with U.S. No testing, getting remains, hostages returned. Decent chance of Denuclearization...

6:40 am: ...Time will tell what will happen with North Korea, but at the end of the previous administration, relationship was horrendous and very bad things were about to happen. Now a whole different story. I look forward to seeing Kim Jong Un shortly. Progress being made-big difference!

February 8, 2019

7:33 pm: My representatives have just left North Korea after a very productive meeting and an agreed upon time and date for the second Summit with Kim Jong Un. It will take place in Hanoi, Vietnam, on February 27 & 28. I look forward to seeing Chairman Kim & advancing the cause of peace!

7:50 pm: North Korea, under the leadership of Kim Jong Un, will become a great Economic Powerhouse. He may surprise some but he won't surprise me, because I have gotten to know him & fully understand how capable he is. North Korea will become a different kind of Rocket—an Economic one!

February 24, 2019

7:58 am: Very productive talks yesterday with China on Trade. Will continue today! I will be leaving for Hanoi, Vietnam, early tomorrow for a Summit with Kim Jong Un of North Korea, where we both expect a continuation of the progress made at first Summit in Singapore. Denuclearization?

8:05 am: President Xi of China has been very helpful in his support of my meeting with Kim Jong Un. The last thing China wants are large scale nuclear weapons right next door. Sanctions placed on the border by China and Russia have been very helpful. Great relationship with Chairman Kim!

8:19 am: Chairman Kim realizes, perhaps better than anyone else, that without nuclear weapons, his country could fast become one of the great economic powers anywhere in the World. Because of its location and people (and him), it has more potential for rapid growth than any other nation!

12:27 pm: So funny to watch people who have failed for years, they got NOTHING, telling me how to negotiate with North Korea. But thanks anyway!

February 25. 2019

7:40 am: Meeting for breakfast with our Nation's Governors—then off to Vietnam for a very important Summit with Kim Jong Un. With complete Denuclearization, North Korea will rapidly become an Economic Powerhouse. Without it, just more of the same. Chairman Kim will make a wise decision!

3:17 pm: Heading over to Vietnam for my meeting with Kim Jong Un. Looking forward to a very productive Summit

February 26, 2019

9:31 pm: Vietnam is thriving like few places on earth. North Korea would be the same, and very quickly, if it would denuclearize. The potential is AWESOME, a great opportunity, like almost none other in history, for my friend Kim Jong Un. We will know fairly soon—Very Interesting!

9:36 pm: The Democrats should stop talking about what I should do with North Korea and ask themselves instead why they didn't do "it" during eight years of the Obama Administration?

February 27, 2019

4:45 am: All false reporting (guessing) on my intentions with respect to North Korea. Kim Jong Un and I will try very hard to work something out on Denuclearization & then making North Korea an Economic Powerhouse. I believe that China, Russia, Japan & South Korea will be very helpful!

10:38 am: Great meeting and dinner with Kim Jong Un in Hanoi, Vietnam tonight. Looking forward to continuing our discussions tomorrow! #HanoiSummit

March 1, 2019

7:49 am: Great to be back from Vietnam, an amazing place. We had very substantive negotiations with Kim Jong Un—we know what they want and they know what we must have. Relationship very good, let's see what happens!

4:03 pm: I never like being misinterpreted, but especially when it comes to Otto Warmbier and his great family. Remember, I got Otto out along with three others. The previous Administration did nothing, and he was taken on their watch. Of course I hold North Korea responsible…

…for Otto's mistreatment and death. Most important, Otto Warmbier will not have died in vain. Otto and his family have become a tremendous symbol of strong passion and strength, which will last for many years into the future. I love Otto and think of him often!

March 3, 2019

3:18 pm: The reason I do not want military drills with South Korea is to save hundreds of millions of dollars for the U.S. for which we are not reimbursed. That was my position long before I became President. Also, reducing tensions with North Korea at this time is a good thing!

March 14, 2019

2:53 pm: The military drills, or war games as I call them, were never even discussed in my mtg w/ Kim Jong Un of NK—FAKE NEWS! I made that decision long ago because it costs the U.S. far too much money to have those "games", especially since we are not reimbursed for the tremendous cost!

March 22, 2019

12:22 pm: It was announced today by the U.S. Treasury that additional large scale Sanctions would be added to those already existing Sanctions on North Korea. I have today ordered the withdrawal of those additional Sanctions!

April 13, 2019

6:54 am to *7:04 am:* I agree with Kim Jong Un of North Korea that our personal relationship remains very good, perhaps the term excellent would be even more accurate, and that a third Summit would be good in that we fully understand where we each stand. North Korea has tremendous potential for...

...extraordinary growth, economic success and riches under the leadership of Chairman Kim. I look forward to the day, which could be soon, when Nuclear Weapons and Sanctions can be removed, and then watching North Korea become one of the most successful nations of the World!

April 26, 2019

6:12 am: No money was paid to North Korea for Otto Warmbier, not two Million Dollars, not anything else. This is not the Obama Administration that paid 1.8 Billion Dollars for four hostages, or gave five terroist hostages plus, who soon went back to battle, for traitor Sgt. Bergdahl

May 4, 2019

8:42 am: Anything in this very interesting world is possible, but I believe that Kim Jong Un fully realizes the great economic potential of North Korea, & will do nothing to interfere or end it. He also knows that I am with him & does not want to break his promise to me. Deal will happen!

May 25, 2019

8:32 pm: North Korea fired off some small weapons, which disturbed some of my people, and others, but not me. I have confidence that Chairman Kim will keep his promise to me, & also smiled when he called Swampman Joe Biden a low IQ individual, & worse. Perhaps that's sending me a signal?

May 28, 2019

4:58 pm: I was actually sticking up for Sleepy Joe Biden while on foreign soil. Kim Jong Un called him a "low IQ idiot," and many other things, whereas I related the quote of Chairman Kim as a much softer "low IQ individual." Who could possibly be upset with that?

June 28, 2019

5:51 pm: After some very important meetings, including my meeting with President Xi of China, I will be leaving Japan for South Korea (with President Moon). While there, if Chairman Kim of North Korea sees this, I would meet him at the Border/DMZ just to shake his hand and say Hello(?)!

June 30, 2019

5:21 am: Leaving South Korea after a wonderful meeting with Chairman Kim Jong Un. Stood on the soil of North Korea, an important statement for all, and a great honor!

July 1, 2019

9:57 am: Thank you to President Moon of South Korea for hosting the American Delegation and me immediately following the very successful G-20 in Japan. While there, it was great to call on Chairman Kim of North Korea to have our very well covered meeting. Good things can happen for all!

5:16 pm: It was great being with Chairman Kim Jong Un of North Korea this weekend. We had a great meeting, he looked really well and very healthy—I look forward to seeing him again soon…

5:17 pm: …In the meantime, our teams will be meeting to work on some solutions to very long term and persistent problems. No rush, but I am sure we will ultimately get there!

August 2, 2019

10:05 am: Kim Jong Un and North Korea tested 3 short range missiles over the last number of days. These missiles tests are not a violation of our signed Singapore agreement, nor was there discussion of short range missiles when we shook hands. There may be a United Nations violation, but...

...Chairman Kim does not want to disappoint me with a violation of trust, there is far too much for North Korea to gain—the potential as a Country, under Kim Jong Un's leadership, is unlimited. Also, there is far too much to lose. I may be wrong, but I believe that...

...Chariman Kim has a great and beautiful vision for his country, and only the United States, with me as President, can make that vision come true. He will do the right thing because he is far too smart not to, and he does not want to disappoint his friend, President Trump!

August 7, 2019

5:21 am: South Korea has agreed to pay substantially more money to the United States in order to defend itself from North Korea. Over the past many decades, the U.S. has been paid very little by South Korea, but last year, at the request of President Trump, South Korea paid $990,000,000.

Talks have begun to further increase payments to the United States. South Korea is a very wealthy nation that now feels an obligation to contribute to the military defense provided by the United States of America. The relationship between the two countries is a very good one!

August 10, 2019

6:58 am: ...seeing Kim Jong Un in the not too distant future! A nuclear free North Korea will lead to one of the most successful countries in the world!

Terrorism and 9/11—2017 News Quotes

Response to a question from David Muir of ABC News, January 26, 2017.
Source: https://www.telegraph.co.uk/news/2017/01/26/
full-transcript-president-donald-trumps-interview-abc-news/

"Well, I have a general who I have great respect for, General [James] Mattis, who said—I was a little surprised—Who said he's not a believer in torture. As you know, Mr. [Mike] Pompeo was just approved, affirmed by the Senate. He's a fantastic guy; he's gonna be the head of the CIA."

Response to a question from David Muir of ABC News, January 26, 2017.
Source: https://www.telegraph.co.uk/news/2017/01/26/
full-transcript-president-donald-trumps-interview-abc-news/

"When they're shooting—When they're chopping off the heads of our people and other people, when they're chopping off the heads of people because they happen to be a Christian in the Middle East, when ISIS is doing things that nobody has ever heard of since medieval times, would I feel strongly about waterboarding?

"As far as I'm concerned, we have to fight fire with fire. Now, with that being said I'm going with General [James] Mattis. I'm going with my secretary because I think [Mike] Pompeo's gonna be phenomenal. I'm gonna go with what they say. But I have spoken as recently as 24 hours ago with people at the highest level of intelligence. And I asked them the question, 'Does it work? Does torture work?' And the answer was, 'Yes, absolutely.'"

Response to a question from David Muir of ABC News, January 26, 2017.

Source: https://www.telegraph.co.uk/news/2017/01/26/
full-transcript-president-donald-trumps-interview-abc-news/

"I don't want people to chop off the citizens' or anybody's heads in the Middle East. Okay? Because they're Christian or Muslim or anything else. I don't want—look, you are old enough to have seen a time that was much different. You never saw heads chopped off until a few years ago.

"Now they chop 'em off and they put 'em on camera and they send 'em all over the world. So we have that and we're not allowed to do anything. We're not playing on an even field. I will say this; I will rely on [Mike] Pompeo and [General James] Mattis and my group. And if they don't wanna do, that's fine. If they do wanna do, then I will work for that end.

"I wanna do everything within the bounds of what you're allowed to do legally. But do I feel it works? Absolutely I feel it works. Have I spoken to people at the top levels and people that have seen it work? I haven't seen it work. But I think it works. Have I spoken to people that feel strongly about it? Absolutely."

Response to a question from David Muir of ABC News, January 26, 2017.

Source: https://www.telegraph.co.uk/news/2017/01/26/
full-transcript-president-donald-trumps-interview-abc-news/

"We're talking about—No, it's not the Muslim ban. But it's countries that have tremendous terror. It's countries that we're going to be spelling out in a little while in the same speech. And it's countries that people are going to come in and cause us tremendous problems. Our country has enough problems without allowing people to come in who, in many cases or in some cases, are looking to do tremendous destruction."

Response to a question from David Muir of ABC News, January 26, 2017.

Source: https://www.telegraph.co.uk/news/2017/01/26/
full-transcript-president-donald-trumps-interview-abc-news/

"You're looking at people that come in, in many cases, in some cases with evil intentions. I don't want that. They're ISIS. They're coming under false pretense. I don't want that.

"I'm gonna be the President of a safe country. We have enough problems. Now I'll absolutely do safe zones in Syria for the people. I think that Europe has made a tremendous mistake by allowing these millions of people to go into Germany and various other countries. And all you have to do is take a look. It's, it's a disaster what's happening over there.

"I don't want that to happen here. Now with that being said, [former U.S.] President [Barack] Obama and Hillary Clinton have, and [John] Kerry have allowed tens of thousands of people into our country. The FBI is now investigating more people than ever before having to do with terror. They—And it's from the group of people that came in. So, look, look, our country has a lot of problems. Believe me. I know what the problems are even better than you do. They're deep problems, they're serious problems. We don't need more."

Response to a question from David Muir of ABC News, January 26, 2017.

Source: https://www.telegraph.co.uk/news/2017/01/26/
full-transcript-president-donald-trumps-interview-abc-news/

"We are excluding certain countries. But for other countries we're gonna have extreme vetting. It's going to be very hard to come in. Right now, it's very easy to come in. It's gonna be very, very hard. I don't want terror in this country. You look at what happened in San Bernardino. You look at what happened all over. You look at what happened in the World Trade Center. Okay, I mean, take that as an example."

Response to a question from David Muir of ABC News, January 26, 2017.

Source: https://www.telegraph.co.uk/news/2017/01/26/
full-transcript-president-donald-trumps-interview-abc-news/

"David [Muir of ABC News], I mean, I know you're a sophisticated guy. The world is a mess. The world is as angry as it gets. What? You think this is gonna cause a little more anger? The world is an angry place. All of this has happened. We went into Iraq. We shouldn't have gone into Iraq. We shouldn't have gotten out the way we got out.

"The world is a total mess. Take a look at what's happening with Aleppo. Take a look what's happening in Mosul. Take a look what's going on in the Middle East. And people are fleeing and they're going into Europe and all over the place. The world is a mess, David."

Response to a question from David Muir of ABC News, January 26, 2017.
Source: https://www.telegraph.co.uk/news/2017/01/26/
full-transcript-president-donald-trumps-interview-abc-news/

"Well, we should've kept the oil when we got out. And, you know, it's very interesting, had we taken the oil, you wouldn't have ISIS because they fuel themselves with the oil. That's where they got the money. They got the money from leaving—When we left, we left Iraq, which wasn't a government. It's not a government now.

"And by the way, and I said something else, if we go in and do this. You have two nations, Iraq and Iran. And they were essentially the same military strength. And they'd fight for decades and decades. They'd fight forever. And they'd keep fighting and it would go—It was just a way of life. We got in, we decapitated one of those nations, Iraq. I said, 'Iran is taking over Iraq.' That's essentially what happened."

Response to a question from David Muir of ABC News, January 26, 2017.
Source: https://www.telegraph.co.uk/news/2017/01/26/
full-transcript-president-donald-trumps-interview-abc-news/

"We should have taken the oil. You wouldn't have ISIS if we took the oil. Now I wasn't talking about it from the standpoint of ISIS because the way we got out was horrible. We created a vacuum and ISIS formed. But had we taken the oil something else would've very good happened. They would not have been able to fuel their rather unbelievable drive to destroy large portions of the world."

Response to a question from David Muir of ABC News, January 26, 2017.
Source: https://www.telegraph.co.uk/news/2017/01/26/
full-transcript-president-donald-trumps-interview-abc-news/

"We should've kept, excuse me. We should've taken the oil. And if we took the oil you wouldn't have ISIS. And we would have had wealth. We have spent right now $6 trillion in the Middle East. And our country is falling apart."

Response to a question from Bill O'Reilly of FOX News, February 7, 2017.

Source:https://www.foxnews.com/transcript/bill-oreillys-exclusive-interview-with-president-trump

"I don't like talking openly about it. I don't like talking openly about it. I can say this, ISIS is bad. They are evil. They cut off heads of Christians and Muslims and anybody else that gets in their way. They drown people in steel cages. This is like not since the medieval times has anything happened like this. And the previous administration allowed it to happen because we shouldn't have been in Iraq, but we shouldn't have gotten out the way we got out. It created a vacuum, ISIS was formed. I was to take the oil. If they would've taken the oil, there would be no ISIS because they used that to—[O'Reilly interrupts.]"

Remarks at 9/11 Memorial Observance, September 11, 2017.

Source: https://www.whitehouse.gov/briefings-statements/
remarks-president-trump-9-11-memorial-observance/

"We're gathered here today to remember a morning that started very much like this one. Parents dropped off their children at school. Travelers stood in line at airports and getting ready to board flights. Here at the Pentagon and at offices all across the country, people began their early meetings.

"Then, our whole world changed. America was under attack. First at the World Trade Center, then here at the Pentagon, and then in Pennsylvania. The horror and anguish of that dark day were seared into our national memory forever. It was the worst attack on our country since Pearl Harbor and even worse because this was an attack on civilians: innocent men, women, and children whose lives were taken so needlessly.

"For the families with us on this anniversary, we know that not a single day goes by when you don't think about the loved ones stolen from your life. Today, our entire nation grieves with you and with every family of those 2,977 innocent souls who were murdered by terrorists 16 years ago.

"Each family here today represents a son or daughter, a sister or brother, a mother or father, who was taken from you on that terrible, terrible day. But no force on Earth can ever take away your memories, diminish your love, or break your will to endure and carry on and go forward. Though we can never erase your pain, or bring back those you lost, we can honor their sacrifice by pledging our resolve to do whatever we must to keep our people safe.

"On that day, not only did the world change, but we all changed. Our eyes were opened to the depths of the evil we face. But in that hour of darkness, we also came together with renewed purpose. Our differences never looked so small, our common bonds never felt so strong.

"The sacrificed [sanctified] grounds on which we stand today are a monument to our national unity and to our strength. For more than seven decades, the Pentagon has stood as a global symbol of American might. Not only because of the great power contained within these halls, but because of the incredible character of the people who fill them. They secure our freedom, they defend our flag, and they support our courageous troops all around the world.

"Among the 184 brave Americans who perished on these grounds were young enlisted servicemembers, dedicated civil servants who had worked here for decades, and veterans who served our nation in Korea, in Vietnam, and in the Middle East. All of them loved this country and pledged their very lives to protect it.

"That September morning, each of those brave Americans died as they had lived: as heroes doing their duty and protecting us and our country. We mourn them, we honor them, and we pledge to never, ever forget them.

"We also remember and cherish the lives of the beloved Americans who boarded Flight 77 at Dulles Airport that morning. Every one of them had a family, a story, and beautiful dreams. Each of them had people they loved and who loved them back. And they all left behind a deep emptiness that their warmth and grace once filled so fully and so beautifully.

"The living, breathing soul of America wept with grief for every life taken on that day. We shed our tears in their memory, pledged our devotion in their honor, and turned our sorrow into an unstoppable resolve to achieve justice in their name. The terrorists who attacked us thought they could incite fear and weaken our spirit. But America cannot be intimidated, and those who try will soon join the long list of vanquished enemies who dared to test our mettle.

"In the years after September 11th, more than 5 million young men and women have joined the ranks of our great military to defend our country against barbaric forces of evil and destruction. American forces are relentlessly pursuing and destroying the enemies of all civilized people, ensuring—And these are horrible, horrible enemies; enemies like we've never seen before. But we're ensuring they never again have a safe haven to launch attacks against our country. We are making plain to these savage killers that there is no dark corner beyond our reach, no sanctuary beyond our grasp, and nowhere to hide anywhere on this very large Earth.

"Since 9/11, nearly 7,000 servicemembers have given their lives fighting terrorists around the globe. Some of them rest just beyond this fence, in the shrine to our nation's heroes, on the grounds of Arlington National Cemetery. They came from all backgrounds, all races, all faiths, but they were all there to dedicate their lives, and they defend our one great American flag.

"They, and every person who puts on the uniform, has the love and gratitude of our entire nation.

"Today, as we stand on this hallowed ground, we are reminded of the timeless truth that when America is united, no force on Earth can break us apart, no force."

Remarks at 9/11 Memorial Observance, September 11, 2017.
Source: https://www.whitehouse.gov/briefings-statements/
remarks-president-trump-9-11-memorial-observance/

"To the family members with us today, I know that it's with a pained and heavy heart that you come back to this place. But by doing so, by choosing to persevere through the grief, the sorrow, you honor your heroes, you renew our courage, and you strengthen all of us. You really do. You strengthen all of us.

"Here on the west side of the Pentagon, terrorists tried to break our resolve. It's not going to happen. But where they left a mark with fire and rubble, Americans defiantly raised the stars and stripes: our beautiful flag that for more than two centuries has graced our ships, flown in our skies, and led our brave heroes to victory after victory in battle. The flag that binds us all together as Americans who cherish our values and protect our way of life. The flag that reminds us today of who we are, what we stand for, and why we fight.

"Woven into that beautiful flag is the story of our resolve. We have overcome every challenge, every single challenge, every one of them; we've triumphed over every evil, and remained united as one nation under God. America does not bend. We do not waver. And we will never, ever yield.

"So here at this memorial, with hearts both sad and determined, we honor every hero who keeps us safe and free, and we pledge to work together, to fight together, and to overcome together every enemy and obstacle that's ever in our path.

"Our values will endure. Our people will thrive. Our nation will prevail. And the memory of our loved ones will never, ever die."

Terrorism and 9/11—2017 Tweets

January 30, 2017

7:16 am to *7:20 am:* Only 109 people out of 325,000 were detained and held for questioning. Big problems at airports were caused by Delta computer outage...

protesters and the tears of Senator Schumer. Secretary Kelly said that all is going well with very few problems. MAKE AMERICA SAFE AGAIN!

7:27 am: There is nothing nice about searching for terrorists before they can enter our country. This was a big part of my campaign. Study the world!

8:31 am: If the ban were announced with a one week notice, the "bad" would rush into our country during that week. A lot of bad "dudes" out there!

February 1, 2017

7:50 am: Everybody is arguing whether or not it is a BAN. Call it what you want, it is about keeping bad people (with bad intentions) out of country!

February 3, 2017

7:51 am: A new radical Islamic terrorist has just attacked in Louvre Museum in Paris. Tourists were locked down. France on edge again. GET SMART U.S.

6:08 pm: We must keep "evil" out of our country!

February 4, 2017

7:59 am: When a country is no longer able to say who can, and who cannot , come in & out, especially for reasons of safety &.security— big trouble!

8:06 am: Interesting that certain Middle-Eastern countries agree with the ban. They know if certain people are allowed in it's death & destruction!

3:44 pm: What is our country coming to when a judge can halt a Homeland Security travel ban and anyone, even with bad intentions, can come into U.S.?

4:44 pm: Because the ban was lifted by a judge, many very bad and dangerous people may be pouring into our country. A terrible decision

February 6, 2017

9:49 pm: The threat from radical Islamic terrorism is very real, just look at what is happening in Europe and the Middle-East. Courts must act fast!

February 8, 2017

12:41 pm: Big increase in traffic into our country from certain areas, while our people are far more vulnerable, as we wait for what should be EASY D!

February 12, 2017

6:55 am: 72% of refugees admitted into U.S. (2/3–2/11) during COURT BREAKDOWN are from 7 countries: SYRIA, IRAQ, SOMALIA, IRAN, SUDAN, LIBYA & YEMEN

March 22, 2017

8:33 pm: Spoke to U.K. Prime Minister Theresa May today to offer condolences on the terrorist attack in London. She is strong and doing very well.

March 23, 2017

10:16 am: A great American, Kurt Cochran, was killed in the London terror attack. My prayers and condolences are with his family and friends.

May 26, 2017

3:26 pm: Terrorists are engaged in a war against civilization-it is up to all who value life to confront & defeat this evil→https://t.co/haeuvCIF6I

April 21, 2017

5:32 am: Another terrorist attack in Paris. The people of France will not take much more of this. Will have a big effect on presidential election!

June 4, 2017

6:19 am: We must stop being politically correct and get down to the business of security for our people. If we don't get smart it will only get worse.

6:31 am: At least 7 dead and 48 wounded in terror attack and Mayor of London says there is "no reason to be alarmed!"

6:43 am: Do you notice we are not having a gun debate right now? That's because they used knives and a truck!

June 5, 2017

5:25 am: People, the lawyers and the courts can call it whatever they want, but I am calling it what we need and what it is, a TRAVEL BAN!

5:37 am: The Justice Dept. should ask for an expedited hearing of the watered down Travel Ban before the Supreme Court—& seek much tougher version!

5:44 am: In any event we are EXTREME VETTING people coming into the U.S. in order to help keep our country safe. The courts are slow and political!

8:49 am: Pathetic excuse by London Mayor Sadiq Khan who had to think fast on his "no reason to be alarmed" statement. MSM is working hard to sell it!

8:20 pm: That's right, we need a TRAVEL BAN for certain DANGEROUS countries, not some politically correct term that won't help us protect our people!

July 11, 2017

7:23 am: Big wins against ISIS!

July 12, 2017

6:05 am: ISIS is on the run & will soon be wiped out of Syria & Iraq, illegal border crossings are way down (75%) & MS 13 gangs are being removed.

August 5, 2017

5:12 pm: "Under Trump, gains against #ISIS have dramatically accelerated" https://t.co/jNtOThOmoL

August 12, 2017

12:19 pm: We ALL must be united & condemn all that hate stands for. There is no place for this kind of violence in America. Lets come together as one!

3:23 pm: What is vital now is a swift restoration of law and order and the protection of innocent lives. #Charlottesville

4:19 pm: We must remember this truth: No matter our color, creed, religion or political party, we are ALL AMERICANS FIRST.

4:49 pm: We will continue to follow developments in Charlottesville, and will provide whatever assistance is needed. We are ready, willing and able.

5:50 pm: Deepest condolences to the families & fellow officers of the VA State Police who died today. You're all among the best this nation produces.

6:25 pm: Condolences to the family of the young woman killed today, and best regards to all of those injured, in Charlottesville, Virginia. So sad!

August 14, 2017

5:29 pm: Made additional remarks on Charlottesville and realize once again that the #Fake News Media will never be satisfied...truly bad people!

August 16, 2017

9:58 am: Memorial service today for beautiful and incredible Heather Heyer, a truly special young woman. She will be long remembered by all!

August 17, 2017

1:00 pm: The United States condemns the terror attack in Barcelona, Spain, and will do whatever is necessary to help. Be tough & strong, we love you!

1:45 pm: Study what General Pershing of the United States did to terrorists when caught. There was no more Radical Islamic Terror for 35 years!

August 18, 2017

7:31 am: Homeland Security and law enforcement are on alert & closely watching for any sign of trouble. Our borders are far tougher than ever before!

8:06 am: Radical Islamic Terrorism must be stopped by whatever means necessary! The courts must give us back our protective rights. Have to be tough!

September 1, 2017

7:58 am: Texas is healing fast thanks to all of the great men & women who have been working so hard. But still, so much to do. Will be back tomorrow!

September 15, 2017

5:42 am: Another attack in London by a loser terrorist. These are sick and demented people who were in the sights of Scotland Yard. Must be proactive!

5:48 am: Loser terrorists must be dealt with in a much tougher manner. The internet is their main recruitment tool which we must cut off & use better!

5:54 am: The travel ban into the United States should be far larger, tougher and more specific-but stupidly, that would not be politically correct!

6:00 am: We have made more progress in the last nine months against ISIS than the Obama Administration has made in 8 years. Must be proactive & nasty!

3:54 pm: Our hearts & prayers go out to the people of London, who suffered a vicious terrorist attack...

September 26, 2017

5:32 pm: I want to express our support and extend our prayers to all those affected by the vile terror attack in Spain last month.

October 4, 2017

10:49 am: I will be landing in Las Vegas shortly to pay my respects with @FLOTUS Melania. Everyone remains in our thoughts and prayers.

6:36 pm: WE LOVE YOU LAS VEGAS!

8:08 pm: On behalf of a GRATEFUL NATION, THANK YOU to all of the First Responders (HEROES) who saved countless lives in Las Vegas on Sunday night.

October 11, 2017

2:49 pm: Happy to announce we are awarding $1M to Las Vegas—in order to help local law enforcement working OT to respond to last Sunday's tragedy.

October 19, 2017

8:43 pm: Keep up the GREAT work. I am with you 100%! "ISIS is losing its grip..." Army Colonel Ryan Dillon CJTF–OIR

October 20, 2017

5:31 am: Just out report: "United Kingdom crime rises 13% annually amid spread of Radical Islamic terror." Not good, we must keep America safe!

October 23, 2017

6:18 pm: We will never forget the 241 American service members killed by Hizballah in Beirut. They died in service to our nation. https://t.co/BaQZDA3s2e

October 31, 2017

9:46 am: "Statement by President Trump on the Apprehension of Mustafa al-Imam for His Alleged Role in Benghazi Attacks" https://t.co/2U7WJmfGlM

5:31 pm: We must not allow ISIS to return, or enter, our country after defeating them in the Middle East and elsewhere. Enough!

5:57 pm: My thoughts, condolences and prayers to the victims and families of the New York City terrorist attack. God and your country are with you!

8:26 pm: I have just ordered Homeland Security to step up our already Extreme Vetting Program. Being politically correct is fine, but not for this!

November 1, 2017

6:24 am: The terrorist came into our country through what is called the "Diversity Visa Lottery Program," a Chuck Schumer beauty. I want merit based.

2:26 pm: We mourn the horrifying terrorist attack in NYC. All of America is praying and grieving for the families who lost their precious loved ones.

3:14 pm: Just spoke with @NYGovCuomo and @NYCMayor de Blasio to let them know that the federal government…

3:14 pm: @NYGovCuomo @NYCMayor …fully supports any and all of their efforts with respect to the West Side attack. #NYCStrong

9:09 pm: Just spoke to President Macri of Argentina about the five proud and wonderful men killed in the West Side terror attack. God be with them!

10:43 pm: NYC terrorist was happy as he asked to hang ISIS flag in his hospital room. He killed 8 people, badly injured 12. SHOULD GET DEATH PENALTY!

November 2, 2017

6:50 am to 6:54 am: Would love to send the NYC terrorist to Guantanamo but statistically that process takes much longer than going through the Federal system...

...There is also something appropriate about keeping him in the home of the horrible crime he committed. Should move fast. DEATH PENALTY!

November 3, 2017

7:03 am to 7:11 am: ISIS just claimed the Degenerate Animal who killed, and so badly wounded, the wonderful people on the West Side, was "their soldier"...

...Based on that, the Military has hit ISIS "much harder" over the last two days. They will pay a big price for every attack on us!

November 5, 2017

3:06 pm: May God be w/ the people of Sutherland Springs, Texas. The FBI & law enforcement are on the scene. I am monitoring the situation from Japan

11:48 pm: ...Americans do what we do best: we pull together. We join hands. We lock arms and through the tears and the sadness, we stand strong...

November 14, 2017

11:34 pm: May God be with the people of Sutherland Springs, Texas. The FBI and Law Enforcement has arrived.

November 17, 2017

10:03 am: Together, we're going to restore safety to our streets and peace to our communities, and we're going to destroy the vile criminal cartel, #MS13, and many other gangs... 'Hundreds arrested in MS-13 crackdown' https://t.co/Mp268d8RaU

November 24, 2017

10:27 am: Horrible and cowardly terrorist attack on innocent and defenseless worshipers in Egypt. The world cannot tolerate terrorism, we must defeat them militarily and discredit the extremist ideology that forms the basis of their existence!

1:49 pm: Will be calling the President of Egypt in a short while to discuss the tragic terrorist attack, with so much loss of life. We have to get TOUGHER AND SMARTER than ever before, and we will. Need the WALL, need the BAN! God bless the people of Egypt.

Terrorism and 9/11—2018 News Quotes

Statement on the Iran nuclear deal, January 12, 2018.
Source: https://www.whitehouse.gov/briefings-statements/
statement-president-iran-nuclear-deal/

"The Iranian regime is the world's leading state sponsor of terror. It enables Hezbollah, Hamas, and many other terrorists to sow chaos and kill innocent people. It has funded, armed, and trained more than 100,000 militants to spread destruction across the Middle East. It props up the murderous regime of Bashar al Assad, and has helped him slaughter his own people. The regime's destructive missiles threaten neighboring countries and international shipping. Within

Iran, the Supreme Leader and his Islamic Revolutionary Guard Corps use mass arrests and torture to oppress and silence Iran's people. Iran's ruling elite has let their citizens go hungry while enriching themselves by stealing Iran's national wealth.

"Last October, I outlined to the American people, and to the world, my strategy for confronting these and other destructive activities. We are countering Iranian proxy wars in Yemen and Syria. We are cutting off the regime's money flows to terrorists. We have sanctioned nearly 100 individuals and entities involved with the Iranian regime's ballistic missile program and its other illicit activities. Today, I am adding 14 more to the sanctions list. We are also supporting the brave Iranian citizens who are demanding change from a corrupt regime that wastes the Iranian people's money on weapons systems at home and terrorism abroad. And crucially, we are calling on all nations to lend similar support to the Iranian people, who are suffering under a regime that is stifling basic freedoms and denying its citizens the opportunity to build better lives for their families—an opportunity that is every human being's God-given right.

"All this stands in stark contrast to the policy and actions of the previous administration. [Former U.S.] President [Barack] Obama failed to act as the Iranian people took to the streets in 2009. He turned a blind eye as Iran built and tested dangerous missiles and exported terror. He curried favor with the Iranian regime in order to push through the disastrously flawed Iran nuclear deal.

"I have been very clear about my opinion of that deal. It gave Iran far too much in exchange for far too little. The enormous financial windfall the Iranian regime received because of the deal, access to more than $100 billion, including $1.8 billion in cash, has not been used to better the lives of the Iranian people. Instead, it has served as a slush fund for weapons, terror, and oppression, and to further line the pockets of corrupt regime leaders. The Iranian people know this, which is one reason why so many have taken to the streets to express their outrage.

"Despite my strong inclination, I have not yet withdrawn the United States from the Iran nuclear deal. Instead, I have outlined two possible paths forward: either fix the deal's disastrous flaws, or the United States will withdraw.

"I am open to working with Congress on bipartisan legislation regarding Iran. But any bill I sign must include four critical components.

"First, it must demand that Iran allow immediate inspections at all sites requested by international inspectors.

"Second, it must ensure that Iran never even comes close to possessing a nuclear weapon.

"Third, unlike the nuclear deal, these provisions must have no expiration date. My policy is to deny Iran all paths to a nuclear weapon, not just for 10 years, but forever.

"If Iran does not comply with any of these provisions, American nuclear sanctions would automatically resume.

"Fourth, the legislation must explicitly state in United States law, for the first time, that long-range missile and nuclear weapons programs are inseparable, and that Iran's development and testing of missiles should be subject to severe sanctions.

"In 2015, the Obama Administration foolishly traded away strong multilateral sanctions to get its weak nuclear deal. By contrast, my Administration has engaged with key European allies in seeking to secure a new supplemental agreement that would impose new multilateral sanctions if Iran develops or tests long-range missiles, thwarts inspections, or makes progress toward a nuclear weapon, requirements that should have been in the nuclear deal in the first place. And, like the bill I expect from Congress, these provisions of a supplemental agreement must never expire.

"I also call on all our allies to take stronger steps with us to confront Iran's other malign activities. Among other actions, our allies should cut off funding to the Islamic Revolutionary Guard Corps, its militant proxies, and anyone else who contributes to Iran's support for terrorism. They should designate Hezbollah, in its entirety, as a terrorist organization. They should join us in constraining Iran's missile development and stopping its proliferation of missiles, especially to

Yemen. They should join us in countering Iran's cyber threats. They should help us deter Iran's aggression against international shipping. They should pressure the Iranian regime to stop violating its citizens' rights. And they should not do business with groups that enrich Iran's dictatorship or fund the Revolutionary Guard and its terrorist proxies.

"Today, I am waiving the application of certain nuclear sanctions, but only in order to secure our European allies' agreement to fix the terrible flaws of the Iran nuclear deal. This is a last chance. In the absence of such an agreement, the United States will not again waive sanctions in order to stay in the Iran nuclear deal. And if at any time I judge that such an agreement is not within reach, I will withdraw from the deal immediately.

"No one should doubt my word. I said I would not certify the nuclear deal, and I did not. I will also follow through on this pledge. I hereby call on key European countries to join with the United States in fixing significant flaws in the deal, countering Iranian aggression, and supporting the Iranian people. If other nations fail to act during this time, I will terminate our deal with Iran. Those who, for whatever reason, choose not to work with us will be siding with the Iranian regime's nuclear ambitions, and against the people of Iran and the peaceful nations of the world."

Remarks as part of a joint press statement with then-President Nursultan Nazarbayev[20] of Kazakhstan, January 16, 2018.
Source: https://www.whitehouse.gov/briefings-statements/
remarks-president-trump-president-nursultan-nazarbayev-kazakhstan-joint-press-statements/

"Thank you. And I'm pleased to welcome President [Nursultan] Nazarbayev who has done a tremendous job in Kazakhstan. And having you at the White House is an honor. Mr. President, thank you for visiting with us, and we have very important discussions going on.

"For more than a quarter century, the United States has seen the strong, sovereign, and independent nation of Kazakhstan as a valued friend

---

20 Nazarbayev resigned in 2019 after nearly 30 years in office.
    Source: https://www.reuters.com/article/us-kazakhstan-president/
    president-of-kazakhstan-nursultan-nazarbayev-resigns-idUSKCN1R01N

and a strategic partner in Central Asia. And we're honored, and we are truly honored to be the first country to recognize Kazakhstani independence on Christmas Day 1991. That's a long time ago, but not that long. You've made incredible strides.

"Since that time, the United States and Kazakhstan have worked together to advance peace and security in the region and far beyond the region.

"Together, we dismantled Kazakhstan's nuclear weapons infrastructure and ensured a safer and healthier future for the children of Kazakhstan and for the world at large. We've pursued opportunities to increase investment in Kazakhstan and the energy sector in particular.

"And today, our strategic partnership with Kazakhstan has advanced my South Asia strategy, which is working, and working far more rapidly than anybody would understand, and providing crucial support for our forces in Afghanistan and denying safe haven for terrorists.

"This cooperation has grown even stronger this month during Kazakhstan's presidency of the United Nations Security Council. And I will say, that's a great honor.

"Today, the President and I have a series of discussions on how our relationship can further the safety, prosperity, and wellbeing of our people. Kazakhstan is a valued partner in our efforts to rid the Korean Peninsula of nuclear weapons. Together, we are determined to prevent the North Korean regime from threatening the world with nuclear devastation.

"I also want to thank the President for his full support for our South Asia strategy, including our efforts in Afghanistan. I greatly appreciate the President's personal assurances that Kazakhstan will continue to provide critical logistical support and access for our troops fighting ISIS and the Taliban, where we have made tremendous strides.

"We also appreciate Kazakhstan's work to train and educate Afghan civilian specialists, and I'm grateful for the President's pledge of additional support to bolster Afghan security. The United States seeks partners who are strong, prosperous, respectful of their neighbors, and in control of their own destinies."

Response to a question from an unidentified reporter before a bilateral meeting with Prime Minister Stefan Löfven of Sweden, March 6, 2018.

Source: https://www.whitehouse.gov/briefings-statements/
remarks-president-trump-prime-minister-lofven-sweden-bilateral-meeting/

"Well, I think we're [Prime Minister Stefan Löfven of Sweden and I are] going to be talking a lot about trade and a lot about the military and protection; a lot about terrorism, which is, unfortunately, a subject we discuss with many countries when they come to the Oval Office. But we'll be discussing many things."

Remarks before a bilateral meeting with President Muhammadu Buhari of Nigeria, April 30, 2018

Source: https://www.whitehouse.gov/briefings-statements/
remarks-president-trump-president-buhari-federal-republic-nigeria-bilateral-meeting/

"It's an honor to be with President [Muhammadu] Buhari of Nigeria. We have many things that we do together, as you know, probably— Especially on terrorism and terrorism related.

"We also have a very big trade deal that we're working on for military equipment, helicopters and the like. We have met before. We have developed a great relationship. And we look forward to our discussion today, very important, but again, especially as it relates to terrorism. And that's terrorism here and terrorism all over the world. It's a hotbed, and we're going to be stopping that.

"Also, we've had very serious problems with Christians who have been murdered, killed in Nigeria. We're going to be working on that problem, and working on that problem very, very hard, because we can't allow that to happen."

Remarks before a bilateral meeting with President Muhammadu Buhari of Nigeria, April 30, 2018

Source: https://www.whitehouse.gov/briefings-statements/
remarks-president-trump-president-buhari-federal-republic-nigeria-bilateral-meeting/

"We have very much decimated ISIS. Much has taken place over the last 12 months."

Remarks before a bilateral meeting with President Uhuru Kenyatta of Kenya, August 27, 2018.

Source: https://www.whitehouse.gov/briefings-statements/
remarks-president-trump-president-kenyatta-republic-kenya-bilateral-meeting/

"We have a tremendous relationship with Kenya. We have terrorism, a lot of trade, getting bigger and bigger all the time."

Remarks before a bilateral meeting with President Emmanuel Macron of France, September 24, 2018.

Source: https://www.whitehouse.gov/briefings-statements/
remarks-president-trump-president-macron-french-republic-bilateral-meeting/

"It's a great honor to have a friend of mine, [French] President [Emmanuel] Macron. And we've had some very good experiences. On occasion, not so good, but 99% very good.

"France is doing very well. We're doing very well. And I think, very importantly, we're doing very well together. We have a lot of trade and we're discussing trade. We'll be discussing it today. We'll be discussing military and defense. And terrorism is a big subject that we're always talking about. And that's why we're here tonight, I think maybe more so than almost anything. And trade.

"So, I just want to thank you for being here. And it's a great honor. We had a tremendous celebration in the White House a number of months ago, honoring the President and Mrs. Macron, and honoring France. And it was something very special."

Response to a question from Chris Wallace of FOX News, November 18, 2018.

Source: https://www.youtube.com/watch?v=rMgJnnG-Nql

"Wouldn't it have been nice if we got Osama Bin Laden a lot sooner than that? Wouldn't it have been nice? You know, living—Think of this, living in Pakistan, beautifully in Pakistan in what I guess they considered a nice mansion, I don't know, I've seen nicer. But living in Pakistan right next to the military academy, everybody in Pakistan knew he was there. And we give Pakistan $1.3 billion a year and they don't tell him, they don't tell him."

From a letter to the Speaker of the House of Representatives and the President Pro Tempore of the Senate, December 7, 2018.

Source: https://www.whitehouse.gov/briefings-statements/
text-letter-president-speaker-house-representatives-president-pro-tempore-senate-5/

"Since October 7, 2001, United States Armed Forces, including Special Operations Forces, have conducted counterterrorism combat operations against al-Qa'ida, the Taliban, and associated forces. Since August 2014, these operations have targeted the Islamic State of Iraq and Syria (ISIS), also known as the Islamic State of Iraq and the Levant (ISIL), which was formerly known as al-Qa'ida in Iraq. In support of these and other overseas operations, the United States has deployed combat-equipped forces to several locations in the United States Central, European, Africa, Southern, and Indo-Pacific Commands' areas of responsibility. Such operations and deployments have been reported previously, consistent with Public Law 107-40, Public Law 107-243, the War Powers Resolution, and other statutes. These ongoing operations, which the United States has carried out with the assistance of numerous international partners, have been successful in seriously degrading ISIS capabilities in Syria and Iraq. If necessary, in response to terrorist threats, I will direct additional measures to protect the citizens and interests of the United States. It is not possible to know at this time the precise scope or the duration of the deployments of United States Armed Forces that are or will be necessary to counter terrorist threats to the United States.

"Afghanistan. Consistent with the strategy I announced publicly on August 21, 2017, United States Armed Forces remain in Afghanistan for the purposes of stopping the reemergence of safe havens that enable terrorists to threaten the United States, supporting the Afghan government and the Afghan military as they confront the Taliban in the field, and creating conditions to support a political process to achieve lasting peace. United States forces in Afghanistan are training, advising, and assisting Afghan forces; conducting and supporting counterterrorism operations against al-Qa'ida and against ISIS; and taking appropriate measures against those who provide direct support to al-Qa'ida, threaten United States and coalition forces in Afghanistan, or threaten the viability of the Afghan government or the ability of the Afghan National Defense and Security Forces to achieve campaign success. Although reconciliation efforts are ongoing, the United States remains in an armed conflict, including in Afghanistan and against the Taliban, and active hostilities remain ongoing.

"Iraq and Syria. As part of a comprehensive strategy to defeat ISIS, United States Armed Forces are conducting a systematic campaign of airstrikes and other necessary operations against ISIS forces in Iraq and Syria. United States Armed Forces are also conducting airstrikes and other necessary operations against al-Qa'ida in Syria. United States Armed Forces are also deployed to Syria to conduct operations against ISIS with indigenous ground forces. In Iraq, United States Armed Forces are advising and coordinating with Iraqi forces and providing training, equipment, communications support, intelligence support, and other support to select elements of the Iraqi security forces, including Iraqi Kurdish Security forces. United States Armed Forces also provide limited support to the North Atlantic Treaty Organization mission in Iraq. Actions in Iraq are being undertaken in coordination with the Government of Iraq, and in conjunction with coalition partners.

"Arabian Peninsula Region. A small number of United States military personnel are deployed to Yemen to conduct operations against al-Qa'ida in the Arabian Peninsula (AQAP) and ISIS-Yemen. The United States military continues to work closely with the Government of Yemen and regional partner forces to dismantle and ultimately eliminate the terrorist threat posed by those groups. Since the last periodic update report, United States Armed Forces conducted a number of airstrikes against AQAP operatives and facilities in Yemen, and supported the United Arab Emirates-and Yemen-led operations to clear AQAP from Shabwah Governorate. United States Armed Forces are also prepared to conduct airstrikes against ISIS targets in Yemen. United States Armed Forces, in a non-combat role, have also continued to provide military advice and limited information, logistics, and other support to regional forces combatting the Houthi insurgency in Yemen; however, aerial refueling of regional forces' aircraft ended in November 2018. United States forces are present in Saudi Arabia for this purpose. Such support does not involve United States Armed Forces in hostilities with the Houthis for the purposes of the War Powers Resolution.

"Jordan. At the request of the Government of Jordan, approximately 2,795 United States military personnel are deployed to Jordan to support Defeat-ISIS operations, enhance Jordan's security, and promote regional stability.

"Lebanon. At the request of the Government of Lebanon, approximately 86 United States military personnel are deployed to Lebanon to enhance the government's counterterrorism capabilities and support the Defeat-ISIS operations of Lebanese security forces.

"Turkey. United States Armed Forces, including strike and combat-support aircraft and associated United States military personnel, remain deployed to Turkey, at the Turkish government's request, to support Defeat-ISIS operations and to enhance Turkey's security.

"East Africa Region. In Somalia, United States Armed Forces continue to counter the terrorist threat posed by ISIS and al-Shabaab, an associated force of al-Qa'ida. Since the last periodic report, United States Armed Forces have conducted a number of airstrikes against al-Shabaab. United States military personnel also advise, assist, and accompany regional forces, including Somali and African Union Mission in Somalia (AMISOM) forces, during counterterrorism operations. Additional United States Armed Forces are deployed to Kenya to support counterterrorism operations in East Africa. United States military personnel continue to partner with the Government of Djibouti, which has permitted use of Djiboutian territory for basing of United States Armed Forces. United States military personnel remain deployed to Djibouti, including for purposes of posturing for counterterrorism and counter-piracy operations in the vicinity of the Horn of Africa and the Arabian Peninsula, and to provide contingency support for Embassy security augmentation in East Africa, as required.

"Libya. Since the last periodic update report, United States Armed Forces conducted a limited number of airstrikes against al-Qa'ida in the Islamic Maghreb (an associated force of al-Qa'ida) and ISIS terrorists in Libya. These airstrikes were conducted in coordination with the Government of National Accord.

"Lake Chad Basin and Sahel Region. United States military personnel in the Lake Chad Basin and Sahel Region continue to conduct airborne intelligence, surveillance, and reconnaissance operations and provide support to African and European partners conducting counterterrorism operations in the region, including by advising, assisting, and accompanying these partner forces. Approximately 730 United States military personnel remain deployed to Niger. United States military personnel are also deployed to Cameroon, Chad, and Nigeria to support counterterrorism operations.

"Cuba. United States Armed Forces continue to conduct humane and secure detention operations for detainees held at Guantánamo Bay, Cuba, under the authority provided by the 2001 Authorization for the Use of Military Force (Public Law 107-40), as informed by the law of war. There are 40 such detainees as of the date of this report.

"The Philippines. United States Armed Forces deployed to the Philippines are providing support to the counterterrorism operations of the armed forces of the Philippines."

Remarks at the Signing Ceremony for H.R. 390, Iraq and Syria Genocide Relief and Accountability Act of 2018, December 11, 2018.
Source: https://www.whitehouse.gov/briefings-statements/remarks-president-trump-signing-ceremony-h-r-390-iraq-syria-genocide-relief-accountability-act-2018/

"In a few moments, I will sign legislation to assist religious and ethnic groups targeted by ISIS for mass murder and genocide in Syria and Iraq. The bill also authorities U.S. government efforts to help bring preparations and perpetrators of these heinous crimes to justice, and to justice very swiftly."

Remarks at the Signing Ceremony for H.R. 390, Iraq and Syria Genocide Relief and Accountability Act of 2018, December 11, 2018.
Source: https://www.whitehouse.gov/briefings-statements/remarks-president-trump-signing-ceremony-h-r-390-iraq-syria-genocide-relief-accountability-act-2018/

"In recent years, ISIS has committed horrifying atrocities against religious and ethnic minorities in Syria and Iraq, including Christians,

Yazidis, Shia, and other groups. And beyond the, beyond the various groups, they've just been devastating to a lot of people.

"And I have to say, we've done a very, very major job on ISIS. There are very few of them left in that area of the world. And within another 30 days, there won't be any of them left.

"Since I took office, we've driven ISIS out of nearly all of the territory it once held in Syria and Iraq, devastating the caliphate. You've been reading about it. It's actually been covered reasonably fairly, which isn't bad.

"This bill continues my administration's efforts to direct U.S. assistance toward persecuted communities, including through faith-based programs. It also allows the government agencies to assist a range of entities in investigating and prosecuting ISIS' despicable acts. And they are very despicable indeed.

"Today, we honor the memory of all those killed by ISIS in Syria and Iraq, and we renew our sacred commitment to religious freedom."

Terrorism and 9/11—2018 Tweets

January 27, 2018

5:59 pm: Taliban targeted innocent Afghans, brave police in Kabul today. Our thoughts and prayers go to the victims, and first responders. We will not allow the Taliban to win!

April 14, 2018

7:21 am: A perfectly executed strike last night. Thank you to France and the United Kingdom for their wisdom and the power of their fine Military. Could not have had a better result. Mission Accomplished!

May 7, 2018

6:04 am: My highly respected nominee for CIA Director, Gina Haspel, has come under fire because she was too tough on Terrorists. Think of that, in these very dangerous times, we have the most qualified person, a woman, who Democrats want OUT because she is too tough on terror. Win Gina!

May 10, 2018

9:33 am: Five Most Wanted leaders of ISIS just captured!

May 13, 2018

7:03 pm: So sad to see the Terror Attack in Paris. At some point countries will have to open their eyes & see what is really going on. This kind of sickness & hatred is not compatible with a loving, peaceful, & successful country! Changes to our thought process on terror must be made.

May 18, 2018

11:34 am: We grieve for the terrible loss of life, and send our support and love to everyone affected by this horrible attack in Texas. To the students, families, teachers and personnel at Santa Fe High School—we are with you in this tragic hour, and we will be with you forever...

May 26, 2018

8:22 am: Good news about the release of the American hostage from Venezuela. Should be landing in D.C. this evening and be in the White House, with his family, at about 7:00 P.M. The great people of Utah will be very happy!

June 26, 2018

9:40 am: SUPREME COURT UPHOLDS TRUMP TRAVEL BAN. Wow!

June 29, 2018

12:59 pm: Before going any further today, I want to address the horrific shooting that took place yesterday at the Capital Gazette newsroom in Annapolis, Maryland. This attack shocked the conscience of our Nation, and filled our hearts with grief…

August 14, 2018

6:42 am: Another terrorist attack in London…These animals are crazy and must be dealt with through toughness and strength!

September 11, 2018

6:59 am: Rudy Giuliani did a GREAT job as Mayor of NYC during the period of September 11th. His leadership, bravery and skill must never be forgotten. Rudy is a TRUE WARRIOR!

10:32 am: #NeverForget #September11[th] https://t.co/l8WZer3UOL

October 25, 2018

6:13 pm: We are gathered together on this solemn occasion to fulfill our most reverent and sacred duty. 35 years ago, 241 American service members were murdered in the terrorist attack on our Marine Barracks in Beirut, Lebanon. Today, we honor our fallen heroes…

6:19 pm: In 1983, roughly 1,800 Marines were in Beirut to keep the peace in a Nation torn apart by Civil War. Terrorists had bombed the U.S. Embassy earlier that year, killing 63 people, including 17 Americans…

6:21 pm: The Service Members who died that day included brave young Marines just out of high school, accomplished officers in the middle of their military careers, and enlisted men who had served in theaters all over the world…

October 26, 2018

9:19 am: Republicans are doing so well in early voting, and at the polls, and now this "Bomb" stuff happens and the momentum greatly slows—news not talking politics. Very unfortunate, what is going on. Republicans, go out and vote!

10:41 am: I will be speaking at the Young Black Leadership Summit in 15 minutes where I will address the investigation into the bomb packages.

12:23 pm: I would like to begin today's remarks by providing an update on the packages and devices that have been mailed to high-profile figures throughout our Country, and a media org. I am pleased to inform you that law enforcement has apprehended the suspect and taken him into custody.

12:59 pm: I want to applaud the FBI, Secret Service, Department of Justice, the U.S. Attorneys' Office for the Southern District of New York, the NYPD, and all Law Enforcement partners across the Country for their incredible work, skill and determination!

October 27, 2018

10:08 am: Watching the events unfolding in Pittsburgh, Pennsylvania. Law enforcement on the scene. People in Squirrel Hill area should remain sheltered. Looks like multiple fatalities. Beware of active shooter. God Bless All!

11:26 am: Events in Pittsburgh are far more devastating than originally thought. Spoke with Mayor and Governor to inform them that the Federal Government has been, and will be, with them all the way. I will speak to the media shortly and make further statement at Future Farmers of America.

2:43 pm: As you know, earlier today there was a horrific shooting targeting and killing Jewish Americans at the Tree of Life Synagogue in Pittsburgh, Pennsylvania. The shooter is in custody, and federal authorities have been dispatched to support state and local police...

4:41 pm: All of America is in mourning over the mass murder of Jewish Americans at the Tree of Life Synagogue in Pittsburgh. We pray for those who perished and their loved ones, and our hearts go out to the brave police officers who sustained serious injuries...

…This evil Anti-Semitic attack is an assault on humanity. It will take all of us working together to extract the poison of Anti-Semitism from our world. We must unite to conquer hate.

November 19, 2018

10:26 am: Of course we should have captured Osama Bin Laden long before we did. I pointed him out in my book just BEFORE the attack on the World Trade Center. President Clinton famously missed his shot. We paid Pakistan Billions of Dollars & they never told us he was living there. Fools!…

10:41 am: …We no longer pay Pakistan the $Billions because they would take our money and do nothing for us, Bin Laden being a prime example, Afghanistan being another. They were just one of many countries that take from the United States without giving anything in return. That's ENDING!

November 26, 2018

2:45 pm: On the ten-year anniversary of the Mumbai terror attack, the U.S. stands with the people of India in their quest for justice. The attack killed 166 innocents, including six Americans. We will never let terrorists win, or even come close to winning!

December 16, 2018

10:03 am: At the request of many, I will be reviewing the case of a "U.S. Military hero," Major Matt Golsteyn, who is charged with murder. He could face the death penalty from our own government after he admitted to killing a Terrorist bomb maker while overseas. @Pete-Hegseth @FoxNews

December 19, 2018

9:29 am: We have defeated ISIS in Syria, my only reason for being there during the Trump Presidency.

December 21, 2018

10:31 am: I've done more damage to ISIS than all recent presidents… not even close!

Terrorism and 9/11—2019 News Quotes

Response to a question from Margaret Brennan of CBS News, February 3, 2019.
Source: https://www.cbsnews.com/news/
transcript-president-trump-on-face-the-nation-february-3-2019/

"I think, let me just say it wasn't so much a report. It was the questions and answers as the report was submitted and they were asked questions and answers. We've done an incredible job with Syria. When I took over Syria it was infested with ISIS. It was all over the place. And now you have very little ISIS and you have the caliphate almost knocked out. We will be announcing in the not too distant future 100% of the caliphate which is the area, the land, the area: 100. We're at 99% right now, we'll be at 100. When I took it over it was a disaster. I think we've done a great job with that. At the same time, at a certain point, we want to bring our people back home. If you look at Afghanistan we're going in very soon we'll be going into our 19th year spending 50 billion dollars a year. Now if you go back and look at any of my campaign speeches or rallies, I talked about it all the time."

Response to a question from Margaret Brennan of CBS News, February 3, 2019.
Source: https://www.cbsnews.com/news/
transcript-president-trump-on-face-the-nation-february-3-2019/

"I'm not telegraphing anything. No, no, no. There's a difference. When [then-U.S.] President [Barack] Obama pulled out of Iraq in theory we had Iraq. In other words, we had Iraq. We never had Syria because President Obama never wanted to violate the red line in the sand. So we never had Syria. I was the one that actually violated the red line when I hit Syria with 59 Tomahawk missiles, if you remember. But President Obama chose not to do that. When he chose not to do that, he showed tremendous weakness. But we didn't have Syria whereas we had Iraq. So when he did what he did in Iraq, which was a mistake. Being in Iraq was a mistake. Okay. Being in Iraq—It was a big mistake to go; one of the greatest mistakes going into the Middle East that our country has ever made. One of the greatest mistakes that we've ever made—[Brennan interrupts.]"

From State of the Union address, February 5, 2019.

Source: https://www.whitehouse.gov/briefings-statements/
president-donald-j-trumps-state-union-address-2/

"When I took office, ISIS controlled more than 20,000 square miles in Iraq and Syria. Today, we have liberated virtually all of that territory from the grip of these bloodthirsty killers.

"Now, as we work with our allies to destroy the remnants of ISIS, it is time to give our brave warriors in Syria a warm welcome home.

"I have also accelerated our negotiations to reach a political settlement in Afghanistan. Our troops have fought with unmatched valor and thanks to their bravery, we are now able to pursue a political solution to this long and bloody conflict.

"In Afghanistan, my administration is holding constructive talks with a number of Afghan groups, including the Taliban. As we make progress in these negotiations, we will be able to reduce our troop presence and focus on counter-terrorism. We do not know whether we will achieve an agreement, but we do know that after two decades of war, the hour has come to at least try for peace.

"Above all, friend and foe alike must never doubt this nation's power and will to defend our people. Eighteen years ago, terrorists attacked the USS Cole, and last month American forces killed one of the leaders of the attack."

Response to an unidentified reporter's question before Marine One departure, March 20, 2019.
Source: https://www.whitehouse.gov/briefings-statements/
remarks-president-trump-marine-one-departure-34/

"No, no. We're—In Syria, we're leaving 200 people there and 200 people in another place in Syria, closer to Israel, for a period of time. I brought this out for you because this is a map of—Everything in the red—This was on Election Night in 2016. Everything red is ISIS. When I took it over, it was a mess.

"Now, on the bottom, that's the exact same. There is no red. In fact, there's actually a tiny spot, which will be gone by tonight.

"So that's ISIS: red, right there, and the bottom one is how it is today. This just came out 20 minutes ago. So this is ISIS on Election Day, my election day, and this is ISIS now. So that's the way it goes."

Response to an unidentified reporter's question before Marine One departure, March 20, 2019.
Source: https://www.whitehouse.gov/briefings-statements/
remarks-president-trump-marine-one-departure-34/

"Pakistan—We'll be meeting with Pakistan. I think our relationship right now is very good with Pakistan."

Response to a question from an unidentified reporter before Marine One departure, September 9, 2019.
Source: https://www.whitehouse.gov/briefings-statements/
remarks-president-trump-marine-one-departure-63/

"They're [The Taliban are] dead. They're dead. As far as I'm concerned, they're dead.

"They [the Taliban] thought that they had to kill people in order to put themselves in a little better negotiating position. When they did that, they killed 12 people. One happened to be a great American soldier, a wonderful young man from Puerto Rico. Family is from Puerto Rico. And you can't do that. You can't do that with me.

"So they're dead, as far as I'm concerned. And we've hit the Taliban harder in the last four days than they've been hit in over 10 years. So that's the way it is."

Response to a question from an unidentified reporter before Marine One departure, September 9, 2019.

Source: https://www.whitehouse.gov/briefings-statements/
remarks-president-trump-marine-one-departure-63/

"No. Actually, in terms of advisors, I took my own advice. I liked the idea of meeting. I've met with a lot of bad people and a lot of good people during the course of the last almost three years. And I think meeting is a great thing. I think that meeting with—You know, you're talking about war. There are meetings with war. Otherwise, wars would never end. You'd have them going forever.

"We had a meeting scheduled. It was my idea, and it was my idea to terminate it. I didn't even—I didn't discuss it with anybody else. When I heard, very simply, that they [the Taliban] killed one of our soldiers and 12 other innocent people, I said, 'There's no way I'm meeting on that basis. There's no way I'm meeting.' They did a mistake.

"And, by the way, they are telling people they made a big mistake. They're saying it loud and clear that they made a big mistake."

Response to a question from an unidentified reporter before Marine One departure, September 9, 2019.

Source: https://www.whitehouse.gov/briefings-statements/
remarks-president-trump-marine-one-departure-63/

"Well, Camp David has held meetings with a lot of people that would have been perceived as being pretty tough customers and pretty bad people. There have been plenty of so-called 'bad people' brought up to Camp David for meetings. And the alternative was the White House, and you wouldn't have been happy with that either.

"So Camp David would have been a good place, but I don't want to meet under circumstances where they [the Taliban] go around and try and make themselves a little bit more important by killing a soldier; by killing, actually, also a great NATO soldier, in addition to our soldier; and also a total of 12 people. I don't want that.

"But, you know, Camp David has had many meetings that, I guess, people would not have considered politically correct."

Response to a question from an unidentified reporter before Marine One departure, September 9, 2019.
Source: https://www.whitehouse.gov/briefings-statements/
remarks-president-trump-marine-one-departure-63/

"Well, my decision was to have a meeting. And I said, 'You know what? I don't like the concept of having it at the White House. That would be a step too far.' There have been many very powerful meetings at Camp David having to do with enemies, real enemies, very big enemies, war, and I thought Camp David would be good, and I still do.

"The only reason I canceled that meeting is because they killed one of our soldiers and they killed a total of 12 people, trying to build up their importance, because they think that's important—Except, to me, it backfired. And they're very upset. They feel that they blew it. And they said it loud and clear. They feel they made a big mistake by doing what they did."

Response to a question from an unidentified reporter before Marine One departure, September 9, 2019.
Source: https://www.whitehouse.gov/briefings-statements/
remarks-president-trump-marine-one-departure-63/

"Afghanistan is a very interesting situation. We've been there for 19 years. Nineteen years. And we're now really policemen in Afghanistan.

"So what's happening is this: we're talking. We're talking to the government. We're talking to a lot of different people. And we'll see. But I canceled Camp David on the basis that they did something that they sure as hell shouldn't have done."

Response to a question from an unidentified reporter before Marine One departure, September 9, 2019.

Source: https://www.whitehouse.gov/briefings-statements/
remarks-president-trump-marine-one-departure-63/

"We haven't discussed it. I'm not looking to discuss it. We've hit the Taliban and our enemy in Afghanistan harder than we have in over 10 years. So I'm not discussing anything right now."

Remarks made at a rally in Tupelo, Mississippi, November 1, 2019.

Source: https://www.c-span.org/video/?465540-1/
president-trump-campaign-rally-tupelo-mississippi

"Al Baghdadi, the founder and leader—Look, you know, you've heard about him for a long time. I kept saying, 'Where is Al Baghdadi; that's the one I want. Where is he?' And then, by the way, the following day we got number two. I don't know if you read about that, but he was the founder and the leader of ISIS, and he's dead.

"And Baghdadi, he was a savage and soulless monster, but his reign of terror is over. American special operators executed a masterful raid that ended his wretched life and punched out his ticket to hell. I guess you could say. He spent his last miserable moments on earth, cowering and trembling, and crying in fear of the American warrior that was right there, going right up. No enemy stands a chance against the righteous might of the United States military."

Terrorism and 9/11—2019 Tweets

January 6, 2019

10:27 am: Our GREAT MILITARY has delivered justice for the heroes lost and wounded in the cowardly attack on the USS Cole. We

417

have just killed the leader of that attack, Jamal al-Badawi. Our work against al Qaeda continues. We will never stop in our fight against Radical Islamic Terrorism!

January 13, 2019

5:53 pm: Starting the long overdue pullout from Syria while hitting the little remaining ISIS territorial caliphate hard, and from many directions. Will attack again from existing nearby base if it reforms. Will devastate Turkey economically if they hit Kurds. Create 20 mile safe zone…

6:02 pm: ..Likewise, do not want the Kurds to provoke Turkey. Russia, Iran and Syria have been the biggest beneficiaries of the long term U.S. policy of destroying ISIS in Syria—natural enemies. We also benefit but it is now time to bring our troops back home. Stop the ENDLESS WARS!

January 14, 2019

5:12 pm: Spoke w/ President Erdogan of Turkey to advise where we stand on all matters including our last two weeks of success in fighting the remnants of ISIS, and 20 mile safe zone. Also spoke about economic development between the U.S. & Turkey—great potential to substantially expand!

January 30, 2019

6:25 am: When I became President, ISIS was out of control in Syria & running rampant. Since then tremendous progress made, especially over last 5 weeks. Caliphate will soon be destroyed, unthinkable two years ago. Negotiating are proceeding well in Afghanistan after 18 years of fighting.

February 1, 2019

8:35 am: …after 18 long years. Syria was loaded with ISIS until I came along. We will soon have destroyed 100% of the Caliphate, but will be watching them closely. It is now time to start coming home and, after many years, spending our money wisely. Certain people must get smart!

February 10, 2019

5:28 pm: The U.S. will soon control 100% of ISIS territory in Syria. @ CNN (do you believe this?)

February 14, 2019

12:30 pm: One year ago today, a horrific act of violence took the lives of 14 students and 3 educators in Parkland, Florida. On this somber anniversary, we honor their memory and recommit to ensuring the safety of all Americans, especially our Nation's children..

February 15, 2019

6:11 pm: Great job by law enforcement in Aurora, Illinois. Heartfelt condolences to all of the victims and their families. America is with you!

February 16, 2019

10:51 pm: The United States is asking Britain, France, Germany and other European allies to take back over 800 ISIS fighters that we captured in Syria and put them on trial. The Caliphate is ready to fall. The alternative is not a good one in that we will be forced to release them…

February 20, 2019

4:05 pm: I have instructed Secretary of State Mike Pompeo, and he fully agrees, not to allow Hoda Muthana back into the Country!

February 25, 2019

2:08 pm: It is my honor today to announce that Danny Burch, a United States citizen who has been held hostage in Yemen for 18 months, has been recovered and reunited with his wife and children. I appreciate the support of the United Arab Emirates in bringing Danny home…

…Danny's recovery reflects the best of what the United States & its partners can accomplish. We work every day to bring Americans home. We maintain constant and intensive diplomatic, intelligence, and law enforcement cooperation within the United States Government and with…

…our foreign partners. Recovering American hostages is a priority of my Admin, and with Danny's release, we have now secured freedom for 20 American captives since my election victory. We will not rest as we continue our work to bring the remaining American hostages back home!

March 15, 2019

6:41 am: My warmest sympathy and best wishes goes out to the people of New Zealand after the horrible massacre in the Mosques. 49 innocent people have so senselessly died, with so many more seriously injured. The U.S. stands by New Zealand for anything we can do. God bless all!

2:14 pm: Just spoke with Jacinda Ardern, the Prime Minister of New Zealand, regarding the horrific events that have taken place over the past 24 hours. I informed the Prime Minister…

…that we stand in solidarity with New Zealand—and that any assistance the U.S.A. can give, we stand by ready to help. We love you New Zealand!

March 18, 2019

8:38 am: The Fake News Media is working overtime to blame me for the horrible attack in New Zealand. They will have to work very hard to prove that one. So Ridiculous!

March 22, 2019

7:57 am: "Our own Benjamin Hall is doing fantastic reporting on ISIS right on the from line (True). ISIS was willing to die but now, because of big pressure, save for a few people in caves, most have surrendered. A testament to our President." Thank you Pete Hegseth

11:15 am: ISIS uses the internet better than almost anyone, but for all of those susceptible to ISIS propaganda, they are now being beaten badly at every level...

...There is nothing to admire about them, they will always try to show a glimmer of vicious hope, but they are losers and barely breathing. Think about that before you destroy your lives and the lives of your family!

April 8, 2019

7:22 am: Uganda must find the kidnappers of the American Tourist and guide before people will feel safe in going there. Bring them to justice openly and quickly!

April 21, 2019

6:20 am: 138 people have been killed in Sri Lanka, with more that 600 badly injured, in a terrorist attack on churches and hotels. The United States offers heartfelt condolences to the great people of Sri Lanka. We stand ready to help!

April 22, 2019

1:05 pm: Spoke to Prime Minister Ranil Wickremesinghe of Sri Lanka this morning to inform him that the United States stands by him and his country in the fight against terrorism. Also expressed condolences on behalf of myself and the People of the United States!

April 27, 2019

4:41 pm: Thoughts and prayers to all of those affected by the shooting at the Synagogue in Poway, California. God bless you all. Suspect apprehended. Law enforcement did outstanding job. Thank you!

5:47 pm: Sincerest THANK YOU to our great Border Patrol Agent who stopped the shooter at the Synagogue in Poway, California. He may have been off duty but his talents for Law Enforcement weren't!

April 29, 2019

5:49 am: I spoke at length yesterday to Rabbi Yisroel Goldstein, Chabad of Poway, where I extended my warmest condolences to him and all affected by the shooting in California. What a great guy. He had a least one finger blown off, and all he wanted to do is help others. Very special!

April 30, 2019

11:31 am: We have 1,800 ISIS Prisoners taken hostage in our final battles to destroy 100% of the Caliphate in Syria. Decisions are now being made as to what to do with these dangerous prisoners…

European countries are not helping at all, even though this was very much done for their benefit. They are refusing to take back prisoners from their specific countries. Not good!

May 5, 2019

7:13 pm: Once again, Israel faces a barrage of deadly rocket attacks by terrorist groups Hamas and Islamic Jihad. We support Israel 100% in its defense of its citizens…

To the Gazan people—these terrorist acts against Israel will bring you nothing but more misery. END the violence and work towards peace—it can happen!

May 8, 2019

12:42 pm: Our Nation grieves at the unspeakable violence that took a precious young life and badly injured others in Colorado. God be with the families and thank you to the First Responders for bravely intervening. We are in close contact with Law Enforcement.

June 1, 2019

9:43 am: Spoke to Virginia Governor @RalphNortham last night, and the Mayor and Vice Mayor of Virginia Beach this morning, to offer condolences to that great community. The Federal Government is there, and will be, for whatever they may need. God bless the families and all!

July 17, 2019

9:16 am: After a ten year search, the so-called "mastermind" of the Mumbai Terror attacks has been arrested in Pakistan. Great pressure has been exerted over the last two years to find him!

July 18, 2019

4:33 pm: This should have been taken care of years ago, the Trump Administration is taking care of these thugs now!

July 28, 2019

10:08 pm: Law Enforcement is at the scene of shootings in Gilroy, California. Reports are that shooter has not yet been apprehended. Be careful and safe!

July 30, 2019

5:38 am: Somali refugees arresed in Tucson on way to Egypt. They were in touch with an agent posing as a terrorist. One of them stated, "The best wake up call is Islamic State to get victory or another 9/11." Get smart people! #MAGA #KAG @foxandfriends

August 3, 2019

3:10 pm: Terrible shootings in ElPaso, Texas. Reports are very bad, many killed. Working with State and Local authorities, and Law Enforcement. Spoke to Governor to pledge total support of Federal Government. God be with you all!

11:19 pm: Today's shooting in El Paso, Texas, was not only tragic, it was an act of cowardice. I know that I stand with everyone in this Country to condemn today's hateful act. There are no reasons or excuses that will ever justify killing innocent people...

August 4, 2019

2:49 pm: …The flags at the White House will be lowered today through Thursday, August 8. Melania and I are praying for all those impacted by this unspeakable act of evil!

August 5, 2019

5:54 am: We cannot let those killed in El Paso, Texas, and Dayton, Ohio, die in vain. Likewise for those so seriously wounded. We can never forget them, and those many who came before them. Republicans and Democrats must come together and get strong background checks, perhaps marrying…

…this legislation with desperately needed immigration reform. We must have something good, if not GREAT, come out of these two tragic events!

11:51 am: The First Lady and I join all Americans in praying and grieving for the victims, their families, and the survivors. We will stand by their side FOREVER!

12:10 pm: Today, I am also directing the Department of Justice to propose legislation ensuring that those who commit hate crimes and mass murders face the DEATH PENALTY—and that this capital punishment be delivered quickly, decisively, and without years of needless delay.

1:12 pm: We must honor the sacred memory of those we have lost by acting as ONE PEOPLE. Open wounds cannot heal if we are divided. We must seek real, bipartisan solutions that will truly make America safer and better for all.

August 9, 2019

7:03 am: Serious discussions are taking place between House and Senate leadership on meaningful Background Checks. I have also been speaking to the NRA, and others, so that their very strong views can be fully represented and respected. Guns should not be placed in the hands of…

...mentally ill or deranged people. I am the biggest Second Amendment person there is, but we all must work together for the good and safety of our Country. Common sense things can be done that are good for everyone!

August 15, 2019

7:59 am: The Philadelphia shooter should never have been allowed to be on the streets. He had a long and very dangerous criminal record. Looked like he was having a good time after his capture, and after wounding so many police. Long sentence—must get much tougher on street crime!

August 22, 2019

6:31 pm: Just concluded a very good meeting on preventing Mass Shootings. Talks are ongoing w/ both Republicans & Democrats. We are likewise engaging with lawful gun owners, survivors, grieving family members, law enforcement, the NRA, mental health professionals, and school officials.

I am hopeful Congress will engage with my Team to pass meaningful legislation that will make a real difference and, most importantly, Save Lives

August 31, 2019

5:35 pm: Just briefed by Attorney General Barr about the shootings in Texas. FBI and Law Enforcement is fully engaged. More to follow.

September 1, 2019

10:07 am: Great job by Texas Law Enforcement and First Responders in handling the terrible shooting tragedy yesterday. Thank you also to the FBI, @GregAbbott_TX and all others. A very tough and sad situation!

September 7, 2019

5:51 pm: Unbeknownst to almost everyone, the major Taliban leaders and, separately, the President of Afghanistan, were going to secretly meet with me at Camp David on Sunday. They were coming to the United States tonight. Unfortunately, in order to build false leverage, they admitted to...

an attack in Kabul that killed one of our great great soldiers, and 11 other people. I immediately cancelled the meeting and called off peace negotiations. What kind of people would kill so many in order to seemingly strengthen their bargaining position? They didn't, they...

...only made it worse! If they cannot agree to a ceasefire during these very important peace talks, and would even kill 12 innocent people, then they probably don't have the power to negotiate a meaningful agreement anyway. How many more decades are they willing to fight?

September 14, 2019

2:02 pm: The Taliban has never been hit harder than it is being hit right now. Killing 12 people, including one great American soldier, was not a good idea. There are much better ways to set up a negotiation. The Taliban knows they made a big mistake, and they have no idea how to recover!

October 7, 2019

6:40 am: The United States was supposed to be in Syria for 30 days, that was many years ago. We stayed and got deeper and deeper into battle with no aim in sight. When I arrived in Washington, ISIS was running rampant in the area. We quickly defeated 100% of the ISIS Caliphate,.

...including capturing thousands of ISIS fighters, mostly from Europe. But Europe did not want them back, they said you keep them USA! I said "NO, we did you a great favor and now you want us to hold them in U.S. prisons at tremendous cost. They are yours for trials." They...

...again said "NO," thinking, as usual, that the U.S. is always the "sucker," on NATO, on Trade, on everything. The Kurds fought with us, but were paid massive amounts of money and equipment to do so. They have been fighting Turkey for decades. I held off this fight for..

...almost 3 years, but it is time for us to get out of these ridiculous Endless Wars, many of them tribal, and bring our soldiers home. WE WILL FIGHT WHERE IT IS TO OUR BENEFIT, AND ONLY FIGHT TO WIN. Turkey, Europe, Syria, Iran, Iraq, Russia and the Kurds will now have to.

...figure the situation out, and what they want to do with the captured ISIS fighters in their "neighborhood." They all hate ISIS, have been enemies for years. We are 7000 miles away and will crush ISIS again if they come anywhere near us!

10:38 am: ...the captured ISIS fighters and families. The U.S. has done far more than anyone could have ever expected, including the capture of 100% of the ISIS Caliphate. It is time now for others in the region, some of great wealth, to protect their own territory. THE USA IS GREAT!

October 9, 2019

11:16 pm: In case the Kurds or Turkey lose control, the United States has already taken the 2 ISIS militants tied to beheadings in Syria, known as the Beetles, out of that country and into a secure location controlled by the U.S. They are the worst of the worst!

October 10, 2019

3:07 pm: We defeated 100% of the ISIS Caliphate and no longer have any troops in the area under attack by Turkey, in Syria. We did our job perfectly! Now Turkey is attacking the Kurds, who have been fighting each other for 200 years...

October 14, 2019

2:10 pm: After defeating 100% of the ISIS Caliphate, I largely moved our troops out of Syria. Let Syria and Assad protect the Kurds and fight Turkey for their own land. I said to my Generals, why should we be fighting for Syria…

…and Assad to protect the land of our enemy? Anyone who wants to assist Syria in protecting the Kurds is good with me, whether it is Russia, China, or Napoleon Bonaparte. I hope they all do great, we are 7,000 miles away!

October 18, 2019

10:42 pm: Just spoke to President @RTErdogan of Turkey. He told me there was minor sniper and mortar fire that was quickly eliminated. He very much wants the ceasefire, or pause, to work. Likewise, the Kurds want it, and the ultimate solution, to happen. Too bad there wasn't…

…this thinking years ago. Instead, it was always held together with very weak bandaids, & in an artificial manner. There is good will on both sides & a really good chance for success. The U.S. has secured the Oil, & the ISIS Fighters are double secured by Kurds & Turkey…

…I have just been notified that some European Nations are now willing, for the first time, to take the ISIS Fighters that came from their nations. This is good news, but should have been done after WE captured them. Anyway, big progress being made!!!!

10:46 am: DEFEAT TERRORISM!

October 29, 2019

8:29 am: Just confirmed that Abu Bakr al-Baghdadi's number one replacement has been terminated by American troops. Most likely would have taken the top spot—Now he is also Dead!

October 30, 2019
12:54 pm: AMERICAN HERO! https://t.co/XCCa2sGfsZ

November 1, 2019

8:39 am: ISIS has a new leader. We know exactly who he is!

November 6, 2019

3:15 pm: Just had a very good call with President @RTErdogan of Turkey. He informed me that they have captured numerous ISIS fighters that were reported to have escaped during the conflict—including a wife and sister of terrorist killer al Baghdadi…

…Also talked about their Border with Syria, the eradication of terrorism, the ending of hostilities with the Kurds, and many other topics. Look forward to seeing President Erdogan next Wednesday, November 13th at the @WhiteHouse!

November 14, 2019

6:34 pm: We continue to monitor the terrible events at Saugus High School in Santa Clarita, California through our ongoing communications with Local, State, and Federal Authorities…

…We send our deepest condolences to the families and friends of those tragically lost, and we pray for the speedy recovery of the wounded.

December 6, 2019

1:16 pm: Just received a full briefing on the tragic shooting at NAS Pensacola in Florida, and spoke to @GovRonDeSantis. My thoughts and prayers are with the victims and their families during this difficult time. We are continuing to monitor the situation as the investigation is ongoing.

2:18 pm: King Salman of Saudi Arabia just called to express his sincere condolences and give his sympathies to the families and friends of the warriors who were killed and wounded in the attack that took place in Pensacola, Florida…

…The King said that the Saudi people are greatly angered by the barbaric actions of the shooter, and that this person in no way shape or form represents the feelings of the Saudi people who love the American people.

December 10, 2019

4:41 pm: Just received a briefing on the horrific shootout that took place in Jersey City, NJ. Our thoughts & prayers are w/ the victims & their families during this very difficult & tragic time. We will continue to monitor the situation as we assist local & state officials on the ground.

December 29, 2019

2:10 pm: The anti-Semitic attack in Monsey, New York, on the 7th night of Hanukkah last night is horrific. We must all come together to fight, confront, and eradicate the evil scourge of anti-Semitism. Melania and I wish the victims a quick and full recovery.

December 30, 2019

7:57 pm: Our prayers are with the families of the victims and the congregation of yesterday's church attack. It was over in 6 seconds thanks to the brave parishioners who acted to protect 242 fellow worshippers. Lives were saved by these heroes, and Texas laws allowing them to carry arms!

December 31, 2019

8:53 am: Armed congregants quickly stopped a crazed church shooter in Texas. If it were not for the fact that there were people inside of the church that were both armed, and highly proficient in using their weapon, the end result would have been catastrophic. A big THANK YOU to them!

9:06 am: President Putin of Russia called to thank me and the U.S. for informing them of a planned terrorist attack in the very beautiful city of Saint Petersburg. They were able to quickly apprehend the suspects, with many lives being saved. Great & important coordination!

Veterans—2017 News Quotes

Remarks at the signing of the Veterans Accountability and Whistle-blower Protection Act, June 23, 2017.

Source: https://www.whitehouse.gov/briefings-statements/
remarks-president-trump-signing-veterans-accountability-whistleblower-protection-act/

"In just a short time, we've already achieved transformative change at the VA [Veterans Administration]. And believe me, we're just getting started."

Remarks at the signing of the Veterans Accountability and Whistle-blower Protection Act, June 23, 2017.

Source: https://www.whitehouse.gov/briefings-statements/
remarks-president-trump-signing-veterans-accountability-whistleblower-protection-act/

"The enthusiasm for the Veterans Administration and for making it right for our great veterans has been incredible. And I want to thank all of them."

Remarks at the signing of the Veterans Accountability and Whistle-blower Protection Act, June 23, 2017.

Source: https://www.whitehouse.gov/briefings-statements/
remarks-president-trump-signing-veterans-accountability-whistleblower-protection-act/

"One of my greatest honors and joys during the presidential campaign was the time I spent going all across the country with our nation's really and truly incredible veterans. In their courage, their dignity, and

431

their selfless sacrifice, they represent the very best of us. Our veterans have fulfilled their duty to this nation and now we must fulfill our duty to them. So, to every veteran who is here with us today, I just want to say two very simple words: Thank you. Thank you. Thank you. You are the warriors and heroes who have won our freedom, and we will never forget what you have done for all of us, ever."

Remarks at the signing of the Veterans Accountability and Whistle-blower Protection Act, June 23, 2017.
Source: https://www.whitehouse.gov/briefings-statements/
remarks-president-trump-signing-veterans-accountability-whistleblower-protection-act/

"As you all know all too well, for many years the government failed to keep its promises to our veterans. We all remember the night-mare that veterans suffered during the VA [Veterans Administration] scandals that were exposed a few years ago. Veterans were put on secret waitlists, given the wrong medication, given the bad treatments, and ignored in moments of crisis for them. Many veterans died waiting for a simple doctor's appointments. What happened was a national disgrace. And yet, some of the employees involved in these scandals remained on the payrolls. Outdated laws kept the government from holding those who failed our veterans accountable. Today, we are finally changing those laws, wasn't easy, but we did have some fantastic help, to make sure that the scandal of what we suffered so recently never, ever happens again, and that our veterans can get the care they so richly deserve."

Remarks at the signing of the Veterans Accountability and Whistle-blower Protection Act, June 23, 2017.
Source: https://www.whitehouse.gov/briefings-statements/
remarks-president-trump-signing-veterans-accountability-whistleblower-protection-act/

"Our Wounded Warriors have given everything they have to this na-tion, and we owe them everything we have in return. And we're tak-ing care of it. Today, we are taking a very historic action to transform the VA [Veterans Administration] by enacting the VA Account-ability and Whistleblower Protection Act. This was not easy. This was not an easy one. And it's one that they wanted to do, Michael

[Verardo]²¹, you know, for a long time. For many years, couldn't get it done. We got it done."

Remarks at the signing of the Veterans Accountability and Whistle-blower Protection Act, June 23, 2017.

Source: https://www.whitehouse.gov/briefings-statements/
remarks-president-trump-signing-veterans-accountability-whistleblower-protection-act/

"This is one of the largest reforms to the VA [Veterans Administration] in its history. It's a reform that I campaigned on, and now I am thrilled to be able to sign that promise into law."

Remarks at the signing of the Veterans Accountability and Whistle-blower Protection Act, June 23, 2017.

Source: https://www.whitehouse.gov/briefings-statements/
remarks-president-trump-signing-veterans-accountability-whistleblower-protection-act/

"VA [Veterans Administration] accountability is essential to making sure that our veterans are treated with the respect they have so richly earned through their blood, sweat, and tears. This law will finally give the VA Secretary, who is, by the way, just doing some job, and he's doing it with this and with the heart. It gives the Secretary the authority to remove federal employees who fail and endanger our veterans, and to do so quickly and effectively. It's been a long time since you've heard those words. Those entrusted with the sacred duty of serving our veterans will be held accountable for the care they provide. It's a big statement."

Remarks at the signing of the Veterans Accountability and Whistle-blower Protection Act, June 23, 2017.

Source: https://www.whitehouse.gov/briefings-statements/
remarks-president-trump-signing-veterans-accountability-whistleblower-protection-act/

"At the same time, this bill protects whistleblowers who do the right thing. We want to reward, cherish, and promote the many dedicated

---

21   Verardo is a U.S. Army veteran who lost his left leg and most of his left arm serving in Afghanistan. Source: https://www.independencefund.org/tiger-team/michael-verardo/

employees at the VA [Veterans Administration]. This legislation also gives the VA Secretary the authority to appoint new medical directors at VA hospitals, something which was almost impossible to do in the past. And these are going to be talented, talented people."

Remarks at the signing of the Veterans Accountability and Whistle-blower Protection Act, June 23, 2017.

Source: https://www.whitehouse.gov/briefings-statements/
remarks-president-trump-signing-veterans-accountability-whistleblower-protection-act/

"Our very sincere gratitude as well to the veteran service organizations who have joined us for this tremendous occasion, and for everything they do for the veterans, and for so long. They've been fighting for this and other things so long. And by the way, other things are happening. We've done a lot. This is a big one. We have a lot of good ones coming."

Remarks at the signing of the Veterans Accountability and Whistle-blower Protection Act, June 23, 2017.

Source: https://www.whitehouse.gov/briefings-statements/
remarks-president-trump-signing-veterans-accountability-whistleblower-protection-act/

"I also want to express our appreciation for Secretary [David] Shulkin, who is implementing the dramatic reform throughout the VA [Veterans Administration]. It's got to be implemented. If it's not properly implemented, it will never mean the same thing. But I have no doubt it will be properly implemented. Right, David? Better be, David. We'll never have to use those words. We'll never have to use those words on our David. We will never use those words on you, that's for sure."

Remarks at the signing of the Veterans Accountability and Whistle-blower Protection Act, June 23, 2017.

Source: https://www.whitehouse.gov/briefings-statements/
remarks-president-trump-signing-veterans-accountability-whistleblower-protection-act/

"Since my first day in office, we've taken one action after another to ensure our veterans, and make sure, have to make sure, that they get world-class care and the kind of care that they've been promised by so many different people for so many years. We've created a new Office of Accountability at the VA [Veterans Administration], which will empower, and really has been empowered by this legislation. We've launched a new website that publishes wait times at every VA hospital. We've delivered same-day mental health services at all 168 VA medical centers. That's a big operation when you think of it."

Remarks at the signing of the Veterans Accountability and Whistleblower Protection Act, June 23, 2017.
Source: https://www.whitehouse.gov/briefings-statements/
remarks-president-trump-signing-veterans-accountability-whistleblower-protection-act/

"We've announced that the VA [Veterans Administration] will finally solve a problem that has plagued our government for decades: seamlessly transferring veterans' medical records from the Department of Defense to the Department of Veterans Affairs. That doesn't sound like such a big deal. It is, believe—That was a big one. We thought this would be easy, but the people, like David [Shulkin] and all that have been here and understand the system, he said that's going to be a tough one. We got it done. So that was a good one. But it is something we're very proud to have been able to do it this quickly."

Remarks at the signing of the Veterans Accountability and Whistleblower Protection Act, June 23, 2017.
Source: https://www.whitehouse.gov/briefings-statements/
remarks-president-trump-signing-veterans-accountability-whistleblower-protection-act/

"I've also signed the Veterans Choice Improvement Act so that more veterans can see the doctor of their choice. Already this year, using the Choice Program, veterans have received nearly double the number of approvals to see the doctor of their choosing."

Remarks at the signing of the Veterans Accountability and Whistleblower Protection Act, June 23, 2017.
Source: https://www.whitehouse.gov/briefings-statements/
remarks-president-trump-signing-veterans-accountability-whistleblower-protection-act/

"And this is only the beginning. We will not rest until the job is 100% complete for our great veterans."

Remarks at the signing of the Veterans Accountability and Whistle-blower Protection Act, June 23, 2017.

Source: https://www.whitehouse.gov/briefings-statements/
remarks-president-trump-signing-veterans-accountability-whistleblower-protection-act/

"So, I just want to thank you, our incredible veterans. We stand with you. We salute you. And with this new legislation, we strive to better support and serve you every single day."

Remarks at the signing of the Veterans Accountability and Whistle-blower Protection Act, June 23, 2017.

Source: https://www.whitehouse.gov/briefings-statements/
remarks-president-trump-signing-veterans-accountability-whistleblower-protection-act/

"So, this is something that we are all very proud to be signing. It's a tremendous honor for me. It's a tremendous honor for everybody on stage. And we're taking care of our veterans, and we're taking care of them properly."

Veterans—2017 Tweets

March 29, 2017

9:12 pm: Today we honored our true American heroes on the first-ever National Vietnam War Veterans Day. #ThankAVeteran…

April 3, 2017

12:56 pm: Looking forward to hosting our heroes from the Wounded Warrior Project (@WWP) Soldier Ride to the @WhiteHouse on Thursday!

April 6, 2017

1:30 pm: It was an honor to host our American heroes from the @ WWP #SoldierRideDC at the @WhiteHouse today with @FLOTUS, @VP and @SecondLady.

April 8, 2017

9:54 am: Congratulations to our great military men and women for representing the United States, and the world, so well in the Syria attack.

April 19, 2017

3:26 pm: Today I signed the Veterans (OUR HEROES) Choice Program Extension & Improvement Act @ the @WhiteHouse. #S544 Watch 45.wh.gov/7x5n53

April 28, 2017

7:15 am: We are making tremendous progress with the V. A. There has never been so much done so quickly, and we have just started. We love our VETS!

May 29, 2017

7:11 am: Honoring the men and women who made the ultimate sacrifice in service to America. Home of the free, because of the brave. #MemorialDay▆

7:35 am: Today we remember the men and women who made the ultimate sacrifice in serving. Thank you, God bless your families & God bless the USA!

7:36 am: I look forward to paying my respects to our brave men and women on this Memorial Day at Arlington National Cemetery later this morning.

June 6, 2017

12:47 pm: Today we remember the courage and bravery of our troops that stormed the beaches of Normandy 73 years ago. #DDay... https://t.co/zhR24dMzYB

8:07 pm: Senate passed the VA Accountability Act. The House should get this bill to my desk ASAP! We can't tolerate substandard care for our vets.

June 13, 2017

6:18 pm: The passage of the @DeptVetAffairs Accountability and Whistleblower Protection Act is GREAT news for veterans! I look forward to signing it!

July 1, 2017

4:38 pm: Getting rdy to leave for tonight's Celebrate Freedom Concert honoring our GREAT VETERANS w/ so many of my evangelical friends. See you soon!

11:47 pm: We will always take care of our GREAT VETERANS. You have shed your blood, poured your love, and bared your soul, in defense of our country.

July 22, 2017

2:22 pm: A ship is only as good as the people who serve on it—and the AMERICAN SAILOR is the BEST in the world. @USNavy #USS-GeraldRFord https://t.co/YmiTLXcCEh

July 25, 2017

11:05 pm: It was my great honor to join our wonderful Veterans at AMVETS Post 44 in Youngstown, Ohio this evening. A grateful nation salutes you!

August 2, 2017

9:09 am: It was my great honor to pay tribute to a VET who went above & beyond the call of duty to PROTECT our COMRADES, our COUNTRY, & OUR FREEDOM! https://t.co/YS6y1WR30G

August 3, 2017

2:07 pm: Our GREAT VETERANS can now connect w/ their VA healthcare team from anywhere, using #VAVideoConnect—available at: https://t.co/WFFHLWn8nF. https://t.co/Dmq4htSps9

August 7, 2017

1:03 pm: On #PurpleHeartDay💜I thank all the brave men and women who have sacrificed in battle for this GREAT NATION! #USA

August 16, 2017

4:35 pm: Today in Bedminster I signed the Harry W. Colmery Veterans Educational Assistance Act of 2017, joined by @DeptVetAffairs @SecShulkin.

August 20, 2017

10:01 pm: Thoughts & prayers are w/ our @USNavy sailors aboard the #USSJohnSMcCain where search & rescue efforts are underway.

August 22, 2017

2:15 pm: We pray for our fallen heroes who died while serving our country in the @USNavy aboard the #USSJohnSMcCain, and their families.

August 23, 2017

5:41 pm: A great honor to sign the Veterans Appeals Improvement & Modernization Act into law w/ @AmericanLegion @SecShulkin.

7:52 pm: Donald E. Ballard, on behalf of the people of the United States, THANK YOU for your courageous service. YOU INSPIRE US ALL! #ALConv2017

August 24, 2017

7:21 pm: A GREAT HONOR to spend time with our BRAVE HE-ROES at the @USMC Air Station Yuma. THANK YOU for your service to the United States of America! https://t.co/4lJ94nxODu

September 15, 2017

2:02 am: NEVER forget our HEROES held prisoner or who have gone missing in action while serving their country. Proclamation: https://t.co/4xBZGjAGj5 https://t.co/yZTr7rlpTV

September 24, 2017

2:32 pm: Courageous Patriots have fought and died for our great American Flag—we MUST honor and respect it! MAKE AMERI-CA GREAT AGAIN!

November 3, 2017

11:54 am: The decision on Sergeant Bergdahl is a complete and total disgrace to our Country and to our Military.

5:44 pm: Getting ready to land in Hawaii. Looking so much forward to meeting with our great Military/Veterans at Pearl Harbor!

November 10, 2017

12:45 am: Just landed in Da Nang, Vietnam to deliver a speech at #APEC2017

November 11, 2017

7:11 am: On this wonderful Veterans Day, I want to express the incredible gratitude of the entire American Nation to our GREAT VETERANS. Thank you! https://t.co/GhQbCA7yII

December 7, 2017

10:04 am: National Pearl Harbor Remembrance Day—"A day that will live in infamy!" December 7, 1941

11:15 am: Today, our entire nation pauses to REMEMBER PEARL HARBOR—and the brave warriors who on that day stood tall and fought for America. God Bless our HEROES who wear the uniform, and God Bless the United States of America. #PearlHarborRemembranceDay

3:04 pm: Today, the U.S. flag flies at half-staff at the @WhiteHouse, in honor of National Pearl Harbor Remembrance Day. https://t.co/LkXsBx2JF8 https://t.co/ogmpydr5LK

3:52 pm: Today, as we Remember Pearl Harbor, it was an incredible honor to be joined with surviving Veterans of the attack on 12/7/1941. They are HEROES, and they are living witnesses to American History. All American hearts are filled with gratitude for their service and their sacrifice. https://t.co/x5LD125o30

4:10 pm: Across the battlefields, oceans, and harrowing skies of Europe and the Pacific throughout the war, one great battle cry could be heard by America's friends and foes alike: "REMEMBER PEARL HARBOR." https://t.co/dfev02TwIr

Veterans—2018 News Quotes

Remarks at a rally in Tampa, Florida, July 31, 2018.
Source: https://www.tampabay.com/florida-politics/buzz/2018/08/01/
heres-a-full-transcript-of-president-trumps-speech-from-his-tampa-rally/

"The veterans' unemployment rate, oh, do we love our veterans, right?

"Has reached the lowest level in 18 years."

Remarks at a rally in Tampa, Florida, July 31, 2018.
Source: https://www.tampabay.com/florida-politics/buzz/2018/08/01/
heres-a-full-transcript-of-president-trumps-speech-from-his-tampa-rally/

"We passed the biggest VA reform in half a century, Veterans Choice. If our veterans can't get the care they need from the VA, they will have the right to go see a private doctor. We'll pay for the doctor. And frankly, we'll save a lot of money. We'll help a lot of vets. Everybody said they've been trying to get it for 45 years.

"Everybody said, 'You can't get it.' Think of it. Think of it. Veterans Choice, they have to stand, our great people. These are our great people. Who's a veteran in this audience? Do you like Trump? Do you like the job we're doing?

"Now, think of it, 45 years, everybody said, 'You'll never get it passed.' And I used to say before I really was well-versed on the veteran situation in healthcare, I used to say all the time, 'Why don't they just let the folks go to a doctor?' They'd wait in line for 7 days, 9 days, 14 days, 21 days. Some of them started off with a very modest problem. They end up being terminal because they can't see a doctor.

"I said, 'Why don't they just let them go see a local private doctor, pay the bill, and take care of it?' It will be a lot less expensive. And it's turned out to be something that the veterans love. And it's passed. It's passed.

"They've been trying to get it passed for 38 years. The other one is 45, and that's VA accountability. If somebody treated our veterans badly, if they stole, if they was, if they were—You know this, if they were sadistic, if they were really bad to our vets, all right? Really, really bad, we couldn't do anything about it. They could steal. They could rob. They could be abusive. You couldn't say, 'You're fired.' Now you can say, 'You're fired.'

"Made a big difference. That was another one they said you'll never get it done between civil service and unions. We love them both. But between civil service and unions they said, 'You'll never get it done. You'll never get it approved.' And by the way, we had virtually no help, very little from Democrats. Very little. Not because it's not right, but because they don't want to give Trump any victory. They'll do everything that's wrong."

Response to a question from Chris Wallace of FOX News, November 18, 2018.
Source: https://www.youtube.com/watch?v=rMgJnnG-Nql

"I don't think anybody's been more with the military than I have, as a President. In terms of funding, in terms of all of the things I've been able to get them, including the vets. I don't think anybody's done more than me."

Veterans—2018 Tweets

January 9, 2018

6:07 pm: Today, it was my great honor to sign a new Executive Order to ensure Veterans have the resources they need as they transition back to civilian life. We must ensure that our HEROES are given the care and support they so richly deserve!

March 25, 2018

8:08 am: Happy National #MedalofHonorDay to our HEROES. We love you!

March 28, 2018

4:31 pm: I am pleased to announce that I intend to nominate highly respected Admiral Ronny L. Jackson, MD, as the new Secretary of Veterans Affairs…

…In the interim, Hon. Robert Wilkie of DOD will serve as Acting Secretary. I am thankful for Dr. David Shulkin's service to our country and to our GREAT VETERANS!

April 27, 2018

6:23 am: So great to have Staff Sgt. Dan Nevins and the incredible WOUNDED WARRIORS with me in the White House yesterday. These are truly brave and special people! @foxandfriends

May 3, 2018

11:39 am: This spring marks 4yrs since the Phoenix VA crisis. We won't forget what happened to our GREAT VETS. Choice is vital, but the program needs work & is running out of $. Congress must fix Choice Program by Memorial Day so VETS can get the care they deserve. I will sign immediately!

May 16, 2018

12:21 pm: House votes today on Choice/MISSION Act. Who will stand with our Great Vets, caregivers, and Veterans Service Organizations? Must get Choice passed by Memorial Day!

May 17, 2018

10:25 am: Congrats to the House for passing the VA MISSION Act yesterday. Without this funding our veterans will be forced to stand in never ending lines in order to receive care. Putting politics over our veterans care is UNACCEPTABLE—Senate must vote yes on this bill by Memorial Day!

May 24, 2018

4:18 pm: Today, it was my great honor to present the #MedalOfHonor to @USNavy (SEAL) Master Chief Special Warfare Operator Britt Slabinski in the East Room of the @WhiteHouse. Full ceremony: https://t.co/2UldFozRh1 https://t.co/R3ACmkWsqJ

May 28, 2018

12:13 pm: Thank you for joining us on this solemn day of remembrance. We are gathered here on the sacred soil of @ArlingtonNatl Cemetery to honor the lives and deeds of America's greatest heroes, the men and women who laid down their lives for our freedom. #MemorialDay https://t.co/YSYAHf7bNu

12:14 pm: The heroes who rest in these hallowed fields, in cemeteries, battlefields, and burial grounds near and far are drawn the full tapestry of American life. They came from every generation from towering cities and wind swept prairies, from privilege and from poverty...

12:19 pm: Our fallen heroes have not only written our history they have shaped our destiny. They saved the lives of the men and women with whom they served. They cared for their families more than anything in the world, they loved their families. They inspired their communities...

June 6, 2018

2:37 pm: Today we mark another milestone: the 74th anniversary of #DDay, the Allied invasion of Normandy. On June 6, 1944, more than 70,000 brave young Americans charged out of landing craft, jumped out of airplanes, and stormed into hell..

3:09 pm: We must always protect those who protect us. Today, it was my great honor to sign the #VAMissionAct and to make Veterans Choice the permanent law of the land!

June 8, 2018

11:22 pm: My thoughts and prayers are with the families of our serviceman who was killed and his fellow servicemen who were wounded in Somalia. They are truly all HEROES.

June 12, 2018

6:21 pm: Tonight, it was my great honor to host a Congressional Medal of Honor Society Reception at the @WhiteHouse!

June 26, 2018

3:12 pm: Today, we tell the story of an incredible HERO who defended our nation in World War Two-First Lieutenant Gatling Murl Conner. Although he died 20 years ago, today he takes his rightful place in the Eternal Chronicle of American Valor...

July 3, 2018

6:52 pm: Tonight we gathered to celebrate the courageous men and women who make freedom possible: our brave service members, and our wonderful Veterans. For 242 years, American Independence...

...has endured because of the sweat, blood and sacrifice of the American Armed Forces—the greatest force for peace and justice in the history of the world!

7:36 pm: Tomorrow, families across our Nation will gather to celebrate the Fourth of July. As we do, we will think of the men & women serving overseas at this very moment, far away from their families, protecting America—& we will thank GOD for blessing us with these incredible HEROES!

July 23, 2018

8:35 pm: Robert will do a great job for our Vets. We also recently won Choice!

July 24, 2018

2:15 pm: I want to thank the @VFWHQ for your devotion to our fallen heroes, unknown soldiers, Prisoners of War, those Missing in Action, and their families. #VFWConvention

July 26, 2018

10:52 pm: The Remains of American Servicemen will soon be leaving North Korea and heading to the United States! After so many years, this will be a great moment for so many families. Thank you to Kim Jong Un.

July 27, 2018

1:16 pm: The @USNavy's first female Admiral, Alene Duerk once said: "It was a nice distinction to have, and to be recognized as the first, but I wanted to make certain that I used that notoriety to do as much positive as I could." Alene did just that, and America is forever grateful!

July 30, 2018

5:44 pm: Congratulations to our new @DeptVetAffairs Secretary, Robert Wilkie!

August 1, 2018

10:32 pm: Incredibly beautiful ceremony as U.S. Korean War remains are returned to American soil. Thank you to Honolulu and all of our great Military participants on a job well done. A special thanks to Vice President Mike Pence on delivering a truly magnificent tribute!

11:47 pm: Thank you to Chairman Kim Jong Un for keeping your word & starting the process of sending home the remains of our great and beloved missing fallen! I am not at all surprised that you took this kind action. Also, thank you for your nice letter—l look forward to seeing you soon!

August 7, 2018

1:25 pm: Today, on the 236th anniversary of the Purple Heart, we honor the members of our Armed Forces for serving as the vanguard of American democracy and freedom around the world. #PurpleHeartDay

September 21, 2018

12:22 am: Throughout American history, the men and women of our Armed Forces have selflessly served our Country, making tremendous sacrifices to defend our liberty. On National POW/MIA Recognition Day, we honor all American Prisoners of War:

3:11 pm: Promises Kept for our GREAT veterans! https://t.co/C0h8cW4FuH

October 2, 2018

11:18 am: Yesterday, it was my great honor to present the Medal of Honor to Ronald J. Shurer II, for his actions on April 6, 2008, when he braved enemy fire to treat multiple injured Soldiers.
Read more: https://t.co/Nrrcp2JJUL https://t.co/A0KLHmIPZs

October 17, 2018

5:03 pm: This afternoon, it was my great honor to present @USMC Sergeant Major John Canley the Medal of Honor in the East Room of the @WhiteHouse!

October 25, 2018

6:13 pm to 6:21 pm: We are gathered together on this solemn occasion to fulfill our most reverent and sacred duty. 35 years ago, 241 American service members were murdered in the terrorist attack on our Marine Barracks in Beirut, Lebanon. Today, we honor our fallen heroes... https://t.co/zPgjSFj9BM

In 1983, roughly 1,800 Marines were in Beirut to keep the peace in a Nation torn apart by Civil War. Terrorists had bombed the U.S. Embassy earlier that year, killing 63 people, including 17 Americans...

The Service Members who died that day included brave young Marines just out of high school, accomplished officers in the middle of their military careers, and enlisted men who had served in theaters all over the world...

November 11, 2018

9:16 am: On this Veterans Day—the 100th Anniversary of the end of WWI, we honor the brave HEROES who fought for America in the Great War, and every Veteran who has worn the uniform and kept our Nation Safe, Strong and FREE! https://t.co/zBvvYRR7XE https://t.co/YO06ztfvNm

November 15, 2018

3:34 pm: It was my great honor to host a @WhiteHouse Conference on Supporting Veterans & Military Families... To everyone here today who has served our Country in uniform, & to every Veteran & Military family across our land, I want to express the eternal gratitude of our entire Nation!

3:39 pm: Last year, I signed the landmark VA Accountability Act to ensure those who mistreat our Veterans can be held fully accountable. Since my inauguration, we have removed more than 3,600 government employees who were not giving our Vets the care they deserve...

3:43 pm: It is our sacred duty to support America's Service Members every single day they wear the uniform—and every day after when they return home as Veterans. Together we will HONOR those who defend us, we will CHERISH those who protect us, and we will celebrate the amazing heroes...

December 7, 2018

9:46 am: Today, we honor those who perished 77 years ago at Pearl Harbor, and we salute every veteran who served in World War II over the 4 years that followed that horrific attack. God Bless America!

December 30, 2018

10:28 am: Veterans on President Trump's handling of Border Security—62% Approval Rating. On being a strong leader—59%. AP Poll. Thank you!

Veterans—2019 News Quotes

Remarks during a visit to the Lima Army Tank Plant in Ohio, March 20, 2019.
Source: https://www.c-span.org/video/?458966-1/
president-trump-delivers-remarks-lima-army-tank-plant-ohio

"[The late U.S. Senator John] McCain didn't get the job done for our great vets and the VA, and they knew it. That's why, when I had my dispute with him, I had such incredible support from the vets and from the military. The vets were on my side because I got the job done. I got Choice and I got Accountability. Accountability—Meaning, if somebody mistreats our vets—For 45 years they were trying—They mistreat our vets, and we say, 'Hey, you're fired. Get out.' You can't mistreat our vets. They never got it done.

"And Choice—For year and years, decades, they wanted to get Choice. You know what Choice is. You're a military person. You're one of our great people. To me, one of the great people. For many decades, they couldn't get it done. It was never done. I got it five months ago. I got it done: Choice. Instead of waiting in line—A vet fought for us, fought in these tanks; fought for us.

"Instead of waiting in line for two days, two weeks, two months—People on line, they're not very sick. By the time they see a doctor, they're terminally ill. We gave them Choice. If you have to wait for any extended period of time, you go outside, you go to a local doctor. We pay the bill; you get yourself better. Go home to your family. And we got it passed. We got it done."

Remarks at the signing of an executive order protecting and improving Medicare for senior citizens, Ocala, Florida, October 3, 2019.
Source: https://www.whitehouse.gov/briefings-statements/remarks-president-trump-signing-executive-order-protecting-improving-medicare-nations-seniors-ocala-fl/

"Under this administration, we believe that every American family has a right of choice—you have a right to choose. Choice. So important. Like what we did with the vets. Choice. Where they can go out and get a doctor instead of waiting in line for three weeks, four weeks, two months. Choice. And you look at the doctor and you look at the plan that is best for you."

Remarks at the signing of an executive order protecting and improving Medicare for senior citizens, Ocala, Florida, October 3, 2019.
Source: https://www.whitehouse.gov/briefings-statements/remarks-president-trump-signing-executive-order-protecting-improving-medicare-nations-seniors-ocala-fl/

"And to care for our great veterans, we passed VA Accountability. You know what that is, right? This is where the great heroes and tough people—But—And, by the way, in their super prime, nobody touched them.

"But they're more vulnerable, and people would take advantage of our veterans. You had sadists. You had people that would rob them and rob the system. You had some horrible people. We couldn't fire anybody. They had, in Arizona, people that got stealing—they got caught stealing $400,000. They couldn't fire them. So now we have VA Accountability. You think that was easy? They've been trying to get it for 50 years. And I got it. I'm good at getting things.

"So now, when they don't take proper care of our vets, we say, 'Jim, get the hell out of here. You're fired. Get out of here.' We can fire them. Get them out. We get them out. We don't have to ask questions. We get them out. If they're bad, they treat our veterans badly, we fire them. That's why you don't hear about—You know, before me, every night you'd see these stories, these horror stories about the VA. I haven't seen one in a long time. Now, I don't want to wish it because the fake news will search the system to find somebody that's not happy. 'We found somebody. We found a vet in Florida who isn't quite happy with everything. Let's do a major story.'

"But do you remember all of the bad stories that used to be about the VA? Now you don't see that because they have accountability. We can fire bad people. We fired a tremendous number of really bad people that should've been fired years ago.

"I don't like firing people, but I like firing people that don't treat our vets great, that aren't doing their job. And they were protected, frankly, by the unions, and they were protected by civil service: very powerful. Do you think it was easy beating unions and civil service? Not too easy. But I explained to them too. I said, 'This is good for all of us. It's good for America.'

"And the other, as I said, is VA Choice, where our veterans no longer have to wait for endless, endless hours, days, even months. We've had cases where a person is on line—Not bad; could be fixed up very easily with whatever treatment it may be, and they end up being terminal by the time they see a doctor. That's not happening anymore. Because now you go out, you find a great local doctor, we pay the bill.

"And, you know, it's interesting, it's totally less important but we also save a lot of money on that. Hard to believe, we save a lot of money. It's much less expensive for us to do that than the other way, and it's saving tremendous numbers of lives. And we have great doctors, frankly, that need the business. Not so bad."

Veterans—2019 Tweets

January 15, 2019

7:16 am: Just announced that Veterans unemployment has reached an 18 year low, really good news for our Vets and their families. Will soon be an all time low! Do you think the media will report on this and all of the other great economic news?

February 9, 2019

8:56 am: It was great meeting some of our outstanding young military personnel who were wounded in both Syria and Afghanistan. Their wounds are deep but their spirit is sooo high. They will recoverer & be back very soon. America loves them. Walter Reed Hospital is AMAZ-ING—Thank you all!

March 5, 2019

Just a few moments ago, I signed an EO addressing one of our nation's most heartbreaking tragedies: VETERANS SUICIDE. To every Veteran—I want you to know that you have an entire nation of more than 300 million people behind you. You will NEVER be forgotten.

March 27, 2019

3:48 pm: We are here today to award America's highest military honor to a fallen hero who made the supreme sacrifice for our nation—Staff Sergeant Travis Atkins…

March 29, 2019

7:48 am: On this Vietnam War Veterans Day, we celebrate the brave Vietnam Veterans and all of America's Veterans. Thank you for your service to our great Nation!

April 9, 2019

10:31 am: On National Former Prisoner of War Recognition Day, we honor the Americans captured and imprisoned by foreign powers while carrying out their duties to defend this great Nation…

April 18, 2019

3:37 pm: Today, I was thrilled to host the @WWP Soldier Ride once again at the @WhiteHouse. We were all deeply honored to be in the presence of TRUE AMERICAN HEROES…

April 24, 2019

11:54 am: Rep. Alexandria Ocasio-Cortez is correct, the VA is not broken, it is doing great. But that is only because of the Trump Administration. We got Veterans Choice & Accountability passed. "President Trump deserves a lot of credit." Dan Caldwell, Concerned Veterans of America

May 13, 2019

6:15 pm: I met Marine Sgt. John Peck, a quadruple amputee who has received a double arm transplant, at Walter Reed in 2017. Today, it was my honor to welcome John (HERO) to the Oval, with his wonderful wife Jessica. He also wrote a book that I highly recommend, "Rebuilding Sergeant Peck."

June 5, 2019

7:18 am: As we approach the 75th Anniversary of D-Day, we proudly commemorate those heroic and honorable patriots who gave their all for the cause of freedom during some of history's darkest hours. #DDay75

June 6, 2019

12:36 pm: Today, we remember those who fell, and we honor all who fought, here in Normandy. They won back this ground for civilization.

To more than 170 Veterans of the Second World War who join us today: You are among the very greatest Americans who will ever live! #DDay75thAnniversary

12:55 pm: To the men who sit behind me, and to the boys who rest in the field before me: your example will never grow old. Your legend will never tire, and your spirit—brave, unyielding, and true—will NEVER DIE! #DDay75thAnniversary

June 25, 2019

3:27 pm: Today, it was my great honor to present the Medal of Honor to Army Staff Sgt. David Bellavia (HERO) for his courageous actions as a squad leader in Fallujah. #MOH

4:38 pm: Staff Sgt. David Bellavia—today, we honor your extraordinary courage, we salute your selfless service, and we thank you for carrying on the legacy of American Valor that has always made our blessed nation the strongest and mightiest in the world!

July 3, 2019

9:47 am: Congratulations to Navy Seal Eddie Gallagher, his wonderful wife Andrea, and his entire family. You have been through much together. Glad I could help!

July 23, 2019

1:43 pm: I was saddened to learn of the recent passing of Bob Morgenthau, a truly great man! Bob served as a Naval Officer in World War II, was an extraordinary US Attorney, Manhattan District Attorney, and always a warrior for our Country that he loved so dearly...

...I got to know him over his many years as Chairman of the Police Athletic League, for which he devoted so much time and energy. Bob Morgenthau, a legend, will be greatly missed!

July 25, 2019

8:00 am: House Republicans should support the TWO YEAR BUD-GET AGREEMENT which greatly helps our Military and our Vets. I am totally with you!

July 31, 2019

5:43 pm: Thank you Bill, say hello to our GREAT VETERANS! https://t.co/toDqIAIQ54

August 7, 2019

9:46 am: Today, we honor all of our Country's Purple Heart recipients, their loved ones, and our Gold Star Families for their immeasurable sacrifice. These American Patriots represent the unyielding and un-matched strength and determination of the U.S. Armed Forces:

August 21, 2019

7:20 pm: It was my honor to sign a Presidential Memorandum fa-cilitating the cancellation of student loan debt for 25K of our most severely disabled Veterans. With today's order, we express the ever-lasting love & loyalty of a truly grateful Nation. God bless our Vets, & God Bless America!

November 11, 2019

8:42 am: HAPPY VETERANS DAY!

2:28 pm: Today, we come together as one Nation to salute the Veter-ans of the United States Armed Forces—the greatest warriors ever to walk on the face of the Earth. Our Veterans risked everything for us. Now, it is our duty to serve and protect THEM every day of our lives!

November 17, 2019

8:43 am: Thank you Pete. Our great warfighters must be allowed to fight. I would not have done this for Sgt. Bergdahl or Chelsea Manning

November 21, 2019

8:30 am: The Navy will NOT be taking away Warfighter and Navy Seal Eddie Gallagher's Trident Pin. This case was handled very badly from the beginning. Get back to business!

November 24, 2019

7:11 am: Navy Seal Eddie Gallagher will be on @foxandfriends this morning at 7:30 A.M. Have no fear, all will end well for everyone!

6:32 pm to 6:33 pm: I was not pleased with the way that Navy Seal Eddie Gallagher's trial was handled by the Navy. He was treated very badly but, despite this, was completely exonerated on all major charges. I then restored Eddie's rank. Likewise, large cost overruns from past administration's...

...contracting procedures were not addressed to my satisfaction. Therefore, Secretary of the Navy Richard Spencer's services have been terminated by Secretary of Defense Mark Esper. I thank Richard for his service & commitment. Eddie will retire peacefully with all of the.

...honors that he has earned, including his Trident Pin. Admiral and now Ambassador to Norway Ken Braithwaite will be nominated by me to be the new Secretary of the Navy. A man of great achievement and success, I know Ken will do an outstanding job!

November 26, 2019

6:33 am: I will always protect our great warfighters. I've got your backs!

November 29, 2019

9:06 am: Just returned to the United States after spending a GREAT Thanksgiving with our Courageous American Warriors in Afghanistan!

December 9, 2019

12:04 am: Let our great soldiers fight!

December 20, 2019

10:30 pm: Last year I signed legislation that gives our Veterans CHOICE, through private providers, and at urgent care facilities! Today we fully funded this $10 billion a year effort that gets our brave Veterans care quickly, and close to home.

10:31 pm: We will always provide for our Veterans and their mental health. I pushed Congress to provide $10 Billion for Vet mental health, suicide prevention outreach, and funding for my PREVENTS Initiative to end Vet suicide. Congress responded. A big win for our Vets!

Honored to finally put an end to the "Widow's Tax" and ensure that our surviving military spouses receive their full benefits. The spouses and families of our fallen heroes have suffered enough and WE must do everything in our power to ease the burden.

10:32 pm: My Administration pushed to include a big expansion to Veteran telehealth in the spending bill so that the brave men and women who served our Country get the care they need. #RuralProsperity

December 31, 2019

7:55 pm: One of my greatest honors was to have gotten CHOICE approved for our great Veterans. Others have tried for decades, and failed.